Informal Metropolis

Confluencias

SERIES EDITORS

Susie S. Porter
University of Utah

María L. O. Muñoz
Susquehanna University

Diana Montaño
Washington University in St. Louis

Informal Metropolis

Life on the Edge of Mexico City, 1940–1976

DAVID YEE

University of Nebraska Press
LINCOLN

© 2024 by the Board of Regents of the University of Nebraska
All rights reserved

The University of Nebraska Press is part of a land-grant institution with campuses and programs on the past, present, and future homelands of the Pawnee, Ponca, Otoe-Missouria, Omaha, Dakota, Lakota, Kaw, Cheyenne, and Arapaho Peoples, as well as those of the relocated Ho-Chunk, Sac and Fox, and Iowa Peoples.

Portions of this work previously appeared as "Shantytown Mexico: The Democratic Opening in Ciudad Nezahualcóyotl, 1969–1976," *The Americas* 78, no. 1 (2021): 119–47; and "The Making of Mexico City's Historic Center: National Patrimony in the Age of Urban Renewal," *Journal of Planning History* 19, no. 2 (2020): 90–111.

Library of Congress Cataloging-in-Publication Data
Names: Yee, David (Historian of Latin America), author.
Title: Informal metropolis: life on the edge of Mexico City, 1940–1976 / David Yee.
Description: Lincoln: University of Nebraska Press, 2024. | Series: Confluencias | Includes bibliographical references and index.
Identifiers: LCCN 2024011480
ISBN 9781496225924 (hardback)
ISBN 9781496240460 (paperback)
ISBN 9781496241184 (pdf)
ISBN 9781496241177 (epub)
Subjects: LCSH: Urbanization—Mexico—Mexico City Region—Case studies. | Housing—Mexico—Mexico City Metropolitan Area—Case studies. | Netzahualcóyotl (Mexico)—Social conditions. | San Juan de Aragón (Mexico City, Mexico)—Social conditions. | Social movements—Mexico—Netzahualcóyotl. | Urbanization—Mexico—Netzahualcóyotl. | Urbanization—Mexico—San Juan de Aragón (Mexico City) | BISAC: HISTORY / Latin America / Mexico
Classification: LCC HT384.M62 M4935 2024 |
DDC 307.760972/53—dc23/eng/20240717
LC record available at https://lccn.loc.gov/2024011480

Designed and set in Minion Pro by Scribe Inc.

To Nina and Charles Yee

CONTENTS

List of Illustrations	ix
Acknowledgments	xi
Introduction	xiii

Part 1. Modernist Metropolis

1. Mexico City at a Crossroads	3
2. Mass Housing in the Mexican Metropolis	22

Part 2. The Origins of Ciudad Nezahualcóyotl

3. Land Politics on the Periphery	43
4. Autoconstrucción in Ciudad Neza	64

Part 3. The Echeverría Years

5. Mortgaging the Revolution: The Early Years of Infonavit	87
6. Strike: The Democratic Opening on the Urban Frontier	106
7. Fineza and Land Regularization	125
8. Serve the People: Liberation Theology in Ciudad Nezahualcóyotl	144
Conclusion	175
Notes	185
Bibliography	225
Index	253

ILLUSTRATIONS

Map 1. Mexico City Metropolitan Area — xxvii
Table 1. Land and property in Colonias del Vaso de Texcoco / Ciudad Neza — 183

Photographs following chapter 4
1. Exterior facade of Unidad Santa Fe, 1957
2. Partial view of San Juan de Aragón Lake and Forest, 1964
3. Raúl Romero Erazo and Jorge Sáenz Knoth, 1965
4. Early home in Ciudad Neza, ca. 1963
5. Early home in Ciudad Neza, ca. 1963
6. Luis Echeverría signing the Fineza Land Trust agreement, 1973
7. Neighborhood association meeting, Ciudad Lago, ca. 1973
8. Promotional materials for Jesuit-run classes and workshops, 1974

ACKNOWLEDGMENTS

Although writing this book has been a long, solitary endeavor, it has brought several incredible people into my life. As time passes, the list of people and places to thank continues to grow, constantly evolving until the very end. This book would not have been possible without the following people.

My foremost debt of gratitude is to my advisor Eric Zolov. With patience and humor, he helped me turn an idea into a project and reminded me to think about what was at stake in the questions I pursued along the way. At Stony Brook, I encountered a vibrant space for scholars through the Center for Latin American and Caribbean Studies. I thank Paul Gootenberg for his insights, guidance, and super sessions. Eric Beverley helped shape how I conceptualize cities in our discussions in the atrium at Lincoln Center. Many of the ideas for this project were developed in between New York and Mexico through endless conversations with Sergio Pinto-Handler, Ashley Black, Gonzalo Romero Sommer, and Brooke Larson.

In Mexico, Catarino Sandoval Uvalle was the most instrumental person in the research for this project. As the director of CIDNE, he gave me unfettered access to archival material on Ciudad Neza's history. A veteran of the subversive seventies and an expert on José María Luis Mora, Catarino's assistance was invaluable. In addition to Catarino, the staff at CIDNE and the Centro Pluricultural de Nezahualcóyotl assisted me in the research for this book. In the early stages of this project, my affiliation with the Centro de Documentación sobre la Ciudad at UAM-Xochimilco was crucial. I am grateful to the staff at the AHDF, AGN, Biblioteca Nacional de México, Toluca's Archivo Histórico del Estado de México, and Biblioteca Miguel Lerdo de Tejada. I would be remiss not to acknowledge my favorite public institution in Mexico, the Cineteca Nacional (the cinema is a good place for cheap introverts). This project was shaped by numerous people from

Ciudad Neza who volunteered their time and energy to talk with me, share old documents, and suggest new contacts in my historical investigation of the municipality. I thank the residents I interviewed for their time, especially Rogelio Vargas Soriano. I was also assisted in this work by Feike de Jong and Carlos G. Vélez-Ibáñez.

In New York, my research benefited from access to documents and material at the New York Public Library and the UN Archives and Records Management Section. The Rockefeller Archive Center awarded me a grant-in-aid to work in their repositories. Furthermore, my research was generously supported with funds from the Tinker Foundation, Lincoln Institute of Land Policy, Swiss National Science Foundation, and Benson Center at the University of Colorado Boulder. I also received support from the history department and the Graduate School at Stony Brook University.

In Denver, I was able to complete this work in a supportive and stimulating environment. As a postdoctoral fellow at University of Colorado Boulder, I was given the rare opportunity to rethink and revise my dissertation in optimal conditions. At Metropolitan State University of Denver, I have been welcomed and supported by my colleagues in the history department. Meg, Matt, Todd, Alex, and Kim have been especially helpful these past few years, though I thank all the familiar faces I see and greet on campus each day. Bridget Barry has been a fantastic collaborator to work with throughout the entire process.

I want to give a special thanks to my friends who have challenged and supported me over the years. I was aided in the process of writing this book by Chris Illum, Kevin Moyer, Ryan Cannava, and Giancarlo Romero. I have only gratitude for Ati Egas and the Conteras-Egas families for opening their doors to me in Quito and Píllaro Viejo. Mil gracias a Mónica and the Gonzalez-Rivera families for opening their doors to me in New York and Neza York. Mónica, thank you for going on this adventure with me, and of course for Mayita. Maya Mia—my brightest light, my guiding light. As I was writing this book, you came into our lives and joined Mark, Brian, Michaels, Liam, and Kellie in a family that stretches from Brooklyn to Rockland and back again. Finally, I am grateful to my parents, Charles and Nina Yee, for their unwavering love and support.

INTRODUCTION

For over a thousand years, rustic settlements dotted the edges of Lake Texcoco. The majestic body of water was once part of five contiguous lakes nestled in the Basin of Mexico's volcanic mountain range. Over time, various kingdoms and empires laid claim to Texcoco as generations of villagers continued to hunt and fish around the edges of the lake. However, after a succession of regimes drained most of its water, the villagers found themselves on the edges of Mexico City.[1] By the middle of the twentieth century, with the former lake bed's land tenure still in question, the newly surfaced land became a violently contested site. This conflict would inevitably shape the area as it grew from a cluster of crudely built shacks into an informal city of over one million people.

Rogelio Vargas Soriano was one of the millions of people who moved out to the former lake beds encircling the capital's eastern periphery. Originally from the Mixteca region of Oaxaca, he moved to Mexico City in 1954 as a teenager. Prior to his arrival, he had spent several days on a bus traveling across the mountain ranges that lie between Oaxaca and the capital. Rogelio arrived in the San Lázaro Terminal with a few pesos in his pocket, the little his family could scrape together after a poor harvest season. He struggled to survive in the city's growing informal economy yet had saved up enough money to purchase a plot of land in a new municipality called Ciudad Nezahualcóyotl (Neza). On the day he met with the land developer, he asked where his property ended. The developer threw a rock into a nearby marsh and told him it ended where the rock hit the water. Despite the lack of formalities, Rogelio signed the contracts, much like thousands of other poor migrants lured to Ciudad Nezahualcóyotl by the prospects of becoming a homeowner.[2]

Raúl Ruiz Bautista arrived in the same terminal nearly ten years prior to Rogelio Vargas. Raúl Ruiz walked for days through the Mixteca's mountainous terrain until he found a train station that connected him to Oaxaca's capital. From there, he continued his journey to Mexico City in 1942. Unlike Rogelio, Raúl Ruiz maintained close ties with his fellow Mixtecs in Mexico City, organized a mutual-aid association to send funds back to the Mixteca, and worked closely with the National Indigenous Institute. Eventually, he found an office job with the Mexican Institute of Social Security, a position that gave him access to an apartment in one of the new housing projects built by the federal government in the 1950s. Located in the middle-class neighborhood of Narvarte, Raúl Ruiz held meetings in Spanish and Mixtec with other migrants from his village in a modern apartment equipped with services and a shopping center on the ground floor.[3]

The parallel journeys of Rogelio Vargas and Raúl Ruiz Bautista reflect a common story shared by millions of Mexicans who left behind their small towns and villages for a new life in Mexico City. The commonalities shared by Rogelio and Raúl are striking, yet at some point their paths diverged and their lives moved in different directions. Why did one poor migrant from the Mixteca region gain access to a modern apartment with an elevator and hot water, while the other built his own home out of recycled materials near a polluted lake? Was the division between Rogelio and Raúl the product of their own decisions, or were there larger forces at play? These initial questions eventually led me to the central theme of this book: the relationship between urban housing and social inequality in mid-twentieth-century Mexico.

Rogelio Vargas's and Raúl Ruiz Bautista's stories are representative of a larger divergence that took place in Mexican society during the middle of the twentieth century. Over the span of two decades, from 1940 to 1960, inequality steadily rose, after which point, the country's levels of inequality precipitously declined until the 1980s. Specifically, inequality peaked around 1963 and sunk to its lowest point in 1983.[4] As one economist in the 1970s observed, "The Mexican miracle appears to have resulted in a redistribution of income in favor of its urban middle-class at the expense of the country's top and bottom sectors."[5] Since then, historians have primarily focused on the nation's "bottom sectors" to highlight Mexico's comparatively high levels of inequality.[6] In many ways, the current study of Mexico's largest shantytown enriches this literature. However, to limit the scope of inquiry to Mexico City's poorest shanty dwellers would overlook a distinctive feature of midcentury Mexico: the persistence of endemic poverty amid prosperity and upward social mobility. This reconfiguration was fully expressed in the crisis surrounding urban housing. As millions of rural migrants settled in Mexico City, housing functioned as a mechanism for upward mobility among the city's incipient middle class at the expense of the informal poor.[7]

Mexico City's expansion was shaped by two kinds of mass housing. The first was the *multifamiliar*, a broad term associated with public housing complexes built for civil servants and middle-class families.[8] Monumental in scale and modernist in style, the multifamiliar provided a national aesthetic for social welfare in midcentury Mexico. The second was the self-built home, a rudimentary shelter constructed by poor families at a distance from the state.[9] As laborers in the informal economy, their precarious positions limited their access to financial credit, social welfare, and citizens' rights. In this period, the multifamiliar and the shantytown were defined by each other, representing two possible futures for the Mexican metropolis. If the multifamiliar symbolized progress, rationality, and the quixotic optimism of high modernity, the shantytown reflected the failures of Mexico's accelerated modernization. Nowhere was this duality more vividly expressed than in the Vaso de Texcoco.

The swampy remains of Texcoco's lake bed became a proving ground for mass housing in Mexico City. It was here where Mexico's largest shantytown, Ciudad Nezahualcóyotl, grew alongside Mexico's largest government housing complex, San Juan de Aragón. I analyze these two contrasting areas to explore the relationship between geographic space and social inequality. In doing so, I argue that a person's position in the formal or informal economy was the most decisive factor in determining where they lived in the metropolis. Beyond state institutions and laws, the inherent biases embedded in Mexico's housing policies were also upheld and defended by the nation's largest labor unions. In particular, the Confederation of Mexican Workers waged several struggles against the government's attempts to provide a more inclusive program for informal laborers. Struggles surrounding housing helped solidify a broader reconfiguration of social stratification in midcentury Mexico.

Informal Metropolis traces the urbanization of the Vaso de Texcoco (Ciudad Neza and San Juan de Aragón) between 1946 and 1976. These years marked a period when the nation's traditionally rural population declined in the wake of mass migrations to urban centers. During this period, in the press and the public imagination, Ciudad Neza represented a deformed, incomplete transition from "the rural" to "the urban." By its sheer size and scale, Ciudad Neza gained particular notoriety as a city of extremes. In the 1970s, it was the site of the largest garbage dump and the largest shantytown in Latin America.[10] It was also home to the largest protest strike for urban land rights and, subsequently, the largest land regularization reform carried out under President Luis Echeverría (1970–76). However, despite the extreme material deprivation evident in Ciudad Neza's early history, a close study of its local archives reveals that the extreme nature of Ciudad Neza's deprivation was more a product of policy than poverty. Though undoubtedly impoverished, Ciudad Neza's extreme features can be traced back to the government's unspoken practice of granting impunity to private developers who embezzled public funds designated for critical infrastructure projects.

Ciudad Neza's historical record challenges many of the myths and common assumptions held about lawless squatters in Third World cities.[11] In fact, most of Ciudad Neza's residents were not squatters—broadly defined as one who settles on property without title or payment of rent—but instead were aspiring homeowners indebted to land developers. Documents held in Ciudad Neza's municipal archives detail the fortunes reaped by private developers who fraudulently sold property lots with nonexistent services to unsuspecting families taken in by the prospects of owning land close to the city.

Nevertheless, a historian's attempt to demystify past stigmas cannot negate the power they once possessed. Though fundamentally symbolic and ephemeral, social stigmas can exert a strong influence on the material conditions of a locale. Whether the Northeast of Brazil or the Southside of Chicago, the stigmatization of a region or area can influence policy decisions, financial investments, policing methods, and levels of corruption.[12] In one poignant example, a former public works director in Ciudad Neza recalled the heartache of receiving a rejection letter from the World Bank for a much-needed loan. According to the official, when Ciudad Neza's unsavory reputation reached the offices in Washington, the lenders became convinced that Ciudad Neza's residents were unreliable and incapable of paying back the loan.[13]

Though influenced by prevailing ideas on international development, these stigmas were fundamentally rooted in local notions of modernity. When Ciudad Neza was officially put on the map in 1963, it lacked the hallmarks of urbanity: the plaza, the department store, the streetcar trolley, the rush of the crowd and all its fleeting excitement. It did not possess the vibrancy of a cosmopolitan city or the tranquility of the rural pastoral.[14] Instead, it was characterized by what I refer to as a *vulgar hybridity*—in this case, a place composed of the worst attributes of the countryside and the city, unidentifiable from each other. The presence of chicken coops, livestock, outhouses, and dirt roads were viewed as signs of the unassimilated "peasant in the city."[15] These rustic symbols produced a visual dissonance when mixed with the sights of crowded subdivisions, discos, bus lines to metro stations, and planes landing in the nearby airport. Over the years, Ciudad Neza's undefinable qualities came to define it. The backgrounds of residents only contributed to Ciudad Neza's perceived vulgar hybridity, as they were neither peasants nor industrial workers. Just as Ciudad Neza's environment was undefinable, its residents were unassimilable into Mexico's consolidated system of labor syndicates, peasant confederations, and civil servant unions. As our narrative moves forward into the 1960s and 1970s, chapters 6 and 7 illuminate how this contradiction was eventually resolved through the popularization of the *colono* (resident of a *colonia*, a neighborhood outside of the city center) as a political category and constituency in Mexican society.

The first four decades of Ciudad Neza's history also overlap with three other timelines. As mentioned, these were the decades when Mexico experienced its own "Great Migration" of rural dwellers leaving the countryside for Mexico City, Monterrey, Guadalajara, Acapulco, and other Mexican cities. For Mexico City's metropolitan area, the population grew from 1.3 million in 1940 to 13 million in 1980.[16] The second timeline encompasses the rise and decline of social inequality in Mexico, steadily rising for the first two decades (1940–60) and then declining for the latter half until the economic crash of 1982.[17] The third overlapping timeline covers the emergence of Mexico's neighborhood associations and urban social movements. While often depicted as appendages of the Institutional Revolutionary Party, this timeline allows for a historical analysis of the 1970s, when there was a partial radicalization and rupture within the movement, both in Ciudad Neza and nationally. As a history of an informal city, the book ends in the mid- to late 1970s, when the federal government began to formalize its lands and install public utilities throughout the entire municipality.[18]

Of the many themes explored in this book, housing provides its main through line. In part 1, the early years of Mexico's social housing programs are analyzed with a collection of archival sources from the government's main housing agency (IMSS) during the 1950s and early 1960s. Part 2 sheds light on how Ciudad Neza's earliest settlers built their own homes in the former Vaso de Texcoco, with research benefiting from unprecedented access to materials in Ciudad Neza's municipal archives (CIDNE). Part 3 covers the Echeverría years, as these were the most pivotal in shaping Ciudad Neza's history. After providing an overview of urban housing in the early 1970s, part 3 details Ciudad Neza's payment strike (similar to a rent strike) and the fallout caused by the strike leaders' compromise with President Echeverría. These chapters reconstruct a new narrative of the strike and its aftermath with the aid of formerly classified government reports (DGIPS) and an untapped collection of materials from a Jesuit grouping based in Ciudad Neza during the 1970s.[19]

In the 1970s, Ciudad Neza gained more attention as an object of study by scholars, social workers, engineers, medical professionals, and political activists. The diversity of documentary evidence and perspectives provided a source base not exclusively tied to official reports from state functionaries, allowing for greater insights into how ordinary people lived, worked, and organized in Ciudad Neza. Among these sources, and in related scholarship, the depiction of the early years of Ciudad Neza (1947–63) tends to be limited to a published collection of testimonials (*Netzahualcóyotl: Testimonios históricos*, 1978) and interviews with residents from on-site fieldwork.[20] *Informal Metropolis* builds upon this scholarship but moves in new directions due to its grounding in archival research.[21] Indeed, neglected archival sites and collections throughout Mexico contained boxes of court documents, local news articles, unpublished memoirs, and recorded interviews that shed new light on Ciudad Neza's origins, including why its first inhabitants moved there, how they survived, and who profited from its settlement.

Conceptually, newly discovered archives and recent advances in urban historiography have enabled me to apply research methods rarely utilized by social scientists in their study of Ciudad Neza or poor urban settlements in Mexico more broadly. A comprehensive survey of newspapers published over two decades (1960–80) gave a clear sense of how Ciudad Neza was represented in the press and how that stigmatization influenced its historical development. Unlike previous scholars who have tended to study Ciudad Neza in and of itself, this work situates its history in relation to urban planning policies and social housing programs implemented in the same period.²² As detailed in the first two chapters, Ciudad Neza's early history is bound up with the government's ambitions to conserve the capital's historic center while constructing a modern metropolis on top of its surrounding hinterlands.²³

In the following, I situate the book's main arguments within broader historiographical debates concerning segregation, race, and social movements.

Space, Place, and Race in Mexican History

Space and *place* are terms that possess similar meanings and are often carelessly conflated together as one. Both terms can denote a physical location, but *space* tends to encompass more abstract and intangible qualities (e.g., virtual space, discursive space). If time is a dimension in which things happen one after the other, then space is "the dimension of things being and existing at the same time in simultaneity. It's the dimension of multiplicity."²⁴ *Place* is "space to which meaning has been ascribed and endowed with value," to draw from Yi-Fu Tuan's popular formulation.²⁵ In general, this book does not seek to complicate space as a theoretical concept. Instead, it aims to clarify the concrete role spatial segregation has played in shaping Mexico's social structure and politics.

Along with regionally based studies, urban history has also contributed to our understanding of space and place in Mexican cities. For postcolonial cities, the privileged period of study has been the years between 1880 and 1940. In surveying the most significant works in the field, the vast majority focus on the central core of Mexico City (neighborhoods of Centro Histórico, Guerrero, Tepito, Juárez, etc.).²⁶ The historiography's geographic focus is a direct result of its temporal scope, as most of the metropolitan area had yet to be urbanized by 1940. However, if we were to historically map out where the most dynamic and consequential urban development occurred in Mexico City after the 1940s, we would inevitably be drawn out to the city's peripheral areas. From the vantage point of the periphery, new questions arise and become more apparent. They include distinct issues of home ownership, transportation networks, *autoconstrucción*, survival strategies (water, electricity), land developers, colono associations, and informal land tenure.

With the outlying periphery as its primary focus, this book contributes to the interdisciplinary field of global metropolitan studies. The metropolitan scale allows for both a wider geographic area and a conceptual framework to analyze the historical development of a city and its surroundings (suburbs, exurbs, hinterlands) as a unified entity.[27] Unlike metropolitan areas in North America, Mexico City's history is not one of urban renewal and suburbanization. *Centro Histórico* and *conurbación* are words that speak to a different social reality, one in which people did not flee from the city but attempted to re-create it on an ever-expanding periphery.[28] The earlier years of this expansion (1880s–1940s) have been detailed by historian Matthew Vitz, while the later years of the twentieth century were analyzed by Emilio Duhau and Angela Giglia in their classic text on urban space in Mexico City.[29] *Informal Metropolis* delves directly into the throes of the century's middle decades to examine when Mexico City passed through a crucible that left it, and the nation, profoundly changed.

As alluded to earlier, the urban periphery is unstable and impermanent, particularly during periods of rapid growth and expansion. While the term *peripheral urbanization* can refer to a way of producing space as opposed to a physical location on the margins of the city, here it does indeed refer to the physical outlying areas surrounding the center of the city.[30] As discussed in chapter 2, the distance from the city center no longer served as a marker for socioeconomic wealth after 1960. Mexico City's midcentury growth was too intense, large, and unwieldy to neatly fit its social geography into any overarching spatial model or pattern. Although Mexico City's social geography defies any broad generalizations, there are varying degrees of organization and coherency in its chaos. In looking back to the origins of many neighborhoods established in the 1950s and 1960s, each locale's status as formal or informal was decisive in its respective development.

At its core, informality is a concept defined in relation to its opposite. In this study, *informality* refers to the "entities and processes unregulated by the institutions of society, in a legal and social environment in which similar activities are regulated."[31] The long-standing prevalence of informality in urban studies has also generated a critical backlash. For some, informality is a fallacy because it "designates by negation" and "does not tell us what it is describing; it only tells us what it is not."[32] In this study, informality is partially defined by absence, but that void also gives rise to distinctive practices. The everyday routines of negotiating the *pipa* system (water distribution), adjusting the *telarañas* (electric utility poles), and communal house-building practices made up the inner workings of Ciudad Neza. These practices, along with several others documented in this book, help refute the argument that informality is simply defined by a state of absence, suggesting the possibility for new economic and cultural practices to emerge from such absence.

Along with state authorities and residents, a third element was critical to the production of informal space in urban Mexico: land speculators. Commonly referred to as a *fraccionador* (a person who subdivides land for financial gain), the fraccionador has been overlooked in the history of postrevolutionary Mexico. More than simply a swindler, the fraccionador was deeply integrated into the political system, closely aligned with church authorities, and reliant upon lethal force carried out by hired gunmen (*pistoleros*).[33] In this light, the fraccionador was somewhat similar to the rural *cacique*—a central figure in Mexican history, defined in the 1960s as "a strong and autocratic leader in local and/or regional politics whose characteristically informal, personalistic, and often arbitrary rule . . . is marked by the diagnostic threat and practice of violence."[34] At the time of Ciudad Neza's rapid growth (ca. 1960), many scholars were skeptical of the cacique's future survival in a country growing more urban and bureaucratic. In hindsight, we can now see urban life did not spell the demise of the cacique but instead created the environment for new forms of *caciquismo* to emerge.[35] For historians Jaime Pensado and Ilán Semo, the *charro* (corrupt union boss) represented a fusion of "the rural and the urban; the campesino culture and the proletarian culture" in the tradition of the cacique and caudillo.[36] The term *charro* does not quite accurately describe Ciudad Neza's fraccionadores, but there are several parallels. Discussed in further detail in chapter 3, it can be said here that the fraccionador was a distinct variant of urban caciquismo.

In studying residential segregation in Mexico City, one confronts a set of challenges centered on race in Mexican history and how it fits into the broader historiography of urban segregation.[37] Specifically, to what degree can historians of urban Mexico draw from research methods employed in North American / North Atlantic cities?[38] To date, there has not been a major work that has demonstrated similar patterns of ethnoracial segregation in Mexico City as found in the United States or Europe, despite the long history of racial discrimination and violent suppression against peoples of Indigenous, Chinese, and African descent in Mexico. The scholarship that does exist on residential segregation in Mexico City has largely focused on personal income or geographic proximity to services (education, medical offices, water).³⁹ The general lack of engagement with broader trends necessitates a return to basic assumptions to reevaluate the determinants responsible for Mexico City's divided landscape. Was personal income the sole determinate or did it function in relation to others?

These questions were central to this project's research agenda. They informed close readings of legal statutes, housing codes, mortgage loans, applications for housing programs, and archival material produced by housing authorities. Race and ethnicity were considered when reviewing maps, land contracts, community newspapers, and memoirs of early residents accepted into Mexico's housing programs. In my research of housing laws and regulations, I did not discover the same kind of racialized policies found in the United States or South Africa, nor anything resembling the racial covenants formed by white residents in U.S. cities.⁴⁰ Census data and studies from the period indicate that families who moved to Mexico's major cities in this period were Catholic, Mexican, and spoke Spanish.⁴¹ For the smaller, but significant, number of monolingual (native language) Indigenous migrants, they remained disparate and scattered throughout the metropolis, never establishing a pattern of segregation.⁴² While one could argue racial discrimination affected a migrant's socioeconomic standing, Mexico's mortgage lending institutions, public/social housing application forms, and rent laws did not possess racial codes or restrictions comparable to North Atlantic countries or former colonies.⁴³

Beyond structural discrimination, there is also the question of interpersonal prejudices held among residents. In reviewing both ethnographic accounts and community papers, there is evidence of contempt for practices associated with the countryside (e.g., maintaining livestock, folk Catholicism) and darker-skinned residents in some cases, but no indication that these personal prejudices formed a pattern of exclusion in housing.⁴⁴ Perhaps the most salient example of prejudice in this period was articulated in the term *naco*. In Mexico, the word *naco* was simply one of many in a long line of popular terms used to describe rustic folk uprooted to the city.⁴⁵ Originally used as a slur against "an Indian peasant in the city," it grew increasingly unmoored from its racial origins in the 1960s to assume a broader meaning: a derogatory term for a poor person (or person of humble origins) lacking in education who makes an unsophisticated attempt to assimilate into modern urban culture.⁴⁶ Difficult to define, its power lies in its ambiguity. Nevertheless, racial undertones are not the same as racial categories, particularly when compared to other countries (the United States, Canada, South Africa, England) where racial categories were more decisive in housing. Thus, race cannot be negated or amplified, only placed among several concomitant determinants. In the case of urban housing, these intersecting lines crystalized into a point most visibly pronounced around the issue of informality.

Mexico's historical realities remained incongruous with the dominant conceptual frameworks for understanding residential segregation in modern cities. In twentieth-century Mexico City, there were no "Little Oaxacas" or "Mayan Towns." There were, however, migrants from Oaxaca or Chiapas who found that their search for a home in the city was circumscribed by their position in the division of labor. Access to social housing programs or mortgage loans was granted to those with occupations recognized and regulated by the state—a principle concretely expressed through regular paychecks, official bank accounts, union dues, and work contracts.[47] These laborers were categorized as *empleados de base* or *trabajadores asalariados*—salaried workers.

The issue of in/formality becomes necessary to factor into an analysis of urban housing after reviewing the costs of living for a resident of a public housing complex (IMSS) compared to a resident in Ciudad Neza. In the 1960s, the rental costs for families in an IMSS housing unit were nearly the same as the monthly fees for families in Ciudad Neza (payments for a land plot and services).[48] The main dividing line was not affordability but in/formality in the workplace. More broadly, the same argument does not apply when measuring differences between the wealthy and the poor.[49] However, for the multitiered lower-to-middle classes, the question of informality was paramount.

Democracy on the Margins

In 1985, President Miguel de la Madrid asked a group of reporters, "Why do we now call it civil society, when before we simply called it *el pueblo* [the people]?"[50] This offhand comment was popularized in Carlos Monsiváis's *Entrada libre*, a now classic work on democracy in 1980s Mexico. De la Madrid's question hinted at a change pulsing across the continent, one that Monsiváis detected in his chronicles of Mexico's growing social movements.[51] Latin America's urban poor were no longer the marginals of modernization or the victims of clientelism.[52] *El pueblo* was now the citizenry in a struggle for democratic rights and social justice.⁵³ But President de la Madrid's question still stands: Why the change in terms? What transpired in the transition from el pueblo to civil society?

A key step in addressing this question is to decenter Mexico's presidential elections as the sole criterion for measuring the nation's state of democracy. This analytical shift assumes a higher importance for the twentieth century, as historical research on democracy, civic associations, the public sphere, and the press in the nineteenth century has received more scholarly attention.⁵⁴ Indeed, the power of *presidencialismo* casts a long shadow over Mexico's twentieth century, one that obscures a richer, more multilayered political history. This book, mainly focused on housing and inequality, highlights the role of popular urban movements in civil society as a crucial component of Mexico's broader democratic transition.

In its most common definition, civil society constitutes a distinct sector independent of state and business interests. Although its viability as a consequential force in midcentury Mexico has been routinely doubted and dismissed, historians have more recently pointed to its sustained existence "in the Tocquevillian sense, as a series of relatively autonomous, horizontally structured organizations and networks . . . and in the Habermasian sense, as independent, if geographically limited, public spheres."⁵⁵ Civil society's broad and amorphous qualities have also drawn criticism from many activists and scholars over the past two decades. This opposition, reflected in titles such as *The Illusion of Civil Society* and *Beyond Civil Society*, finds civil society organizations too riven by antagonistic class divisions, or too easily co-opted by wealthy interests, to act as loci for real change.⁵⁶ These limitations are as evident today as they were in the past. Even with these limitations, civil society remains a crucial component for the kind of debate, dissent, and solidarity necessary for self-governance. Civil society is not a guarantor of democracy but a requisite of it. Mexico's urban social movements played an instrumental role in revitalizing facets of civil society and can be observed most saliently through their popular neighborhood associations.

In most major cities, the neighborhood association came to represent the organizational expression of Mexico's urban social movements.⁵⁷ Although the neighborhood association provided a forum for residents to air their grievances, in the end, it served to legitimate and strengthen the PRI's dominance during the 1950s and much of the 1960s.⁵⁸ This dominance would be challenged at the end of the 1960s, when the stirrings of a new social movement (Movimiento Urbano Popular) exploded onto the scene after expectations were raised by the arrival of President Luis Echeverría (1970–76).[59] Echeverría's populist discourse and public support for urban land rights propelled a national movement forward and, in the process, inadvertently turned Mexico's urban shantytowns into political spaces where the PRI's patronage system mixed uneasily with embryonic forms of local democracy.[60] This phenomenon could also be witnessed in Cuernavaca, Monterrey, Durango, and Torreón.[61] Initially spurred by demands for land titles and basic services, the urban social movements from this period would ultimately achieve more lasting significance as precursors to the formation of a new urban citizenry in Mexico.

Mexico's urban social movements and poor settlements also offer an alternative interpretation of Mexican politics, particularly during the volatile years of Luis Echeverría's presidency. Echeverrismo, with its blend of revolutionary rhetoric, social reform, and violent repression, has often been portrayed as a kind of disingenuous populism marred by dirty war operations and limited results.[62] Though largely true, the tendency to focus on the intentionality of President Echeverría's reforms, or their failure to reach projected goals, has limited our understanding of how they affected the lives of ordinary citizens. While Echeverría's fiery speeches may ring hollow to historians today, we must not overlook how such discourse was received and interpreted throughout Mexican society at the time. In the case of Ciudad Neza, this dynamic was most vividly expressed in a strike waged by residents in the early 1970s.

The chapters covering Ciudad Neza's strike build upon recent scholarship aiming to move "beyond '68" by situating the student movements of 1968 as one part of a larger historical moment, not the center of it.[63] Moreover, this book seeks to broaden the scope of study even further, enlarging the historical lens beyond armed struggles and radical groupings to incorporate the overlooked history of everyday life and politics as experienced by residents of a Mexican shantytown. A close study of this strata produces a different starting point and timeline when compared to the divergent trajectories of the era's student radicals and revolutionary guerrillas.

By moving away from the most extreme expressions of violent resistance and repression, this work joins a small but growing number of studies concerned with the growth of grassroots Indigenous movements, democratic labor struggles, feminist collectives, and urban social movements. Indeed, when the various movements from the 1970s are brought together more systematically, a new political panorama comes into focus.[64] The scholarly attention directed to Mexico's "new social movements" and "birth of civil society" in the 1980s has failed to account for the gathering of independent political forces in the 1970s prior to the economic crises and neoliberal turn of the 1980s.[65] More than simply an issue of chronology, the implications of the revised timeline run much deeper: the rise of organized political and cultural forces independent of the PRI prior to the economic crises of the 1980s indicates a "birth" or "revitalization" of Mexican civil society not solely conditioned (or less conditioned) by economic causes (financial collapse, decline of social services, neoliberal policies), as currently argued, and instead suggests a greater role for ideology and political consciousness in the expansion of Mexico's civil society.

With Ciudad Neza as the book's central protagonist, this work enters an interdisciplinary body of scholarship focused on politics among the urban poor. This scholarship shares a common pursuit of more deeply understanding the varied political subjectivities that arise out of the struggle to build one's own home at a distance from the state.[66] It also follows those individuals as they band together into larger collectives to demand formal rights to the lands upon which those homes were built. The struggles over property rights and public utilities in Ciudad Neza were indicative of a broader, global shift in politics. Specifically, the rapid growth of cities in the Global South produced a new set of circumstances in which the urban poor's demands shifted from labor to land—a shift in which the struggles of poor city dwellers were posed "much more in terms of everyday resources than in terms of the kinds of conflict between labor and factory discipline that characterized working-class movements in Europe during the last century."[67] Chronologically, Ciudad Neza's popular urban movements overlapped with similar mobilizations in Peru, Brazil, Chile, Argentina, and Uruguay.[68] Thus, it is a local history with global resonance.

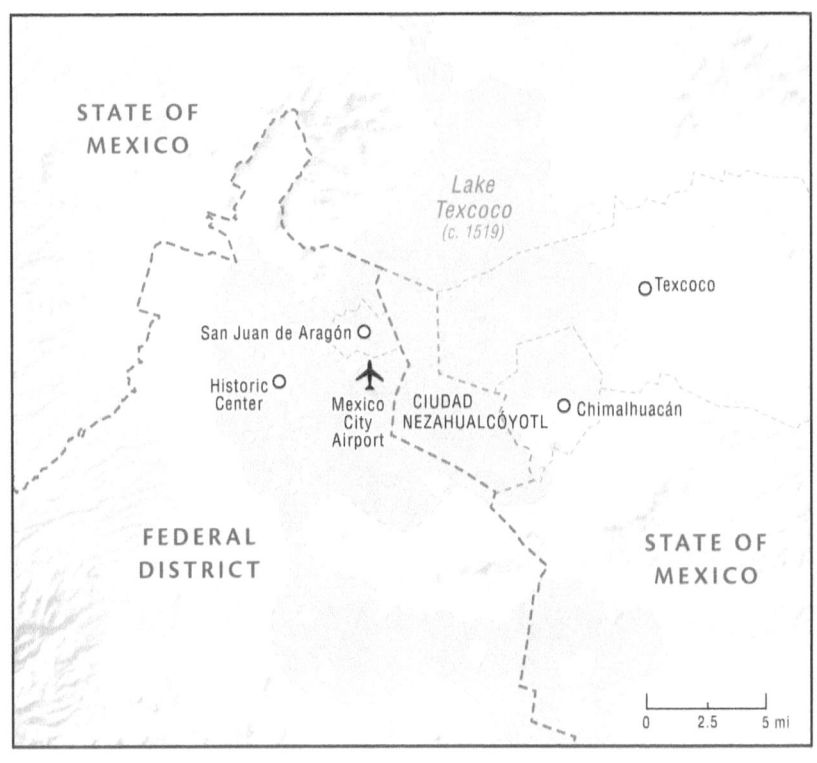

MAP 1. Mexico City Metropolitan Area. Map created by Erin Greb.

Informal Metropolis

PART 1

Modernist Metropolis

1

Mexico City at a Crossroads

Standing in the center of Zócalo Square, one cannot help but feel overwhelmed by a sense of history amid the rush of the crowd. The Zócalo is the central square of the oldest capital city in the Americas. Its origins date back to 1325, when the Mexicas settled in the region. It was here where Spanish conquistador Hernán Cortés laid the foundations for the capital of New Spain in the 1520s. The Zócalo has been a place where crowds have gathered to praise deities and leaders over the past seven centuries: the Aztec gods of war and water, the Holy Trinity in the Metropolitan Cathedral, and the president at the National Palace on the eve of each Independence Day.

By the 1950s, the Zócalo's centrality began to weaken and diminish. Mexico City's outward expansion produced new urban centers and heralded the emergence of a modern metropolis. This chapter identifies three main factors behind this transformation: migration, historic preservation, and urban planning policies. The millions of rural migrants arriving in Mexico City constituted more than a demographic shift. With El Centro's housing stock on the brink of collapse, the capitol's entire social geography was called into question. Local demands to curtail urban development in the face of escalating housing shortages forced officials to look beyond the urbanized core to the surrounding hinterlands for solutions. Overall, I frame this history as a simultaneous process of *centralization* and *decentralization*.

The *centralization* aspect describes a national phenomenon and refers to the extreme spatial concentration of industry, media, government, commerce, and people in one singular location. The disproportionate number of people in Mexico City led to a situation where 20 percent of the nation's population lived on 1 percent of the nation's territory in 1970.[1] In addition, Mexico City was also the seat of federal government, the nation's industrial center, the headquarters for the national media, and the main site for the film industry—it was Washington, Detroit, New York, and Hollywood all in one.

The *decentralization* aspect refers to historical changes on a local scale. In this case, decentralization applies to an actual place (El Centro) and does not suggest the loss of "a center" for public life and civic culture due to suburbanization. The chapter examines a decisive struggle over an urban renewal project slated to demolish large swathes of the capital's historic quarters. At the beginning of the 1950s, a movement to defend Mexico City's cultural patrimony blocked a massive urban renewal project from moving forward, subsequently intensifying the city's expansion toward its peripheral areas. As a result, midcentury Mexico City would not grow vertically with the construction of new skyscrapers but horizontally through uncontrolled sprawl. It was this intense expansion that eventually gave rise to the colonias of Ciudad Neza.

The first part of this chapter provides an overview of Mexico City's unique land tenure system before turning to the main driving force behind Mexico City's housing crisis: rural-to-urban migration. It then highlights the contentious discussions over the city's escalating housing deficit. In tracing the debates surrounding the city's chaotic growth, the chapter uncovers the lost history of the Federal District Planning Commission (1950–53)—a body of urban experts assembled by Regent Fernando Casas Alemán (1946–52) to redraw El Centro's street grid and modernize its colonial environs.

Land Tenure in Revolutionary Mexico City

During the 1870s and 1880s, Mexico City's social geography was changed by two crosscurrent migrations: the incoming migration of poor families streaming into the city from the surrounding countryside, and the outward movement of wealthy families toward new neighborhoods (colonias) west of the Zócalo. Although too slow to be considered an exodus, the gradual development of homes along the elegant Paseo de la Reforma boulevard gave new expression to wealth and prestige during the Porfiriato period (1876–1911). Most importantly, the Beaux-Arts mansions along the Paseo de la Reforma marked an important shift away from traditional Spanish influences and toward more contemporaneous French designs.[2]

The movement of wealthy families to the western colonias left their former estates empty and abandoned. This development occurred shortly after the passage of several reforms that sanctioned the expropriation and privatization of church properties, including several large estates around the La Merced neighborhood.[3] The combined effect left hundreds of abandoned properties ready to be bought up, subdivided, and converted into single-room tenements. For several generations, this type of housing would be known as a *vecindad*—a designation still used today. The vecindad became the symbol for Mexico City's urban poor, a term that immediately conjures up images of squat buildings and large patios filled with clotheslines, wash bins, and children. In 1895, approximately one hundred thousand people, or one-third of Mexico City's population, lived in tenements surrounding the Zócalo.[4] As writer Salvador Novo observed, "The proletariat lives in tenements made from surviving buildings, which in Argentina are still called 'little convents' [*conventillos*] and which in Mexico, with their huge patios and their dark cells, represent the transformation of convents into dwelling places."[5] A residential structure intended for one extended family and their servants quickly deteriorated under the pressures of over twenty families under the same roof.

Public health became the dominant paradigm to analyze Mexican cities during the Porfiriato. Government reports and articles in the press from the late nineteenth century drew direct links between sanitary conditions, morality, and social behavior among the urban masses. For criminologists of the period, unsanitary and overcrowded homes directly led to immoral public behavior. While empirical evidence and scientific investigation did not hold much sway among most city dwellers, it did set the agenda for the small cadre of *científicos* responsible for transforming the capital into a modern city.[6] Beyond the sphere of housing, engineers and planners confronted a city besieged by chronic flooding, dust storms, and contagious diseases.[7]

Porfirio Díaz invested heavily in large-scale public works projects designed to modernize Mexico City. Among the Porfiriato's numerous monuments of progress, the Grand Canal reigned supreme. The Grand Canal was the most celebrated feature of a larger drainage system implemented in the Valley of Mexico at the end of the nineteenth century. Lauded as an extraordinary feat of hydraulic engineering, these public works projects were fueled by two objectives: (1) to create a sewage system capable of carrying waste and contaminated waters out of the city's environs and (2) to drain large portions of Lake Texcoco to decrease the rate and intensity of flooding in the capital.[8]

Though effective, the massive hydraulic works did not eliminate all the flooding and ultimately exacerbated the area's ferocious dust storms, as the desiccation of Texcoco exposed the former lake bed's brittle soil to strong winds from the east. The disappearance of close to half of Lake Texcoco produced a massive new surface area that became a site for experimental agricultural centers and saltpeter mineral extraction. The former lake bed would remain mostly barren until residential settlements began to form on its desert plains in the 1940s and grow into what would become Ciudad Neza.

Despite the project's limited success, the partnership between the Porfiriato regime and British engineers still projected a technical prowess widely revered by the capital's elite families and intelligentsia. At the time of the Grand Canal's inauguration (1900), Alberto J. Pani was one of the many young engineers who supported Díaz's public works projects.[9] Pani would later grow into a public figure with multiple lives. In the early decades of the twentieth century, Pani was a civil engineer, a revolutionary exile, a diplomatic ambassador, and most famously, a central figure in the design of Mexico's postrevolutionary financial system. In 1917, he authored the influential *Hygiene in Mexico* at the request of President Venustiano Carranza. After surveying data on Mexico City's climate, dwellings, transit, medical facilities, and mortality rates, Pani lamented, "Mexico City . . . is assuredly the most unhealthy city in the whole world."[10] For Pani, "the tenements and lodging houses of Mexico . . . are indeed sinks of physical and moral infection."[11] Pani's proposals for a "sanitary city" would have to wait several years, as the devastation wrought by the Mexican Revolution combined with the fragility of new institutions blocked any path for comprehensive urban reform.

Although the countryside was the main theater of war for the Mexican Revolution, the capital experienced its own share of military battles, destruction, and political fervor throughout the ten years of violent upheaval. Revolutionary ideas animated the workers' movement, which later gained important labor and housing rights through the 1917 constitution.[12] By far, the most significant and lasting outcome of the revolution in Mexico City is also perhaps the most surprising: the *ejido*. With deep roots in Mexican history, the ejido is a form of land tenure broadly defined as communal land owned corporately by agricultural communities. The ejido was distinct from private property and governed by specific legislation established for its own particular kind of land tenure. Article 52 of the Federal Law for Agrarian Reform states, "The rights over agrarian lands held by the ejido communities are inalienable, inextinguishable, and cannot be mortgaged or sold."[13] Although ejidos and agrarian reform are most commonly associated with President Lázaro Cárdenas (1934–40), a vast majority of the ejidos surrounding Mexico City's urban core were created in the 1920s (74 percent of the Federal District's ejidos were created between 1918 and 1929).[14] Later in 1940, it was estimated that 117 square kilometers of the Federal District were urbanized and 1,381 square kilometers were rural.[15] For those rural areas surrounding the urban core in 1940, 66 percent of those lands were ejidos.[16] This staggering figure was crucial to Mexico City's urban expansion. It also makes Mexico's history of urbanization unique in comparison to the rest of Latin America. Instead of the traditional hacendado landowner found throughout much of Latin America, Mexico's poor settlers resisted and negotiated more directly with the Mexican state over their land rights.

As the violent phase of the revolution began to subside, Alberto Pani left Mexico to serve as the ambassador to France for the postrevolutionary regime.[17] Alberto's nephew, Mario Pani, would later follow in his footsteps—first to Italy, then to France to study at the École nationale supérieure des Beaux-Arts. After Europe, the two Panis would travel down different paths: Alberto as a prominent economist who led the efforts to establish a national banking system, and Mario as a leading architect and urban planner. When Mario moved back to Mexico City in 1934, he returned to a city still reeling from the economic consequences of the Great Depression and recovering from years of internal unrest. Although the mass migrations from the countryside had not begun in earnest yet, the city's growth provoked officials to commission a "master plan" for the Federal District. Still years away from the moment when he would get his own chance to craft a master plan for the capital (1950), Mario began his career by completing his uncle Alberto's Hotel Reforma in 1936. The prestige of the hotel was elevated (perhaps subverted) by the inclusion of a mural by Diego Rivera. Rivera's sweeping depiction of Mexican history (*Carnival of Mexican Life*) typified the contradictory nature of Mexican art and design in the 1930s. In this period, the tensions between revolutionary nationalism and urban cosmopolitanism shaped the work of a new generation of architects and civil engineers who were confronted with the daunting challenge of resolving Mexico City's severe housing shortages.

A Migrant's Search for a New Home

In the 1940s, mass migration from the countryside was the main engine of growth and change in Mexico City. Internal migration to Mexico City had always existed, yet never on the scale witnessed in the 1940s. Between 1940 and 1950, Mexico City grew by 1.5 million people, representing a larger population growth in ten years than the previous forty years combined (Mexico City grew by just 30,000 people during the revolution).[18] Over the course of the 1940s, 845,000 people migrated to Mexico City, accounting for close to one-third of the total population.[19] In the poor neighborhood of La Merced, studies found that 70 percent of residents were born outside of the Federal District.[20] Each day hundreds of migrants would arrive in the Buenavista and San Lázaro Terminals to begin their new lives in the capital. They came from every state in the country, with most hailing from Hidalgo, Guerrero, Veracruz, Michoacán, Guanajuato, and Oaxaca.[21]

What fueled this mass migration? A combination of a decline in opportunities in agriculture and a turn toward industrialization has been a standard response and remains overwhelmingly true. Shifts in the economy were undoubtedly at the heart of the migrations, yet it was the government's conscious policies underlying these economic shifts that accounted for their intensity. In her classic study of urban development in Mexico, Diane Davis highlights the spatial dimensions of President Manuel Ávila Camacho's strategy to restructure the relationship between capital, labor, and the state in a "national pact." Davis writes, "To ensure the success of such a pact, given the regional conflicts that divided the nation's economic elite, Ávila Camacho grounded it geographically in the region where the economic elite was most likely to support him and where he had the greatest institutional control over labor: Mexico City."[22] Between 1945 and 1955, fiscal incentives were extended to heavy industries to establish their operations in Mexico City. Government-owned rail lines offered the best freight rates within the capital. Public subsidies were placed on tortillas, bread, electricity, and public transportation to attract workers and offset low wages.[23] Several housing laws were passed throughout the 1940s that established and solidified a "rent freeze" on apartment units for working-class families to help keep wages low for employers.²⁴ Within the swirl of chaotic growth, there were concrete policies that contributed to the concentration of industries, institutions, and people in Mexico City's metropolitan area.

The extreme concentration of business, government, cultural institutions, mass media, and population in Mexico City represents the *centralization* of the nation in the capital. For an area that constitutes no more than 1 percent of the nation's territory, Mexico City was the site of 50 percent of Mexico's economic activity in 1970.²⁵ As the "unchallenged industrial capital of the nation," Mexico City accounted for 30 percent of national employment in manufacturing, 90 percent of commerce in industrial materials, and 45 percent of aggregate industrial value in 1965. In the years after President Ávila Camacho's national pact, Mexico City went on to absorb 82 percent of the nation's wholesale business and 43 percent of investment in manufacturing by the 1960s.²⁶ The changes reflected in these figures required a large base of industrial workers in a historically agrarian society. While the number of rural migrants who arrived at the capital proved to be much greater than the actual demand for industrial labor, there were still hundreds of thousands of former campesinos who were absorbed into the steel, glass, automotive, textile, and cement industries.

The strong agglomeration of industry and government was mutually reinforcing and only served to magnify Mexico's spatial centralization. More than simply the seat of government and home to the nation's president, Mexico's expanding state apparatus was physically anchored in the capital as well. The headquarters for IMSS, the National Indigenous Institute, the National Hydrocarbons Commission, Pemex, the Ministry of Public Works and Communications, the Ministry of Finance and Public Credit, and dozens of other agencies were all based in Mexico City. Behind their towering facades, these bureaucratic institutions employed thousands of people as desk clerks, secretaries, engineers, nurses, switchboard operators, legal aids, social workers, and hundreds of other jobs that kept the state machinery in operation.²⁷ Their presence reminds us that the state is not simply an abstract entity but also an administrative network powered by the labor of hundreds of thousands of workers. In many cases, these *empleados* were the product of the Cárdenas-era educational reforms that expanded the number of formally educated workers across Mexico. By 1970, Mexico City accounted for 70 percent of workers employed by the government.²⁸

Of course, the list does not end with industry and government. Mexico's major television networks (Telesistema Mexico / Televisa), movie studios (Estudios Churubusco), museums (National Museum of Anthropology), universities, and financial firms were located in the capital. After taking into account the historical legacy of the capital and the policies surrounding the Camacho-era national pact, one can observe a form of exponential growth that escalated Mexico City's expansion ("everybody's here because everybody's here"). The concept of spatialized centralization in Mexico City should not be interpreted as an implied superiority of the capital. Mexico City is not a substitute for the whole, nor is it representative of the nation in its totality. Here the point is to emphasize the concrete economic and political factors that undergirded the nation's great lopsidedness.

By 1970, 1 percent of the nation's land housed 20 percent of Mexico's population.[29] The mass migration to Mexico City encompassed the entire nation and drew individuals and families from every state in Mexico. In this sense, Mexico City was not a representative of the whole but more of a condensed composite image. Although the majority of migrants were poor farmers, when dealing with a quantity in the millions, even a relative minority of educated professionals and office workers (empleados) can amount to a significant absolute number of people. Across class lines, the migrants who initially arrived in Mexico City in the 1940s tended to be more skilled, healthier, and younger compared to the next generation of migrants who followed them in the 1960s. In some cases, such as with migrants from Los Altos in Jalisco and the Mixteca in Oaxaca, hometown associations were formed to ease the transition of city life and maintain connections with their native towns.[30]

In the aftermath of the revolution, leaders proposed a national highway system intended to develop regional roads between provincial urban centers and Mexico City. At the time of planning, Mexico only possessed seven hundred kilometers of road in 1928. The first interregional roads connected port cities (Veracruz, Acapulco) to Mexico City, and there was one between Monterrey and Nuevo Laredo. In just six years, close to four thousand kilometers of drivable roads were introduced into Mexico's road system.[31] By 1940, thirty-three cities were connected to the capital by ten thousand kilometers of road laid down to enable the movement of people and goods.[32] The creation of roads did not, however, automatically lead to widespread bus travel. Rail lines remained the main form of transportation to Mexico City until a sufficient number of bus companies made long-distance travel a viable option. In some cases, residents in small cities could take a taxi to the bus station, store their luggage, and board a bus bound for Mexico City. In other cases, villagers in more remote areas were often forced to walk for days until reaching a road that could connect them to a larger regional highway system.[33] Overall, the broad starting point for thousands of towns narrowed and narrowed until each migrant arrived at one of the two central transportation hubs in Mexico City: Buena Vista or San Lázaro Terminal.

The image of the humble peasant arriving in the city with a small satchel, sombrero, and sandals (or barefoot) became a common sight in 1940s Mexico City. The degree to which they shed their past or held on to tradition defies any easy categorization or pattern. Subjective feelings about their initial encounters in the city are difficult to assess, but it was undeniable that their access to electricity, education, medical services, and a broader variety of foods (particularly meat) increased upon arrival to the city.[34] As a whole, the majority of migrants were poor, lacked formal education, and were from towns centered on agriculture. A significant portion (40 percent in 1960) were classified as "marginal"—defined by low-pay work absent of contracts, state regulation, and social security benefits.[35] This 40 percent does not include working-class laborers who were part of the powerful Confederation of Mexican Workers (Confederación de Trabajadores de México, CTM). Documentation of internal migrations was scarce among scholars, whereas it was pervasive in popular culture. Indeed, the paucity of investigative studies on rural migrants is only magnified when compared to the innumerable depictions of in comic strips and movies, most notably in the work of actor Cantinflas.[36]

The films of Cantinflas resonated with audiences, yet both the press and scholars have failed to recognize the large number of formally educated migrants who also arrived in Mexico City. The concentration of government institutions and new business headquarters in the nation's capital exerted a strong pull on high school and university–educated empleados in provincial cities throughout the country. Although figures do not exist for earlier waves, estimates for the 1960s indicate that 16 percent of the roughly eight hundred thousand migrants who settled in Mexico City during this decade were college graduates (virtually the same portion as people born in Mexico City, 17 percent).[37]

The families who constituted this lower segment of the middle class were widely considered, or referred to, as *la gente decente*. More than simply income, their cultural values, reputation, their place within the division of labor, and the manner in which they comported themselves in public were all integral parts of what constituted and demarcated a person of la gente decente. The first tenants of Mario Pani's original multifamiliar apartment complex, Conjunto Urbano Presidente Alemán, were all civil servants who migrated to Mexico City from various parts of the country. Many of Multifamiliar Alemán's first residents originally migrated to Mexico City from the central and southern states of Oaxaca, Chiapas, Veracruz, and Hidalgo.[38] One longtime resident of Multifamiliar Alemán initially disliked the scale and uniformity of the buildings. She remembered, "In *mi tierra*, Tehuantepec in Oaxaca, we never saw such tall buildings, it was new, but each person on my floor liked their new place, and as more people came, I eventually grew to like the building."[39] Described as an "exceptional geographic mosaic of the country," the multifamiliar's residents held parties and *kermesses* (a traditional outdoor festival with games, food stands, and dance troupes) where residents organized displays that featured traditional culture and regional food from Oaxaca, Veracruz, Jalisco, and Guanajuato.[40] In addition to the economic pulls outlined previously, the National Autonomous University of Mexico (Universidad Nacional Autónoma de México, UNAM) and the National Polytechnic Institute of Mexico (Instituto Politécnico Nacional de México, IPN) universities drew young people from different parts of the country. The experiences of moving to the capital to study found their way into the canon of midcentury Mexican literature through the works of Rubén Bonifaz Nuño (Veracruz), Jaime Sabines (Chiapas), Sergio Pitol (Veracruz), José Agustín (Guerrero), Jorge Ibargüengoitia (Guanajuato), and Ricardo Garibay (Hidalgo).

The Mexican Revolution and subsequent agrarian reforms reconfigured the spatial distribution of Mexico's aristocracy. Prior to 1910, close to two-thirds of the nation's aristocratic families lived in Puebla, Zacatecas, Guanajuato, Chihuahua, Xalapa, Durango, Oaxaca, Guadalajara, Tampico, and Mérida.[41] These landed elite families occupied large estates and operated haciendas in their regional power bases. Due to the work of anthropologist Hugo Nutini, we know that prior to 1910, roughly 750 aristocratic families lived in Mexico's provincial cities, while 300 were located in Mexico City.[42] The period between 1920 and 1950 witnessed a slow but steady stream of aristocratic families migrating to Mexico City. Nutini divides the migration stream into two categories: "(1) those whose haciendas had suffered the greatest destruction and whose land had either been given legally to peasants or who had been overrun illegally; and (2) those who had been steadily losing their lands throughout the Porfiriato and whose financial base was by then mainly urban, that is, commercial and industrial."[43] By the 1950s, close to 80 percent of Mexico's provincial aristocracy had relocated to Mexico City, including all the families from Chihuahua, Durango, Tampico, Oaxaca, and Xalapa. Mexico City's traditional aristocracy accepted the newcomers by virtue of their old genealogical ties and positions as hacendados, leading to a moment when "the aristocracy experienced a veritable renaissance in Mexico City."[44]

The diversity of Mexico's rural-to-urban migration was fully expressed on the streets of downtown Mexico City during the 1940s. In this period of transition, the traditional delineations that separated poor and middle-class areas were challenged and weakened by the surge of migration to the central districts of the city. It was a moment when different layers of those struggling to survive in the city—from the indigent street vendor to the elementary school teacher—lived relatively close to one another in crowded neighborhoods lying west and south of the Zócalo. The compact heterogeneity was volatile and could only last for so long. For observers who evoked the image of "a ticking time bomb" in describing the tensions on the crowded streets of El Centro, the resolution to their metaphor did not produce a destructive explosion so much as a diffusion of tensions facilitated by the outward movement of families frustrated with the loud noise and overall chaotic nature of life in El Centro.[45] Although desirable rent-controlled apartments and persistent migration to Mexico City would ensure that El Centro remained crowded and lively, its decline and deterioration were key factors for understanding why large numbers of its residents abandoned it for the undeveloped peripheral areas of the metropolis.

Housing in Midcentury Mexico City

By the end of the 1940s, migrants arrived in a city paralyzed by a severe housing shortage commonly referred to as *la crisis*. Low-rise vecindades and tenements were filled to capacity. The city's downtown remained impervious to urban renewal, a barrier that caused the city to grow more horizontally than vertically. New middle-class colonias such as Narvarte and Portales drew office workers away from El Centro, while the working-class colonias proletarias scattered around the outlying areas absorbed 25–30 percent of the city's population.[46] Nevertheless, the center of gravity remained in the tenement belt that encircled the Zócalo from north, east, and south (*la herradura de tugurios*). Data from 1952 found that one-third of Mexico City's population (993,000) lived in cramped tenements surrounding the Zócalo. Of that nearly 1 million people, 400,000 lived in a one-room apartment with an average of 5 people per unit. Housing shortages had become so dire that 315,000 people were forced to build temporary shacks (*jacales*) out of cardboard and recycled materials after failing to find an apartment.[47]

Mexico City's escalating housing crisis fed into a larger set of concerns over public health and crime in the city. Regardless of one's place of residence, disease spread by dust storms, flooding, vermin, and crowded tramways or buses was an immediate threat to the entire city. The fear of disease was part of a larger existential angst over the decline of the capital, a foreboding feeling that the "City of Palaces" was deteriorating into a squalid slum. In 1944, journalist Carlos Vargas reported from colonia Morelos, where he could hardly believe the sight of "thousands of Mexicans living in such misery so close to the heart of the city, just five minutes from the Zócalo."[48] Ten years later, *El Nacional* ran an editorial entitled "The Face of the Times," which depicted a city government powerless in the face of crime, pollution, traffic, and squatter settlements.[49]

In these conditions, privacy was scarce and communicable diseases were rampant. In some cases, up to one hundred families could be forced to share the same communal water source and bathroom. A study found 21 percent of the apartments in the tenement belt lacked a single window, a deficiency that created the conditions for harmful bacteria to thrive and spread in overcrowded units.[50] The absence of sanitation services, lack of refrigerators, and close-quarters living made vermin infestation a daily part of life. In the densely packed tenements, you were only as clean as your neighbor. Despite the mounting pressures, the daunting tasks of rebuilding the country, stabilizing the economy, and managing the simmering discontent of the nation's peasantry after a violent revolution did not make for the best conditions to conduct systematic investigations into "the urban question." Notwithstanding newspaper investigations and the efforts surrounding a 1933 "master plan," the first thorough and detailed account of housing conditions in postrevolutionary Mexico City can be found in the National Urban Mortgage and Public Works Bank (Banco Nacional Hipotecario Urbano y de Obras Públicas, BNHUOP) studies from the late 1940s. In the years before the Mexican Institute of Social Security (Instituto Mexicano del Seguro Social, IMSS) and the National Institute of Housing (Instituto Nacional de Vivienda, INV), Alberto Pani led the BNHUOP to become the main public institution in Mexico's urban affairs, particularly in the realm of public works projects.[51]

In 1948, President Miguel Alemán commissioned the BNHUOP to carry out a comprehensive study of Mexico City. The study would attempt to provide a scientific and objective analysis of life in the capital, covering multiple socioeconomic classes, housing types, and geographic locations. In an attempt to cover as much ground as possible, the agency deployed thirty architects and engineers from IPN to carry out surveys of thirty-six neighborhoods in the Federal District.[52] Close attention was paid to neighborhoods considered emblematic of a particular kind of urban environment: tenement buildings (Tepito), working-class settlements (Gómez Frías), informal shantytowns (Buenos Aires), traditional middle-class apartments (Santa María la Ribera), and wealthy condominiums (Polanco).

Taken as a whole, the BNHUOP study presents a city undergoing an unprecedented period of uneven development. In part, these changes can be observed in the growing concentration of wealth dispersed across a larger geographic area yet limited and constrained by an even more intense growth of poverty-stricken neighborhoods. Although social inequality generally increased in these years, the absolute number of wealthy or middle-class families located in the capital gradually rose and expanded in new directions beyond El Centro. The average income for each neighborhood had a strong correlation to its access to public services, population density, and residents' quality of health. In terms of average income, the breakdown reveals a wide division between the upper and lower strata of Mexico City. The average income for the head of the household in 1950 was 217 pesos in a typical shantytown, 248 pesos in a tenement (including both vecindad and tugurio), 360 pesos in a working-class settlement (colonia proletaria), 830 pesos in a middle-class neighborhood like Santa María la Ribera, and 6,388 pesos on average in the wealthy Lomas de Chapultepec.[53] Unsurprisingly, studies found a majority of residents in Santa María la Ribera and Lomas de Chapultepec had access to electricity, drainage, and running water. For the urban poor, the breakdown of access to services by area was more complicated and multifaceted. In general, tenants in the central-city districts (vecindad, tugurio) paid less in monthly fees and received more access to services when compared to working-class settlements (colonia proletaria) built outside of the city center.[54]

The depths of poverty found in the old tenement quarters of La Merced, Tepito, and Lagunilla had a profound effect on the young architects who studied the neighborhoods' buildings, talked with their residents, and photographed their crowded marketplaces. By reordering the architects' individualized accounts, found interspersed throughout the report's various sections, one can begin to form a mental map of their street-by-street observations. The authors describe Adolfo Gurrión Street on the lower end of La Merced, where "the slums [tugurios] offer the observer the spectacle of malnutrition, disease, and vice." In our mental map, we move north to 44 Calle Rosario, where over one hundred people share one bathroom and the "leaks and humid moisture in the rooms can be found where bronchitis is pervasive; pneumonia and tuberculosis are easily generated in this environment."[55] We continue north a few buildings to 72 Calle Rosario, where the architects assess the building's conditions: it is a vecindad of thirty-one units, of which nine are habitable while the rest have already fallen into a state of disrepair.[56] They end up at Plaza de la Candelaria, where one of the authors observes, "Vice and religion seem to be the only consolation for these people. Vice for men; religion for women.... One regularly encounters *pulquerías* on the streets. Religious images, simplistic in their consultation or condemnation, adorn their bedrooms."[57] As the rate of new migrants in the city's old quarters grew over the years, calls for urban renewal gained momentum among public officials and planners who were alarmed by the capital's steady deterioration.

Historic Preservation in El Centro

The housing crisis sparked a sharp debate across a broad spectrum of Mexican society. For tenant associations, store owners, bus drivers, city planners, architects, scientists, and environmental conservationists, the situation was intolerable. These circumstances set the stage for polarizing debates that would ultimately shape the future of the metropolis. Discussed and formulated in seemingly neutral, technocratic language, the resolution of these debates was guided by local political dynamics.

In surveying the many critical junctures in Mexico City's long history, the beginning of Uruchurtu's tenure represents one of the most consequential. With the city at a crossroads, the future of El Centro would be decided in the years between 1950 and 1953. Politically, it was a time of transition, one which witnessed a new president, Adolfo Ruiz Cortines (1952–58), and a new regent, Ernesto P. Uruchurtu (1952–66). Ideologically, the early 1950s marked a moment when both cultural nationalism and modernism approached their respective high points in Mexican history. In Mexico City, these two high points came into direct conflict with each other when the Federal District Planning Commission unveiled its plans to rebuild the city's historic center into a modern downtown and provoked a major outcry of opposition by historic preservationists. The historic center's compact zone of cultural patrimony produced an affective sense of national identity strongly tied to its built environment. The defense of cultural patrimony embedded in Mexico City's downtown streets had its own limits, even among the most ardent preservationists. As the Planning Commission's urban renewal project reveals, the vast majority of Mexico's urbanists all agreed on the need to transform Mexico City. The question of to what extent the city's historic center should be destroyed and modernized caused the many forces to diverge and form points of conflict.

With housing and traffic problems growing dire, Regent Fernando Casas Alemán established the Federal District Planning Commission in 1950. The Federal District Planning Commission (1950–53) was a body of engineers, planners, architects, and business leaders assembled by Casas Alemán to resolve Mexico City's most pressing problems through scientific research and technical expertise. The commission consisted of fifteen members with voting power and an additional fifteen individuals who served as consultants without voting power. Architects Mario Pani and Pedro Ramírez Vázquez, engineer Luis Ángeles (Department of Public Works), Carlos Novoa (Banco de México), and Fernando Valdés (Property Owner's Defense League) were among the fifteen representatives with voting power over the commission's resolutions.[58] The main feature of the commission's city plan was the creation of a new roadway system in the center of Mexico City. Frustrated with an antiquated street grid from the 1500s, the leading figures in the Planning Commission proposed a system of wide boulevards designed to cut through Mexico City's colonial-era streets that were to be connected by a series of *glorietas* (roundabouts). The commission's engineers envisioned a modern landscape of towering buildings and department stores to accompany the new boulevards in the central and eastern sections of the capital.

Engineer Luis Ángeles emerged as the most vocal proponent for "destroying the city in order to save the city."[59] The commission's urban renewal project consisted of the widening and expansion of the Paseo de la Reforma, Tacuba Street, Guerrero Street, Palma Street, and Veinte de Noviembre Avenue. The plan required the destruction of seven hundred buildings, leaving over thirty thousand people homeless. Of those seven hundred buildings, at least twenty-six were registered as historic landmarks by the colonial monuments division of the National Institute of Anthropology and History (Instituto Nacional de Antropología e Historia, INAH).[60] Buildings that represented the foundations of Catholicism in the Western Hemisphere (Convento de la Encarnación), bastions of the enlightenment in New Spain (Real Seminario de Minería), and the vibrancy of the modern era (Café de Tacuba) were all set to be destroyed to remake El Centro. On October 21, 1950, the Planning Commission approved Luis Ángeles's plan to modernize El Centro's street grid.[61] As the Federal Commission's internal process proceeded smoothly, negative coverage in the press (particularly in *El Universal* and *Novedades*) turned public opinion against the Planning Commission's new road system. At the beginning of 1951, tenant associations began to mobilize, and prominent figures from the INAH began to jump into the fray.[62] Journalist Adrián García Cortés wrote, "If these attacks against the spirit of Mexico, expressed in the stone of past centuries . . . are executed, then the plan will be seen not only as an affront to our culture and our history, but to humanity itself."[63] The discontent among small business owners, emboldened by preservation laws for Mexico's cultural patrimony passed in the early 1930s, gained the upper hand. At an impasse, the Planning Commission suspended future meetings and used the indefinite recess to privately discuss how to turn the tide back in their favor.[64]

The Planning Commission's plans proved to be futile after Ernesto Uruchurtu was selected to be the Federal District's new regent (*regente*) in 1952.[65] At the time of his inauguration, the Planning Commission's project was widely unpopular among residents and contributed to Fernando Casas Alemán's steep decline in popularity. Shortly after Uruchurtu took office, he announced the cancellation of the Planning Commission's proposal to widen Tacuba Street, reasoning that "it's a beautiful project but not possible . . . it is necessary to first resolve the problem of flooding and lack of drinking water."[66] With that, the project was largely scrapped, and only a partial extension of the Paseo de la Reforma was carried out under Uruchurtu.[67] The technocratic dream of a rational and modern downtown could not overcome the weight of tradition.

Uruchurtu's Antiurban Growth Platform

Uruchurtu's reign as regente was fueled by a potent blend of political populism and cultural nationalism. He staked his political career on the city's middle class and rooted it in a nostalgia for the past.[68] Globally, from New York to Manila, slum clearance and urban renewal characterized the tenor of the times.[69] Unlike most major cities in the postwar era, Mexico City's built environment was defined not by urban renewal but by urban restoration. The investment and implementation of urban services (drainage, running water, electricity) were integrated into El Centro's preexisting built environment to retain both its historic ambiance and middle-class residents. Mexico City's housing problem would not be resolved through the "verticalization" of its downtown. Uruchurtu's nostalgia for the city's former glories, combined with the pressing problems of the day, contributed to his reluctance to fully accept the major changes that lay ahead in the future. This outlook was most concretely expressed in his 1953 Ley de Planificación y Zonificación del Distrito Federal (Federal District Planning and Zoning Law), a sweeping measure intended to stem and control urban growth in the Federal District.

At the end of 1953, Uruchurtu introduced several amendments to the city's main body of zoning and planning laws to prohibit the establishment of new subdivisions within the limits of the Federal District. The prohibition on new subdivisions was, in reality, a selective ban that empowered the Federal District's local government (Departamento del Distrito Federal, DDF) to decide which new subdivisions or developments would be granted approval.[70] The amendments raised the fees for building permits, made building codes more stringent, and lengthened the legal process to develop residential units on vacant lands. In effect, the amendments created a large number of prerequisites and building codes that would require significant capital investment, thus leading to high rental fees beyond what Mexico City's urban poor could afford. In practice, it strengthened the local government's control over authorizing new housing developments, thereby determining where the city would be obligated to invest in public utilities and infrastructure.[71] The 1953 law functioned as a barrier to land regularization for poor subdivisions (*fraccionamientos*) and was a key factor in exacerbating the urban poor's settlement beyond the bounds of the Federal District into the neighboring State of Mexico.

Uruchurtu's arrival would prove decisive for Mario Pani's career. Under Uruchurtu, the poles of contention in urban politics became more clearly defined and consolidated, a clarifying moment that shaped Pani's outlook and influenced how he would proceed in the years ahead.[72] For Pani, the void left by the Federal District Planning Commission's disintegration was quickly filled by the construction of UNAM's new Ciudad Universitaria (University City). The largest single government project since the Porfirian Grand Canal, the relocation of UNAM's new campus on the southern edge of the city was driven by a utopian impulse.[73] UNAM's Ciudad Universitaria "not only represented the projection of collective work for the transformation of [the] nation through the focus on higher education but also served as an expression of modernization" attained by Mexico at the time of its construction.[74] The palpable energy and anticipation surrounding UNAM's Ciudad Universitaria further convinced Pani of the direction forward after the Planning Commission debacle: the future of the city was on the frontier.[75] The events surrounding the Federal District Planning Commission and UNAM's Ciudad Universitaria moved Pani to collaborate more closely with various government agencies in the construction of several massive public works projects often envisioned as "cities outside of the city."[76]

In the 1950s, the idea of "cities outside of the city" would take shape in the new housing complexes built by IMSS in various cities across Mexico.[77] The social housing project (*unidad habitacional*) would come to symbolize Mexico's rising urban middle class. In Mexico City, the new unidades habitacionales would also help contribute to the middle class's eventual abandonment of El Centro. Mexico City's housing projects would be constructed not over the rubble of downtown tenements but on the empty plains of the outlying periphery.

Today, Calle Tacuba continues to retain the historical ambiance that was once threatened by the Federal District Planning Commission. A short stroll from the legendary Café de Tacuba leads one to a large plaza containing the excavated ruins of the Aztec Templo Mayor. A UNESCO World Heritage Site and popular tourist destination, the impressive ruins of the temple would have been buried under four lanes of highway leading to the airport if the Planning Commission's street grid would have passed through Uruchurtu's administration. The various factors discussed in this chapter prevented the Planning Commission's new expressway to the airport, yet it did not prevent the capital's poor families from beginning to settle on the open fields surrounding the airport. In fact, it accelerated it. Uruchurtu's urban agenda was not the cause of Mexico City's outward sprawl, but it intensified its reach and made the settlement of the Vaso de Texcoco (later Ciudad Neza) more plausible.

Facing a housing crisis at the end of the 1940s, the city's surrounding periphery began to function as an escape valve for overcrowding in El Centro. As Mexican leaders increasingly sought to modernize and centralize Mexico's economy, their aspirations were reflected in the modernist housing complexes being constructed around the outlying areas of Mexico City. In the following chapter, we turn to the first public housing complexes built by IMSS and the criteria developed for their initial residents.

2

Mass Housing in the Mexican Metropolis

Before the 1950s, Mexico experimented with an assortment of models for popular housing. The first phase (1933–38) was pioneered by several collectives of avant-garde architects who melded functionalism, socialist realism, and Mexican nationalism into a small number of housing cooperatives during the 1930s.[1] At the end of the 1940s, Mario Pani broke new ground with his adaptation of Le Corbusier's Radiant City housing complex in the heart of Mexico City.[2] Architects and government officials gravitated toward Pani's multifamiliar, but they eventually recognized that his singular model lacked the kind of organization and structure necessary for a national housing program with a comprehensive financial system, centralized administration, and legal protocol. This undertaking became the domain of the Mexican Institute of Social Security (IMSS). IMSS developed the criteria for prospective tenants, making union membership and proof of a regular salary two necessary requisites. Structurally, the criteria played a fundamental role in solidifying divisions between urban workers in Mexico's social hierarchy. Culturally, the state's housing complexes provided a national aesthetic for the built environment of social welfare.

The following chapter details the decisive role IMSS played in Mexico's early years of social housing. It then explores the influence of the Alliance for Progress on Mexico's housing programs in the 1960s. It concludes with a close study of a government-built housing complex in the former Vaso de Texcoco called Unidad Habitacional San Juan de Aragón. Neighboring Ciudad Neza, San Juan de Aragón offered workers the promise of home ownership, marking a significant shift away from the initial rental units built by IMSS in the 1950s.

IMSS and Social Housing in Mexico

The Mexican Institute of Social Security was officially established on January 9, 1943. When Abel Morales Rodriguez became the first person to receive an IMSS membership card on July 12, 1943, Mexico's social security system only covered 2 percent of the country's population.[3] Initially dormant, social security programs were enacted and implemented as part of diffusing a series of labor conflicts in the summer of 1944. The programs' language and ideals called upon the spirit of the revolution to raise the standard of living for Mexican workers through a national network of affordable housing, health insurance, and pension savings.[4] Initially, IMSS's insurance and benefits were limited to government employees, nurses, unionized electricians, and the highly organized sugarcane workers in Veracruz.[5]

In 1945, the Executive Committee for Social Security passed a resolution to allot 20 percent of IMSS's budget for housing. The committee stated, "Housing can be transformed into an instrument for social security" and envisioned newly constructed worker cities as physical expressions of the revolution.[6] These lofty ambitions were met with limited success. For its first ten years, IMSS was primarily focused on the creation of a national health care system, and plans for housing construction did not begin in earnest until 1954.[7]

As IMSS focused on health insurance and medical facilities during the 1940s, Mario Pani continued to champion the multifamiliar as a solution to Mexico's housing problem. After the success of several experimental projects, many public officials were convinced as well. Pani's Unidad Modelo (1948), Multifamiliar Alemán (1949), and Multifamiliar Juárez (1952) projected a sense of progress and momentum to both local residents and international audiences.[8] With limited funds, Pani was able to re-create Le Corbusier's Radiant City for federal employees on an empty field to the south of the city center (Multifamiliar Alemán). Pani's emphasis on the increased density and height of residential towers allowed for more surface area to build playgrounds, parks, gardens, and parking spaces for residents. For the Multifamiliar Juárez, Pani integrated plastic arts and colorful murals into the exterior facades, foreshadowing the consolidation of cultural nationalism in midcentury Mexican architecture. These early projects provided the template for future housing programs developed under presidents López Mateos (1958–64) and Díaz Ordaz (1964–70).

The IMSS housing system was created at a time when developmentalism was in ascendancy around the world.⁹ The prospects of rapid economic development through the application of science and technology held sway among leaders in IMSS's housing division. In the postrevolutionary state's efforts to transform Mexico's "rustic and uneducated population," the built environment was an essential component of the formation of a new citizenry. More than simply housing, the complexes were also viewed as ideal locales to build new hospitals, medical clinics, parks, sports arenas, theaters, supermarkets, and schools for both residents and the general public. In terms of "citizenry," the issue of democracy was generally absent or vague in the available reports, speeches, and ephemera produced by IMSS in the late 1950s.¹⁰ Neither anticommunism nor liberal democracy were featured in the numerous newsletters, posters, brochures, or educational materials produced by IMSS from this period.¹¹ The absence or lack of anticommunism in IMSS literature does not negate the significance of the Cold War in Mexico but instead points to an alternative political orientation promoted by IMSS officials. The less explicit political dimensions of 1950s public housing were expressed around questions of gender norms, health, hygiene, identity, and history. The planning meetings, designs, speeches, and pedagogical materials found in IMSS's archives demonstrate these questions were framed around a mixture of nationalism, secular humanism, and patriarchal values. The manifestation of these overarching ideas will be further explored in the actual construction and habitation of Unidad Santa Fe. However, before turning to the architectural aspects of Unidad Santa Fe, it is necessary to examine the selection process for its tenants and their initial reception to the new housing complex.

The Selection Process for Social Housing

The selection process for Unidad Santa Fe established the procedures and prerequisites for future social housing programs. IMSS's housing laws and application forms stated that residents must show proof of a salaried wage (pay stubs or stamped checks) and have a bank account, an IMSS membership card, and no criminal record.¹² Although not explicitly stated, it was highly unlikely that a person would be admitted unless they were part of a recognized labor union (trade, teacher, professional employee). Here, along with the absolute income of an applicant, it was equally important to show proof of a stable income through formal banking records and pay stubs.[13] While government-built housing would extend beyond workers insured by IMSS after 1963, the prerequisites of personal bank accounts, verifiable pay stubs, and available credit continued to present barriers for those who worked in the informal economy.

Direct government assistance also meant direct government supervision. This was enforced through rules, regulations, social workers, educators, security guards, spatial design, and the all-powerful *chisme* (gossip). Unregulated marketplaces, cantinas, dance halls, and livestock (all staples of poor settlements, or vecindades) were banned from social housing complexes.[14] Children went to public schools, day cares, and after-school programs that were located near their apartment buildings. As Mexico's primary social service agency, IMSS integrated its separate social worker program into its housing system.[15] At Unidad Santa Fe, social workers were assigned to periodically meet with tenants. The training manuals IMSS produced for social workers detail the steps that should be taken with each visit, including noting observations of each family's living conditions, holding workshops for mothers on hygiene and food preparation, and organizing cultural events among neighbors.[16] Beginning in 1960, IMSS began to utilize social workers to interview prospective tenants.[17] These examples illustrate a filtering process for tenants that was carried out over the course of several months, if not years, by IMSS and related agencies.

The story of the Padilla family is illustrative of Unidad Santa Fe's selection process. At the time of Santa Fe's inauguration, the Padilla family was featured in several magazines and newspapers as Santa Fe's first tenants. The family was originally from the Gulf Coast city of Tampico and moved from the port city after it was battered by a powerful hurricane. The patriarch of the family, José Manuel Padilla González, worked from 7 a.m. until 1 p.m. at the Radio Mex station and then worked a second job in the offices of the Departamento de Afiliación del IMSS until 9:30 at night. At forty-seven, José had the look of a man "tanned by the sun of the Gulf Coast and hardened by the pressures of work in the capital."[18] The move to Unidad Santa Fe was viewed by the family as "a blessing." The mother, Carlota Aleman Padilla, told a reporter, "We have everything here, a dry cleaner, a laundromat, markets, a butcher shop, a post office and telegraph, and our own police station."[19] With a lower rent fee (90 pesos a month), José was relieved that the monthly rent payments would no longer "eat up [his] pay check."[20] Overall, 65 percent of the families in Unidad Santa Fe paid a subsidized, low-cost rent of 100–150 pesos. As one journalist wrote, "The story of the Padilla family . . . is the same for thousands of workers who live permanently haunted by economic anguish as a result of being a large family in a city with high rent costs."[21] The profile of the Padillas gives us a more living sense of the families moving into Unidad Santa Fe at the time of its opening on July 16, 1957.

Unidad Santa Fe Opens

Located to the west of El Centro in a forested area called Lomas de Santa Fe, Unidad Santa Fe was built along the foothills of a mountain range that separates the Federal District from the State of Mexico.[22] At the time of its opening in 1957, Unidad Santa Fe was the largest housing complex in Mexico City, containing 2,100 housing units for roughly 13,000 people.[23] It was frequently touted as the first project in Latin America to fully integrate social service facilities into a public housing complex.[24]

Unidad Santa Fe was divided along an east-west axis, with its civic plaza functioning as a central convergence point. Each home's interior was organized by function (food, rest, personal hygiene), and each home was part of a set of residential buildings surrounded by schools and medical clinics. The schools and clinics were encircled by supermarkets, parks, and finally, the main roadways linking the complex to the rest of the city. Organized on a superblock grid, children could walk along a series of tree-lined pathways from their homes to school without crossing potentially dangerous roadways designed for cars.[25] Santa Fe's apartments were mechanized and austere yet clean, safe, affordable, and equipped with basic services. Fully functioning drainage systems, running water, and electricity for each unit were installed to enable the kinds of sanitary habits and physical hygiene that officials sought to promote among Mexican families. Each zone had a supermarket, park, athletic field, administration building, parking lot, day care, and elementary school. In addition, the complex had a hospital and several clinics.[26] Overall, Santa Fe was a planned urban community with the necessary infrastructure and services to be relatively self-contained and semiautonomous.

Unidad Santa Fe merged Mario Pani's modernist designs with IMSS's social agenda. In one example, Santa Fe's Social Center offered cooking classes and childcare workshops to young women in an effort to instill and reinforce gender norms through everyday domestic activities. In a report on the social center's construction, Julián Díaz Arias stated, "The wives and daughters of workers . . . will find their daily dilemmas and problems solved through Santa Fe's shopping market, access to nutritionists, doctors, social workers, and teachers who will help guide them to create the most efficient household."[27] IMSS's social programs arose at a contradictory moment when technological advances were adapted to maintain traditional gender roles. This general orientation was adopted for young people in both education and athletics. As IMSS's housing program progressed, athletics and social programs for youth continued to be a central focus. This can be seen most clearly in a series of youth centers built by IMSS in the early 1960s. With Unidad Morelos as its flagship site, IMSS intended to mold the children of migrants into model citizens while at the same time addressing the growing anxieties over juvenile delinquency.[28]

In Mexico, modernism provided the visual aesthetic for social welfare. In this specific context, "modern" was a turn away from ornate exteriors to functional facades; the cathedral and the plaza were replaced by the public school and civic center; standardized piping and running water were hailed as major steps toward improved hygiene; sports facilities and playgrounds were viewed as healthy antidotes to the lethargy of cantinas.[29] It was not the case, however, that Mexico's modernist marvels were completely aligned with the core characteristics of modernist architecture. In contrast to modernism's ahistoricism and opposition to ornamentation, Mexico's midcentury housing complexes were historicized landscapes adorned with Aztec symbols, statues of national heroes, and homages to pre-Hispanic civilizations.[30] Modernism's "rebellion against historicism" had been adapted to Mexico's national project in a hybridized form of mestizo modernism.[31] Beyond architecture and aesthetics, the housing projects reflected a notion of modernity distinct from Western modernity due to its ancestral connections to ancient cities and civilizations formed before contact with Europe.[32]

After Unidad Santa Fe, IMSS began to build more housing complexes in Mexico City, Sonora, and Hidalgo. By 1963, IMSS constructed thirteen complexes for 10,853 families (roughly 50,000 people). In addition to IMSS, projects built by Banobras (Alemán, Juarez, Modelo, Reloj, Esperanza) contributed another 15,000–20,000 units throughout Mexico.[33] On both local and national levels, this number was minuscule when measured against the country's housing deficit. However, with each publicized inauguration and ribbon-cutting event, the Mexican state could point to concrete measures it was taking to address the housing problem in its major cities.

The pressures to produce more housing only intensified as Mexico entered the 1960s. As the new decade approached, many of the same dynamics that led to the construction of Unidad Santa Fe were still at play as the Mexican government began to draw up a set of plans to urbanize the former Vaso de Texcoco—notably, the sections within the bounds of the Federal District. At the far reaches of the Federal District, where a previous generation of engineers and agronomists failed to turn the former lake bed into prime farmland, a new wave of engineers and architects set out to build a new city within the city: the Unidad Habitacional San Juan de Aragón.

The Cold War and Modernism in the Vaso de Texcoco

Mexico's housing program was internationalized in the early 1960s due to the confluence of several different factors. Objectively, officials estimated the need for approximately 250,000–300,000 new homes each year to absorb the growing housing deficit.[34] Politically, President López Mateos saw social housing programs as a means to directly improve the lives of Mexican workers and visibly demonstrate "the fruits of the Mexican Revolution."[35] Internationally, the Cuban Revolution had sent shockwaves around the world, and the United States was recalibrating its foreign policy in Latin America. In the wake of Cuba's alignment with the Soviet Union, President John F. Kennedy launched the Alliance for Progress as an economic assistance program for Latin America.[36] Under the aegis of the Alliance for Progress, funds were channeled to new housing projects throughout Mexico—including in the Vaso de Texcoco. Before turning to the Mexican government's urban developments in the Vaso de Texcoco (San Juan de Aragón), the following section provides a brief sketch of Washington's role in Mexico's urban housing programs.

The Alliance for Progress provides a fruitful focal point for assessing changes to Mexico's housing programs during López Mateos's presidency. A charter for the alliance was established at an inter-American conference held in Uruguay during the summer of 1961. The participating countries agreed to implement policies that would promote literacy, democratic institutions, land reform, industrialization, and overall economic development (an annual increase of 2.5 percent per capita income).[37] Within this ambitious agenda, low-cost housing was viewed as a tool for foreign policy, a bulwark against social unrest, and an opportunity to expand the region's housing industry, both domestically and internationally. As one 1962 report for the United States Agency for International Development (USAID) revealed, "Home ownership (e.g., savings and loans institutions, self-help programs, cooperatives) may stimulate investment that may not otherwise take place . . . poor housing may be a significant factor in matters of health, family, stability, moral values, and political unrest."[38] Mexican officials didn't need to be convinced that the nation had a "housing problem"; the question was how and where to prioritize it within the aid package.

In 1962, roughly 40 percent of the Federal District's population (5.1 million people) lived in dwellings of just a single room, with most of those rooms lacking adequate bathroom facilities.[39] Despite the housing units built by public agencies between 1949 and 1960, studies carried out by the INV, IMSS, and USAID in the early 1960s all predicted that Mexico City's housing deficit would continue to soar unless drastic measures were taken by the government.[40] Between 1958 and 1963, a series of publications and internal memos by the INV concluded that Mexico City's population explosion was heading toward catastrophic levels; if housing was left solely within the domain of the private market, then wages would need to be dramatically raised for most of the city's residents to be able to afford decent housing, and although it was not directly stated, the reports implied that the PRI was at risk of losing a crucial constituency if the housing problem was not resolved in the near future.[41] Building from the foundation created by IMSS, López Mateos made urban housing a central component of his political agenda for social reform as Cold War tensions escalated throughout the hemisphere.

Between January 1961 and September 1964, direct U.S. assistance to Mexico totaled 72 million dollars.[42] Initially, the United States agreed to lend Mexico 20 million dollars to establish a supervised agricultural credit program for small farmers, consisting of low-interest productivity loans.[43] In the end, 40 percent of U.S. aid to Mexico under the Alliance for Progress was directed toward low-cost housing (20 million from USAID and 10 million from the Inter-American Development Bank). As a direct result of this foreign aid, the Mexican government constructed forty-two housing projects, primarily in Mexico City and Morelos.[44] Beyond the tens of thousands of homes created through the program, Mexico's collaboration with agencies linked to the Alliance for Progress served as an impetus for the creation of the Fund for Housing Operations and Finance (Fondo de Operación y Financiamiento Bancario a la Vivienda, FOVI), a federal entity designed to grant financial support to credit institutions working in the housing industry.

FOVI is a financial trust that was established on April 10, 1963, by the federal government and the Banco de México. Partially modeled after the U.S. Federal Housing Administration (FHA), FOVI dramatically revised Mexico's mortgage laws for dwellings that were considered *vivienda de interés social* (roughly translated as "social housing"). In order to qualify as vivienda de interés social, the housing unit could not cost more than 62,500 pesos in the Mexico City area or 55,000 for the rest of the country. Banking institutions that participated in FOVI entered into a legal agreement that considered the whole program for low-cost housing had a social character and, therefore, were barred from engaging in financial speculation or excessive banking profits that could be detrimental to credit subjects.[45] Shortly after FOVI was created, López Mateos passed several laws that required both commercial banks and mortgage lending institutions to allot 30 percent of their available savings or mortgage bonds for low-cost housing.[46]

FOVI opened mortgage lending to an entirely new demographic of the population. Prior to FOVI, saving departments of commercial banks could not grant mortgage loans, and mortgage banks required a guarantee of 40 percent of the total amount from the home buyer. Under the new banking and credit laws that accompanied FOVI, banks were now authorized to make loans for low-cost housing for up to 80–90 percent of the value of the guarantee. Short-term amortization plans (mortgage payment plans) were lengthened from five to twenty-five years, thus making monthly payments feasible for families who would otherwise be priced out of home ownership in a major city.[47] In the case of Unidad Kennedy, a family could make a down payment of 1,944 pesos for a home valued at 55,000 pesos and pay off the rest at 565 pesos per month over the next twenty years.[48]

In its first five years of existence, FOVI funded 39,370 low-cost housing units in twenty cities.[49] A mixture of public and private entities was responsible for this total number: a miners' union in Sonora, the U.S.-based AFL-CIO for Unidad Kennedy, the DDF for San Juan de Aragón, and several petroleum worker unions in Veracruz and Tamaulipas. In general, FOVI did widen the accessibility of low-cost housing beyond people employed or insured by IMSS but remained inaccessible to the majority of the urban poor. Even the subsidized rates of 550–750 pesos per month were too high for most impoverished families; FOVI was only open to people who earned three times the minimum wage—roughly 30 percent of the Mexican population in 1964.[50] Like IMSS, housing for FOVI required work references, bank account numbers, and in many cases, membership in an officially recognized labor union.[51]

Most fundamentally, FOVI shifted the focus of social housing from apartment rentals to home ownership. In places like San Juan de Aragón, the prospects of home ownership (being a *propietario*) enhanced the appeal of apartments or *unifamiliares* that were part of the FOVI program. In addition, home ownership increased the family's equity and tended to make them wary of, or opposed to, radical politics. FOVI was the financial institution through which residents of San Juan de Aragón bought into housing built by the Mexico City government.

San Juan de Aragón, Satellite City

Today, San Juan de Aragón is most commonly known as the green-and-blue oasis at the edge of the city. The blue fragments that can be seen when arriving at the nearby Mexico City airport make up parts of the San Juan de Aragón Lake. It is one of the world's largest artificial lakes, built on top of what was once a natural lake—a work of true modern irony. The lake is surrounded by Mexico City's "greenbelt"—a public works project consisting of soccer fields, playgrounds, gardens, picnic grounds, and walking paths that wind through the park's 14,730 trees. Within the park are eight biosphere facilities for over 135 different species contained, labeled, and on display in the San Juan de Aragón Zoo.[52] Beyond the park and zoo are some twenty thousand homes that house roughly 130,000 people.

The San Juan de Aragón of today is a far cry from its origins as an arid plain dotted with small ejidos and outlined by canals. The complicated history of the land that now constitutes the San Juan de Aragón housing complex is one that twists and turns over the course of six centuries. Beginning in 1435, the water and lands were part of the Tlatelolco city-state (*altepetl*) either in the form of self-rule or as the República de Indios de Santiago Tlatelolco (established in 1524 after the Spanish conquest). In general, the northwestern sections were productive and supported several small pueblos (villages) that were able to cultivate a variety of grains. However, like Ciudad Neza, much of what is now San Juan de Aragón was underwater before 1880. As a series of regimes depleted more of Lake Texcoco, the land expanded, though it suffered from high deposits of salt that made land cultivation impossible or tenuous at best. By the mid-1800s, the roughly 450 people who lived in Pueblo de San Juan de Aragón survived through hunting, fishing, salt extraction, or small crop production.[53]

The 1930s marks a turning point in the history of San Juan de Aragón. During this decade, the postrevolutionary state set out to eradicate the unrelenting dust storms that plagued Mexico City through a combination of land cultivation and afforestation projects. These projects were to be carried out primarily in San Juan de Aragón and the neighboring Peñón de los Baños.[54] As Matthew Vitz details in his history of the area, substantial investments into land reclamation projects failed to convert the former Texcoco lake bed into a center for agriculture.[55] An aerial photo of San Juan de Aragón from 1945 reveals large tracts of land that were barren and desolate.[56] Much like the feeble crops that clung to the arid soil, the hopes of a thriving, green hinterland slowly withered away. The afforestation carried out in San Juan de Aragón proved to be a more effective and longer-lasting public works project. Long rows of newly planted poplar and eucalyptus trees weakened the velocity of powerful wind gusts that carried dust clouds from the desiccated Texcoco lake bed to the Federal District. As the years passed, these trees began to function as Mexico City's "second lung" through their provision of oxygen and absorption of carbon dioxide. Although these forest reserves were man made, their upkeep required significantly less human attention than crops in a setting such as the former Vaso de Texcoco.

As the city expanded and radiated outward from El Centro, the remote plains of San Juan de Aragón seemed less and less distant by the end of the 1950s. What may be panned as a failure in land cultivation can be viewed as a fundamental building block for urbanization. The scientific investigations, afforestation, canal construction, soil washing, and rudimentary road construction in the parts of the Vaso de Texcoco that fell within the bounds of the Federal District created better conditions for urban settlements when compared to the very minimal investment that went into the Colonias del Vaso de Texcoco (Ciudad Neza) in the neighboring State of Mexico.

The land of San Juan de Aragón was expropriated by the federal government on February 22, 1962.[57] Mexico's land laws stipulated that ejido land could be repossessed by the government if it was determined to be "within the public interest."[58] The government and remaining *ejidatarios* in San Juan de Aragón reached an agreement that guaranteed compensation for the expropriated lands (still a matter of dispute among some ejidatarios who claim they have not received their full compensation). In all, the government expropriated 1,110 hectares (2,718 acres) of land to begin building a new housing development. The expropriation in 1962 signaled an end to land cultivation and marked the beginning of San Juan de Aragón's urbanization.[59] The Federal District's Department of Planning and the Oficina de Habitación Popular (Office of Popular Housing) officially designated the land for urbanization and began to assemble a team that would be responsible for the planning and construction of a satellite city. In a matter of weeks, San Juan de Aragón's land gained the same kind of formal recognition that the residents of Ciudad Neza struggled to gain over the course of twenty years.

The construction of San Juan de Aragón brought together several key urbanists who were at the forefront of the modernist movement in Mexico. Most notably, Héctor Velázquez Moreno was the principal figure who coordinated the various government institutions in the creation of San Juan de Aragón (the housing, roadways, infrastructure, park, zoo, and police). At the time of San Juan de Aragón's construction phase, Velázquez was the head of the DDF's Popular Housing Department and president of Mexico's National Society of Architects.[60] In his search for someone to lead the San Juan de Aragón project, he selected an up-and-coming urban planner named Enrique Cervantes Sánchez.[61] His approach to urban planning diverged from Mario Pani, of whom he was highly critical: "The architect Mario Pani thought that *urbanismo* was simply making architecture on a grand scale, and that is incredibly reckless."[62] In conceptualizing the urbanization of San Juan de Aragón, Cervantes Sánchez parted ways with the towering multifamiliar model and looked abroad in search of an alternative. In the end, he gravitated toward the "neighborhood-unit" models developed by Clarence Perry and Clarence Stein.

The neighborhood unit was adapted to San Juan de Aragón through a series of sections Cervantes Sánchez called *unidades vecinales*. He designed seven unidades vecinales that each contained four to six neighborhoods.

In one example, Unidad Vecinal I's borders are defined and encircled by 508th and 503rd Avenues, with the center containing a traffic-free space where two schools, a medical clinic, restaurants, a cultural center, shops, and a few offices are located. Unidad Vecinal I itself is divided into six neighborhoods, with each one containing a minicenter that has a school, commercial area, and offices. Along the western edge of Unidad Vecinal I is a sports center (Campo Deportivo Francisco Zarco), a large park that features a playground and recreational facilities.[63] The unidad vecinal model operated under the assumption that family life has universal needs, that those universal needs have similar parts performing similar functions, and that "in the neighborhood-unit system, those parts have been put together as an organic whole."[64] Unidad Vecinal I alone required 15 supervisors and 150 laborers to work day and night constructing 3,229 homes, a children's medical center, commercial spaces, water fountains, one elementary school for each of the six *supermanzanas* (large block), and athletic fields, which included a stadium, sixteen basketball courts, five soccer fields, four volleyball courts, and a playground.[65] The northern edges of Unidad Vecinal I are surrounded by Unidad Morelos, an immense community center independently run by IMSS that began construction in 1962. At the end of 1964, San Juan de Aragón was ready to be inaugurated by President López Mateos.

November 1964 was a watershed moment in the history of Mexico City. On November 5, López Mateos arrived via helicopter to the opening of Viveros de la Loma. The project was built by the INV and consisted of 1,116 units.[66] On November 16, the headlines proclaimed, "A New City Is Born in the Federal District," and every major newspaper in the capital featured photo layouts of San Juan de Aragón's new park, zoo, and housing units. In its first phase of development, San Juan de Aragón contained 9,927 homes.[67] Two days later (November 17), Robert Kennedy landed in Mexico and joined López Mateos in a ceremony to inaugurate Unidad Kennedy. Opened only a few days before the first anniversary of John F. Kennedy's assassination, Unidad Kennedy brought together the designs of Mario Pani and the funding of the AFL-CIO and USAID to provide housing for members of the Unión de Obreros de Artes Gráficas de los Talleres Comerciales (3,107 units).[68] In the short time that elapsed between John F. Kennedy's 1962 visit to Mexico and his brother Robert's trip in 1964, the Mexican government funded and/or built approximately 60,000 housing units. Of those 60,000 units, 11,000 were part of Mexico's most iconic housing complex: Tlatelolco. In his final week as president, López Mateos inaugurated the monumental Unidad Nonoalco–Tlatelolco on November 22.[69] The housing complex, most associated with the 1968 massacre, was exceptional in that it was part of a slum-clearance campaign and not located in a peripheral area. Put into historical perspective, more social housing units were built in the last years of López Mateos's administration than between 1925 and 1958 (57,228).[70]

San Juan de Aragón was the most ambitious and comprehensive housing complex built in Mexico during the 1960s. It was a projection of power that transformed the former Vaso de Texcoco into a showcase for mestizo modernism. In the case of San Juan de Aragón, nature was viewed by planners not as an obstacle to be destroyed but as a contradiction to be controlled. In contrast to the anarchic shantytowns that exhibited the worst of both worlds—the absence of parks and green space yet at the mercy of flooding—the residents of San Juan de Aragón would benefit from a life in the city enlivened and beautified by a curated nature.

As Héctor Velázquez Moreno and Enrique Cervantes Sánchez oversaw San Juan de Aragón's design and construction, local governmental agencies (part of the DDF) and FOVI representatives led the selection process for its residents. Contrary to the description of San Juan de Aragón as being a "new urban model for the popular classes," it was originally intended as a mixed-income housing development. *Popular*—a broad term that is politically advantageous but deeply flawed as a descriptor for a highly stratified sector of society—flattens out the diversity of the thousands of families who moved to San Juan de Aragón in 1964. San Juan de Aragón's original residents arrived there through a rigorous application process or by dispossession: the destitute and the aspiring middle class, civil servants and former squatters, public school teachers and poor families who inhabited crumbling tenements slated for demolition. Unlike Unidad Santa Fe and other IMSS housing units, San Juan de Aragón's residents originally included a substantial number of the informal poor.

San Juan de Aragón was originally conceived as a development that would provide housing for people in two broadly defined categories: bureaucrats and families displaced by public works projects. Specifically, the homes were designated for people who were displaced by the construction of the Mexico-Pachuca highway and for those who resided on land that was taken over by the Tepeyac National Park. A random sampling of 250 of the 1,010 housing contracts stored in the Federal District's archives (AHDF) indicates that 32 percent of the new residents were categorized as *obreros* (workers), 29 percent as federal employees, and 10 percent as *albañiles* (carpenters). Among the other jobs or categories were hairdressers, bus drivers, commercial vendors, electricians, and *dedicada al hogar* (housewife).[71] Roughly 25 percent of the residents were originally from the Federal District, while the large majority were born outside of the capital in the states of Oaxaca, Puebla, Guanajuato, Morelos, and Guerrero.[72] The statistics are limited in that they do not present a total picture of all the residents, but they do reflect similar characterizations of residents described by journalists and scholars.

Beyond those who were displaced by public works projects, announcements about San Juan de Aragón were circulated through memos or bulletins in the offices of public administration buildings, the Federation of Colonias Proletarias, and by word of mouth. In the weeks leading up to San Juan de Aragón's opening, dozens of applicants would line up each day at a provisional DDF office to find out if their applications were approved or rejected. A reporter who visited the lines outside of the DDF offices observed a sense of anxiety and anticipation in the air.[73] One person on line commented, "Some people who put in their application a long time ago didn't get it, and others who put it in a few months ago were reviewed favorably. . . . I don't know why. . . . I think they pick those who have a fixed salary and are *empleados de base* [roughly translated as 'employees who are salaried and have contracts']."[74] Some left disappointed, while others "left happy. A diverse set of *empleados*, wives of police officers and transit workers, [and] meat packers emerged victorious with their housing cards."[75] Successful applicants were issued identification cards by the DDF that included their name, address, and monthly payment quota. The most common response for why applicants wanted to move to San Juan de Aragón was simple: to become a homeowner. A meat cutter who waved his card around commented, "Even though I have to pay 175 pesos a month, maybe more, I will have a decent house to live in, no matter what the price, I know it will be mine as I pay it."[76]

Explicit rules and regulations prohibited several kinds of establishments and cultural practices in San Juan de Aragón. Single mothers were not eligible to gain access to a home regardless of income. Dance halls and bars were banned from the housing complex.[77] Contracts specifically stipulated that its residents were not allowed to own pigs, goats, rabbits, or any form of livestock.[78] This last prohibition was officially justified on the grounds of hygiene, but it was also motivated by the conviction to eliminate a cultural and economic practice synonymous with impoverished shantytowns (one can also point to its rustic character as well). The ban on owning chickens or rabbits, a practice so pervasive in a place like Ciudad Neza that most homes were designed around both people and animals, sent a clear message to prospective residents. The prohibition on animals (excluding dogs and cats) not only was stipulated in the contracts but was also enforced by city workers who inspected the moving trucks that transported the items of displaced families from Tepeyac.[79]

The change in San Juan de Aragón's socioeconomic composition was a gradual shift. Census data and surveys taken in the 1970s clearly indicate a definite change, but the documentation of this process is limited to faint traces in the press, academic surveys, and personal accounts of families who remained in San Juan de Aragón. In 1965, *Excélsior* polled families being transported in from Tepeyac and found some willing to stay, while others stated that they were planning on leaving because of the costs and restrictions.[80] Some of the families who subsequently moved back to Tepeyac were later found injured as the result of heavy flooding that inundated the area in July 1971.[81] As the years passed and demand for homes in San Juan de Aragón increased, many of the poorer families secretly moved back to their previous apartments but maintained their property titles in order to rent out their homes to middle-class families who were eager to find a place in the development. In one example, COPEVI (a Mexican institute focused on housing) carried out an investigation where they found one family living in a rent-controlled apartment in Tepito while renting out their house in San Juan de Aragón.[82]

Social pressures exerted a strong influence on San Juan de Aragón's transition. Families who worked for the government went into debt from the costs of remodeling their homes. In order to differentiate themselves from the displaced families, they built extensions and extra floors, decorated the exterior facades, and purchased cars in textbook examples of conspicuous consumption. Many of the poorer families, particularly in Unidad Vecinal VII, traveled long distances on Sundays to attend Mass at various churches in the adjoining area because they felt so alienated and judged at the local church.[83]

In 1970, when sociologist Susan Eckstein interviewed a former squatter who moved to San Juan de Aragón, he complained, "I feel intimidated by my new neighbors. They see that I am of a lower status, because they see I am poorly dressed."[84] In 1968, a group of more well-to-do families used their ties with a neighborhood priest who had leverage in the DDF to pressure the government to evict one hundred reputed pickpockets or thieves (*rateros*). Writing at the time, Eckstein observed, "Interclass relations here are highly formalized. Dress, skin color, house size, house décor, and on occasion, automobiles serve as visible cues to the degree of intimacy lower, working, and 'middle' class neighbors can expect from each other."[85]

As families displaced by public works projects slowly streamed out of San Juan de Aragón, new housing units built after 1968 were designated for laborers in the formal work sector. Police officers, airline pilots, electricians, radio announcers (this grouping may seem odd, but they were highly organized and numbered in the hundreds in Mexico City), and members of the large CTM union federation began to stream into the new unidad vecinal.[86] In 1970, FOVI was responsible for constructing an additional five thousand homes in San Juan de Aragón. The expansion of the complex increased San Juan de Aragón's population by roughly twenty-four thousand people, making it the largest housing complex in Mexico (by 1972, San Juan de Aragón's population surpassed the number of residents at Tlatelolco).[87]

San Juan de Aragón was shaped through a combination of economic pulls and social pressures that were driven by government agencies, residents, and Mexico's political economy. In many respects, one finds the same patterns of inclusion and exclusion in the history of San Juan de Aragón as with other housing complexes built by the government in the 1960s. However, the inclusion of several hundred families who were displaced by public works projects created the conditions for a community rife with social divisions and conflicts that were rarely witnessed in other housing complexes. The antagonisms found in the early years of San Juan de Aragón's history were not created by the conditions of the housing complex, nor were they unique to Mexican society in general. However, the complex's distinctive social composition, and the ethnographic studies that documented it, provide historians with a rare view into a place where those antagonisms became more condensed and visible than in other new housing developments. If San Juan de Aragón failed to become "a new urban model for the popular classes," it succeeded as a direct form of government assistance to a crucial sector of Mexican society.

Notwithstanding their political and symbolic value, Mexico's public housing system failed to resolve or alleviate the nation's housing crisis. The IMSS system was effective for public sector workers but unsustainable for the "marginal majority." Mexico simply did not have the level of domestic resources or political wherewithal necessary to replicate Unidad Santa Fe on a scale commensurate with the severity of the deficit.

In 1962–63, Mexico's housing program was internationalized through the Alliance for Progress. At this pivotal moment, Mexico decided to proceed along the same trajectory as before. Modernist multifamiliares and unidades habitacionales continued to urbanize the periphery as Adolfo López Mateos presided over the construction of the Unidad Kennedy and San Juan de Aragón projects, along with the more central Tlatelolco. With the creation of FOVI in 1963, López Mateos transformed home payment amortization in Mexico by lowering down payment fees and authorizing the government to act as a guarantor for their loans. FOVI significantly increased the number of people eligible for government-built housing yet continued to favor salaried workers at the expense of the informal poor. In surveying this continuity, one possible argument can be offered: the Mexican government based its housing program on a particular demographic (la gente decente) and from that foundation conceived of its architectural designs, not the other way around. Form followed political function.

PART 2

The Origins of Ciudad Nezahualcóyotl

3

Land Politics on the Periphery

In 1955, Mexican president Adolfo Ruiz Cortines faced a dilemma over the future of the Vaso de Texcoco. Flash flooding, dust storms, rent strikes, assassinations, and widespread land fraud had put his plans to urbanize this former lake bed near Mexico City in serious jeopardy. Two years earlier, Ruiz Cortines issued a presidential decree that upheld the desiccated lake bed's status as federal property and mandated the area be used for housing Mexico City's working class.[1] Now in 1955, major flooding had caused one-third of its inhabitants to abandon their homes, while the remaining residents were locked in a bitter struggle over basic infrastructure and services. President Ruiz Cortines debated evacuating the Vaso de Texcoco's thirty thousand residents as proposals for reflooding the former lake were floated out in the press.[2]

The president turned to Eduardo Chávez Ramírez, a prominent engineer in the government, and asked him to conduct a rapid investigation into the viability of urbanizing the Vaso de Texcoco. Chávez Ramírez interviewed residents, analyzed the extent of the flood damage, and even used a military plane to survey the land from above. He told the president that it was the most inhospitable land in the Valley of Mexico and not fit for human habitation. Contrary to advice from government officials, Ruiz Cortines decided to move forward with the urbanization of the former lake and told reporters, "It would be unpatriotic for me to evict 30,000 Mexican citizens."[3] Ruiz Cortines's dilemma reveals a hidden feature in Mexico City's history, one where the government had a stake in the future of what would be Mexico's most infamous shantytown: Ciudad Nezahualcóyotl.

This chapter is organized chronologically and geographically, united by three narrative threads that follow the city's eastward expansion into the former remains of the Vaso de Texcoco. The first section (1945–48) details the early career of Ciudad Neza's ultimate powerbroker, Raúl Romero Erazo.

The history surrounding his first attempts to subdivide and sell plots of land provides a crucial insight into how Ciudad Neza's first fraccionadores (land developers) learned how to exploit Mexico's weak judicial system and corrupt political culture to legitimize their fraccionamientos (subdivisions). Next, I focus on Colonia El Sol (1948–57), the center of an explosive struggle waged by the first settlers to receive public utilities and services. Finally, the chapter moves farther east to Colonia Aurora (1957–63) to more closely investigate the means of land expropriation and the impact of the 1958 Ley de Fraccionamientos on the Colonias del Vaso de Texcoco.[4] The origins of Ciudad Neza illustrate how land politics in the urban periphery were integral to the development of a new phase of residential segregation in Mexico City.

Godfather of the Colonia

In 1946, when the former Vaso de Texcoco was still a desert, Raúl Romero Erazo surprised a group of local villagers after he told them he was surveying the area to build a city that would be bigger than Toluca (capital of the State of Mexico). The group shook their heads in disbelief and went back to fishing in what was left of Lake Texcoco. To the surprise of many, Ciudad Neza surpassed Toluca's population in 1964.[5]

By the end of the 1930s, the Romero brothers had perfected the art of land fraud. Following the footsteps of their father, they began on the fringes of Iztapalapa, where they purchased land from desperate ejidatarios that they in turn subdivided and sold to poor families being squeezed out of El Centro.[6] The Romeros' initial forays into subdividing small pockets of cheap land in Iztapalapa soon extended outward to the Vaso de Texcoco in the neighboring State of Mexico. In the case of the Vaso de Texcoco, it was the younger brother, Raúl Romero, who would spearhead the drive to establish and maintain the area's first settlements.

Raúl Romero discovered Texcoco's dried-out lake beds by chance. According to a brief memoir, Romero first encountered the area when a friend asked him for assistance in resolving a land dispute.[7] As the events of the land invasion came to light, Romero saw the dispute as an entryway into something larger—an opportunity to capitalize on undeveloped land that was outside the Federal District's jurisdiction but only a forty-minute drive from the Zócalo (the city's central square).

The desiccated lake beds of Texcoco became an obsession for Raúl Romero. During the day, he meticulously reviewed Texcoco's public registry of property records and land titles. He sought out families with historic ties to the land in order to understand how property changed hands over the decades. Through sheer persistence and charisma, he was able to persuade longtime resident Don Dionicio to copy (mimeograph) his box of land contracts, maps, census data, and title deeds that Dionicio had accumulated over the years. Romero also met with José Guzmán Guzmán, who, according to local legend, was the first person from the Federal District to settle in the former Vaso de Texcoco in 1945.

At night, Raúl Romero drove his Buick convertible up and down the Mexico-Puebla highway. He wrote, "From El Centro you would pass the San Lázaro train station followed by a deserted aviation camp owned by the military [Campo Militar de Aviación]; it was a short drive through the poor Moctezuma neighborhood and then an open road through the dark desert." He continues, "The occasional sewage canal could be seen in the distance, but other than that, nothing, nothing until you reached the edge of Lake Texcoco."[8] The desert that unfolded before Romero as he drove at night was initially envisioned as a breadbasket by Mexico's postrevolutionary leaders. Those hopes faded after numerous attempts at cultivating the land ended in failure as a result of the arid soil. The drainage of Lake Texcoco's salty waters (about half of the lake by 1895 and then 40 percent of that half by the 1940s) left behind a loose, briny soil that was largely unproductive.[9]

The feeling of desolation described by Raúl Romero was real but not completely accurate. In fact, the remnants of a once thriving civilization that can be traced back to 1259 still existed in the form of Indigenous *comuneros* (one who subsists on commonly shared land). Ethnographic studies from the 1930s found that the comuneros used the same kind of spears (*atlatl*) and long nets to hunt for waterfowl as was described by European travelers in the early 1820s. They possessed a local knowledge passed down over centuries that enabled them to collect aquatic insects such as *palomeros* and *cuatecones* (sold in large quantities as livestock feed), hunt ducks, and fish.[10] Every few months they would navigate their canoes through a series of canals and causeways that connected Texcoco to Mexico City's eastern marketplaces. Still numbering in the hundreds after most of the lake's waters were depleted (primarily in Chimalhuacán, a municipality in the State of

Mexico), their resiliency would eventually pose an obstacle to the urbanization of the former Vaso de Texcoco.[11] However, for Romero, it would end up being another group of Indigenous families who played a more decisive role in his initial attempts to urbanize the former Vaso de Texcoco.

In October 1946, Raúl Romero met with a group of settlers that had recently invaded and occupied a small tract of land near the border that separated the Federal District from Chimalhuacán. They were a collection of families from Mexico City who originally came from the states of Oaxaca and Puebla. Romero arranged to meet them at night alongside the Mexico-Puebla highway. He followed a group of Indigenous women wrapped in *rebozos* (shawls) and children carrying lanterns to a meeting in the temporary encampment. In what can be seen as a precursor to the years that would follow, Romero won over the settlers by falsely claiming that he was in close contact with the local officials and he could arrange for the transfer of legitimate land titles to the invaders.[12]

In a scramble, Raúl Romero met with political leader Dr. Nestor Herrera in Chimalhuacán and Governor Alfredo del Mazo Vélez in Toluca. Soon after, Romero orchestrated a backyard Sunday fiesta attended by both residents and local politicians where the "steaks, *carnitas*, *barbacoa*, and *pulque* [alcohol] flowed in abundance."[13] On February 7, 1947, a deal was struck, and it was agreed that each lot would be sold for 875 pesos. The official documents and contracts pertaining to the fraccionamiento are, however, more revealing of what is missing from them. Romero's name never appears on the contracts. Instead, one finds the name "Fernando Lopez Carona," someone who was either paid to have his identity used for the public record or possibly completely fabricated.[14] Furthermore, the wording found in the main document is highly ambiguous, never clearly indicating if the land is meant to be used for agriculture or residency.[15] Nevertheless, the process of buying cheap land to be subdivided into lots had been legitimated in the eyes of local officials. The formal recognition of Romero's Colonia México helped pave the way for an intense period of urbanization in the years to come.

The approval of Raúl Romero's subdivision stemmed from his intimate knowledge of Mexico's corrupt political culture. The formal contracts and stamps of approval that remain with us today are the sanitized, outward expressions of social interactions far removed from any courtroom or board meeting. In 1950s Mexico, many of those decisive meetings took place in the backrooms of restaurants or in a backyard on a Sunday afternoon, places where the "barbacoa and pulque flowed in abundance."

The First Neighborhood Associations

The approval of Raúl Romero's new subdivision signaled a green light to fraccionadores in Mexico City (Federal District). Fraccionadores also utilized local and federal decrees printed in the pages of the *Diario Oficial* to their advantage. On February 12, 1949, President Miguel Alemán issued a decree on the land and water tenure of the Vaso de Texcoco. The president placed the lake and its immediate surroundings under the jurisdiction of the Ministry of Hydraulic Resources (Secretaría de Recursos Hidráulicos, SRH) while transferring over roughly 4,000 hectares (9,800 acres) of land south of the lake to the Federal District's local government (DDF) for the purposes of urbanization. The presidential decree specifically directs the SRH to hand over the lands to the DDF to "urbanize them to establish working-class settlements on those lands as part of solving the housing problem for the working class."[16]

The decree opened the floodgates to the new land's urbanization. After several months of inactivity on behalf of the DDF, a Junta Regional de Planificación y Zonificación (Regional Planning and Zoning Council) was formed by local officials to fill the void and functioned as a regulatory body tasked with the oversight of the colonias. Despite the fact that none of the colonias met the requirements necessary for approval (electricity, paved roads, water pumps, sanitation services), all were granted authorization by the local council.[17] The facade of legal propriety exerted a powerful force on poor families desperate for cheap land.

The first colonias were located along the boundary line that separated the Federal District from the State of Mexico. Raúl Romero's Colonia México is generally considered the first urban fraccionamiento.[18] Colonia México began to sell residential lots in 1947 and was followed shortly after by four other colonias: Estado de México, Maravillas, Tamaulipas, and El Sol.[19] The colonias began in the southern section and then moved north until they reached the Bordo de Xochiaca (a flood-control levee) and the shores of Lake Texcoco. The closer to the lake, the higher the risk of flooding in summer months, when torrential downpours caused the lake's water levels to rise and overrun the Bordo de Xochiaca. In 1949, it was estimated that approximately two thousand people had settled in the newly established colonias (referred to then as the Colonias del ex–Vaso de Texcoco, or just Vaso de Texcoco).[20]

The residents of the Colonias del Vaso de Texcoco were at the mercy of nature. Between October and May, the former lake bed turned into a dust bowl. Strong winds from the northeast swept across its barren plains, creating dust storms (*tolvaneras*) that enveloped residents with dirt and salt. When geologists from UNAM conducted one of the first comprehensive studies of the dust storms, they found that 41 percent of the topsoil was carried away by wind currents.[21] A resident recalled, "When the mud dried out, it was practically pure salt, it irritated the eyes, dried your lips, and weakened your spirit."[22] At night, powerful wind gusts were strong enough to blow away roofs and doors, exposing families to dust storms until the following morning.[23] Poorly constructed homes made for highly porous structures that left interior surfaces covered in dust until the tolvaneras gave way to the summer rainstorms.

Each year when June approached, residents braced for the rainy season. Although the Valley of Mexico receives more annual rainfall than London, nearly all the rain is concentrated into just four months of the year between May and August.[24] During these months, torrential downpours and flooding covered large swathes of the former Vaso de Texcoco, eventually settling into large saline ponds and temporarily forming a scattered series of marshlands closer to the lasting remains of Lake Texcoco.

Constant rain and flooding took a heavy toll on the lives of colonos. In 1953, an entire row of homes was washed away with floodwaters.[25] Former resident Margarita Lopez recalled, "The only thing I can say is it was very hard to live here, only the bravest stayed."[26] After the rains subsided, colonos were forced to fend for themselves. A former lake bed without a drainage system naturally absorbs and holds water for weeks unless it is mechanically pumped out. Roads were unpassable, and movement to and from the Federal District could be paralyzed for days. Discarded garbage left by colonos and waste from latrines were swept up with rising floodwaters and remained in newly formed lagoons. Pools of stagnant water and waste created the perfect set of conditions for mosquito infestations. The sight of mosquitoes hovering around a body of standing water was so common that one of the former Vaso de Texcoco's first newspapers was named *El Mosquito*.[27] Of all the initial colonias founded in the first decade, El Sol was the most notorious for both flooding and evictions.

Colonia El Sol was founded by César Hann Cárdenas, a young fraccionador from Mexico City who decided to stake his fortune on a tract of land located between the Bordo de Xochiaca and Lake Texcoco.[28] As one can imagine, settling people on empty land sandwiched between a lake and a levee was an extremely dangerous and daunting endeavor. Yet César Hann set out to do just that in 1948. Because César Hann's Colonia El Sol was located on a site slated to become a sewage treatment facility, the settlement and urbanization of El Sol was a contested affair. Political conflict over the future of this strip of land generated the first neighborhood associations and eventually led to the first payment strike in the former Vaso de Texcoco.

The establishment of neighborhood associations along the boundary of the Federal District and the State of Mexico in the middle of the 1940s introduced a new set of circumstances for local figures in the PRI. The previous decade's experience of two public agencies responsible for the supervision of working-class settlements in the Federal District (Reglamento de Colonias en el Distrito Federal and the DDF's Oficina de Colonias) provided some precedent and foundation for the Vaso de Texcoco.[29] Nevertheless, for local officials in the State of Mexico, the actual inner workings of rule over undefined spaces composed of residents who did not easily fit into a PRI-led peasant league or industrial worker union was still uncharted territory. In this political terra incognita, the degrees of power exerted by competing interests (residents, Indigenous comuneros, private land developers, public PRI officials) had to be forged and established through practice—in this case, the urbanization of the former Vaso de Texcoco. It was a process shaped by land speculation, corruption, violent repression, and political patronage that eventually culminated in the 1957–58 Ley de Fraccionamientos de Terrenos del Estado de México. The Ley de Fraccionamientos declared a new set of regulations and codes for subdivisions created in the State of Mexico after 1957 and was the result of a struggle that originated in Colonia El Sol.

The former Vaso de Texcoco's lands were federal property, first given out in parcels to native inhabitants who fished and hunted around the remnants of Lake Texcoco. In a development that defied legal logic, some of those federal lands were beginning to be sold by native inhabitants to private real estate developers at the end of the 1940s.[30] Records from the State of

Mexico's public works department (Dirección de Comunicaciones y Obras Públicas) and individual land contracts demonstrate the relative ease with which fraccionadores purchased land from Indigenous comuneros during the 1940s and 1950s. Dozens of property contracts authorized by the same public notary official in Mexico City, Rafael del Paso Reinert, were signed, stamped, and filed away in accordance with all legal norms.[31] The process left the lands of the former Vaso de Texcoco in the hands of three distinct parties at the same time: (1) the federal government, (2) the fraccionadores, and (3) the residents who technically had property titles and were paying off their "mortgages." The legal ambiguity was ultimately advantageous for the fraccionadores, who could simultaneously stall court proceedings while employing violent force with impunity. The manipulation of Mexico's weak legal system laid the basis for land fraud that was sustained through minor concessions and violent repression.

The 1953 Colono Strike

In 1951, the governor of the State of Mexico, Alfredo del Mazo Vélez, grew concerned when he began to hear reports about clusters of colonos forming neighborhood groups to petition for services and to protest looming evictions. After del Mazo received a flurry of letters from a group in El Sol, including one that threatened a payment strike, he sent Felipe Lopez Beltran to El Sol in order to keep the colono group isolated and focused on minor reforms.[32] Felipe Lopez Beltran worked in the police division of the Secretaría de Recursos Hidráulicos and was a friend of Governor Alfredo del Mazo.[33] Beltran moved to El Sol with his family in May 1951 and formed the Comité Pro-Mejoras del la Colonia del Sol.[34] The organization took on the character of a mutual-aid society; members pooled individual contributions together to pay for housing materials and the construction of a small church. Felipe Beltran, now a local deputy, was there to facilitate donations of cement from the PRI and to negotiate the daily delivery of buckets of water from César Hann. However, before Beltran could settle into his role as a political intermediary between the PRI and colonos, a change in state governors would dramatically reverse his standing in local politics.

In September 1951, Salvador Sánchez Colín became the governor of the State of Mexico. Unlike Alfredo del Mazo, Sánchez Colín viewed Beltran with suspicion and concluded he posed a threat to his rule. First, he organized a group of colonos to destroy Beltran's house. Then he sent out orders for the police to intimidate Beltran's family until he stepped down from his position as local deputy.[35] With Beltran out of the way, Sánchez Colín set out to establish a system of political bodies designated to represent the fraccionadores and colonos. He selected the mayor of Texcoco's brother, Eugenio Alonso, to create a unified colono group called the Federación de Colonos del Vaso de Texcoco in October 1952. Felipe Lopez Beltran, recently pushed out of his post as a local deputy, was able to retain his position as a neighborhood leader in El Sol and was selected as El Sol's representative in the wider colono federation. After all the local associations were grouped together into the Federation of Colonos, Sánchez Colín formed the Committee of Urban Subdivisions for the Texcoco District (Comité de Fraccionamientos Urbanos para el Distrito de Texcoco). The committee was the central administrative body that authorized land sales in the Vaso de Texcoco. Its creation signified a definitive shift in government policy: Sánchez Colín intended to give full support for the urbanization of the Vaso de Texcoco. Although the Indigenous comuneros would preserve some of their land rights in the years to come, Sánchez Colín gave fraccionadores free rein to advertise and sell plots of land without legal obligations to contract agreements that guaranteed urban services.

The Committee of Urban Subdivisions was led by Ruben Ortega Lopez, a shadowy figure with ties to both Governor Sánchez Colín and President Ruiz Cortines. As president of the committee, Lopez was responsible for carrying out public works projects and reporting on their progress to President Ruiz Cortines.[36] Beyond his official duties of coordinating power line installations and property negotiations, Lopez was unofficially charged with neutralizing any discontent among colonos, a position that put him in direct conflict with Felipe Lopez Beltran.

Tensions between Beltran and Ruben Ortega Lopez began to flare up at the beginning of April 1953. That March, the SRH posted eviction notices throughout Colonia El Sol, warning residents that the area was scheduled to be flooded in June.[37] Beltran formed a defense committee and secured the official backing of the Federation of Colonos president Eugenio Alonso. The SRH eventually backed down from flooding El Sol, but the incident alarmed Ruben Ortega Lopez. The case revealed to him that key leaders in the Federation of Colonos were willing to publicly oppose the federal government's decision on a controversial matter. In September, Ruben Ortega sent a letter to President Ruiz Cortines that outlined his plans to regain control over the renegade federation: "In view of the seriousness of the situation, I need to establish friendly relations with the leadership . . . that will allow me, little by little, to destroy and eliminate the leadership cadre of the Federación de Colonos del Vaso de Lago de Texcoco." Ruben Ortega adds, "The unscrupulous elements such as Eugenio Alonso, Felipe Lopez Beltran, Jorge F. Carmona and others, these are the individuals who are opposing normal, working relations between colonos and the government . . . fortunately as has been the case, Salvador Sánchez Colín has given me full backing."[38] Ruben Ortega Lopez sent Eugenio Alonso to Toluca, where Governor Sánchez Colín stripped Alonso of his position as president of the Federation of Colonos. The abrupt removal of the well-respected Alonso caused an uproar among the social leaders of all the neighborhood associations, a development that pushed Governor Sánchez Colín to appoint Felipe Lopez Beltran as the new president of the federation in an attempt to diffuse the rising tensions.

The selection of Felipe Lopez Beltran brought about a moment of political calm that was short-lived and fleeting. The minor concessions that came in the form of water buckets and cinder blocks did little to address the colonos' growing list of grievances. An unaffiliated group of colonos wrote to the president, stating, "Since the foundation of the first colonias in this place, we have lacked all the sanitary services accorded by law to urban zones despite the fact that we pay monthly quotas for such services."[39] The aforementioned monthly quotas were collected by the Committee of Urban Subdivisions in addition to the monthly installments colonos paid to their respective fraccionadores (an amount that ranged between 30 to 80 pesos per month). On average, each family paid 10 to 15 pesos per month to the Committee of Urban Subdivisions to "urbanize" their neighborhoods by providing paved roads, electricity, running water, drainage, and sanitation services. Aside from a few communal wells and marketplaces, nothing was constructed. It is estimated that Ruben Ortega Lopez embezzled 3.5 million pesos through the Comité de Fraccionamientos.[40] By the end of the 1960s, the systematic theft of public funds became a rallying cry for colonos, featured regularly on flyers and community newsletters that detailed how local officials embezzled large sums of money to pay for luxury cars and vacation homes in Acapulco.[41]

The misappropriation of public funds and lack of transparency reached a boiling point in the summer of 1953. The rift between the leadership of the Federation of Colonias and the state government was beyond repair. Colonos from El Sol, Tamaulipas, Estado de México, Romero, Juarez Pantitlán, and Evolución held a series of meetings where they united around a payment strike (*huelga de pagos*) until urban services were installed. A "declaration" letter sent from Colonia Romero stated that monthly payments were to be suspended until their contracts were honored and urbanization projects (potable water, electricity, drainage systems) were carried out by Raúl Romero.[42]

The first wave of repression came with the arrest of the strike's leaders and a sudden spike in evictions. Police commander Guadalupe Chavira rounded up the leaders of the neighborhood associations in Colonias Tamaulipas and Evolución and threw them in jail.[43] After arbitrarily evicting twelve families from their homes in El Sol, he arrested and jailed Felipe Lopez Beltran on murder charges. When Beltran's gun and identification were found ten kilometers from the murder scene, the evidence weighed too heavily in Beltran's favor even for the Vaso de Texcoco. Shaken but undeterred, Beltran was released and continued to lead the strike.[44]

When Beltran was released from jail, he returned to El Sol to discover that his leadership position was usurped by Aureliano Ramos, a local pistolero who worked for the governor's secretary. On four different occasions, Aureliano Ramos and his men systematically attacked women active in the strike.[45] A climate of terror hung over El Sol and the Vaso de Texcoco, with one resident recalling, "Daily conversations and exchanges revolved around who was the most recent person to be arrested. . . . I remember people had to gather at night and in different locations."[46] Water supplies were cut off in El Sol in an act of collective punishment that endangered the lives of hundreds of colonos, particularly young children. True to form, Ruben Ortega Lopez candidly wrote, "Given the peculiarly poor economic conditions in the area, we tried to adopt a system of corporal punishment and retribution and only used monetary fines in rare cases."[47] The Federation of Colonos had openly rebelled against the party that created it; the renegade leadership had failed to convince colonos to pay their monthly quotas for urbanization projects and were instead mobilizing them to withhold their payments.

As the strike entered its second year, its momentum began to dissipate due to several factors. First, despite the sacrifice and heroism exhibited by striking colonos, it remained politically isolated and received little attention in the press. Ruben Ortega Lopez's excessive use of "corporal punishment" combined with an escalation of arbitrary evictions proved to be effective in weakening the strike and creating an overall climate of fear. Internally, differences over whether to publicly criticize Governor Sánchez Colín resulted in a split with the Federation of Colonos. As internal divisions continued to weaken the colono groupings and with an unofficial bounty on his head, Felipe Lopez Beltran fled to nearby Tepeyac in October 1955, marking the end to the strike.[48] The demands for running water and electricity were unsuccessful, and the colonos' material deprivation continued with little change. At the end of 1957, the Federation of Colonos of the Vaso de Texcoco officially disbanded.

The early years of Ciudad Neza (Colonias del Vaso de Texcoco) demonstrate that its extreme levels of scarcity could be found in causes not solely reducible to the poverty of its inhabitants. Each home contributed monthly funds to a financial trust created for the stated purposes of "urban colonization" (investments into public utilities, infrastructure, police services). The absence of urban services was not the result of an illegal land occupation by defiant squatters but the product of systematic embezzlement carried out by government officials. Even when local judges ruled in favor of the comuneros, the fraccionadores simply steamrolled ahead with their plans.

The most concrete and consequential outcome of the payment strike was the 1958 Ley de Fraccionamientos. On December 20, 1958, the State of Mexico's new governor, Gustavo Baz Prada, publicized an official law on urbanization that stated, "Land cannot be the object of sale, or promise of sale, if the services and urbanization projects are not completed and approved by the state executive."[49] The 1958 law was applauded by colonos and appeared to be a measure taken by the government to ensure fraccionadores would provide basic services for the lands they sold for residence.

In the years to come, the 1958 Ley de Fraccionamientos would be consequential not for the infrastructure it constructed but for the resentment it created. The practice of land fraud and broken promises following the law added insult to injury and only temporarily quelled discontent among colonos. As a result, the fraccionadores began to channel the discontent of colonos in a different direction: cessation and independence from Chimalhuacán. In the years between 1958 and 1963, fraccionadores sought to locate the problems of the Colonias del ex–Vaso de Texcoco in the old-guard leadership of the Chimalhuacán municipality. According to this logic, the only solution to their problems would be the creation of a new municipality independent of the Indigenous leaders in Chimalhuacán's municipal offices. That new municipality would eventually become Ciudad Nezahualcóyotl in 1963. No other colonia represented the years leading up to the creation of Ciudad Neza better than Colonia Aurora.

Colonia Aurora and the Ley de Fraccionamientos

Colonia Aurora extended the urbanization of the Vaso de Texcoco to its eastern limits. When the boundary lines of Ciudad Neza's municipality were drawn in 1963, Colonias Aurora and Villada made up most of the land directly next to the Chimalhuacán municipality. The development of Colonia Aurora contains two distinct characteristics. Due to its location, Aurora encroached upon lands actively used or valued by the Indigenous comuneros, producing a more antagonistic and violent process of urbanization than in previous colonias. The second element stems from when Aurora was established (1957) in relation to the 1958 Ley de Fraccionamientos. Although Aurora was technically given approval several months before the law was ratified, it provides an optimal example for scholars to examine the application of the State of Mexico's first major set of laws, codes, and policies for urban fraccionamientos.

The Aurora Company was founded in the Federal District in 1955.[50] The business was led by Bernardo Eckstein Salz and Abraham Slotnick, two immigrants who arrived in Mexico during the Second World War. While less is known about Slotnick, Eckstein was born in Germany in 1928 to parents who migrated from Rymanów, Poland. Eckstein's family records indicate his family left the Pale of Settlement before Nazi Germany invaded Poland and remained in Germany until 1933—the year Bernardo Eckstein's younger brother was born in Saarbrücken. A gap in the records exists until 1942, at which point the Eckstein family formally registered with the Mexican government in the Federal District. The dates and locations typed into Mexico's bureaucratic forms depict a Jewish family seeking refuge in Mexico after being driven out of Europe by the Third Reich's genocidal onslaught.[51]

At some point in the late 1940s, Bernardo Eckstein settled in Puebla, forged close ties with the city's small Jewish community, and became friends with Abraham Slotnick. Like many other enterprising immigrants, they tried their hand at any venture that showed promise: a small pots-and-pans factory, military uniforms, a mezcal distillery, and real estate.[52] When Eckstein and Slotnick caught wind of a land scheme on the outskirts of Mexico City, they decided to move their operations up to Mexico City. However, before they went to try their luck in the *gran ciudad*, they paid a visit to Germán Aréchiga Ruiz, a Jalisco-born engineer who moved to Puebla for a public works project.[53] Not only did Eckstein and Slotnick need a qualified engineer for their fraccionamiento; they needed to "Mexicanize" the public face of their operations. Although Eckstein and Slotnick were legally naturalized Mexican citizens, they were aware of the potential backlash a group of foreigners could incur by exploiting communal lands for personal gain.

In 1956, Eckstein and Slotnick assembled a team of engineers and lawyers to square away all the legal and political obligations. They decided to buy a section of land on the eastern plains of the former lake bed, far removed from the other colonias. The location placed them within the area where Indigenous comuneros still hunted for ducks and *chichihualcote* (small birds) during the rainy season.[54] Aurora's fraccionadores would need to gain the consent of the comuneros and arrange a land transfer deal. In addition, to acquire a tract of land of this size, they would need to get permission from Ruben Ortega Lopez and the Romero brothers. In the interim, they met at night in a run-down cantina in El Centro where they mapped out the colonia's street plan and brainstormed slogans for ad campaigns. The grid followed a geometric pattern, and names from popular *rancheras* and *boleros* like "La Bamba," "Rancho Grande," and "Aguila Negra" were chosen for the streets in order to attract a wider audience.[55]

On July 10, 1957, Governor Salvador Sánchez Colín authorized the Aurora fraccionamiento, granting the full two thousand acres of land.[56] For Eckstein, it was just the beginning. The Aurora Company went on to buy three more sections of equal or greater size in the next five years. One section, Aurora Oriente, was co-owned with Raúl Romero, starting a partnership that would later include Colonia Esperanza.

The lands were expropriated by three different methods. The first was to buy the land, as in the case of the first section. When negotiations failed,

Aurora's fraccionadores forged documents and stole property records from Texcoco's public registry. A land contract from 1961 contains the signatures of four people who were not the previous owners, yet the document was stamped and approved by Rafael del Paso Reinert.[57] Third, Aurora's land developers commonly hired pistoleros (gunmen) to intimidate and murder uncooperative comuneros. On December 13, 1960, a judge from Texcoco ordered the Aurora Company to suspend sales, since the land in question was under judicial review. Aurora's fraccionadores simply ignored the judge's verdict and continued to sell property lots, a move that led to a bloody confrontation between the company's pistoleros and incensed comuneros.[58] When a group of comuneros tried to stop the company from demarcating the land with tractors in 1961, the company's pistoleros ambushed the group and cleared the way for the workers to move forward with the land invasion.[59]

The main source of anger and frustration for Aurora's residents was the absence of urban services deemed mandatory by the 1958 Ley de Fraccionamientos. In addition to the state law, the Aurora Company specifically indicated on the urbanization certificates they gave to each colono that their land plot would have electric and potable water services. Later, an ad hoc group of colonos from Aurora sent a letter to the president, stating, "We bought our homes in these marshy lands with the firm promise that they would be urbanized with services: water, light, drainage. It has been several years, and we still do not see these services despite the fact that we paid a fairly high price for the land."[60] *Services* and *urbanization* became synonymous in the political language of Aurora's settlers. After Aurora's colonos registered their complaints and contacted local news publications, the government remained passive and indifferent; the housing contracts were left unfulfilled.[61]

In Aurora, the cramped conditions in most homes drove residents, particularly men, to find solace and refuge in other neighborhood spaces. Like other colonias, bars were one of the few things that flourished and thrived in Aurora's desertlike conditions. Generic-named bars like La Palmera and El Rancho sprung up in Aurora and served as second homes for men who squandered their day's earnings on a night of drunken comradery. Unlike other colonias, Aurora was unique in that it was the site of an arena built to stage professional bullfights.

Colonia Aurora's Plaza de Toros was inaugurated on January 20, 1963. The arena was born out of a need to attract more families to buy lots in Aurora. After three years of existence (1957–60), Aurora's owners had only sold fifty of the thirty thousand available lots.[62] Business had begun to pick up in 1961 as a result of an increased presence on the airwaves and the introduction of a free bus service that brought potential buyers to and from the colonia. Eckstein and Slotnick held meetings in their offices every Thursday to brainstorm new advertising schemes: slogans, posters, and even aerial advertising through planes carrying banners over sports stadiums. It was in one of these brainstorming sessions that engineer Germán Aréchiga Ruiz proposed the idea of building a bullfighting arena. Germán Aréchiga Ruiz's idea was met with howls of laughter and was deemed absolutely ludicrous. Nevertheless, Aréchiga Ruiz persisted and pleaded with Eckstein and Slotnick for an entire year until they were worn down and persuaded to undertake the risky business venture.[63]

The construction of a bullfighting arena in the middle of a desert was truly surreal. Despite the problems posed by high winds and a spongy underlying soil, construction neared completion by the end of 1962. The structure could hold up to five thousand people when filled to capacity and was outfitted with several generators that ran power to the arena's sound system. After a successful opening, Eckstein and Slotnick quickly realized that they would need to expand and diversify the arena's programming in order to keep the business afloat. After concluding they were in over their heads, they reached out to a company that specialized in hosting festivals, Parties and Events of Mexico (Diversiones y Espectáculos de México, DEMSA). DEMSA was run by Angel Vazquez, a Cuban immigrant who made a name for himself in Mexico by throwing extravagant parties and coordinating neighborhood festivals. Aurora's fraccionadores gave him complete control over the arena's planning and promotion in exchange for a monthly fee and a small percentage of the profits.[64] Soon, the Plaza de Toros hosted bullfighters, ranchera singers, comedians, beauty pageants, boxing matches, and of course, *la lucha libre* (wrestling).

With a population of roughly 120,000 people in 1965, Ciudad Neza was now a large enough audience to hire some of the biggest names in Mexican film and music. Popular singers like Javier Solís performed at Day of the Dead festivals, and actors such as Julio Alemán, Freddy Fernández (El Pichi), and Shilinsky entertained the crowds before boxing matches or bullfights.[65] Colonia Aurora even had its own local legend, Armando Soto la Marina, better known as El Chicote. A rising star during the 1940s, he was eventually relegated to smaller roles after too many alcohol-fueled shooting sprees (one in which he pulled a gun on actor/singer Jorge Negrete and challenged him to a duel). El Chicote's violent escapades made him a persona non grata in Mexico's film industry. After making the occasional appearance at the arena before a boxing match or lucha libre, he stumbled home with a complimentary liquor bottle in hand.[66] Sunday afternoons were usually reserved for bullfights, featuring homegrown matadors ("El Palmeño" Jesús López Moyano) and aging legends from Jalisco.

With the success of the Plaza de Toros, Eckstein and Slotnick opened the Cine Aurora movie theater. This was the third theater opened after the first two (Cine Maravillas and Cine Lago) were established by Colonia Maravillas's fraccionador, Benjamín Cemaj. Like Eckstein, Cemaj was a Jewish immigrant from Eastern Europe.[67] Undoubtedly, for an area composed of mainly migrants from the countryside, the presence of immigrants from another country was conspicuous. More than their Jewish backgrounds, it was their foreignness that critics attacked and vilified in the press. Save for one article in a local daily from 1961, Eckstein was always identified as "a foreigner" as opposed to "a Jew."[68] In another rare article, perhaps the only one with antisemitic undertones, the author lambastes fraccionador Cemaj for being a "Jewish businessman" guilty of perverting the minds of children by screening "pornographic" movies at his cinema.[69] The movies in question were not pornographic but simply Hollywood films with some risqué content. The article's implications are not difficult to discern: two Jewish fraccionadores (Eckstein and Cemaj) both operated the only movie houses in Ciudad Neza and were just as responsible for corrupting Mexican youth as Hollywood moguls.[70] Nonetheless, to fixate on the Jewish backgrounds of Eckstein and Cemaj would be to lose sight of the principal religious actor in the making of Ciudad Neza: the Catholic Church. As chapter 8 shows, the leaders of Ciudad Neza's local churches were supportive of the various fraccionador associations. When the colonos finally decided to strike in 1969, church authorities condemned the movement and worked closely with the fraccionadores to put down the revolt.[71] One would be hard-pressed to find a more fitting example than a photo in a local paper displaying a line of colonos making their monthly payments in Romero's office located in the outer walkway (*paseo*) of Mexico City's main cathedral.[72] When the fraccionadores embarked on a campaign to make the Colonias del Vaso de Texcoco an independent municipality, they received the church's blessing.[73]

From Colonia to Municipality

The historical significance of the 1958 Ley de Fraccionamientos has been typically dismissed by scholars. Though nominal and hollow, it did raise the expectations of colonos and imbued their cause with a sense of legitimacy and moral certitude. In their eyes, the law was on their side. Though the fraccionadores abdicated their legal obligations, they were aware of the risks under these new circumstances. The fraccionadores' support for a new municipality not only deflected criticism away from them; it also opened up an opportunity to create a new municipal government composed of friendly officials with mutual interests.

The creation of Ciudad Nezahualcóyotl as the 120th municipality in the State of Mexico is one of the most documented periods in its local history. As historian Pedro Ocotitla Saucedo argues, it seems the movement for "municipal independence" was initially a grassroots effort that the fraccionadores quickly recognized could play to their advantage.[74] The nascent demands for a new municipality developed into a new colono organization in March 1961 with the formation of the Central Executive Committee for a Free Municipality in Colonias del Vaso de Texcoco. Along with local demands for public utilities, the colonos made sure to cite the inspiration they gained from President López Mateos: "The citizenship and patriotism that our children learn in the free textbooks that President López Mateos has provided us must serve as a framework for a municipal, democratic, revolutionary, and direct government."[75] Various associations of colonos, merchants, teachers, and fraccionadores merged into a coalition for municipal status. Unsurprisingly, three Romero family members held leadership positions in the new coalition. A lengthy two-year process of rallies, meetings, petitions, legal filings, and poster campaigns finally led to the official creation of Ciudad Nezahualcóyotl in April 1963.

A statement issued in *El Gallo* (a local newspaper) in April 1963 is one of the most illuminating texts from the period. The statement depicts a scenario in which the progressive, forward-looking colonos' efforts to build an urban municipality are thwarted by the traditional, rural caciques in Chimalhuacán: "The majority of those living in the colonias are salaried workers who commute to the Federal District and who have used their regular paychecks to construct their own homes in this area; the inhabitants of Chimalhuacán are dedicated to agriculture, artisanal products, and other diverse realms of the economy; they are totally different."[76] Notwithstanding the fact that 97 percent of the colonos were not salaried workers, the statement expressed what they aspired to be and what they sought to distance themselves from—namely, their rural past.

The Colonias del Vaso de Texcoco became Ciudad Nezahualcóyotl on April 23, 1963. Gathered in front of a provisional city hall, Raúl Romero stood with the city's first mayor, Jorge Sáenz Knoth, to address a cheering crowd of residents from the new municipality.[77] Sáenz Knoth was a Oaxacan-born engineer of Dutch ancestry who arrived at the former Vaso de Texcoco at the beginning of the 1950s. A leading figure in the struggle for the creation of an independent Ciudad Nezahualcóyotl, Sáenz Knoth would later become a prominent spokesperson for the main association of fraccionadores in Ciudad Nezahualcóyotl. A widely publicized photo of Raúl Romero and Sáenz Knoth standing in front of a plaque that commemorated the establishment of Ciudad Nezahualcóyotl depicts the intimate and unequal relationship between the private fraccionadores and public officials.[78] The frail Sáenz Knoth listlessly pointing to the plaque while the domineering Romero stands to his left foreshadowed the power that the fraccionadores would exert over local officials who either remained complicit or actively participated in the fraccionadores' land fraud and malfeasance.

The open collusion between local politicians and land barons produced endemic levels of corruption that became normalized in Ciudad Nezahualcóyotl over the next ten years. Ultimately, the independent municipal status given to Ciudad Nezahualcóyotl only served to strengthen the power of the fraccionadores; resistance from Indigenous comuneros and local officials in Chimalhuacán had been neutralized, and the lands controlled by the fraccionadores were now under the jurisdiction of a new, abetting political body.

In the years to come, the fraccionadores in Ciudad Neza would gain an even greater level of power and impunity. As previously mentioned, the fraccionador was a distinct variant of urban caciquismo. They operated on a geographical scale that ranged from the neighborhood to the municipal level, rarely reaching anything that would be considered regional.[79] In many ways, they fit the conventional description of "a local or regional boss whose eminently personalist domination typically rests on a combination of family... alliances and patron-client networks, control over patronage resources, and coercive sanctions."[80] The urban fraccionador was not, however, a corrupt labor leader or political intermediary.[81] This fact distinguished them from both the charros of labor unions and the political functionaries analyzed by sociologist Wayne Cornelius in his work on "urban squatter settlements" in Mexico City (including in Ciudad Neza).[82] For Cornelius, the cacique of an informal settlement was a figure who shaped public opinion (in the neighborhood) and occupied a leadership position in a neighborhood or improvement association (*junta de mejoras*), discussed here in the section on Colonia El Sol.[83] While a neighborhood's political intermediary could have been a cacique, previous scholarship on urban caciquismo has largely ignored the fraccionador—in many ways an "entrepreneurial cacique" in land speculation and urban development.[84] The limitations of focusing on a single case (Neza) point to the need for more studies in various locations to draw any broader generalizations.

This chapter has presented the fraccionadores as an important, yet overlooked, force in urban politics after the 1920s. The events and actors detailed here only speak to one collection of informal settlements near Mexico City. At the same time, Ciudad Neza was not an isolated case, and one can find similar histories of fraccionadores in every major Mexican city by the 1960s. Who were these men? How can we assess the degree to which they influenced Mexican cities on a national scale?

Most fundamentally, the fraccionadores wielded power for profits and entered into the political arena on that basis. The fraccionadores were businessmen who developed deep ties with political figures and local authorities (police officers, judges, land surveyors) to benefit their private land speculation. The distinction is all the more important when the lines separating elected officials, business leaders, and the rule of law became blurred and seemingly indistinguishable in the 1960s. Fraccionadores such as Raúl Romero and Bernardo Eckstein built their urban fiefdoms with impunity from the law. The fraccionadores' power reached into virtually every aspect of public life in the former Vaso de Texcoco: they controlled the local press (*El*

Heraldo del Valle de México), church leaders, athletic clubs, bathhouses, and cinemas. Romero himself was a common fixture at neighborhood baptisms, where he became the godfather to dozens of children throughout the colonias.[85] The fraccionadores were individuals who did not come from wealthy families and tended to lack the level of education needed for professional positions in Mexico at the time. They were unified in their willingness to bribe public officials, commit land fraud, hire pistoleros, threaten journalists, and abdicate any responsibility for the inhuman conditions in their colonias. With the exception of Romero, whose father was a fraccionador, these were aspiring businessmen who could see the potential in land speculation but did not have the kind of capital or clout necessary to invest in valued lands through proper channels. Oddly, this scenario shared some similarities with the residents; they were both outcasts compelled to take a risk in the Vaso de Texcoco despite its harsh environs.

4

Autoconstrucción in Ciudad Neza

For a vast majority of Ciudad Neza's residents, building their own homes was the natural order of things. As migrants from Mexico's small towns and villages, it would have been likely that their childhood homes were one-story structures made of adobe bricks.[1] The long history of poor people constructing their own homes (or inheriting one from a previous generation) took on a new meaning when the practice became "massified" in major cities.[2] Thus, the term *autoconstrucción* (self-construction) emerged in relation to more conventional structures associated with urban living (apartment buildings, vecindades). For the millions of people who built their own homes on Mexico City's periphery, autoconstrucción not only fulfilled a basic human need but also represented "the kind of commitment to and imagination about the future that property ownership engenders."[3] The appeal of agency over one's living circumstances and the powerful sense of self-worth that came from being a *propietario* (property owner) were powerful factors for migrants frustrated by the lack of vacancies in the center of Mexico City.

After focusing on fraccionadores and land politics in the previous chapter, we now turn to residents and autoconstrucción. The self-constructed home provides a focal point to examine the lived experiences of residents in an informal city. These everyday experiences provide the material to pursue four key questions: Who moved to Ciudad Neza? Why did they move there? How did they survive? And finally, how were they stigmatized for living there? Before addressing these key questions, I provide a brief sketch of autoconstrucción in Mexico City in the middle of the twentieth century.

Autoconstrucción

In Mexico City, when a poor family could not find shelter, they made it. After foraging for materials, they improvised makeshift homes near railroad tracks, factories, highway overpasses, vacant lots, open fields, or anywhere else they could find. In 1952, it was estimated that roughly 315,000 people inhabited *jacales*, or temporary shelters.⁴ They were generally viewed as more precarious and temporary structures compared to sociospatial formations called *colonias proletarias* or *colonias populares*.

The term *colonia proletaria* was officially adopted by the government in 1949 to refer to a working-class or poor subdivision built outside of the city center.⁵ A self-built home in a colonia proletaria represented the largest growth of any housing stock during the 1950s, more than doubling their numbers in the Federal District from housing 420,000 residents in 1952 to 1.5 million in 1964.⁶ Although still subject to debate, most accounts identify Colonia Agrícola Oriental as one of the first colonias proletarias (1925). Like other colonia proletarias in the Federal District, Agrícola Oriental was remote, informal, and settled by poor families.⁷ On the one hand, colonias proletarias were subject to more repression in the Federal District compared to the State of Mexico, especially during the Ernesto Uruchurtu years. On the other hand, colonias proletarias in the Federal District were more likely to gain services and formal recognition from public authorities due to the Oficina de Colonias del DDF, an agency that increasingly grew to support colonias proletarias as a viable solution to the capital's housing crisis.

The single most important housing item in the initial phase of construction was the roof. It was generally the first item procured and the last to be installed. This was the case not only in Mexico but in much of the world. In the 1950s, housing expert Charles Abrams worked on roof-lending programs in Ghana and Bolivia after he identified its fundamental importance in the process.⁸ In Mexico City, most roofs were either sheets of corrugated steel or thick pieces of cardboard (*lámina de carton*). Just two years after *Excélsior* shocked its readers with an exposé on Mexico City's "Cardboard City" (Colonia Buenos Aires), Venezuelan poet and activist Alí Primera sang for the urban poor in his song "Techos de cartón" (Cardboard roofs).⁹ His lyrics speak to the fear and dread provoked by the sound of rain falling on a cardboard roof: "How sad, to hear the rain fall on cardboard roofs / There the rain falls and the suffering comes / Yes, the rain passes, but when does the suffering pass?"¹⁰ Rain, once a blessing from the sky for those who tilled the land, was now a looming threat.

For the structure of the house, the most important material was *tabique*. Tabique is a locally produced clay brick that is light but durable. With the passing of time, more hardware stores and material depots were established for residents. As peripheral neighborhoods and colono associations grew, the PRI channeled more resources into subsidized supply centers where items such as cement, wood, mortar, glass, rebar, and tabique were sold at fixed, discounted rates. Even with these subsidies, costs ran high, and construction tended to move slowly.

Ciudad Neza's history of autoconstrucción moved at two different speeds. From a demographic standpoint, there are only a few places in the world that have witnessed the same kind of rapid growth as Ciudad Neza during the 1970s. It would require looking at China's Pearl River Delta region or Lagos, Nigeria, to find another comparable case.[11] The population soared from 60,928 in 1963 to 605,104 in 1969. After 1970, we can zoom in even closer and track its change year by year: 1974 added 163,926 new residents; 1975 added 134,484; and 1976 added 182,871. In comparison, Toluca, the capital of the State of Mexico, added 55,000 people between 1960 and 1970.[12] The rapid growth made a mockery of any infrastructural improvements. After the inauguration of a needed water well or public faucet intended to serve a subdivision of four hundred people, that subdivision's population would likely double in a span of a year.

For residents, autoconstrucción moved painstakingly slowly. The construction of the house's core structure was just the first step in a long, ongoing process. A pallet of bricks in a front yard may lay dormant for months until more money or materials are obtained. Water damage from flooding could set back a new addition to the house. For these reasons, these homes can be described as products of incremental architecture. The incremental nature of autoconstrucción provided a narrative of time through the bricolage of materials used to build the house. A second room built in anticipation of a new child or a new mattress purchased with money from a Christmas bonus functioned as physical markers of time in the development of a family and their home. The slow pace of home construction was reflected in a colonia's infrastructure. As detailed in chapter 6, the major lag between population growth and infrastructural investment was disastrous and, at times, deadly for Ciudad Neza's colonos.

The colonos who built their modest homes in Ciudad Neza were not dissimilar from the colonos in Ecatepec, Santo Domingo, Santa Úrsula, Isidro Fabela, or any of the hundreds of other occupants of informal settlements in the Mexico City metropolitan area.[13] They shared common backgrounds and attitudes, bowed in reverence to the same religious altars, and walked with the same weariness from crowded *pipas*. But who exactly were the early settlers of Ciudad Neza? What did it mean to labor in Mexico City's informal economy, and how was that connected to living in an informal settlement? In the following, I mainly focus on the backgrounds of early residents (1947–63) while utilizing some data from later in the 1970s.

Labor and Living in the Vaso de Texcoco

The precarious nature of life in the former Vaso de Texcoco was mirrored in the jobs of its residents. They scrambled to survive among an ever-expanding constellation of jobs that spanned across Mexico City's informal economy. The instability and disorder of the buses that brought them into the city for work set the tone for much of the day ahead. Between 1947 and 1956, the buses dispatched by the San Rafael Martinez company left from the Colonias del ex-Vaso de Texcoco at erratic hours in the morning. Silver-plated buses lined the Zaragoza Highway at dawn and left at the whim of the driver (usually when the bus was filled to capacity).[14] Unregulated by schedules or any government agency, bus fares fluctuated at a great frequency, though they were typically more expensive than in the Federal District. Routes changed often, either to accommodate new colonias or to avoid bodies of water during the summer months.[15] The danger and desperation of this bus system were vividly captured in the regular images of men dangling from the doors and roofs of packed buses as drivers barreled down the highway toward the city.

Passengers usually rode the bus (*chimeco*) until the last stop in La Merced, where they disappeared into the bustling crowds of the marketplace. Most went their separate ways, but all carried something for work: a hammer, an accordion, cleaning supplies, buckets of flowers, baskets of food, and for many women, infants who could not be left at home unattended. The constellation of jobs reached down into every member of each family: the boys who roamed the Zócalo with shoeshine boxes, the girls who sold flowers and gum outside of Sanborns, the young men who hauled pieces of furniture on their backs to and from distributors (*cargadores*), the army of dust-covered men responsible for building Mexico's metropolis (*albañiles*), the young women who cleaned the luxury apartments surrounding Chapultepec Park, and the tired old women who spent their last years of life selling candies and *palanqueta* on the sidewalks of El Centro. Taken together, they formed a visual spectacle of urban poverty in modern Mexico.[16]

Hidden from this public spectacle were the women who worked in the numerous garment factories (*talleres de costura*) that dotted El Centro. In dozens of nondescript and unassuming buildings, thousands of women labored over sewing machines to make the clothes that were sold on the streets of Tepito, La Merced, and commercial districts spread out across central Mexico. Exact figures for these workshops (basically sweatshops) do not exist for the 1950s, but by 1970, the Mexican government estimated that there were approximately forty thousand clandestine sweatshops operating in Mexico City.[17] A woman from Ciudad Neza who worked in a sweatshop overlooking the Zócalo (on República de Uruguay) explained that she was paid based on the number of jackets she made per week. When asked if she had any form of job security or a work contract, she responded, "I have no social security [IMSS], my boss loaned me money to buy the machine I work on and he deducts a percentage from me each month . . . for Christmas we get a small bonus."[18] The interviewee went on to explain how her job was simply one part of a longer day that consisted of commuting, caring for her children, cooking, and doing housework.

Prior to 1960, documents detailing the backgrounds of the former Vaso de Texcoco's inhabitants were mainly anecdotal. Census data from the State of Mexico (1960) found that 97 percent of residents in the Colonias del Vaso de Texcoco consisted of albañiles, domestic workers, commercial vendors, and the unemployed. Only 2 percent of the population (medical workers and teachers) could have been covered by social security and represented by major trade unions (the last 1 percent consisted of the remaining comuneros).[19] Asked to describe El Sol, a resident said, "Our colonia was for the poor . . . workers, people who had a stand in some marketplace, albañiles."[20] Another longtime resident of Colonia Metropolitana recollected, "These colonias were for the poor—those who work with their hands, the humble ones . . . who lacked social security and credit."[21] Just as there was no dominant regional or ethnic identity in the former Vaso de Texcoco, there was no primary source of employment for its early residents.

Later, a study carried out by engineer Jorge Tamayo in 1970 found 92 percent of male workers were in the broad category of "working class," consisting of carpenters, electricians, albañiles, and street vendors. In this working-class grouping, 40 percent were listed under the general subcategory of *obrero* (worker), which could mean anything from an assembly line worker at a bottling company to a truck driver for an auto-parts importer.[22] Of the women who carried out paid labor (the study doesn't include the portion of women in this category), the bulk of the positions were domestic worker and cleaner (28 percent), street vendor (20 percent), and seamstress (6 percent).[23] Two notable changes can be observed between the 1960 and 1970 studies. First was an increase in residents listed as professionals (from 2 percent to 5 percent), and second was an increase in the portion of people who worked in Ciudad Neza (from 2 to 28 percent).[24] Less of a "bedroom community" in the 1970s compared to the 1950s, virtually all of the early residents engaged in paid labor commuted to the Federal District for work.

In this light, we can begin to observe a growing tension found among a segment of the population geographically excluded from the formal city by residence yet highly integrated into it by work. This was not simply the transference of rural poverty to the city. Unlike poor villagers in the countryside, Ciudad Neza's residents were regularly immersed in various class settings and surroundings through the course of a regular workday (especially for domestic workers, security guards, and construction workers in the capital's affluent neighborhoods). As a result, Ciudad Neza's residents had access to a wide array of construction materials, scrap metal, recycled bits and pieces, and mass-produced consumer goods. In some cases, they possessed an intimate knowledge of designs, layouts, and products found in middle- to upper-class homes. Undoubtedly, their access to those materials and goods was severely limited due to their paltry earnings, but they could still slowly improve their circumstances with time and patience. In many cases, the construction workers who helped build the new corporate headquarters and government buildings downtown were the same individuals who constructed their own homes on the city's periphery.

Long commutes to work were not exclusive to poor colonias in the former Vaso de Texcoco. Colonos in Ciudad Neza suffered from long commute times, as did residents in Coyoacán, Tlalpan, and Iztapalapa.²⁵ But Ciudad Neza's particularly harsh environment and its position outside of the Federal District represented two major obstacles to attracting settlers to the area—even poor ones who could have just as easily found a land plot on the eastern fringes of the Federal District. For some initial settlers, the painful realization of being swindled and stranded on a deserted plain led them to abandon their land and suffer the financial loss. Early resident Margarita Lopez recalled, "This was a large plain. When it rained, a white foam would rise from the ground, some said it was saltpeter. . . . I don't know, the only thing I can say is it was very hard to live here. Only the bravest stayed."²⁶ Why did those "brave" families stay? What originally brought them to the former Vaso de Texcoco / Ciudad Neza? As migrants in the center of Mexico City moved toward the outlying periphery, Ciudad Neza's fraccionadores played a decisive role in directing the movement of that outward migration.

Advertising the New Colonia

Advertisements were instrumental to the growth of the Colonias del Vaso de Texcoco. César Hann Cárdenas of Colonia El Sol was one of the first examples of a fraccionador who relied heavily on advertising to increase land sales. "César Hann's form of selling land was very *populachera*," explained a local journalist. "He would send teams of sellers to poor neighborhoods and markets with flyers . . . he targeted the poorest ones who couldn't defend themselves."²⁷ A promotional flyer for Colonia Estado de México assures readers, "The land that you can buy for a few cents today will be worth a fortune tomorrow!"²⁸ For a largely illiterate demographic, the radio waves were crucial. Castro Ortega, an early resident of El Sol, remembered that he moved there in 1949 after he heard an ad on the radio: "They offered the popular sectors of Mexico City a chance to buy lots that claimed to have the best urban services."²⁹ César Hann did not require bank account statements, references, or proof of income in order to buy a land plot in El Sol; with a down payment of 80 pesos, a person like Castro Ortega could become a propietario overnight.³⁰

Later, at the end of the 1950s, Colonia Aurora came to prominence through its heavy-handed ad campaigns. The company's memorable ads saturated the airwaves and were incessantly played on stations such as XEN, XEW, and XEB. In between songs and soap operas, Aurora's radio spot announced,

"Aurora, Aurora, new and modern, with 24-hour security and lands improved by science!"[31] In time, the fraccionadores developed a second radio ad that included a catchy jingle that ended with the soon-to-be-famous slogan: "Aurora, a colonia where a child is born every day!"[32] In radio ads and newspaper inserts, Aurora was touted as a place to start a family far from the overcrowded slums of El Centro. Despite extreme levels of poverty, television antennas began to crown the rooftops of vecindades and shacks throughout the city's poor neighborhoods by the 1950s. As the "TV boom" made television sets more accessible to *capitalinos*, the Aurora Company diversified its advertising campaign to include television commercials that featured the family's well-being and happiness as a central theme and selling point.[33]

Aurora's advertisements promised running water, paved streets, drainage, and electricity. To stay competitive, they offered free blueprints and sold construction materials at a discount rate. A photo in the pages of *El Día* depicting a worker standing in front of Aurora's offices offers a rare glimpse into a familiar scene in Mexico City's popular marketplaces throughout the 1960s and early 1970s. The banner's message was simple and appealing: "Land and a Home for Your Family in Aurora."[34] The prospects of owning a home and retaining all the services offered by the city exerted a strong pull on rural migrants frustrated by the lack of privacy and space in the city's tenement districts. Eventually, Aurora's advertising blitzes captured the attention of a journalist agitated by the land developers' sensationalistic ads.

In 1961, one of the earliest articles about Aurora was published in the press. *La Extra* published a reporter's firsthand account of Aurora, in which the writer proclaims, "They [the fraccionadores] announce spacious and modern residences, but the public will only find filthy huts." The reporter wrote, "In any country where the laws are respected, commercial advertisements based on lies are subject to intervention by the authorities and the perpetrators are found guilty of fraud."[35] In Aurora, nothing changed. The article was a blip in the news and mainly fell on deaf ears. Its circulation through government offices prompted an investigation by the Secretaría de Hacienda y Crédito Público that turned out to be a minor inconvenience.[36] It was an example of how the unseen workings of corruption account for the gaps in the historical record.

The prevalence of Aurora's posters and radio spots illustrates how advertisements can legitimate the illegitimate. Even for a skeptical public, the uncontested nature of Aurora's claims lent an air of credibility to the company. Their colorful logos were prominently displayed above their offices in the Federal District and in the passageways of the city's main cathedral, where the public could see them operate openly and without disruption. When a business engages in an intense ad campaign over the course of several years and draws little public scrutiny, the absence of any backlash or controversy helps the company maintain a veneer of legitimacy.

The incongruity between the real Aurora and the one advertised on the radio was a major source of anger and discontent for its residents. In one letter, Aurora resident Gregorio Cervantes complained, "I'm practically living out in the open; my wife and children are exposed to all of the health dangers that come with the strong currents of air that penetrate the house with dust. When it rains . . . the water seeps in through the sheets that cover the roof and the windows." Cervantes made a simple demand: "I want to be given a house that meets the conditions stipulated in the contract."[37] A series of housing surveys carried out in the late 1950s and early 1960s indicate that Cervantes's letter was indicative of nearly all the residents in Aurora and Ciudad Neza more broadly.

Architecture of Necessity

One of the first studies of the Colonias del Vaso de Texcoco can be traced back to a 1958 report on Colonia El Sol by the Ministry of Hydraulic Resources. Of the 377 lots with some level of construction, 73 were uninhabited, indicating a family who abandoned their lot or who lived in another location as they built their home.[38] The SRH found three common materials for the homes: tabique bricks (walls), cardboard (roof), and dirt (floor).[39] Unsurprisingly, these materials could rarely withstand a summer of rain and flooding without damage or destruction. Later in 1962, IMSS carried out another housing survey in El Sol and several adjacent colonias (Romero, Maravillas, Estado de México). They found that most (88–90 percent) of Ciudad Neza's residents lived without running water, separate bathrooms, or drainage.[40] Roughly half of the dwellings were built on the bare ground, with no foundation or floor (*pisos de tierra*). When the same survey was conducted in the middle-class neighborhood of Santa María la Ribera, the housing conditions were completely reversed: roughly 90 percent of Santa María la Ribera's residents had running water, drainage, and separate bathrooms. Despite the extreme difference in housing conditions, 30 percent of residents from both areas (Santa María la Ribera and Ciudad Neza) overlapped in the same income bracket.[41]

Autoconstrucción was a physical extension of the family. The home represented the collective work of a family, and each new addition contributed to an ongoing story told among family, friends, and neighbors. For family members, each new room or major improvement marked a moment in time since moving to a particular colonia. For rural migrants uprooted from the familiar faces of their town plaza and local church, life in the city would test the bonds of traditional family relations.

Contrary to predictions of increased alienation and individualism brought on by city life, the challenges and hardships in Mexico City drew migrant families closer together. In a study of rural migrants in Mexico City carried out in the 1950s, anthropologist Oscar Lewis noted, "Family life remains strong in Mexico City.... Household composition is similar to village patterns except that more extended families live together in the city."[42] The state of a particular family—broadly defined as nuclear, extended, *compadragazo* (system of godparenting), or some combination of the three—strongly influenced the pace and quality of construction. In most cases, the father was the principal figure in obtaining the materials, determining the design, and carrying out the initial construction with friends and hired hands. Children assisted their parents by gathering materials, laying down bricks, fetching water, and helping with any unforeseen problems that arose in the construction process.[43] The entire family, many times joined by neighbors and *cuates* (close friends), worked as a collective unit on Sundays to build, expand, or fix their homes.[44] Less visible, though equally important, were the minor and gradual modifications made by women in their day-to-day domestic labor. The placement of potted plants hanging from windows, outdoor clotheslines, water basins, chicken coops, and interior furniture were typically responsibilities of the mother.

At first glance, the early images of the Colonias del Vaso de Texcoco depict an empty dust bowl sparsely populated with a few homes. The deserted landscape was real, but the solitude was a mirage. At home, overcrowding remained a way of life for families in the former Vaso de Texcoco. While the vast stretches of barren land gave its inhabitants space and privacy from their neighbors, an average family of five to eight people shared a one-room shack during their initial years in the area.⁴⁵ Many times, a thin sheet was spread across the room at night, dividing the room by gender with the father sleeping with the boys and the mother sleeping with the girls. In December and January, piles of blankets and human warmth from sleeping together helped children survive those cold nights when the temperature dropped and the winds howled across the open, treeless flats.⁴⁶ Even for homes with little furniture, a table was an essential item to own. The table served as the place to care for babies, make and sort goods to be sold in the city, do homework, eat meals, and socialize.⁴⁷ The interior of homes accumulated more furniture and possessions as time passed. The initial *petate*— a traditional bedroll woven from palm fibers—was eventually replaced by a cushioned mattress, and the charcoal-fueled *fogón* (cooking fire pit) was exchanged for a kerosene stove. In time, a dirt floor was covered with a concrete foundation and cluttered with toys, radios, shoes, and items from work. Without fail, every home possessed an assortment of flowers, candles, and rosaries that were placed around the image of the Virgin of Guadalupe.⁴⁸

For the exterior, many residential lots shared a common spatial layout as well. A simple wall of stacked rocks surrounding the perimeter of the property served as a fence or enclosure. Typically, a ditch was dug around the rock wall to alleviate flash floods. Overwhelmed with nostalgia, a mother remembered, "My children placed all the rocks and rubble around the house . . . from that first room we saw our house grow, we used tabique as a walkway across the mud, we began to make the floor so we wouldn't be covered in mud, we used wood that we found and brought back to the house."⁴⁹ In 1957, Oscar Lewis took extensive notes of a more advanced self-built home in a nearby colonia also located in the former Vaso de Texcoco.⁵⁰ He describes a gray, fortresslike exterior wall with a narrow doorway near the road that led to an open-air patio. The patio was formed by the empty space between the exterior wall near the road and the home itself. In the patio area, the owner built a rudimentary cement staircase to the roof of the home (also made of reinforced concrete). The open space under the staircase was used for a *lavadero*—a space set aside for water basins, buckets, soap containers, dry racks, and clotheslines. Walking past the core housing unit, a small enclosed structure was built for human waste (outhouse). While the cement staircase was not typical in the 1950s, the general layout of the home was common throughout the former Vaso de Texcoco in this period.⁵¹

Domesticated animals and livestock were central to the design and layout of self-built homes on the periphery. In a back patio or extended room, it was common for a family to have a chicken coop or a sty for pigs.[52] In the home, Oscar Lewis observed, "beyond the laundry, two rooms for the animals ranged along the right side of the rectangle, first a room for the pigeons, then one for the pigs."[53] The livestock and fowl represented a clear continuity between "the countryside" and "the city" disparaged by outside observers. For the residents, this "vulgar hybridity" was a way to supplement their incomes, along with providing a familiar affective comfort or routine tied to their past lives in the countryside. A similarity can be found with dogs. There were the emotional bonds forged with a dog, but the family also looked to the dog as a form of protection. When night fell, a pack of dogs sleeping on the roof or near the door of a house was the first line of defense in a poor colonia nearly void of police or security.[54]

The lack of services forced residents to pirate electricity from the Federal District. The process was technically illegal and physically dangerous. The city's official grids were accessed not through trespassing and vandalism but through whispered conversations and bribery. Longtime resident Angel Ramirez discussed his role in talking with the electric company and learning how to handle the wiring from the closest transformer. The main cable was installed into the base of the transformer, stretched along a row of wooden poles, and split into twenty outlets on a large wood board (essentially a makeshift circuit breaker). Ramirez said, "I knew it wasn't possible to have people climb and stick their hands into each electric source, so I lowered it down to the ground and divided it on box made of wood. . . . This is how the famous *telarañas* [literally, 'spider webs'; makeshift utility poles and wires] were born."[55] As one can imagine, the electricity was sporadic and unreliable, especially as the population grew larger. The telarañas became ubiquitous in the former Vaso de Texcoco, highlighting the gap between the residents' needs and their material conditions.

Along with the image of a flooded settlement, the sight of Ciudad Neza's telarañas also left a lasting impression on visitors. In a descriptive passage from Ignacio Pichardo Pagaza's memoir, he recalls the "surreal" quality of Ciudad Neza's landscape. In an attempt to capture the magnitude of the telarañas, he compares them to a busy seaport: "It seemed like we were at the edge of a long wharf for fishermen on some faraway beach in the Pacific.

Dozens, hundreds, perhaps thousands of wooden posts of different dimensions had been placed every 25 meters along the avenues. In the distance, they looked like the masts of fishing boats anchored in a dry lake."[56] He goes on to explain how the system worked: "Instead of sails, the posts supported hundreds of thin cables carrying electrical currents generated from strategically placed transformers. The colonos connected a cable to the devices, one by one, to carry the energy across hundreds of meters to each of their modest homes. Almost all tied a colored ribbon to their conducting wire at a certain number of meters."[57] He concludes, "The result was a dense web of little flags with dozens of cables in each transformer, for each street, and in each post."[58] The absence of electricity and potable water stole valuable time and energy from colonos who were forced to go to extreme lengths to survive in such hostile environs.

Space, Time Constraints, and Gender

Time has been an object of inquiry across academic disciplines since their respective inceptions. More specifically, studies about "the relationships between the workings of power and the experience of time" have enriched our collective understanding of social divisions and inequalities in modern societies.[59] These works cover a broad range of themes and questions, probing how time is experienced (collectively or personally); how power relations are expressed through the organization of calendars and clocks; and how time is given meaning through ritual, memory, labor, war, politics, and art.[60] Javier Auyero's work in Buenos Aires is particularly significant in elucidating how gender inequalities and social domination structure the everyday experiences of women waiting in welfare offices for public assistance.[61] The time allotted to waiting is one of the temporal categories used in the current analysis of women's labor and survival strategies in Ciudad Neza.

The increased attention to gender roles and divisions among scholars during the 1970s and 1980s in Mexico provides part of the empirical foundation for the inclusion of temporality as a factor in the perpetuation of inequities. These studies were principally concerned with the division of labor (at home and in the workplace) between men and women in cities to more deeply understand how gender inequality was reproduced on a day-to-day basis. Feminist scholars interested in the everyday experiences of women in metropolitan centers documented the disproportionate number of hours women invested into unpaid domestic work (cleaning, childcare, food preparation) compared to their male counterparts. Study after study demonstrated the extra burdens and barriers placed on women's time in various neighborhoods throughout Mexico City in the 1970s.[62]

By reviewing the documentation of Ciudad Neza's infrastructure in conjunction with testimonials and comments from residents, one can begin to discern the outlines of a common daily routine among women in Ciudad Neza during the 1960s. While differences existed between women who commuted to the Federal District and those who stayed behind in the colonias, there were several consistent and nearly uniform demands facing both groupings. These demands, and the challenges they posed, burdened Ciudad Neza's women with time-consuming tasks not shared by residents in Mexico City's government-built housing complexes, vecindades, or affluent neighborhoods.

For most women in Ciudad Neza, their first waking moments began in the murky hours between night and morning.[63] The hours right before dawn are always the coldest in the Valley of Mexico, which is usually still dark before 6:00 a.m. with a chill in the air regardless of the season. In those moments, the procurement of water was always urgent and necessary. During the summer months, rainwater might have been collected in a basin, but this partial reserve did not negate the fact that the entire day hinged on water. With few exceptions, the responsibility of water procurement fell to the woman of the house. Often, the children would accompany their mother to a public faucet or *pipa* distributor to assist with the heavy lifting and transportation of water.[64] Due to the fact that Ciudad Neza was never just a neighborhood but a collection of neighborhoods and later a municipality, the distances for residents vary and consequently produce different time spans. Most accounts state they walked between thirty and ninety minutes in the morning for water.[65]

After they arrived at a water distribution point, each person would have to wait anywhere from thirty to ninety minutes. Again, wait times could vary based on a person's position in the line, if there was a heavy rainstorm the previous night, or the pipa distributor's schedule.[66] Women and children lined up their empty water basins and buckets along Zaragoza Highway each morning at dawn and anxiously waited for a pipa tanker truck to arrive. Along with the mobile water tankers, there were semifunctional public faucets. As one resident later recalled, "The first public water faucet was the only one for ten blocks." She goes on to say, "Then you can imagine, given the overdensity of families. . . . We had to queue for several hours."[67]

The walk back home was always slower than the first part of the journey. This was for the simple reason that the buckets and basins were now full of water, requiring more physical lifting and a steady hand (or shoulder) to prevent spillage. In this back-and-forth process, the environment must be considered as well. Without streetlights or paved roads, the trek for water in the darkness or early morning light was rendered even more dangerous. Devoid of vegetation and fresh water, one could walk for long stretches of time (twenty to forty minutes) without passing a single tree or blade of grass. In the distance, there might have been a row of power lines or a faint, pulsing red light from one of the airport towers, though it was more likely to have been the same dusty plains stretching out to the mountain ranges on the horizon. In these moments, the silent darkness of the former lake bed made the desolation even more palpable. The bitter irony of trudging across a lake bed to obtain water was not lost on the women of the colonias. The environment also placed women in precarious positions. Walking alone or with children, they were regularly forced into potentially dangerous situations where they were more vulnerable to theft and sexual assault.

While the procurement of water in Ciudad Neza could take up to a few hours, the process in an IMSS housing complex was a matter of a few seconds. Water was available in each apartment's bathroom and kitchen area for cooking, cleaning, bathing, removing waste (toilet), and in many cases, washing clothes.[68] The cost was free, and its regularity was close to certain.[69] This simple difference saved a tenant sixty to ninety minutes each day. Of course, there is no way to predict or ascertain what each person would do with that time, but it leaves the possibility open to each person and provides a competitive advantage over a peer in another part of the metropolis.

The daily struggle of finding water, then competing, paying, and petitioning for it, constituted a portion of the myriad tasks and demands that confronted women in the Colonias del Vaso de Texcoco / Ciudad Neza. Along with water procurement, there was the extra time spent digging ditches for flooding, petitioning officials for electricity, and traveling to the market for perishables that could not be refrigerated (lack of regular electricity). These examples are not based on the unevenness found between men and women performing domestic tasks in general. They more specifically highlight the notable differences in the time that one group of women must allot to perform a set of daily, menial tasks to survive while the other grouping does not, solely based on where they live. In terms of time, the cumulative effect could mean a difference of two to four hours—significant enough to be used to carry out paid work, care for children, learn a desired skill, rest, gather one's thoughts, read, or any other of the many possibilities given the circumstances.

The lack of systematic documentation and challenges of estimating an average amount of lost time oddly strengthens the study's argument in an unanticipated way. One of the most common themes running through the various interviews and accounts of daily life in Ciudad Neza was uncertainty.[70] The uncertainty was a direct result of the infinite contingent factors and unpredictable problems that arose from Ciudad Neza's lack of basic services and infrastructure. One day a wait for water could be thirty minutes; the next day it could stretch out to two hours. The bus could arrive at one's stop at 7:00 a.m. on Monday and arrive at the same place at 7:35 a.m. on Tuesday. The instability and uncertainty revolving around basic life necessities made it extremely difficult to hold on to a job with a fixed schedule and lent itself to work in the informal economy. Undoubtedly, there are numerous examples of jobs in Mexico City's formal economy with unfixed schedules and women from Ciudad Neza who worked in positions with fixed schedules in the Federal District. Notwithstanding these notable exceptions, the freedom and independence promised by work as a street vendor (food, clothes, mass-produced goods, artisanal crafts) or part-time domestic work did not extend to work in a factory or office. In many cases, the chaotic nature of daily life in peripheral colonias formed an insurmountable obstacle and counterweight to upward social mobility.

In the public imagination, the image of a woman carrying a bucket of water down a dirt road after the 1950s symbolized not the rise of a new urban underclass but a nation still mired in the primitivism of its rural past. Of course, transporting water from a store or natural body of water was the norm for all classes for most of Mexico City's history (the upper classes had servants manually retrieve water until the beginning of the twentieth century, with nearly all wealthy homes connected to the city's water supply by 1910).[71] The preexisting stigma grew and took on a new meaning after various public works projects implemented by Uruchurtu made domestic potable water generally accessible for middle-class families.[72] As the following will demonstrate, basic services such as water and electricity were associated with urbanity in popular discourse.

Vulgar Hybridity

Around the world, poor urban areas share many of the same stigmas. They are often portrayed as breeding grounds for crime, vice, disease, social dysfunctionality, and political corruption.[73] All these stigmas find their own distinctive expressions based on each place's particular history and culture.[74] In Mexico's press, Ciudad Neza's novel and ambiguous built environment (or lack thereof) left writers simultaneously perplexed and appalled, fearful of what the outlying frontier could portend for the future.[75]

A typical depiction of Ciudad Neza in the press can be found in a *Novedades* article from 1970 entitled "Marginalized from Progress Just outside of the Metropolis." Like many articles from the period, its stigmatization of Ciudad Neza is based on conjecture and partial truths articulated by bureaucrats or engineers visiting the area. The article features David Castillo Salas, an engineer working on the construction of a school facility in an unnamed colonia. He begins by falsely claiming that most of Ciudad Neza's residents are *paracaidistas* (literally, "parachutists"), a colloquial term for an illegal squatter meant to invoke the image of poor families swooping down and invading an empty tract of land.[76] Although Ciudad Neza witnessed a wave of paracaidismo from 1973 to 1977, it was a rare occurrence when this article was published in 1970. Most residents had purchased their plot of land in a fraccionador's office, but the stigma surrounding Ciudad Neza led the average reader to assume that residents were paracaidistas.

Already shrouded with an air of illegality, the engineer goes on to lament that most of Ciudad Neza's youth are juvenile delinquents and criminals due to the municipality's lack of urbanization. Without any evidence, the engineer asserts, "[Neza] is a place characterized by having a large population of youth, a lot of whom lack orientation, and as a result, [they] get caught up in vandalism, getting drunk, or just doing nothing."[77] The engineer then provides a logic for this situation: "There are no clean and safe places to play . . . no nearby schools or community centers."[78] Aside from the problem of criminalizing an entire generation of youth based on brief observations and hearsay, the idea that a newly built environment could overcome and negate the multitude of socioeconomic factors at play (extreme poverty, malnutrition, bleak job prospects, etc.) was a frequent talking point not solely limited to engineers. The article's attention to Ciudad Neza's "criminality" is the most salient example of territorial stigmatization, but its opening lines allude to another damming attribute in the eyes of the engineer. Referring to Ciudad Neza, Castillo Salas says, "The city, if you could call it that."[79] In the engineer's skepticism, one can begin to see the derision and scorn heaped on Ciudad Neza for its failure to mirror the image of a traditional city. In the press, Ciudad Neza's lack of urban character was not only a source of crime but also the reason colonos suffered from its toxic environment.

Ciudad Neza's toxic environment had its symbolic repercussions as well. The regular presence of stagnant floodwaters and dirt roads was perceived as "unurban" in the public imagination by 1970. For both officials and residents alike, the solution was to *urbanizar* the area. In addition to images associated with the countryside, where one lives "in nature," Ciudad Neza's lack of urban character was also magnified by its lack of control over nature. The relative absence of human mastery over nature in Ciudad Neza contributed to what I have referred to as its vulgar hybridity.[80]

Ciudad Neza's vulgar hybridity was on full display in a five-part series in *Novedades* at the beginning of 1971, ominously titled "El fin de la leyenda negra" (The end of the black legend). "The black legend of Ciudad Neza" was a term primarily used by journalists in the early 1970s to refer to Ciudad Neza's ill repute.[81] The series contained the kind of sensational details and lurid stories one could expect from a daily tabloid. The graphic images and photo layouts accompanying the series displayed gullies filled with sewage runoff and women carrying buckets of water across mud-drenched passageways. In a follow-up article published later in the year, a line of boldfaced text proclaimed, "Every morning, same thing: avoid puddles, inhale dust, and pray to God you don't get sick."[82] In another installment of the series, a group of children are photographed walking back from school. The silhouette-like figures are dwarfed by the wide panorama of a flooded plain, its turbid waters broken into two sections by a narrow land bridge used by colonos.[83] The images of marshy landscapes, hand-built huts, empty plains devoid of life, and women washing clothes on the side of dirt roads formed the impression that this was not a city. A headline from the series that read "Nezahualcóyotl: The Whole Problem Begins Only

5 Kilometers from the Zócalo" highlighted Ciudad Neza's proximity to the city center, and in doing so, disabused the reader of the notion that Ciudad Neza was located in some distant province (the distance is more accurately twelve to fifteen kilometers).[84]

The territorial stigmatization of a place marks the people who call it home. Based on oral histories and published interviews, along with the author's own conversations with residents, the stigmas associated with Ciudad Neza were pervasive and tangible. They were experienced and made evident on both individual and collective levels. For a person going through the process of a job interview or application, writing down "Ciudad Nezahualcóyotl" for one's home address carried a set of negative connotations generally seen as a strike against the applicant. Those negative connotations and assumptions were also carried over into policing. Regardless of appearance or position, informing a police officer that one was from Ciudad Neza left a person more open to harassment or discriminatory practices, particularly for young people. Salvador Nava Méndez, proprietor of a restaurant in Ciudad Neza since 1950, stated, "It made me sad to say that I [am] from Neza, people in the Federal District always humiliated us; they said that it was a *ciudad perdida* and that there was crime."[85] Later in the interview he goes on to say, "Before, people didn't want to come to Nezahualcóyotl; they called it Nezahualpolvo or Nezahualodo [*polvo* meaning 'dust' and *lodo* meaning 'mud']."[86] In Ciudad Neza's stigmatization, dust and mud were just as present as crime and vice.

More broadly, the black legend surrounding Ciudad Neza influenced policy decisions and loan applications. As previously mentioned, the World Bank turned down a critical loan application for water piping due to Ciudad Neza's notorious reputation. In Ignacio Pichardo Pagaza's memoir about his years as a secretary general under Carlos Hank González (1969–75), he writes, "Our ability to make payments on loans was not recognized at the time by the World Bank. Through Banobras, we repeatedly requested a long-term loan from that international organization for Ciudad Neza. Following reports from several fact-finding missions, they negatively advised its then president, Robert McNamara. His advisors said that the residents would definitely not pay back their loans because they didn't have the capacity to save funds."[87] Ignacio Pichardo Pagaza goes on to relate the story of a compunctious World Bank advisor who made a trip to Ciudad Neza later in the 1980s and expressed his regret for turning down their loan requests.[88] By that point, Ciudad Neza's advances in infrastructure and services put an end to the original black legend surrounding it, though new stigmas emerged and grew stronger than ever. Ciudad Neza's street crime and violence continued to fill the pages and screens of news outlets; however, the skepticism surrounding its urban character and the vulgar hybridity described in this chapter had largely disappeared by the end of the 1980s.

In the middle of the twentieth century, the portion of Mexico City's residents who lived in rented apartments began to decline in the face of rising homeownership. Around 1960, when Mexico became a nation of more urban dwellers than rural residents for the first time in its history, more of Mexico City's residents lived in individual single homes than apartment buildings (in the Federal District and greater Mexico City).[89] One of the main forces behind the dramatic surge in homeownership was autoconstrucción.

Massive in scope, autoconstrucción was a highly contradictory process. It was a collective endeavor that required the labor of family members, friends, and neighbors. The absence of basic services forced neighbors to pool their resources together while also compelling them to join forces on larger projects such as land excavation (wells or ditches) and the construction of telarañas. Later, neighborhood associations promoted horizontal decision-making among members and acts of solidarity with other colonias. Their refusal to accept miserable living conditions put them in direct conflict with state authorities and gave rise to a powerful protest movement. These acts of solidarity and resistance could not, however, alter the central demand of the movement: private property. Though colonos were motivated by desires for better, dignified living conditions, their actions were objectively part of transferring public lands into the private real estate market.[90] With the arrival of President Luis Echeverría at the beginning of the 1970s, these contradictions were put into sharp relief and began to show the potential to challenge the status quo.

Fachada Poniente.

Edificio tipo "C", el más grande del conjunto. Consta de 100 departamentos. En su planta inferior, a nivel de la plaza baja, se aloja la zona comercial principal. El acceso a los departamentos se hace por cinco circulaciones verticales que se comunican con la plaza por medio de cuatro puentes.

Fachada Poniente y Zona Comercial Central.

FIG. 1. Exterior facade of Unidad Santa Fe, 1957. From *Arquitectura México*, no. 59 (September 1957).

Bosque y lago de San Juan de Aragón.

Las circulaciones principales del conjunto están ligadas con el sistema vial de la ciudad por medio de tres puentes sobre el Canal del Desagüe y por medio de la conexión hacia el sur con las avenidas Río Consulado y Oceanía. En un futuro próximo este conjunto quedará comunicado en su extremo oriente con el anillo periférico.

La estructura general de esta unidad urbana consiste en un grupo de unidades vecinales y de supermanzanas, cada una de ellas con sus respectivos servicios, establecidos alrededor de un gran centro comercial y cultural.

Cada "unidad vecinal" está constituida por un grupo de supermanzanas y un centro de servicios comunes. El mercado es el elemento más importante de este centro y el que define la extensión de la unidad vecinal, ya que es necesario considerar que el recorrido máximo conveniente desde una vivienda hasta el mercado es de 80 mts. Complementan el centro vecinal diferentes locales comerciales y de servicios, así como zonas recreativas, plaza cívica, etc.

Plaza de supermanzana y andador arbolado.

cluido aquí, como en cualquier parte del mundo, en que para poder dotar de casa a todas las familias que carecen de ella, es indispensable la construcción en serie, y en que además hay que solucionarla a base de habitación multifamiliar, concentrando los servicios y las instalaciones, puesto que la multiplicación de ellas se hace en cada casa unifamiliar, multiplica igualmente los costos. Si quisiéramos concretar diríamos que la demanda de habitación puede ser resuelta mediante la iniciativa del Estado respaldada en una industria poderosa y construyendo edificios multifamiliares en serie.

Posteriormente a nuestras experiencias de los años treinta y dos, el déficit de habitación veía impulsarse vigorosamente la solución. Los conjuntos Alemán y Juárez son la prueba de que se habían asimilado los primeros intentos, superándolas en grandes conjuntos que tenían de 4 a 14 variantes diferentes a fin de que cualquier familia encontrara acomodo en alguna de ellas.

Ojalá que San Juan de Aragón cambie el curso de la brújula y los conjuntos ya no se destinen a la clase media, cuya posición no obstante sus escasos recursos es muchas veces superior a la de las masas trabajadoras que en almacenes, fábricas y ejidos impulsan al país.

Para solucionar la necesidad de vivienda en todos ellos, el Departamento Central construyó un conjunto habitacional en San Juan de Aragón, que consta de siete unidades vecinales, de las cuales han sido construidas tres, con un total de diez mil viviendas, de dos, tres y cuatro recámaras. El mercado, la escuela primaria, la guardería, el hospital infantil, la secundaria, la plaza principal, el cine y los jardines, no distan más de cuatro cuadras de cualquier casa.

—Como los muchachos están de vacaciones —proseguía—, todos los días se la pasan jugando aquí enfrente de la casa, en la calle, o se van al bosque y al lago. Ojalá que los podamos inscribir en la secundaria que está a tres cuadras de aquí, junto al mercado.

FIG. 2. Partial view of San Juan de Aragón Lake and Forest, 1964. From *Calli*, no. 15 (January 1965).

FIG. 3. Raúl Romero Erazo (*left*) and Jorge Sáenz Knoth at the inauguration of Ciudad Neza's Palacio Municipal, 1965. Courtesy of the Centro de Información y Documentación de Nezahualcóyotl.

FIG. 4. Early home in Ciudad Neza, ca. 1963. Courtesy of the Centro de Información y Documentación de Nezahualcóyotl.

FIG. 5. (*above*) Early home in Ciudad Neza, ca. 1963. Courtesy of the Centro de Información y Documentación de Nezahualcóyotl.

FIG. 6. (*opposite top*) President Luis Echeverría signing the Fineza Land Trust agreement, 1973. Governor Carlos Hank González stands to his right. Courtesy of the Centro de Información y Documentación de Nezahualcóyotl.

FIG. 7. (*opposite bottom*) Neighborhood association meeting, Ciudad Lago neighborhood, ca. 1973. Courtesy of the Centro de Información y Documentación de Nezahualcóyotl.

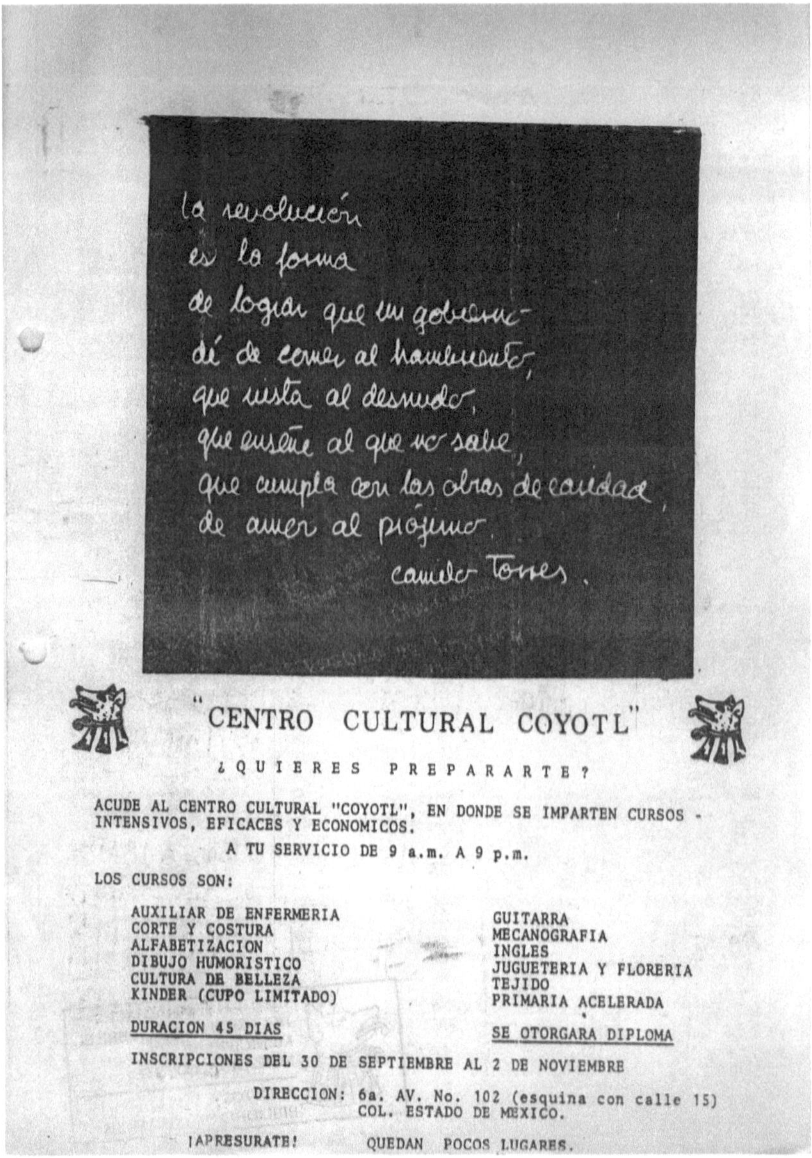

FIG. 8. Promotional materials for classes and workshops at a cultural center led by a Jesuit group in Ciudad Neza, 1974. The image features a quote by Colombian priest Camilo Torres on the need for revolution. From the independently produced pamphlet *El Despertar del Pueblo*.

PART 3

The Echeverría Years

5

Mortgaging the Revolution

The Early Years of Infonavit

"Salvador Allende Arrives!" "Unity!" "Viva América Latina!" The headlines were abuzz with the news of Salvador Allende's arrival in Mexico in 1972. At the end of November, Allende made a short stop in Mexico before delivering a major speech at the United Nations. After a busy itinerary of speaking with students in Guadalajara and meeting with political leaders in Mexico City, Allende found himself in the heart of Iztapalapa—the eastern section (*delegación*) of Mexico City known in the press for poverty, crime, and popular Holy Week processions.[1] Allende was there to help inaugurate the Unidad Habitacional Vicente Guerrero with President Echeverría and the directors of Infonavit, a new institute touted as "the Mexican solution to the nation's housing problem."[2] The Unidad Habitacional Vicente Guerrero was Infonavit's first major housing project and a harbinger of Echeverría's new housing initiative.

A decade earlier, John F. Kennedy had stood with President López Mateos to celebrate the opening of Unidad Independencia near the affluent suburbs of Jardines del Pedregal. Now on the other side of town, the inauguration of Unidad Vicente Guerrero stood in stark contrast to the festivities of the past. Pan-American unity was replaced with Latin American solidarity; the Third World was now favored over the Free World. Salvador Allende lauded Echeverría's role behind drafting the United Nations Charter of Economic Rights and Duties of States, while Echeverría praised Allende for steering Chile toward "true economic independence."[3] In fact, both championed economic independence as a path toward liberation from the "vestiges of colonialism" still present in Latin American societies.[4]

The leaders' political discourse was not the only thing that changed since President Kennedy's visit to Mexico in 1962. The modernist marvels of the López Mateos era had been replaced with drab housing units that had all of the function and none of the flair of their predecessors. Unidad Vicente Guerrero was a bare-bones housing complex that lacked the same kind of Aztec-themed statues and colorful mosaics found in Unidad Independencia. It was only one year earlier when Echeverría announced at a press conference, "We are not going to build anymore Tlatelolcos or Villa Olímpicas!"[5] The costs of the middle-class housing complexes built under López Mateos were at odds with Echeverría's vision for simplified "worker" units capable of housing Mexico's growing population on an even larger scale.

Infonavit represented a new phase in social housing and was the centerpiece of President Echeverría's urban agenda. The new housing agency drew on Mexico's constitution (Article 123) to redirect a portion of each employee's wages into a federal fund for home mortgages. With the creation of Infonavit, Echeverría dissolved the Instituto Nacional de la Vivienda (Mexico's main housing institute), discontinued new IMSS housing projects, and scaled back the budget for FOVI. Infonavit was the way forward.

The chapter presents a panorama of Mexico's housing crisis at the beginning of the 1970s and highlights Mexico's turn to the south (Brazil) as opposed to the north (the United States) in its search for a new housing model for the nation. While Infonavit's demands on the private sector galvanized opposition from Mexico's business leaders, it also drew fierce criticism from labor leaders in the powerful Confederation of Mexican Workers for entirely different reasons. Why would labor unions wage a campaign against Echeverría for expanding workers' rights and benefits? Addressing this key question helps us more deeply understand the latent antagonisms within Mexico's multitiered working class and how they were manifested in the struggle over new housing policies introduced by President Echeverría.

Housing at the Beginning of the 1970s

In the early 1970s, the common sight of overcrowded, makeshift settlements in Mexico City was now becoming more visible and widespread in other Mexican cities. Regional centers including Guadalajara, Ciudad Juárez, and Durango were also beginning to witness precarious housing take on a mass character. The gradual accumulation of migrants seeking new lives and opportunities in the growing industrial hubs centered on Monterrey, Toluca, and Querétaro produced overcrowding and sprawl that began to outstrip local resources and services. It was at this time that the urban housing crisis began to develop into a national question.

While the mortgage lending reforms, budget increases, and pioneering housing projects carried out under President López Mateos helped expand the housing market, Mexico's rapidly growing population continued to outpace housing production. Mexico's deficit grew from 3.4 million housing units to 5.1 million in 1970, of which 1.9 million units were in urban areas.[6] Census data from 1970 indicates 28.5 million people lived in one- to two-bedroom units that lacked bathrooms.[7] For urban housing, experts estimated that production would need to increase to 250,000 units per year to keep pace with the demographic growth.[8]

The complexity of Mexico's housing crisis presented several distinct problem areas. Echeverría's grand ambitions to expand social welfare programs, state agencies, and government jobs would also require an increase in the number of housing units for public employees in accordance with provisions outlined by the social security system for state employees, the Institute of Social Security and Services for State Workers (Instituto de Seguridad y Servicios Sociales de los Trabajadores del Estado, ISSSTE). Second, there were large sectors of low-paid, salaried workers (e.g., factory workers, bus drivers, security guards) who would rarely qualify for social housing programs and were largely dissatisfied with their living conditions. Third, hundreds of rural communities were in need of new homes and infrastructure, particularly those that saw increases in migratory and seasonal laborers. Finally, the most pressing issue remained informal settlements (*ciudades perdidas* or *colonias populares*) primarily composed of unsalaried workers who tended to not belong to a trade union or employee federation. In the 1970s, the proliferation of ciudades perdidas presented the most difficult challenge to Echeverría's ambitious urban reform agenda.[9]

Although the exact origins of the term *ciudad perdida* remain unknown, it began to appear in the press as early as 1950 and more regularly by the early 1960s. One of the first appearances of the term can be found in a 1950 article about an encampment of two thousand families along the San Joaquín River, not too far from where Carlos Slim's Soumaya Museum is located today. Although amorphous, the term generally implies an isolated and informal settlement of poor families that lacks infrastructure, services, and recognized streets. The government legally defined them as *fraccionamientos clandestinos* (clandestine subdivisions). On December 5, 1964, the Federal District's supreme court established the following characteristics of a fraccionamiento clandestino: "A subdivision that consists of numerous lots.... The subdivision contains unauthorized streets or roads.... When a piece of land has been divided for residence without official authorization, it will be considered a fraccionamiento clandestino."[10]

The socioeconomic composition of the ciudad perdida posed a serious challenge to Infonavit. For Mexican sociologists and directors of Infonavit, residents who labored in the informal sector were categorized as *trabajadores no asalariados* (TNA; unsalaried workers).[11] These unsalaried workers lacked a consistent employer to pay into Infonavit's housing fund, and they did not possess the proper financial records necessary to establish credit for mortgage lending institutions. When Echeverría took office in 1970, the number of unsalaried workers was on the rise in every part of Mexico. Unsalaried workers in the informal economy grew in tandem with urban-bound migration patterns, with Mexico's urban workforce increasing from 23 percent unsalaried in 1960 to 31 percent unsalaried by 1970.[12]

Although informal laborers and poor campesinos constituted the two largest sectors in need of humane housing, Mexico's growing urban middle class also lacked housing options. Echeverría's fiery discourse could not obscure the on-the-ground realities he faced when assuming the presidency in 1970. The middle class, broadly defined, played a powerful role in shaping public opinion, occupied key sectors in Mexican society (education, small business, engineering, health care, office work, etc.), and was indispensable to Echeverría's ambitions for a stronger state apparatus.[13] Symbolically, the mestizo middle-class family was widely portrayed as the realization of the revolution's goals ("the fruit of the revolution").[14] It was still unknown whether the more stable middle sectors would be incorporated into a single national program or directed into an expanded version of FOVI. Nevertheless, the previous decade made it painfully obvious that providing modernist housing complexes for civil service employees was a losing strategy incapable of meeting Mexico's pressing housing needs.

The early 1970s marked a period when Mexico's housing policy was developed with a more conscious recognition that Mexico could not replicate the U.S.-European model for mass housing. Echeverría's overhaul of Mexico's national housing programs would more closely scrutinize previous domestic policies and look to Mexico's southern neighbors for possible models and solutions.

The Brazilian Connection

In the 1960s, one of the main debates among Mexico's housing experts was over the unifamiliar and the multifamiliar. In this period, the term *multifamiliar* (multifamily) became synonymous with large-scale apartment buildings that were at least four stories tall and were laid out on a superblock axis.[15] The unifamiliar was a stand-alone house occupied by one family and was typically one to two floors.[16] The residential towers built for Multifamiliar Alemán are quintessential examples of the multifamiliar, while the homes in Mexico City's San Juan de Aragón housing complex are archetypes for the unifamiliar in Mexico—prefabricated homes with private garages and backyards, also laid out on superblocks in a collection of neighborhood units.[17] Under López Mateos, both models were constructed fairly evenly, with Mexico City's Unidad Independencia serving as an example of a housing complex that combined both multifamiliares and unifamiliares.[18]

At the beginning of the 1970s, the prospects of a new national housing program revitalized the debate over housing models in the press. In an article entitled "A Solution for the Housing Problem," Ramón Torres Martínez pointed to the success of prefabricated homes in postwar France. Torres Martínez, the director of UNAM's School of Architecture, stated, "The only way to solve the housing problem is through the technical use of prefabricated houses."[19] For Torres Martínez, the unifamiliar was more appealing to Mexican families because it offered more privacy and a sense of personalized ownership. Although Torres Martínez designed both the unifamiliares in San Juan de Aragón and the multifamiliares in the Villa Olímpica, by 1969, he leaned toward the unifamiliares as Mexico's solution to the housing crisis.[20] However, for many, the unifamiliar was utopian. Here, *utopian* implied the idealistic view that the government could meet the desires of Mexican families to own their own homes while still conserving land against sprawl and speculation.[21] For the unifamiliares' detractors, the stand-alone home was the source of the horizontal growth patterns that were eating up land and required more resources to extend water pipes, sewage canals, and electric wiring over greater distances of land.[22] In an article on housing in 1970, Angel Escalante Baranda praised the design of Brasília for its emphasis on tall, vertical buildings.²³ Brasília's orderly towers and open spaces held a certain appeal to urbanists in Mexico who argued for the "verticalization" of the city in order to reduce crowding and sprawl. Angel Escalante was not alone in looking to Brazil for solutions. As Echeverría searched for a new model for a national housing program, Brazil's National Housing Bank (Banco Nacional da Habitação, BNH) program offered a viable alternative that could work within Mexico's constitutional framework.

Mexico's adoption of Brazil's housing finance system can be traced back to the Committee for the Study of the National Housing Programs Abroad. The committee sent research teams to Spain, Sweden, Yugoslavia, West Germany, France, Italy, and Brazil. Investigators met with banking experts, architects, and directors of national housing institutes in European cities and along the Brazilian coast.²⁴ References to Brazil's housing finance program began to be raised in a regional planning meeting in San Luis Potosí in 1970.²⁵ The construction executives in the business wing of Infonavit gradually coalesced around the model found in Brazil's National Housing Bank. Created in 1964 under the newly installed military dictatorship, Brazil's BNH supplied mortgage funds for low-income groups and organized favela-eradication campaigns. BNH was the product of the federal government's intervention in the housing market after roughly three years of growing inflation and a decline in the construction industry.²⁶ BNH worked through various government agencies to finance housing projects in an effort to "direct, discipline, and control financing of a housing system aimed at promoting home ownership for Brazilian families, especially among low-income groups."²⁷ It was funded from two sources—one forced and one voluntary. The first was the Guaranteed Employment Fund, a form of obligatory savings to which employers contributed 8 percent of the wages of their employees. The second savings program was a voluntary system based on the sale of housing bonds issued by the government.

For a section of Mexican business leaders, Brazil's National Housing Bank represented the ideal blend of state regulation and private enterprise for a Latin American country. In one report, the Mexican committee stated, "Brazil . . . has characteristics similar to ours, and it has had success in its experience of housing construction with the BNH since 1964."²⁸ Indeed, between 1964 and 1972, a total of 875,000 housing units had been financed by BNH throughout Brazil.²⁹ The Mexican committee compared data from both countries and concluded, "The creation of a National Fund for Housing through a 5 percent contribution from each worker's paycheck is a solution that will solve our problem."[30] As the planning stages progressed, Infonavit's directors agreed on a 5 percent bimonthly payroll tax, in contrast to Brazil's 8 percent rate.

Infonavit's role in housing production marked a crucial difference between the two housing finance systems. Brazil's system was created in a time of high inflation and was intended to revive the nation's construction industry. Infonavit reached beyond financial mediation to directly intervene in the location scouting, contracting, planning, building, and supervision of new housing projects.[31] Although Infonavit would evolve into mainly serving as a mortgage lending institution, the initial vision behind Infonavit expanded the role of the state in housing construction. In the years to come, the state subcontracted deals with pipe manufacturers, cement plants, and lumberyards for the raw materials needed to produce tens of thousands of homes around the country.[32] Infonavit's leaders followed Echeverría's general plan of "decentralizing" urban growth and placed a stronger emphasis on building housing developments in areas targeted for industrial growth.

By the beginning of 1972, the drawn-out planning meetings between business, state, and labor sectors finally reached their last stages. The final terms and language for the law to create Infonavit were drafted in time to be passed in conjunction with the International Workers' Day celebrations on May 1.

May Day 1972, the Birth of Infonavit

As in previous years, Mexico City's Zócalo Square shook with excitement on International Workers' Day in 1972. By noon, hundreds of thousands of demonstrators filled the massive plaza and surrounding streets in El Centro for one of the nation's most observed holidays. The increase in newly hired teachers and civil servants swelled the ranks of workers carefully organized into local union contingents. In keeping with tradition, President Echeverría was there to greet the crowds and champion the humble worker as the heart of Mexican society. That year, President Echeverría linked the continuation of the revolution with the launch of Infonavit in his speeches, press conferences, and visits to construction sites around Mexico City.[33]

Infonavit figured prominently in the 1972 May Day celebrations. Earlier that day, Echeverría visited two sites loaded with symbolic value. The first was located in Cuautitlán Izcalli, State of Mexico, where he adjudicated 225 new homes to workers from a nearby factory. Cuautitlán Izcalli was a planned city intended to serve as "a growth pole"—an industrial city built to divert migration flows away from a major city. Later, Echeverría held a press conference where he presented thirty-six veterans of the Mexican Revolution with "keys" to their future homes in the Unidad Habitacional Vicente Guerrero. The elderly militants were once part of the La Casa del Obrero Mundial—the heart of the labor movement in the capital during the early twentieth century.[34] Echeverría's symbolic gesture intended to highlight the state's new plan for housing Mexico's laborers.

Most of the press coverage of Infonavit the following day focused on the founding legal principles of the institute and how employers' tax works in practical terms. The Constitution of 1917 and the Federal Labor Law of 1970 formed the legal foundations for Infonavit. Article 123 of the Mexican constitution includes a provision that requires factories employing more than one hundred workers to supply housing for their employees. The stipulation was an empty decree from its inception until 1970, when the Federal Labor Law amended it to include all employers. Between the approval of the 1970 Federal Labor Law and the passing of Infonavit's resolutions in April 1972, the system's division of labor was reconfigured several times. Due to protests from the business wing of the tripartite commission, employers would no longer be responsible for purchasing the land and supplying the homes as originally mandated in the 1970 law—these tasks now fell on Infonavit's shoulders.[35]

On April 29, 1972, Echeverría announced that Jesús Silva-Herzog would be the general director of Infonavit. As the son of a renowned Mexican intellectual, Silva-Herzog gravitated toward economics in his studies and his career. At twenty-seven, he worked as an economist for the Inter-American Development Bank (1962–63) before joining the economics department at UNAM and Colegio de México for the remainder of the 1960s.[36] In 1971, Silva-Herzog found himself working in close contact with the president as the director of Mexico's most ambitious housing program. At the time of its launch, Silva-Herzog announced a goal of five hundred thousand new homes by the end of Echeverría's term in 1976. This audacious goal would come back to hound Silva-Herzog's tenure as the general director for the next three years. Later in May, Silva-Herzog identified housing as a tool to address three key problems: (1) geographic decentralization of urban centers, (2) land regularization for informal settlements, and (3) overpopulation in major cities. By the 1970s, the excesses of industrialization and urban sprawl finally began to be seriously factored into national housing programs and urban planning policies.[37]

By the end of its first year, Infonavit had made several significant advances yet was far behind its projected goals. After one year, it was responsible for constructing 51,196 housing units in twenty-nine cities. The geographic diversity of Infonavit's operations, from Ciudad Juárez to Mérida, signaled an impressive expansion of social housing and an expression of Infonavit's decentralization approach.[38] Along with construction projects, Infonavit distributed credits to 20,100 workers.[39] More than simply supplying land and materials, Infonavit had to influence public opinion in a contentious atmosphere. On one side, a majority of employers were still noncompliant with the new payroll tax or were still in a grace period before they were obligated to participate in the new arrangement. On the other side, there was still a sense of skepticism and reluctance among many workers to participate in a government program that was unfamiliar and possibly corrupt. In the summer of 1973, Silva-Herzog agreed to an in-depth interview with writer Elena Poniatowska in an effort to explain Infonavit's program to a broader audience.

Herzog and Poniatowska on La Reforma

In June 1973, Elena Poniatowska met with Jesús Silva-Herzog to write a series on Infonavit for *Novedades*. At the time, she was recognized as "the literary voice of the student movement" for her groundbreaking coverage of the Tlatelolco student massacre in *La noche de Tlatelolco* (1971).[40] The book fused investigative journalism, witness testimonials, and personal narratives into a *crónica* style that Poniatowska later explored with her accounts of Mexico's urban underclass.[41] Expecting to visit the same kind of poor settlements she encountered as a journalist in Mexico City at the end of the 1960s, Poniatowska was surprised to meet Silva-Herzog in a chic restaurant on the Paseo de la Reforma. The incongruity between worker housing and Mexico's most elegant boulevard disturbed Poniatowska. Although Silva-Herzog offered a reasonable explanation for Infonavit's location, the symbolic contrast only reinforced Poniatowska's suspicion that Infonavit was simply one more manifestation of Mexico's corrupt bureaucracy.

The interview covered a wide range of issues: the legal aspects of Infonavit, labor disputes, the applicant selection, the payment process, and corruption. Poniatowska, who was coolly pessimistic at the beginning of the interview, asked Silva-Herzog, "What makes the law that gave birth to Infonavit new or any different than the law passed many years ago? Why will bosses comply this time around?" Silva-Herzog contended, "Because it has established a structure of bilateral relations between the business sector and workers ... it expands and gives rise to social insurance institutions."[42] Unlike the previous 1917 law that was only applicable to workplaces with more than one hundred employees, the Infonavit law did not set a minimum or maximum number of employees as part of its criteria. This revision widened the reach of Infonavit from roughly 850,000 workers (the number of people who were employed in a workplace with more than one hundred people in 1970) to 4 million workers.[43] After one year in operation, 97 percent of the companies that were registered with Infonavit employed less than 100 workers.[44]

No longer a topic "off the record," the problem of corruption within Mexico's housing programs was now openly discussed in the press. For Poniatowska, the issue of corruption was the ultimate litmus test for Infonavit's claim to "be an authentic worker's institution." She directly asked Silva-Herzog, "So there are no bribes [*mordidas*] under the table? There's no '*Compadre*, you get me a house like that, and you will see I know how to thank a person who does a favor for me?'"[45] Later, the question of corruption surrounding the INV was raised by Poniatowska. Indeed, the INV earned an unsavory reputation for embezzling public funds and for the common practice of its head directors to contract work from construction companies they owned or profited from indirectly.[46]

Infonavit's main defense against corruption was the new Centro de Cómputo Electrónico del Infonavit (Electronic Computing Center of Infonavit), the nerve center for Infonavit's application process. Initially housed on UNAM's campus, it was an 80-million-peso computer system that analyzed each worker's application (a card) and evaluated if the applicant was eligible for housing credits. After each worker filled out their card and submitted it to Infonavit, it was put through the computer system. The computer then factored each applicant's income, number of family members, address, credit rating, living conditions (size of apartment, private bathroom), and union membership.[47] The novel quality of the computer was reflected in Poniatowska's bewilderment when she asked, "How can one confront a problem of human or social character with technological instruments?"[48] Yet for Silva-Herzog, it was this very technological feature that permitted Infonavit to overcome past human flaws. He affirmed, "I can assure you that the machine is always impartial. We give credits for houses through the computer system so that there aren't any outside influences or *compadrazgo*."[49] *Urbanismo* had entered the Information Age.

As the conversation was winding down and the table was being cleared, the issue of corruption continued to linger. In particular, Poniatowska's skepticism reflected a general distrust of state institutions, which were viewed by many at the time as bloated bureaucracies. If the new, towering headquarters of Mexico's social welfare agencies were designed as monuments to progress, the high levels of poverty that continued to persist throughout the country cast a different, more sinister light on the meanings of their monumentality. For some, like Poniatowska, the extreme aggregation of governmental buildings in Mexico City (IMSS, Pemex, ISSSTE, CONASUPO), represented the extreme concentration of wealth and power in the nation's capital. In the interview, Poniatowska commented to Silva-Herzog, "There are institutions where you feel there is a huge difference between them and those that they are supposed to serve. For example, it amazes me to think about the misery of the Indigenous people in this country and then see a parking lot full of new foreign cars outside of the National Indigenous Institute's headquarters."[50] And yet one can find shades of genuine reform in the initial years of Infonavit's operations.

The first five years did not represent a fundamental rupture with past practices but did alter and widen the demographics of those who benefited from the state's largess. Beyond its technological novelty, Infonavit's "supercomputer" did temporarily reform the relationship between housing agencies and applicants by limiting the reach and influence of the unofficial compadrazgo system. Although the shadowy nature of compadrazgo in housing left behind few traces in the archives, the most visible feature of its existence can be found in Infonavit's fiercest critic, CTM president Fidel Velázquez Sánchez. When Poniatowska alluded to the mounting tensions between Infonavit and Fidel Velázquez in the interview, Silva-Herzog brushed it off as a minor flare-up between colleagues.⁵¹ Despite Silva-Herzog's causal dismissal of Poniatowska's question, Velázquez's criticisms of Infonavit were growing louder in the press. The animosity between Infonavit and the CTM was the product of Infonavit's reforms and mirrored the broader dynamics of state-labor relations under Echeverría.

Organized Labor and Social Housing in the 1970s

Fidel Velázquez Sánchez was no stranger to Silva-Herzog. Silva-Herzog's father (who shared the same name) was a prominent economist and longtime rival of Velázquez. This fact was not lost on Echeverría when he appointed Silva-Herzog at the helm of his new housing program. At the time of Infonavit's founding, Fidel Velázquez was the secretary general of the CTM, a position he held from 1941 to 1997. Fidel Velázquez symbolized "the social pact between organized labor and the postrevolutionary Mexican state" in the 1940s and 1950s.⁵² When the student movement erupted in 1968, he organized labor leaders to defend the government's repression of student activists. Velázquez epitomized the corrupt charro—a labor leader who acquiesced to government demands, oversaw the repression of independent unions, and profited from a system of political patronage.

Notwithstanding a few disagreements over payment plans for mortgages, labor representatives were generally supportive of Infonavit in the period that led up to its creation. On December 22, 1971, at a meeting of the National Tripartite Commission (the precursor to Infonavit), Fidel Velázquez addressed the attendees and said, "One can believe in this [Infonavit]. It is a way for us to fulfill our promises to improve the lives of the working class . . . it is a struggle, one that has produced some fruit, although much work remains."⁵³ However, schisms within the National Tripartite Commission began to publicly emerge at the inauguration events for Infonavit. In a speech delivered to the press and state officials on May 1, 1972, Silva-Herzog said, "Employees of the country, whether or not they are unionized, have the right to own a home by obtaining credits appropriate to their economic activity."⁵⁴ By the summer of 1973, rumblings in the union exploded into a fierce battle between the CTM's leadership and Infonavit for the next four years.

It was only two days after *Novedades* ran Elena Poniatowska's final interview with Jesús Silva-Herzog (June 17, 1973) when Fidel Velázquez launched a public campaign against Infonavit and its leadership. Speaking at a national assembly for sugarcane workers, Velázquez tore into Infonavit's leadership and policies. He summed up Infonavit's first year in operation as a "resounding failure" and went on to point out its failure to meet its annual goal of constructing one hundred thousand homes. He sought to distance the CTM from Infonavit: "Even though we were major actors in its creation, we have been discouraged by the way it is managed."[55] Velázquez's condemnation of Infonavit—a major initiative of the president—caused a commotion among attendees and marked the opening salvos against the new housing institute. Although CTM members applauded for Velázquez, his searing criticism of the president's housing program was as troubling as it was confusing for rank-and-file members.[56] For a union leader who aligned himself with previous presidents on nearly every controversial issue (the union unrest in 1948, the 1959 railway workers strike, the 1968 student massacres), why did Velázquez come out so strongly against the centerpiece of Echeverría's social welfare agenda? Why would a labor leader stand in opposition to housing for Mexico's working class? The events that unfolded on May Day 1973 offer several insights into the causes of the conflict and portend the problems ahead.

On May 1, 1973, as the crowds began to stream into the Zócalo, President Echeverría was concluding a tour of Infonavit's new computer center, the Centro de Cómputo Electrónico del Infonavit. Located a few kilometers from UNAM's campus, the president strolled around the facilities with Silva-Herzog and the center's director, Sergio Ahumada Rivera, who dazzled him with facts about the computer's precision and technical wizardry. More than a fast "number cruncher," the computer system was heralded for its impartiality and unbiased nature. In August, the computer system initially processed 300,000 applications and subsequently selected 23,000 applicants in sixty minutes.[57] With a push of a button from a remote corner in Mexico City, 1.2 billion pesos in housing credits was assigned to 23,000 workers in thirty-seven cities.[58] The majority of recipients were within the range of minimum-wage earners to slightly above minimum wage (1.5), and more than half were nonunionized workers. This trend would continue until 1976, when it was estimated that 46 percent of Infonavit's contributors were unionized workers and 53 percent were nonunionized workers.[59] Although union membership was still one of the ten factors weighed by the computer's rubric, variables such as income, family size, and preexisting credit were given higher priority. Some families were surprised by a process absent of favors or the need for inside contacts. While some viewed these developments as promising signs of reform, Fidel Velázquez saw Infonavit's computer selection as a serious threat.

Improvements in impartiality and efficiency through new technologies were unacceptable to the CTM's leadership. Infonavit's computer selection undermined forms of clientelism and charro leadership established in Mexico's labor sector since the 1940s. In the case of Infonavit, the fact that these government reforms circumvented union mediation only served to weaken the position of labor leaders in a national project for workers. The centralization of credit distribution strengthened the state but diminished the role of labor leaders as intermediaries between the state and rank-and-file members.

The exact motivations behind Echeverría's support and defense of Infonavit's applicant selection remains unclear and a point of debate among scholars. Sociologist Lisa Robinson suggests Echeverría viewed the rising independent labor movement, particularly the Democratic Tendency spearheaded by Rafael Galván, as a possible ally and counterweight to the CTM's hegemony. The Democratic Tendency created a temporary rift within the labor movement in the mid-1970s, but it is unlikely that Echeverría would have based his housing program on the success of the Democratic Tendency movement. Another possible explanation points to the natural instinct or rationale to strengthen the power of the state over a labor sector characterized by an extreme concentration of power in a few hands. Finally, another aspect that has not been considered is the possibility that the leadership of Infonavit viewed the computer selection as a concrete reform against corruption, and Echeverría reasoned he could weather the storm around the controversy such a move would cause among labor officials.[60]

The CTM leadership waged their campaign against Infonavit on several different fronts. First, they sought to portray Infonavit as a flawed institute that could only be remedied by "the workers themselves." For the CTM's leadership, the computer system's vaunted impartiality was deemed inhumane and elitist. According to Fidel Velázquez, union leaders were the most in touch with the workers and therefore had the best understanding of their living situations, interests, concerns, and aspirations.[61] Second, Velázquez took every opportunity in the press to point out that Infonavit had failed to meet its own goals. It is doubtful that Silva-Herzog and Echeverría would have imagined Infonavit's pledge to build one hundred thousand homes per year would later be held up to as much scrutiny as it was in the press between 1973 and 1976. In years past, the consistent, almost predictable, failure of the government to achieve its lofty housing goals was typically mentioned in passing with little condemnation. This lack of accountability took a turn as a result of Velázquez's determination to turn public opinion against Infonavit.

In these years, the numbers were in Velázquez's favor. At a CTM conference in November 1973, Velázquez noted Infonavit completed less than 25 percent of the units it promised to workers that year.[62] Throughout 1974 and most of 1975, Velázquez was consistent, yet constrained, in his exposure of Infonavit's slow pace and inability to meet its projected goals. Toward the end of 1975, Velázquez intensified and expanded his struggle against Infonavit's policies. This escalation might have been attributed to Echeverría's surprising attack on Silva-Herzog in the annual presidential address (1975), where he faulted Silva-Herzog's leadership in meeting the institute's goals. It also could have been provoked by the prospects of a new president who might be more open to restoring past relations between labor and the government. Nevertheless, Velázquez went on the attack. At a national meeting for cement workers, Velázquez demanded Infonavit change how it selected its recipients and how the housing units were constructed. Velázquez remarked, "At the current rate, the grandchildren of workers will still be waiting for their homes!"[63]

In 1976, Velázquez also drew attention to the poor quality of Infonavit's housing units. At a press conference held at his office, he told reporters, "The workers feel affected by the bad quality of the construction carried out by Infonavit."[64] In this period, the El Rosario complex was singled out by the press as a symbol of Infonavit's gross incompetence in housing construction. El Rosario was the last *gran unidad habitacional* built in Mexico City, rivaled only by San Juan de Aragón and Tlatelolco. In the construction of El Rosario, the rush to meet Infonavit's ambitious goals left the interiors in substandard conditions. Instead of a festive inauguration, El Rosario had a gradual "rollout" that featured news coverage of residents complaining of "thin walls covered with cardboard, leaking roofs, and doors that fell off their hinges."[65] A spate of articles in 1976 portrayed unidades habitacionales as breeding grounds for crime and warned that Infonavit's housing complexes could lead to a rise in crime for the capital.[66]

Fidel Velázquez alternated between declarations against poor housing conditions and criticism of the "elitist" policies practiced by Infonavit. These policies consisted of the computer selection, the lottery system, and the construction contracts. As previously discussed, the computer center stripped CTM leaders of their power to decide who among the rank and file would receive housing benefits. The lottery system, a procedure where applicants' cards were randomly picked and awarded housing credits, was also opposed by the CTM's leadership. Velázquez challenged the lottery system and said it "is a discriminatory and unjust mechanism that doesn't resolve the housing problem."[67] Third, the CTM lobbied to be in charge of Infonavit's construction division. At the time, Infonavit employed its own amalgamation of construction firms to solidify its control over the various stages of housing production. Given the scale and scope of Infonavit's goals, the construction contracts for such a massive undertaking would have been a gold mine for the CTM. Velázquez joined angry residents in El Rosario to use their protests as a platform to demand the CTM be put in charge of construction.[68]

Infonavit rarely engaged in Velázquez's "war of words." When reached for comments in response to Velázquez's accusations against Infonavit, Silva-Herzog was reported to "continue the policy of not responding to Fidel Velázquez's attacks."[69] At times, leaders or representatives close to Infonavit but not directly employed by the institute would refute Velázquez's claims in the press. For example, the head of the Chamber of Commerce for Mexico City, José Luis Ordoñez, defended the housing lotteries Infonavit used to select recipients. On a trip back from a United Nations housing conference with President Echeverría, Ordoñez told reporters, "It would be unjust to eliminate the lottery because there are groups of workers that don't belong to the CTM and they have the same rights to a decent home."[70] He also added that Infonavit was beneficial for the economy by stimulating the construction industry and acting as a stabilizing force in the market against potential downturns.

In 1976, Fidel Velázquez elevated the struggle against Infonavit beyond simply words. CTM functionaries organized paracaidista invasions on Infonavit construction sites. Squatters erected makeshift homes around half-finished projects and, in some cases, occupied unsold homes. The union also organized residents to protest issues surrounding poor construction, the lack of community services, inadequate security, and insufficient maintenance.[71]

Although these were manipulated protests, they were not in response to fabricated problems. As a result of Infonavit's breakneck speed, it was not difficult to find deficiencies, sometimes severe, in Infonavit's housing stock. In locales as diverse as Mérida and Chihuahua, faculty electric wiring, water shortages, and thin walls provided ripe conditions for CTM organizers to stage rallies, particularly when the residents were CTM members.[72]

Infonavit's strategy rested on the political discourse and material benefits that were at the heart of the initiative. After a drawn-out debate over the private sector's obligation to play a direct role in worker housing, Echeverría was able to negotiate a major housing reform in the name of Mexican workers. In some cases, such as El Rosario, the shoddy construction work and lack of services caused a public uproar among residents. However, in the larger scheme of things, tens of thousands of Mexican citizens became first-time homeowners as a direct result of government assistance. By the end of Echeverría's term, 150,000 housing units were constructed in 125 cities. Of the total number of units constructed, 72,000 were already inhabited by workers registered with Infonavit.[73] In less than four years, roughly four million workers were registered with Infonavit and contributing to a fund (in conjunction with employers) that was valued at approximately 6 billion pesos. For the business sector, noncompliance and evasion were still problems, though close to 240,000 businesses were actively participating with Infonavit by 1976.[74]

Despite its unprecedented levels of housing production, Infonavit's accomplishments were overshadowed by its failure to even come close to its much publicized goals—the institute completed 150,000 of 500,000 homes it promised to construct by 1976. These goals were not arbitrary figures but corresponded to the number of units necessary to overcome Mexico's housing deficit (100,000 homes over the course of five years). The numbers were irrefutable, yet Infonavit's "colossal failure" also produced several important breakthroughs. A national mortgage system for low-income families was established and activated in over 125 cities. Unlike previous housing programs that were primarily geared toward public employees and/or middle-class families in Mexico City, Infonavit decentralized its operations and expanded the number of people with access to social housing benefits. Under Infonavit, the first social housing developments arrived in Juchitán, Oaxaca; housing projects sprung up around manufacturing plants in Querétaro and

Toluca; and apartments designed for tropical climates were built in Veracruz.[75] Initial flare-ups and problems with housing structures could be and many times were repaired after residents placed pressure on regional directors. Problems in El Rosario persisted over the years, but after bad press, the National Chamber of the Construction Industry oversaw its maintenance and resolved the major issues that plagued the complex.[76]

In this period, CTM workers benefited from Infonavit. Throughout the country, union members enrolled in the program and received housing credits in the same manner as eligible, nonunionized workers. This reality was at odds with Velázquez's campaign in the name of rank-and-file CTM members. The visible gap lays bare the true issue of the matter: political patronage.

In 1978, the Mexican government finally yielded to the CTM's demands. Under President López Portillo, the CTM was awarded a large share of the construction contracts for Infonavit housing, and the computerized selection process for homeowners was terminated.[77] The union federation weathered the storms of an internal uprising (Democratic Tendency) while simultaneously pressuring the PRI to restore its control over state-sponsored housing contracts and extending benefits to its membership.[78] Infonavit recipients now tilted toward unionized workers, with 25 percent of the credits reserved for CTM members alone.[79] The episode is a clear example of the divisions found within Mexico's urban working class. Moreover, it demonstrates how the inequities of Mexico's social housing programs were not solely perpetuated by the state but also reinforced by sectors of civil society (unionized labor, in this case) in order to maintain those inequities (what Charles Tilly has referred to as "hoarding").[80]

Under Echeverría, Infonavit became the nation's main housing agency. It represented a shift from IMSS's rent-subsidized apartments to a new system of home ownership maintained through a public-private alliance. Very few Infonavit housing complexes could be found in Ciudad Neza in these years, and relatedly, very few of its residents demanded entrance into Infonavit's system. In the 1970s, the parameters of the "housing problem" expanded to encompass the question of land regularization. The conversion of informal land plots into regulated property titles was elevated in its importance as government officials conceptualized Mexico's national housing plan. After a few disparate protests for land regularization in Chihuahua and the Federal District (Iztapalapa), a mass movement for land regularization exploded in Ciudad Neza at the end of 1969. In the following chapters, we examine Ciudad Neza's movement for land regularization from multiple angles to further explore its impact on social inequality and urban politics during the Echeverría years.

6

Strike

The Democratic Opening on the Urban Frontier

On June 19, 1970, presidential candidate Luis Echeverría visited Ciudad Nezahualcóyotl at a moment when the municipality was embroiled in a bitter land conflict. Since the 1940s, various fraccionadores were able to take advantage of the area's multiple land tenure systems—federal, private, communal—to sow discord and confusion among residents and local officials. However, in the summer of 1969, after decades of abysmal living conditions, negotiations, nominal legal reforms, and widespread corruption, the residents of Ciudad Nezahualcóyotl launched a payment strike to demand Mexico's federal government expropriate the land from the private land developers. The movement's demand was viewed as a means to gain urban infrastructure, municipal services, and property titles for their land plots. The strike evolved into the first mass movement of poor shantytown residents in Mexico, spanning across four years (1969–73) and giving rise to a coalition of over fifty neighborhood associations in Ciudad Neza. Despite violent repression and entrenched corruption, the residents' hopes were lifted and sustained by President Echeverría's public support for the strike.

It was during Echeverría's visit to Ciudad Neza when a thirty-year-old resident named Rogelio Vargas Soriano pushed his way through the crowd of onlookers to shake the hand of the PRI's presidential candidate. True to form, Rogelio Vargas did not intend simply greet the presidential candidate; Vargas grabbed Echeverría's hand and refused to let go until he felt he fully conveyed the severity of Ciudad Neza's problems.[1] It would only be one year later when Rogelio Vargas found himself at the same table with President Echeverría in the National Palace to discuss the demands of the Settlers' Movement for Land Restoration (Movimiento Restaurador de Colonos, MRC).[2] Echeverría's fiery discourse inadvertently unleashed a social movement from below. The strike forced residents, private land developers, local politicians, and federal officials into an intense struggle over the lands in Latin America's largest informal city.[3]

The emergence of the neighborhood association as a vehicle for mass mobilization in Mexico's poorest shantytowns presents a new perspective on the much-debated "democratic opening" under President Echeverría.[4] In particular, there has been a tendency to focus on the intentionality of Echeverría's social reforms without analyzing how they affected the lives of ordinary citizens. The historical assessment of Echeverría's "democratic opening" has mainly been based on an analysis of official policies and state institutions.[5] To evaluate "the opening" through the lens of high politics overlooks how political discourse "from above" took on a life of its own throughout Mexican society. The payment strike in Ciudad Neza highlights why an analysis of the democratic opening needs to assess how, and to what degree, Echeverría's official discourse influenced Mexican citizens to participate in the affairs of the day. In sum, this chapter seeks to move beyond '68 and below Echeverría.

Infrastructure and Public Health in Ciudad Neza

By the beginning of the 1970s, Ciudad Neza began to enter the national consciousness. It became a symbol for the failures of accelerated urbanization in Mexico—a perceived site of lawlessness and a visual trope for the dark side of the Mexican miracle. Intellectuals lamented the symbolism of television antennas installed on top of corrugated steel roofs: "A complimentary symbol of the new order, a sea of television antennas . . . that is one of the features of our barbaric modernization, access to the transistor culture without going through the culture of the alphabet."[6] Neither urban nor rural, Ciudad Neza was still stigmatized as a vulgar hybridity.

After Ciudad Neza became an independent municipality in 1963, it grew at an astonishing rate. With complete support from the municipality's new administration, fraccionadores were given free rein to establish settlements, evict residents, and commit widespread land fraud. The fraccionadores' public offices, payment centers, and newspaper advertisements lent an air of legitimacy to Ciudad Neza in the eyes of poor families desperate to leave Mexico City's cramped tenements. As a result, the area's population skyrocketed from 60,928 in 1960 to 605,104 in 1970.[7] Once a small collection of wood-and-stone shacks scattered along the banks of Lake Texcoco,

Ciudad Neza was now a municipality composed of nearly fifty different colonias. Dramatic population growth presented the fraccionadores with a risky contradiction: while an increase in land sales meant an increase in profits, the rise in population also heightened the possibility of discontent and mass mobilizations among residents.

Ciudad Neza's growth also led to another new development in the 1970s. In this period, a small number of middle-class professionals and students started to study, and provide services to, the people of Ciudad Neza. Beginning in 1969, the Jesuit Order sent young priests and seminary students to live and work in Ciudad Neza.[8] Dr. Gregorio Valner worked on a project about the social psychology of Ciudad Neza's youth, while David Fox conducted a study of its infant mortality rate with his colleagues from the University of Manchester in the early 1970s. Medical and social work students from UNAM accompanied health brigades in Ciudad Neza as they performed semiannual vaccination drives in the main plaza of the Palacio Municipal.[9] Teachers in training (*normalistas*) based their fieldwork in Ciudad Neza's elementary schools (twenty-two theses are held in CIDNE's archives).[10] One engineer expressed the shock he felt after his first tour of Ciudad Neza: "[It was] depressing and heartbreaking. It generated a feeling of guilt in me. 'Why did my family, like millions of other middle-class Mexicans, live in conditions of comfort so far removed from millions of our fellow Mexicans?' I wondered. Children who were the same age as mine who played with stray dogs on top of garbage heaps, on the streets without sidewalks, next to mud puddles."[11] These kinds of powerful sentiments were common among visitors, but those numbers were relatively small. For most Mexicans, Ciudad Neza was out of sight and out of mind. That status would be temporarily challenged by the MRC movement after it was able to provoke a broader discussion about land rights for colonos.

The MRC's demand to expropriate the land forced the government to carry out a series of investigations to assess the viability of a land regularization program and to weigh the costs of such a sweeping measure. A newly constituted government agency called AURIS began to carry out a series of preliminary investigations in the summer of 1969 with the municipality's planning committee. AURIS visited 1,107 homes spread out over forty-five neighborhoods for the expressed purpose of determining how many residents paid for their land plots and whether residents paid for services. They also documented the conditions of urban services in Ciudad Neza.[12] Initial surveys found that 97 percent of roads were unpaved, 54 percent of the homes lacked drainage, 64 percent lacked running water, and 59 percent lacked electricity. Roughly 55 percent of interviewees paid for water installation, while the remainder expressed a willingness to pay for services but were skeptical of the fraccionadores.[13] The widespread distrust and skepticism among residents was reflected in the fact that 64 percent of the households in the survey refused to sign any forms or petitions requesting service installations.

In 1972, three years after the AURIS survey, Ciudad Neza's population grew from 605,104 to 839,533 people. The dried-out lake bed had been divided and occupied by approximately 81,500 families.[14] A small fraction (7 percent) had installed tiled floors and added a second floor—a new and rare sight in Ciudad Neza. Most homes (88 percent, or roughly 72,000 units) were constructed with cinder blocks, metal doors, dirt floors, and corrugated steel roofs weighed down with rocks and sometimes adorned with a television antenna. Within this category, only 20 percent of the homes had both a bathroom and a kitchen. The large number of homes made of cinder blocks or concrete bricks marked an improvement from the early years of wooden shacks. Despite these gradual improvements, in 1972 there were still approximately 4,000 families with makeshift homes made of stacked rocks covered with recycled cardboard.[15] Overall, the government made some progress in installing a rudimentary drainage system in most of the neighborhoods, and all but ten neighborhoods had access to electricity.[16]

Water was the most vexing problem in Ciudad Neza. The most basic element of life, Neza's water problem included both its consumption and its containment. In 1969, little had changed for a municipality where, as *El Día* reported, "the lack of drinking water in the majority of neighborhoods in Netzahualcóyotl increases with each day. . . . In the face of desperation, hundreds of families impatiently await the arrival of the water distribution trucks [*pipas*]."[17] Reports in the press depicted a different situation than official studies, which touted increases in water distribution for the municipality. In consulting government studies from this period, it becomes clear that their fundamental flaw was overlooking the fact that a large portion of potable water reaching Ciudad Neza was diverted to slaughterhouse facilities and bathhouses (bathhouses were private businesses, many owned by Gonzalo Barquín Díaz, who was the municipal president from 1970 to 1972).[18]

In the 1970s, diseases and infections related to water were the leading causes of death in Ciudad Nezahualcóyotl. A 1973 study from the Department of Epidemiology (Dirección General de Epidemiología, DGE) found that the leading cause of death in Ciudad Neza was diarrhea. In a single year, nearly one thousand people died of diarrhea and intestinal diseases caused by contaminated water; homicide was ranked eighth, with ninety-two deaths.[19] The World Health Organization indicates, "People, particularly children, who die from diarrhea often suffer from underlying malnutrition, which makes them more vulnerable to diarrhea. Each diarrheal episode, in turn, makes their malnutrition even worse."[20] As one of the young Jesuit students who went to live among the poor in Ciudad Neza, Martín de la Rosa remembered a time when he helped a couple in Colonia Aurora make funeral arrangements for their youngest child, who died at six months old. Before the funeral services, the doctor turned to Rosa and confided, "The illness on the death certificate was just a pretext, starvation and poverty killed the baby."[21] In these conditions, the numerous infrastructure projects carried out by the state between 1970 and 1973 raised the expectations of residents, which in turn fueled a movement of resistance from below.

The Origins of the MRC Movement

Popular discontent finally boiled over into a large-scale payment strike in the summer of 1969. The initial sparks for the payment strike began on May 20, 1969, with two public demonstrations. The first demonstration took place in Mexico City's Zócalo Square, while the second protest was organized by a group of teachers in Neza's Aurora. The protests were largely uneventful and failed to gain any momentum. Nevertheless, the small protest in Aurora piqued the interest of a local carpenter named Artemio Mora Lozada. Emboldened by the teachers' protest, Mora Lozada saw an opening to organize neighborhood association leaders to take a more militant stand. The following month, several neighborhood committees united to form the MRC on July 17, 1969, and elected Mora Lozada as the organization's president.[22] The central demand called for the federal government to expropriate Ciudad Neza's land from the private land developers. After years of broken promises and brute repression, the MRC tied the imprisonment of the land developers to their struggle for land rights. Frustrated with symbolic protest, the group decided to mobilize residents to stop making monthly payments on their land plots. The controversial demand captured the imagination of several young men on the fringes of local politics, and a twenty-three-person executive committee was established that summer. The committee included three key leaders: Angel Garcia Bravo, Odón Madariaga Cruz, and Rogelio Vargas Soriano.[23]

The individuals who emerged as the core leadership of the MRC represented a new generation of social leaders in Mexico's informal settlements. When the student movement erupted in Mexico City on the eve of the 1968 Olympics, they watched from afar as young fathers who had recently settled down on small plots of land in Ciudad Neza. The rustic towns and villages they left behind were part of their past, and their homes in Ciudad Neza were their future. On Saturday nights they scraped together the little money they had to go out on the town. They made their rounds at the local pool halls and ramshackle dance clubs, wore sunglasses at night, and preferred the Rolling Stones over the Beatles, drinking over marijuana, mezcal over pulque (when they could afford it)—only to go back to their shacks at dawn before another week of commuting into Mexico City to work as carpenters, street vendors, security guards, and mechanics. Like most residents in Ciudad Neza, they knew their options to move ahead in life were slim but found some hope in the small plots of land they "owned" and could gradually transform into respectable homes through their own labor and willpower.

When the first rumblings of the payment strike began, Rogelio Vargas was just one of the thousands of individuals who had placed his hopes in a new home in Ciudad Neza. Rogelio was born into a poor family of farmers at a time when much of Mexico's rural areas were bereft of major roads and highways (1939). His family mainly spoke Spanish peppered with Mixtec and lived in the Mixteca Baja region of Oaxaca. As a young man, he traveled for days on badly paved roads until he arrived at the San Lázaro Bus Terminal in Mexico City in 1954. After several years of living in a tenement near Tepito, Rogelio moved to Ciudad Neza in 1963, the same year it became the State of Mexico's 120th municipality. When asked why he moved to Ciudad Neza, his response was simple: "To become a homeowner and not rent."[24] After signing the contract to his lot, he asked the salesman where his property ended; the salesman threw a rock into a lagoon—his property ended where the rock had splashed in the water.[25] Despite the area's harsh environment, Rogelio never involved himself with the local neighborhood association until the announcement of the payment strike. It was at this moment that he first met Odón Madariaga Cruz.

When the payment strike began, Odón Madariaga Cruz was a twenty-six-year-old handyman who had recently bought a plot of land in Aurora with his wife and two children. As a teenager, he walked for miles through the sierra in Huasteca until he reached a highway that connected the region to Mexico City. The Huasteca, a region located along the Gulf of Mexico, is home to several Indigenous communities that include the Nahua, Totonaco, Huastec (Mayan), and Otomi. Odón's family were Otomi corn farmers who had lived in the Sierra Huasteca for several generations. When Odón Madariaga turned twenty years old, his father gave him 50 pesos and told him, "Listen, son, here in the Huasteca, you are going to live and die like I have lived and like I will die: with nothing, without learning anything, without knowing anything, and never making it out of poverty. Go to Mexico City. There you will be able to make something out of yourself, God willing."[26]

After a few years of living in the Federal District, Odón Madariaga tried his luck in Ciudad Neza's Aurora colonia, a relatively new settlement established on the barren plains of Ciudad Neza's eastern section. Colonia Aurora had grown by leaps and bounds since land developers Bernardo Eckstein and Abraham Slotnik established it in 1957.[27] Over the course of ten years, Aurora expanded from a few dozen families to thirteen thousand, although roughly sixteen thousand lots still remained vacant in 1969. Like many of Aurora's residents, Madariaga was attracted to the area by the radio ads and brochures that promised modern services, a cinema, a bullfighting arena, and most importantly, one's own home. When Odón Madariaga bought his lot, he made an initial down payment of 1,332 pesos and signed a standard contract that stipulated a monthly fee of 437 pesos for land and services, spread out over fifteen years.[28] Far from squatters who operated beyond the law, Ciudad Neza's informal settlements were lucrative businesses intimately bound up with local officials.

Forces in the Field, 1970–1972

For the first several months, Ciudad Neza's payment strike failed to gain any traction and was shrouded in uncertainty. The residents had a personal stake in their plots of land and were aware of the land developers' power. Land developer Raúl Romero had virtual control over the local police force, judiciary, school officials, priests, and pistoleros and close ties with the governor Juan Fernández Albarrán in Toluca. The MRC began small and organized through the quotidian activities of residents: in marketplaces, bus stops, churches, and bars. Soon they were a regular and visible force in Ciudad Neza's neighborhoods, slowly rolling down unpaved streets in pickup trucks with megaphones and flyers, holding rallies, knocking on doors, and organizing neighborhood meetings at night.[29]

The repression was swift and predictable, but only sporadic in the beginning. Activists publicly associated with the MRC were evicted from their homes, and several leaders were temporarily jailed in nearby Texcoco. At times, the MRC was able to confront the land developers' repressive apparatus through direct-action tactics. When a single mother was evicted from her home by the police, Odón Madariaga and Angel Garcia Bravo led a crowd of five hundred people to reclaim the land. Madariaga later recounted, "There were two police officers guarding the door of the house. . . . Five hundred people ran toward the police with rocks and *garrotes* [clubs]. We said to the woman: 'Don't go. You are going to keep living in your house. We are going to defend you.' We put her furniture and things back into the house and stood guard out front. The police had disappeared out of sight. It was like a miracle. In 15 days, we got thousands of members."[30] Similar actions became more frequent, and the strike gained momentum.

In 1970, the MRC released a five-point program that was subsequently published in the *El Día* newspaper. In addition to the land's status as federal property, the MRC pointed to a statewide law passed by the governor that affirmed land developers were legally responsible for providing colonos with the services stipulated in their contracts (the Ley de Fraccionamientos passed in 1957 and was amended in 1958).[31] Here we find an example of how a nominal law hastily passed by the PRI to weaken political unrest could later be revived to legitimate the demands for land rights.

By the end of 1970, the colonos' moral certitude was translated into collective political action. In December 1970, the MRC held a rally attended by nine hundred people in front of their offices in Colonia Metropolitana. People in the crowd carried signs that read "The problems of Ciudad Nezahualcóyotl can only be resolved through one way—EXPROPRIATION!" and "The Fraccionadores are the Enemy of the People."[32] Speakers appealed to the crowd to stop making payments to the fraccionadores and praised

President Echeverría for his courage to stand with the people. As the MRC grew, observers commented it was common to see armed guards in front of their offices and at the home of Artemio Mora Lozada. Neighborhood disputes were settled by the MRC's ad hoc tribunals, and monthly payments were collected by subcommittee leaders. Roughly one year after the strike began, the MRC had deposited 1 million pesos in Nafinsa (as an escrow account). At the end of 1970, nearly twenty thousand homes joined the strike, and the MRC had forty-eight subcommittees.[33] More than a social movement, the MRC was beginning to establish an alternative authority and parallel bodies of informal governance.

What factors explain the emergence and ascendance of the MRC? Unlike other examples in history, the movement was not caused by a dramatic event. In this case, the stirrings of the masses coalesced into a movement when a sense of change in the government started to become palpable among those at the bottom of society. First, the victory of Carlos Hank González as governor of the State of Mexico (1969) signaled a possible shift in policies to the people of Neza. Today, Carlos Hank is seen as the personification of modern corruption in Mexico; it is widely believed he used his political career to build a business empire, along with several high-profile scandals that linked him to organized crime. However, in 1969, Carlos Hank González was most associated with his role as the general director of the National Company of Popular Goods (Compañía Nacional de Subsistencias Populares, CONASUPO), a government-run food program that subsidized basic goods sold in CONASUPO stores across Mexico. Carlos Hank toured the country as the public face of CONASUPO, appeared regularly on television to promote food security for the poor, and became a regular fixture in the State of Mexico's political scene.[34]

Shortly after Carlos Hank assumed his position as governor, Luis Echeverría visited Ciudad Neza on his presidential campaign. Echeverría's decision to publicly support the MRC (whether he was sincere or not) gave sustenance to the movement in trying times of repression and chaos. One MRC document states, "We organized a large number of people to support Luis Echeverría's candidacy and we developed a broad campaign in our municipality to spread his ideology and thought and to fortify our hope in the message of our current president that his government would be a government of the poor."[35] When citizens heard the president talk about "a democratic opening" or saw him in a colonia proletaria distributing formal land titles, those presidential acts had real consequences regardless of Echeverría's intentions. As Carlos Monsiváis once noted, President Echeverría spoke on September 1, 1971, and "emphasized the necessity to legalize the land tenure [for informal settlements] on public lands and pledged the federal government's commitment to support those who lived in the worst conditions." Three days later, four thousand families, some twenty thousand people in total, invaded a swath of land near UNAM's University City.[36] It was the largest single land invasion in Latin America at the time.

The period's political volatility generated several urban social movements around the country. Though Ciudad Neza's MRC movement was the largest, it was not the first. Most scholars and activists identify a colono strike in Chihuahua in 1968 as the first spark in what would become Mexico's Popular Urban Movement (Movimiento Urbano Popular, MUP). Shortly after, strikes and protests erupted in Durango, Iztapalapa, Monterrey, Cuernavaca, Culiacán, and several other cities by 1970.[37] In some cases, student activists were instrumental in mobilizing the protests, and in other cases, the movements were initiated by the colonos themselves. In Ciudad Neza, there appeared to be little interaction and coordination with other cities in the early 1970s. Relatedly, there is no evidence of Ciudad Neza's MRC leaders reaching out to student activists or the radical left during the payment strike.

The student movement in Mexico City played a contradictory role in the mobilizations for land rights and services in Ciudad Neza. The visible rebellion among middle-class youth gave the urban poor in Neza more "breathing room" and carved out more political space for them to maneuver under a repressive regime. While the student movement's open challenge to the PRI's authority created new openings for the MRC, the 1968 Tlatelolco massacre also had a chilling effect on some leaders in the MRC. The violent repression of students served as a warning to Ciudad Neza's social leaders and convinced them to orient their movement within the framework of constitutional rights and nationalism in order to avoid another bloodbath.[38] The presence of left-wing students was viewed more as a hindrance than a help by MRC leaders.

In the realm of public opinion, the fraccionadores displayed little interest in directly combating the core arguments made by the MRC movement. Instead, they adopted a strategy of vilifying MRC leaders, either as communists or as criminals. The only public forum where the fraccionadores articulated their views was in a local newspaper called *El Heraldo del Valle de México*. It was the only periodical to assume a profraccionador position during the strike and provides rare insights into their rationalization for massive land fraud and endemic malfeasance. For the fraccionadores, their business operations were protected by the sanctity of private property. In their narrative, their wealth was the product of their bold determination and personal intuition to take a high-risk gamble on unwanted lands.[39] The MRC movement was calling not simply for reforms but for complete land expropriation; the fraccionadores were prepared to fight for their livelihoods at all costs.

Divide and (Partially) Conquer

The rhythms of the MRC payment strike resembled the movement of waves—periods of slow activity that gathered, crescendoed, crashed, and withdrew to slowly build up again, yet always in motion. Their daily activities consisted of holding neighborhood meetings, collecting payment, writing press releases, and building alliances with shopkeepers, bus companies, and lawyers. They remained in close contact with Juan Ugarte, a director in the Department of Colonization and Agrarian Affairs (Departamento de Asuntos Agrarios y Colonización, DAAC) and the main person in charge of the land investigation. In private correspondences with Carlos Hank, Ugarte assured the governor that he verified four records on file in the public registry, along with five presidential decrees published in the *Diario Oficial*, that definitively proved most of the land (8,819 hectares, or 21,792 acres) was communal or federal property.[40] The MRC's favorable relationship with the head of the DAAC, Echeverría's public support of the movement, and Carlos Hank's condemnation of the land developers were all factors that merged together and buoyed the hopes of Ciudad Neza's residents.

The movement crescendoed in the summer of 1971. Shortly before the rainy season, the MRC organized a rally in front of the Palacio Municipal (town hall) in March. The rally was attacked by the police, followed by protesters retaliating with bricks and bats, burning police cars, and shutting down the main intersection. Three days later, the MRC mobilized six thousand people to protest the repression in Mexico City's Zócalo.[41] The rally marked a turning point for the MRC—it was the first major protest organized in the capital. The crowd took over the adjacent cathedral and occupied the space until they moved to demonstrate in front of an office building for the Departamento Agrario (a government agency that settled rural land disputes). On June 22, 1971, a crowd of five hundred protesters shutdown Bucarelli Street in Mexico City to demonstrate in front of a judicial assembly that was meeting to discuss the land tenure system in areas of the State of Mexico surrounding the Federal District.[42]

The MRC sought to counter increasing political repression by forging ties with allies outside of Ciudad Neza. Various members of the MRC later indicated that the organization received legal advice on various occasions from José Guadalupe Zuno, a progressive lawyer from Guadalajara who was also the father of President Echeverría's wife, María Esther Zuno.[43] The MRC movement also reached out to the neighboring Chimalhuacán comuneros. On October 9, 1971, the headlines announced "Colonos and Comuneros Unite against the Fraccionadores" and featured a photo of the elderly comunero leader Severiana Buendía.[44] The very image of Severiana Buendía at the press conference highlighted the long history of lakeshore communities surrounding Lake Texcoco, evoking a rustic past that strengthened the MRC's case for land restoration. The MRC utilized the press to not only project their message but also remain visible in the public eye at a time of increasing repression. First, they drew on the connections Rogelio Vargas made with the staff at *El Día* from the years when Rogelio worked as a security guard in the building where the newspaper's offices were located. The MRC cultivated a relationship with Hugo Sánchez, a journalist for *El Día* who published one to two articles each week on Ciudad Neza in the paper's Metropolitan section. Sánchez was considered an ally to the movement, had access to leaders and private meetings, and consistently wrote in favor of the movement between 1971 and 1973.[45]

The specter of the masses descending upon the capital from Ciudad Neza became more tangible in the summer of 1971. The government grew concerned about the prospects of losing control of the movement, and officials began to think of Ciudad Neza as a powder keg. In a private meeting with a consortium of wealthy businessmen, Carlos Hank warned the group, "Don't you know it's possible that one day these people could think it would be better to live around your homes in Las Lomas or Pedregal de San Ángel instead of the outskirts of Nezahualcoytl [sic]? And they wouldn't have to go too far. What would happen if 500,000 or 600,000 people from Neza simply marched into Mexico City?"⁴⁶ At the end of July 1971, a private meeting was held between Echeverría, Carlos Hank, and representatives of the DAAC at Los Pinos to analyze and discuss possible solutions to the land tenure problem in Ciudad Neza. Those present came to an unofficial agreement that it was in the best interests of the parties involved to move in favor of land expropriation.⁴⁷

At a moment when twenty-five thousand households were active in the payment strike, the MRC split in two. The division was made public during a neighborhood meeting on July 8 in Colonia Maravillas, where Artemio Mora Lozada denounced Odón Madariaga and Ángel Ávila Jácome for being "radical extremists of the left." Although a definitive reason for the split remains uncertain, it is most likely that Artemio Mora Lozada's aspirations of gaining a seat in the municipal government gave rise to internal power conflicts within the MRC. After the split, Artemio Mora Lozada retained a slim majority of the subcommittees (roughly 60 percent) and Odón Madariaga held on to the rest, mainly subcommittees in the eastern sections of Ciudad Neza. Odón Madariaga, Rogelio Vargas, and Angel Garcia Bravo quickly formed the Executive Committee of the MRC (Comité Executivo del MRC, CE-MRC) and stepped up their militancy in the colonias.⁴⁸

It was in this period when both wings of the movement gravitated closer to state officials and the inner circles of the PRI. The CE-MRC (Odón Madariaga's faction) was incorporated into the PRI's National Peasant Confederation (Confederación Nacional Campesina, CNC), while Artemio Mora Lozada's MRC aligned itself with the ruling party's National Confederation of Popular Organizations (Confederación Nacional de Organizaciones Populares, CNOP).⁴⁹ The split pushed the CE-MRC to seek allies with a broader array of figures outside of Ciudad Neza's local political milieu. Although the MRC never officially opposed the PRI, the movement was independent and unaffiliated with any political party up until this point. For the fraccionadores and local authorities, they viewed the MRC split as an advantageous time to intensify their repression against the movement.

As the summer rainstorms began to abate, a sense of terror and violence hung over Ciudad Neza. The land developers attacked the MRC leaders and their supporters on multiple fronts. Raúl Romero and Bernardo Eckstein routinely paid for private planes to fly over Ciudad Neza to drop flyers on the roofs and yards of residents to notify them that anyone who did not make their monthly payments would be evicted from their homes.[50] The bombardment of flyers was more than a threat; hundreds of people were displaced from their homes in 1971 and 1972. A principal who ran several schools in Colonia Reforma and who was allied with the land developers froze the teachers' payments in an effort to turn public opinion against the strike.[51] Like many others, Rogelio's house was bulldozed to the ground. "They threw me and my family on the street," he said. "They threw us out into the rain with nothing; they destroyed the house I built myself. Can you imagine?"[52] It was becoming more common for the police to arbitrarily harass, assault, and arrest residents walking home at night from work. An article published in August reported, "Among the abuses that the local police commit, residents tell of being arbitrarily arrested, beaten in jail until they confessed to crimes they did not commit, and paying fines without ever receiving any paperwork for them."[53] The systematic abuse of residents was neither condemned nor condoned in public by the federal government.

After the split, the paths taken by the MRC movement were shaped by internal divisions and external repression. Mora Lozada's MRC and the separate CE-MRC were now competing with each other for the support and allegiance of Ciudad Neza's residents. The CE-MRC escalated the militancy of their actions in a show of force intended to appeal to the anger and frustration felt among residents who were growing impatient with the endless meetings and rallies. Between August and November of 1971, the CE-MRC led hundreds of angry residents to burn down the land developers' collection booths that were set up throughout Aurora, Esperanza, Agua Azul, and Vincente Villada. The collection booths, typically small offices or kiosks where residents could make their monthly payments, were destroyed with Molotov cocktails and crowbars, sometimes by CE-MRC leaders and sometimes spontaneously by residents, particularly women during the daytime.[54]

Beyond the political struggles waged by the CE-MRC, the leaders and members of the coalition were close friends united by a common cause and shared history. They attended each other's birthday parties, saint's days, and children's christenings. Members of neighborhood associations, or committees, were imbued with a collective sense of egalitarianism. Regular gatherings were held to distribute communal foodstuff and potable water. Weekly meetings provided a space to make collective decisions over practical matters of daily life. Flyers, bulletins, and community newsletters were discussed as part of maintaining a necessary level of unity in the face of political repression.[55]

The month of March was punctuated with celebrations after the DAAC definitively announced that Ciudad Neza sat on communal lands and federal property. On March 17, 1972, the DAAC announced, "The land where Ciudad Nezahualcóyotl was founded is communal land."[56] Over five thousand people took to the Zócalo to celebrate the news, with festivities continuing on through the night in all of Ciudad Neza's neighborhoods. The CE-MRC's leadership decided it was time to seize the momentum. The following week, they organized a rally of three thousand residents to march down Adolfo López Mateos Avenue toward Ciudad Neza's Palacio Municipal. Scuffles broke out along the route, and by the time they reached the plaza, the crowd was staring down a police force with guns drawn and aimed at the front of the crowd. Odón Madariaga eased the tensions and slowly dispersed the crowd amid the chaos and shouting.[57]

Now that the verdict on the land was publicly announced, Echeverría had to move beyond empty promises and decide how to proceed in light of the DAAC's decision. After the DAAC's announcement, Echeverría began a series of private conferences and planning sessions to determine how to move forward with the land expropriation. Starting on July 24, 1972, the DAAC and Carlos Hank held a series of meetings to review and discuss laws for land expropriation, what legal instruments were required to transfer the property lots, and a systematic account of all the land "owned" by the fraccionadores corresponding details of their property (vendor, cost of purchase, year, size). Daily briefings were sent to Echeverría as he met with Mexico's leading figures in urban affairs: Pedro Ramírez Vázquez, Mario Pani, various lawyers who specialized in property disputes, and even author Carlos Fuentes.[58] Behind closed doors, it was decided that the land would be converted into national property under the jurisdiction of the federal government. A community land trust managed under the Nacional Financiera would serve as a fiduciary to distribute the payments made by residents. For each resident with an outstanding balance on their land, the remaining balance payment would go into a land trust called Fineza, where 40 percent would go to the fraccionadores to compensate for their losses, while the rest (60 percent) would go to the federal government to be utilized for urban services and infrastructure. Intended as a compromise to appease both sides, the federal government's decision to compensate the land developers was the most controversial clause of the agreement, considering most residents thought the developers should be imprisoned for land fraud.[59]

The rumors of a resolution vis-à-vis a new land trust (Fineza) put the movement's leaders on edge. In public, both factions of the MRC denounced the land trust agreement; however, internally, the prospects of a partial victory and a chance to end the struggle produced intense debates within the inner circles of the movement.[60] In the period when the preliminary proposals for the land trust were being circulated, Odón Madariaga was offered an official position in the municipal government as the *tercer regidor* (comparable to a city councilman).[61] The cracks in the CE-MRC's public facade became apparent to its supporters when Rogelio Vargas split from the CE-MRC and formed the Coalición Depuradora de Comités del Movimiento Restaurador de Colonos (*depuradora* roughly translates to "cleansing"; CDC-MRC). Rogelio Vargas's decision to leave was prompted by Odón Madariaga's plans to sign the agreement and invade empty tracts of land to sell them to new families in the interim period when the lands would be in between the fraccionadores and the federal government (described in more detail in what follows). With his departure, Rogelio took most of the neighborhood committees from Aurora under his wing. On the precipice of signing an agreement, the movement for land restoration was on the verge of self-destruction.

As the public announcement of the Fineza Land Trust agreement drew near, Odón Madariaga and Angel Garcia Bravo decided it was time to close ranks and neutralize any dissent. They shot up a meeting house used by a subcommittee in Colonia Aurora (Third Section) and later hired gangs of youth to attack a committee meeting in Colonia Vicente Guerrero due to their refusal to go along with the land trust agreement.[62] The divisions between Odón and Rogelio exploded into violence on the evening of March 22, 1973. In the days leading up to the shoot-out, Rogelio's group (CDR-MRC) distributed flyers that demanded the arrest of Odón Madariaga, Aristeo Pérez López, and Ángel Ávila Jácome for "stealing and selling land plots, charging monthly payments for the land, and extorting local businesses for paid protection [*protección gangstertil*]."[63] Rogelio held a late-night meeting in Colonia Las Flores to discuss plans for the land trust. By 10:00 p.m., roughly two hundred people had gathered in a heavily settled section of Las Flores. A group of forty men arrived with the CE-MRC leader, Ángel Ávila Jácome, who traded insults with Rogelio until scuffles broke out between the two groups, and shots were fired back and forth. Both sides took cover on neighboring rooftops and adjacent alleyways below. At some time after 1:00 a.m., Rogelio escaped on foot and made his way to the Federal District.[64] After the gunfire subsided, two men were found dead from gunshot wounds, dozens were injured, and four cars were still on fire when the Red Cross arrived on the scene.[65] News of the gun battle appeared in all of Mexico City's dailies, with one local headline stating, "Four Hours of Gunfire in Ciudad Nezahualcóyotl."[66] State officials later questioned Rogelio Vargas about the shoot-out the following morning at the Hotel Cadillac. Government reports indicate several leaders from the CE-MRC—Odón Madariaga, Aristeo Pérez López, Salomon Aleman Garcia—were spotted waiting in a café a block away from the Hotel Cadillac.[67] "That was it. It was over," Rogelio remembered.[68]

The Federal Government Expropriates the Land

On March 28, 1973, President Echeverría signed the Fineza Land Trust agreement along with Odón Madariaga of the CE-MRC, Rogelio Vargas of the CDR-MRC, and Severiana Buendía of the Asociación de Comuneros de Chimalhuacán. Artemio Mora Lozada positioned himself to the left of Odón Madariaga and refused to support the Fineza agreement. On March 31, 1973, Augusto Gomez Villanueva, head of the DAAC, held a press conference to announce the signing of the agreement and plans to invest 1,200 million pesos into Ciudad Neza's urban infrastructure. The head of the DAAC told reporters that thirty-four fraccionadores were going to turn over their land (officially categorized as *carreteras de credito*), and the land trust would now be the only entity through which payments for land and services could be made in Ciudad Neza.[69] Raúl Romero sat in front of a row of microphones as the reporters pestered him about the process of the land transfer.[70] The reign of the fraccionadores in Ciudad Nezahualcóyotl was over.

The signing of the Fineza Land Trust marked the end of one stage in Ciudad Neza's history and the beginning of another. The fraccionadores' speculation, sale, and control of the land in Ciudad Neza was coming to an end. For the residents who still had outstanding balances for their land plots (the majority), they now had to pay into the Fineza Land Trust until they fulfilled the full amount stipulated in their contracts. Of that total amount, 60 percent went to the federal government and 40 percent went to the land developers. Under the Fineza Land Trust, the residents' land titles would be recognized in court and among state agencies, the arbitrary threat of eviction dissipated, and the federal government was now responsible for the installation of urban services and infrastructure.[71] The March 31 announcement reverberated through the Ciudad Neza's settlements, bringing both celebrations and protests.[72] The hatred for the land developers was deep and widespread; to lead a movement against them and then grant them a degree of legitimacy at the negotiating table was a tricky proposition.

Despite the solid agreement reached between the federal government, the fraccionadores, and the movement leaders, the viability of the land trust was still dependent upon the support and participation of Ciudad Neza's residents. Most of the organized neighborhood associations supported the land trust; however, three (Villada, Evolución, and Perla) refused to cede any legitimacy to the land developers. The three initial holdouts did not fundamentally alter the Fineza agreements but were substantial enough to constitute a base of residents in opposition to the compromises reached by the federal government and the MRC movement. As in past experiences, the partial reforms offered by public officials could have been just enough to force residents to temporarily acquiesce, await the changes, and eventually recede back to everyday life (this happened previously in the area in 1953).[73] This time, however, the moral certitude residents acquired over years of struggle ran deep enough for a segment of the movement to break from past experiences of compromise and alignment with the PRI. In this case, the residents' demands were legitimated by legal norms, popular notions of land rights, and the president's public position in favor of their struggle.

The events surrounding the Fineza Land Trust culminated in a rally organized by President Echeverría on May 10, 1973. Tens of thousands of people gathered in the Unión de Fuerzas (Neza's civic plaza) to celebrate the regularization of Ciudad Neza's land. Under a rainy sky, President Echeverría, Governor Carlos Hank González, and Municipal President Oscar Loya Ramírez proclaimed that a new day was dawning in Ciudad Neza. Echeverría outlined a new plan to urbanize Ciudad Neza, invest in a new technical college, and create a large park equipped with playgrounds, soccer fields, and lakes. Later on, when pressed by reporters to explain why a compromise was made with the land developers, Echeverría responded, "Unfortunately, we can't deliver all of the land to the people, that's what the laws of Mexico say, as a government, we cannot transgress the law or we will fall into anarchy."[74] Despite the land trust's shortcomings and flaws, it represented a major victory for Echeverría. The land had been legalized, the fraccionadores had been expelled, urbanization projects were in the works, much of the social movement was contained, and an advance was made in overcoming the sulfurous stigma surrounding Ciudad Neza.

On the eve of the Fineza Land Trust agreements, Odón Madariaga used his new position in the municipal government to lead a series of land invasions in which thousands of families settled on empty plots of land (colloquially referred to as paracaidismo). Rogelio Vargas refrained from the illegal land grab and watched his former friends grow in wealth and power while he languished as a low-level PRI functionary. Rogelio's opposition to the land invasions placed him at odds with his former friends in the CE-MRC, while his affiliation with the PRI discredited him in the eyes of the revolutionary left, who opposed both the Fineza agreements and the PRI. At the end of 1974, roughly sixty thousand land plots had been invaded and sold by the core leadership of the CE-MRC.[75] Although this represented the main dynamic for the rest of the 1970s, the capitulation of the CE-MRC leaders created fertile grounds for political collectives steeped in revolutionary politics to organize a restless base of colonos. In 1973, the struggle subsided but was not completely extinguished yet.

The MRC strike highlights the role of neighborhood associations in urban politics at a moment when the informal city acquired a mass character in Mexican society. Echeverría's "democratic opening" was met with less cynicism among the urban poor than the student movement, and in the case of Ciudad Neza, it galvanized residents into a movement that went beyond the bounds of Luis Echeverría's discourse. The urban social movements that arose in every major city during the 1970s underscore the need to widen the scope of inquiry to gain a richer and more comprehensive picture of the democratic opening across Mexican society.

7

Fineza and Land Regularization

The Fineza agreements represented a nodal point in Ciudad Neza's local history. Under the federal government, the agreements approved a massive transfer of land from private fraccionadores to the Mexican government. In addition, the agreements provided a legal framework for granting formal property titles to Ciudad Neza's residents and functioned as a conduit to channel monthly payments by "homeowners" into public utilities (60 percent) and to the fraccionadores (40 percent). The Fineza agreements also marked the first large-scale land regularization project in Mexico at a time when President Echeverría made informal land regularization a central feature of his urban agenda. The high-profile case of Ciudad Neza was viewed as a monumental undertaking with the potential to influence public opinion on the question of land regularization for informal settlements in Mexican cities.

This chapter details the Mexican government's attempt to transfer over one hundred thousand land plots fraudulently owned by private fraccionadores to thousands of families in Ciudad Neza. What was the process like for an ordinary household registered with Fineza? To what degree did the program benefit residents, and conversely, how did it perpetuate sources of inequality deeply ingrained in Mexican society? These questions are addressed through a close study of Fineza's operations from 1973 to 1977. Throughout the chapter, Fineza's official documents are examined in conjunction with news coverage and internal government reports on the violent struggles between various political groupings over unsettled lands. The divisions that emerged between the MRC leaders prior to the Fineza agreements (Odón Madariaga Cruz, Rogelio Vargas Soriano) intensified afterward and continued to shape the development of what was now the fourth-largest city in Mexico: Ciudad Nezahualcóyotl.

Land Invasions and Fineza Agreements Fallout

On May 30, 1976, Mexico's news outlets announced the details of President Echeverría's trip to Canada for the United Nations Conference on Human Settlements (Habitat I).[1] As Echeverría's flight took off that morning, Odón Madariaga was nearby in the sprawling shacks surrounding the airport. For Odón Madariaga, Echeverría's flight could have been any of the dozens of planes flying overhead that morning as he went about his day in Ciudad Neza. The press touted Echeverría's prominent role as a keynote speaker at the first major international conference on human settlements. Echeverría planned on utilizing the international platform to champion his vision for a new international economic order and to extol the land regularization programs Mexico implemented in places like Ciudad Neza.[2] Later that week, as UN delegates and prime ministers listened to Echeverría's speech on Mexico's land regularization reforms, Odón Madariaga was breathing in Ciudad Neza's dusty air and reaping the rewards of its land regularization program.

By 1976, Odón Madariaga built a powerful fiefdom in Ciudad Neza. He had overseen more than a dozen land invasions and collected fees for each of the thousands of land plots divided and distributed in the aftermath of the land grabs.[3] The first step in the process commenced when a family made their down payment on a plot of land (200 pesos). Then each family paid Madariaga and his men for their "protection" for an indefinite period of time—usually after the property title was officially recognized and transferred to state authorities.[4] In the following pages, the details of Madariaga's land invasions are examined in relation to the government's Fineza Land Trust.

Odón Madariaga's financial gains grew in tandem with his political advances. In 1973, Odón Madariaga became the *tercer regidor* (like a city councilman) in Ciudad Neza's municipal government.[5] Unlike the fraccionadores of Ciudad Neza's past, Madariaga was a public official with the PRI, a standing that granted him another layer of protection for his illegal land grabs. In addition, he stood as one of the three colono representatives on the executive board of the Fineza Land Trust. After the Fineza negotiations, Madariaga's political capital extended well beyond land fraud. As a city councilman, he wielded power to grant business licenses, approve building codes, assist municipal judges, resolve interpersonal disputes, and utilize the local police force to his benefit. Madariaga strengthened his political power through the selection of his most loyal men for future political positions. The names previously listed in police files as dangerous agitators—Odón Madariaga Cruz, Angel Garcia Bravo, Aristeo Pérez López—were now displayed on plaques in the lobby of Ciudad Neza's municipal building. In 1969, Madariaga helped launch a movement to bring down Ciudad Neza's fraccionadores and corrupt politicians—now, he was both.

Rogelio Vargas, who elected another path, was not as lucky. In fact, Madariaga's swift ascent was directly tied to Rogelio's tragic demise. When Rogelio Vargas broke with the CE-MRC, the rupture represented more than an act of political fragmentation. Rogelio Vargas was now the head of a rival faction and posed a direct threat to Odón Madariaga. Once close friends, Madariaga now viewed Vargas as an enemy to be isolated, neutralized, and attacked with rumors, arrests, and open violence. After his break with the CE-MRC, Vargas sank into a prolonged period of stagnation punctuated with bouts of alcoholism and debilitating panic attacks.

What was the driving force behind the dispute and Rogelio Vargas's subsequent decline? As briefly noted in the previous chapter, Vargas stood firmly opposed to Madariaga's decision to invade and sell land plots in the eastern sections of Ciudad Neza. On the eve of the Fineza agreements (March–May 1973), Odón Madariaga, Angel Garcia Bravo, and Aristeo Pérez López were ready to exploit their political power for financial fortunes. At a moment when the land tenure was in transition between the fraccionadores and state authorities, the movement's leaders could mobilize those eager to settle on their own plot of land and take advantage of the legal confusion accompanying the transition. By all accounts, Vargas could have shared in the bounty but refused to partake on moral grounds. Even today when asked about it, it is clear the decision weighs heavily on his mind. He tells me his parents raised him not to betray his beliefs and his people (*pueblo*).[6] Even in the most intense moments of the MRC strike, Rogelio was able to step back and see his friends slowly degenerating into the corrupt land barons they once opposed together. "I just couldn't live with myself if I did it," Rogelio simply said.[7] For Rogelio Vargas, he didn't survive three shoot-outs and multiple arrests in a struggle for land rights only to betray that cause and steal the land in question.

Rogelio Vargas's exclusion from Ciudad Neza's centers of political power was reflected in his home life. Unlike his former *compañeros*, Vargas still lived in the same house as before the Fineza agreements. Located a short walk from the Palacio Municipal, the "Frente Unido de Colonos del Valle de México–CNC" banner in Rogelio's front yard was the only visible sign that distinguished his house from the rest on the street. The yard was cluttered with water buckets, used car parts, piles of leftover lumber, chicken coops, and flowerpots. Like his surrounding neighbors, the absence of running water and indoor plumbing forced Rogelio to build a basic outhouse near the side of the yard. After the rock wall and yard, the self-built house stood at the back of the property lot. The home was made of cinder block and covered with a cardboard roof weighed down with piles of bricks and debris.[8]

The interior resembled what one might imagine for a poor, low-level political broker in Ciudad Neza. The common area was completely utilitarian in nature: the furniture consisted of a few chairs and sofas used for the ongoing meetings that stretched out through the day and into the night. The unpainted cinder block walls were completely bare save for a small beer poster and a framed photo of Rogelio standing next to President Echeverría, illuminated at night by a single lightbulb hanging from a worn cable. The bottoms of the walls were lined with stacks of flyers, pamphlets, old press clippings, a bullhorn, parts of an outdoor sound system, and of course, back issues of the popular *Kalimán* comic book series. The kitchen was the domain of Rogelio's wife, Soledad. Soledad used the rudimentary kitchen not only for domestic purposes but also to attend to the constant stream of people visiting the home for assistance. With Rogelio gone for most of the day, his wife's presence and work in the home were indispensable to the survival of the family.[9]

Rogelio Vargas relied on the personal contacts he cultivated as a *lider social* (social leader) to survive in a web of networks built around reciprocity. In 1974, he still maintained active ties with Ciudad Neza's taxi driver cooperatives and Chimalhuacán's Indigenous comuneros (the latter also opposed the land invasions).[10] He was constantly on the move—in Neza, in Toluca, in the Federal District, in meeting rooms, bars, offices, street corners, homes, and notary offices. In many cases, favors were repaid with favors. A store owner might have needed a particular license or permission to build an extension to their business from the municipal government. Vargas's direct access and influence over local politicians could be leveraged for official approval. If successful, Vargas's compensation could come in the form of store credit or goods of value to his family.[11] In one example, Governor Carlos Hank gifted Rogelio ten valuable taxi licenses he was able to parlay for both financial and social gain.[12] If a PRI leader in the Federal District or the State of Mexico needed to quickly pull together a street protest, Vargas could be called upon to mobilize his constituency at a moment's notice. Although Vargas's public reputation and presence formed the basis for his survival, he tells me that it would have all collapsed without the labor of his wife, Soledad, who attended to the daily visits of friends and neighbors in search of Rogelio's assistance.[13]

Both Rogelio Vargas and Odón Madariaga's personal histories epitomize the inner workings of Mexican politics under the dominance of the PRI. In many ways, they illuminate the multiple processes and sociopolitical networks anthropologist Carlos Vélez-Ibáñez termed "rituals of marginality." Carlos Vélez-Ibáñez, who carried out his field work in Ciudad Neza in the early 1970s, described the rituals of marginality as a set of relations "expressed in repetitive forms such as patron-client relationships, brokerage, political friendships of convenience, and other favor-producing exchanges."[14] It was the main mode of dominance exercised by the PRI in Mexico's informal cities. The rituals of marginality were the set of relations Ciudad Neza's MRC social movement challenged in the early seventies, and they were the same set of relations the movement's leaders eventually joined. Vélez-Ibáñez's observations and analysis of Neza's local politics at the time (1971–74) have been further borne out and generally validated over the years by the historical record.

However, three key questions remain from the period. One, where do the various independent, grassroots movements from the period after 1973 fit into the rituals of marginality? This question is addressed in chapter 8. Two, what actually happened when this set of new historical actors entered into Ciudad Neza's entrenched rituals of marginality? In surveying the history of the Vaso de Texcoco over the course of the twentieth century, the first half of the 1970s stands out as a pivotal period when large-scale public works projects finally installed permanent and planned infrastructure, when tens of thousands of formal land titles were granted to residents, and when media hype surrounding the Fineza agreements spurred Ciudad Neza's first and only wave of land invasions. Most importantly, what were the results of Fineza and how did it impact Ciudad Neza's residents? These questions are addressed in the following sections by focusing on the period's land regularization programs, the formation of Fineza and its organizational structure, the number of lots it regulated, and the effects of illegal land invasions on the overall regularization process.

Urban Informality and Land Regularization

In the early 1970s, Mexico's shifting direction in urban housing policy was concretized through the establishment of several new state institutions. These institutions were primarily geared toward the regularization of informal settlements built on ejido or communal lands. The key distinction between the new state institutions was the geographical scope of their respective legal jurisdiction—national, statewide, municipal. In the following section, I outline the key characteristics of AURIS (Estado de México) and CORETT (federal) before providing a detailed account of Fineza (municipal) during its first four years of operation. These three key institutions would become mutually constitutive and set the parameters for Ciudad Neza's land regularization.

As the epicenter of informal urbanization, it should come as no surprise that the Estado de México produced the first government institution for urban land regularization. In 1969, the AURIS Institute was founded by Governor Carlos Hank González to investigate and assess the legal status of contested lands adjacent to the Federal District.[15] Although limited in reach, AURIS soon became a center for cutting-edge research and urban policy. It preceded the flowering of democratic politics on the city's periphery and constituted a rare instance of experimental urbanism in Mexico, comparable only to the Inter-American Center for Housing and Planning (Centro Interamericano de Vivienda y Planeamiento, CINVA) in Colombia or John F. C. Turner's housing experiments in Peru.[16] In one revealing example, AURIS was the first Mexican institution to use the term *human settlements*.[17] More than simply a point of terminology, this term was reflective of a leadership body immersed in global planning trends veering away from the dominant paradigms of the postwar era.

AURIS's innovative work can be traced back to two crucial factors. First, it possessed a certain freedom and autonomy characteristic of any initial pilot program. Second, it was led by a group of young architects, sociologists, anthropologists, and psychologists who drew on their international experiences and connections to take advantage of their novel position. Roberto Eibenshultz and Gregorio Valner were two key links in this formation. The children of Jewish immigrants who fled to Mexico as the Third Reich consolidated its power in Europe, Eibenshultz was a young architect affiliated with the National Indigenous Institute. Gregorio Valner was an up-and-coming social psychiatrist who had the fortune to study in a program established by German émigré Erich Fromm at UNAM. Eibenshultz's graduate training at the International Center for Aerial Survey and Earth Sciences in Holland led to a fruitful collaboration between AURIS and Rotterdam-based Bouwcentrum, a technical institute established to help design and plan the reconstruction of Holland's cities after the Second World War.[18] Although Valner primarily focused on land tenure and construction materials in his position as the general director of AURIS, his specialization in public health led to various clean-water projects and a series of studies on the social psychology of children of Ciudad Neza.[19]

Eibenshultz and Valner were joined by architects Julio Garcia Coll, Eduardo Rincón Gallardo, Hugo Manza, and Alor Calderon.[20] AURIS's leadership body was primarily composed of the first generation of architects trained at UNAM's new facilities in Ciudad Universitaria. They were part of a generation who came of age during Mexico City's grand expansion and entered the National School of Architecture at a time when the urban shantytown had already become a permanent fixture in Mexican society. Even when AURIS settled into the more mechanized tasks of land titling, census gathering, and technical oversight, it continued to be one of the few public entities in Mexico to publish guides on autoconstrucción and establish sites that sold building materials (cement, lumber, tabique bricks) at a subsidized rate.[21]

Of all the land regularization institutions created in this period, the Commission for the Regularization of Land Tenure (Comisión para la Regularización de la Tenencia de la Tierra, CORETT) was by far the largest and most consequential. Initially composed of a few committee members in 1973, CORETT was expanded into a national commission the following year and placed under the leadership of the Department of Colonization and Agrarian Affairs (Departamento de Asuntos Agrarios y Colonización, DAAC).[22] On a practical level, CORETT's alignment with the DAAC granted it the ultimate authority over land tenure cases; symbolically, the coexistence and collaboration between the DAAC and CORETT represented a bureaucratic expression of Mexico's transition into a predominantly urban society. Beginning in 1974, CORETT functioned as the main judicial body to evaluate and determine if ejido land holdings should be converted into private land plots for residential purposes. In this process, CORETT was considered an interim owner of the land and served as a bridge between the ejido and the informal settlement under review for regularization. As the sole national institution responsible for this process, CORETT gradually accumulated enormous tracts of land still pending approval for regularization. As historian Antonio Azuela observed in 1989, "CORETT is the most important urban landowner in the country.... Being the beneficiary of expropriations of ejido and communal lands occupied by human settlements, this commission concentrates ownership of an increasingly large proportion of the land that is being incorporated into the urbanizing process."[23] A similar outcome can be observed in Ciudad Neza.

Fineza and the Formalization of an Informal City

Ciudad Neza was Mexico's first case of land regularization in a singular locale on a mass scale. Ciudad Neza's circumstances posed several legal, political, and environmental problems to Mexican officials. First, Ciudad Neza's land tenure was complicated by the fact that large tracts of land were considered federal property as opposed to communal ejidos.[24] Second, the geological features and environmental factors of the land (particularly the soft, brittle soil) proved to be incredibly vexing for engineers responsible for "urbanizing" an informal city of more than a million residents. Third, the unresolved contradictions left over from the MRC movement made for a particularly charged political atmosphere. Finally, the sheer number of land plots slated for regularization was overwhelming on any scale—local or national. For these reasons, Fineza continued to operate as the main financial and judicial body for Ciudad Neza's land regularization program as opposed to CORETT or AURIS.

Fineza was initially formed as a community land trust (*fideicomiso*) in March 1973 and began operations in May 1973.[25] More than simply a land regularization program, Fineza also functioned as a trust where funds were extracted by the government to invest in public works projects (*obras de beneficio social*). At the end of 1974, approximately 40 million pesos were either utilized or allotted for road construction, drainage projects, and a new park.[26] Funds earmarked for public works projects only represented a portion of the funds deposited (60 percent). The rest of the trust's funds were designated for Ciudad Neza's fraccionadores to compensate for any outstanding balances owed to them by residents. After the fraccionadores turned over the land rights and financial records (*portfolio de credito*), it was determined the government had to reimburse the fraccionadores 623,607,249 pesos in total (approximately 50 million dollars in 1973).[27]

The problems that arose from Ciudad Neza's legal complexity were compounded by its immense size. By the end of its first year of existence, forty-five thousand land contracts were submitted by residents to Fineza for review.[28] The clandestine nature of lot sales in Ciudad Neza made property deed evaluation and verification a tedious process, with one report stating, "Many colonos finished 100 percent of their payments to the fraccionador but don't have the proper paperwork [*escritura*] to prove it."[29] Document verifications, notarizations, court procedures, community consultations, public relations, and financial management exhausted the labor of Fineza's thirty-eight-person staff stationed in offices spread out through Ciudad Neza in Colonias El Sol, Estado de México, Metropolitana, and Esperanza.[30] A major source of frustration stemmed from the numerous *doble ventas*, or occasions when fraccionadores sold the same property lot to multiple parties in order to increase their profits. The widespread practice of doble ventas dragged down the process, as it required extra time to legally mediate and determine which party was the rightful owner of the land. As Fineza assumed responsibility for the lands, doble ventas continued at an average rate of twenty-seven a month in 1973 and 1974.[31] Out of 150,000 total lots in the municipality, only 1,800 were regularized by 1974.[32] The source of frustration did not solely stem from the corrupt and disorganized land tenure system built up over the years under the fraccionadores. The lack of Fineza's progress can also be attributed to the land invasions carried out by a new incarnation of fraccionadores in the form of social movement leaders. Once again, Odón Madariaga was at the head of the pack.

The Rise of Odón Madariaga

Despite the PRI's attempts to move forward, the unjust terms of the Fineza agreements remained a point of contention that was too strong to simply fade away. The contradictory logic was fundamentally flawed at the most basic level: If the settled lands were originally federal or communal properties, how could the fraccionadores legitimately claim those lands as private property? If the 1958 Law of Fraccionamientos required "owners" (fraccionadores) to install electric and water services, how could the fraccionadores claim to be within the law after fifteen years of malfeasance and neglect? The denial of justice produced a deep bitterness shared among the tens of thousands of colonos.

The lingering bitterness over the fraccionadores' impunity was magnified by the financial terms of the agreements. After years of paying the fraccionadores for fraudulent land titles and nonexistent services, now they had to continue paying for newly promised services and the outstanding balances on their land plots. As the first large-scale regularization project, its fragile foundations were a cause for concern for PRI leaders who gambled on its success as a powerful legitimizing force. In this period, the prospects of failure due to negative public opinion and lack of participation made the PRI dependent on Odón Madariaga to mobilize residents to participate in Fineza's program. As for the means of mobilization, the PRI was willing to turn a blind eye to Madariaga's machinations.

After May 1973, several distinct groupings formed a united opposition to Fineza. Though in the minority, the opposition's message reached a wide audience and established a pole of opposition to its terms of regularization. Among residents, three neighborhood associations refused to concede to the Fineza agreements and continued to abstain from their monthly payments. As a spokesperson for the dissident neighborhood associations in La Perla, Reforma, and Villada stated, "At this moment, the fraccionadores and the government should be paying for the urbanization and services. . . . We're poor, we've paid enough."[33] Along with the previously mentioned neighborhoods, unorganized individuals opposed to Fineza could be found scattered across Ciudad Neza's colonias.

As a result of Rogelio Vargas and Odón Madariaga's public support for Fineza, a political vacuum grew for who would organize the breakaway neighborhood associations and scattered groupings. The Independent Popular Front (Frente Popular Independiente, FPI), Authentic Restoration Movement of Settlers (Auténtico Movimiento Restaurador de Colonos, AMRC), and General Union of Workers and Farmers of Mexico (Unión General de Obreros y Campesinos de México, UGOCM) all sought to build their own political base among angered residents unwilling to stop their payment strike. The heightened press coverage of the MRC strike and Fineza agreements attracted the interest of the UGOCM. Established in 1949, the UGOCM represented part of the Mexican left's "old guard."[34] What they lacked in local contacts and fresh ideas, they compensated with national contacts and decades of experience in land invasions, albeit with campesinos for agrarian purposes. The UGOCM opposed Fineza yet engaged in land invasions, a position that directly threatened Odón Madariaga's interests.[35]

A smaller grouping composed of local youth influenced by the Cuban and Chinese Revolutions began to organize as the FPI. Small yet determined, they took to Ciudad Neza's gray, monotonous walls with spray paint, stencils, and wheat paste to publicize their message against Fineza. In many ways, they were the opposite of the UGOCM: young, new, local, and embodying the politics of "revolutionary China" over the "stodgy Soviet revisionism" of the UGOCM. They sporadically worked with the AMRC, a renegade faction of the CE-MRC that appears to have been heavily infiltrated by the PRI in 1974.[36]

The most consistent and articulate opposition to Fineza came from a collective of young Jesuits and their allies (detailed in the next chapter). Based in Ciudad Neza since 1969, the group of young Jesuits used their education centers, religious services, and monthly bulletin (*El Despertar del Pueblo*) to organize residents against Fineza. In an article entitled "How Legal Is the Land Trust?" they implored residents to boycott Fineza (*fraudecomiso*) and pointed to it as an example of the PRI's alignment with the most corrupt elements of society.[37] Enrique Maza, a Jesuit and ally to the group, wrote in *Excélsior*, "If the lands don't belong to the fraccionadores . . . they have committed fraud. . . . A massive fraud of tremendous importance, since it costed human lives. They deserve jail time, not a land trust. The land trust legalizes and covers up fraud and makes the government accomplices with the fraccionadores."[38] In both graffiti and op-eds, opposition to Fineza was growing louder.

Odón Madariaga was the primary colono representative on the executive board of Fineza. Despite his occasional denunciations of Fineza at public rallies (i.e., raised fees, poor services), Odón Madariaga mandated the CE-MRC support Fineza in their leaflets and directed all its members to enroll in the program. The thirty to thirty-five subcommittees still active under Odón Madariaga and Angel Garcia Bravo, combined with Rogelio Vargas's constituency and Artemio Mora Lozada's supporters (now in favor of Fineza), served as important "levers" between the PRI and the colonos.[39]

Disruption to Fineza's operations by dissident neighborhood associations or committees risked violent reprisals from Odón and his pistoleros. In one example, Odón's associate Aristeo Pérez López ordered a hit on the leader of a neighborhood association in La Reforma for openly opposing Odón's use of Fineza as a smokescreen for extortion. Grisly photos of the leader's bloodied corpse found their way into a local newspaper, along with a lengthy depiction of Madariaga and Garcia Bravo as tyrannical figures in Ciudad Neza.[40] In describing Madariaga and Garcia Bravo's repressive acts, Enrique Maza reported, "They sell land that has already been sold and homes that have already been inhabited. They violently evict people in the middle of the night. They strike and assault people. They imprison them in clandestine jails. They rob them of their belongings. It is impossible to detail case by case."[41] The task of detailing each case found in the archives is as daunting of an endeavor. Even more elusive is the political and affective demoralization neighborhood colono leaders must have felt after their brief, shared moment of social solidarity and local democracy suddenly turned into a familiar version of despotism and coercion.

The most dramatic and visible sign of CE-MRC's degeneration was their move toward land invasions in 1973 and 1974. This time, the colloquial term *paracaidista* (parachuter) for squatters was fitting, as thousands of poor families seemingly "swooped down" on empty pockets of land around the eastern sections of Ciudad Neza. With 80 percent of Ciudad Neza's land occupied at the beginning of 1973, roughly 15 percent lay open for settlement.[42] In some cases, the paracaidismo was small and spontaneous. The majority of land invasions, however, were organized, large, and exploited by Odón Madariaga. They first started when the rumors of a fideicomiso began to percolate in April 1973 and dissipated by the end of 1974 after most of the municipality's lands had been occupied by homes or businesses. In this time span, similar invasions took place in Monterrey, Tijuana, Cuernavaca, and the Federal District—some led by political activists, most by ambitious fraccionadores seeking to make a profit.

The first documented land invasion can be traced back to April 5, 1973, when close to seven thousand people descended en masse onto an arid plain and staked out approximately fifteen hundred land plots.[43] At the beginning of May, a second round of invasions temporarily occupied two thousand lots. The total number of lots occupied in the beginning of May is difficult to determine because it is one of the few cases where hundreds of police officers from other jurisdictions were dispatched to arrest the leaders and evict the invaders. It appears as if a small group of local residents not affiliated with MRC movements started a rumor that all unoccupied lots could be claimed by families in need of housing and then proceeded to organize a large land invasion in the early hours of May 2. One factor that may have led to the crackdown was how close it occurred to the planned May 10 celebrations for the fideicomiso; a second factor may have been due to local residents attempting to circumvent the CE-MRC's authority.[44] The land grabs continued on a small scale in Colonias Aurora, Villada, and Reforma in June. For each lot of land, a paracaidista had to pay 200 pesos for an identification card (*credencial*) issued by Odón Madariaga.[45] The invasions created a climate of anarchy in Ciudad Neza, with one report stating, "It's evident that the chaotic situation that prevails in Ciudad Neza has manifested itself in the minds of colonos and has created a state of confusion in respect to the legality and benefits of the fideicomiso."[46] As land values soared and images of humble families holding their land titles became more prevalent in the press, collective land invasions intended to circumvent the slow wheels of bureaucracy possessed a strong appeal to poor *capitalinos* willing to use illegal and direct force in order to secure a property lot.[47]

In October 1974, Odón Madariaga's men clashed with long-terms residents of Ciudad Lago after they invaded unsettled lands and subdivided them into 150 land plots.[48] The symbolism of Madariaga's invasion in Ciudad Lago speaks volumes. Ciudad Lago rivaled El Sol as the most inhospitable and dangerous settlement in Ciudad Neza, stigmatized by both the press and neighboring residents. It was a remote corner of land wedged between the Periférico Highway and the airport's runways, highly susceptible to flooding and the least serviced colonia in the municipality. The fact that Odón Madariaga was reduced to trafficking lands in Ciudad Lago signals his desperation and the exhaustion of paracaidismo in the area. The flow of invasions had dried up, and the large swathes of open lands were gone.

The newly occupied lands became battle zones for rival political factions. The UGOCM made their first forays into Ciudad Neza in 1973 and soon began to encroach upon Odón Madariaga's territory. The UGOCM's incursions were met with angry mobs and pistoleros. On September 23, 1973, Odón and Angel led a crowd of two hundred supporters to attack and disrupt a large

UGOCM assembly meeting with bricks, bats, and a few pistols.[49] In the melee, Aristeo Pérez López and Ángel Ávila Jácome stole a UGOCM member's car and plowed into a crowd of hundreds of people as they attempted to flee the scene. In the end, seventeen people were detained and hauled off to a nearby jail.[50] Oliverio Aguilar, a member of the UGOCM and local leader of the neighborhood association in Colonia Maravillas, was detained and tortured in police custody in the hours following the melee.[51] That week, a pistolero brought in from Guerrero assassinated a journalist from *Pugna* (a local paper that was critical of Fineza) and a bystander.[52]

To echo a sentiment articulated by Enrique Maza in his coverage of Ciudad Neza during this period, "it is impossible to detail case by case."[53] Conflicts over invaded lands were resolved through late-night assassinations and backdoor meetings only alluded to in the press and internal police files. Traces of Oliverio Aguilar's detention and torture exist in the archival record because he was a recognized leader in a national organization (UGOCM) with the resources to directly petition the president and secure meetings with left-leaning figures in the PRI.[54] Less documentation and details are available for the anonymous colonos who were "arrested and locked up in clandestine jails" or evicted from their homes as a form of retribution.[55] Short of public scandals, the PRI could tolerate Madariaga's violent attacks on the UGOCM. The security and safety of UGOCM activists in Neza had less to do with the rule of law and more to do with the rumors of their gun caches, whether true or false.[56] Rogelio Vargas's life was threatened in four shoot-outs with Odón Madariaga's men between 1973 and 1975. While we can say his survival was partially based on luck, it was also partially based on the fact that he shot back. When the rule of law and even a semblance of justice failed to function, the threat and use of physical violence structured local politics more powerfully than ever before. It was, however, only one factor in a much larger process. The stakes remained high for the government to regularize Ciudad Neza's land tenure and put an end to its leyenda negra.

Leaders in the PRI were acutely aware that the success of Fineza was as much of a political question as an economic one. As a result, they made public promotion a cornerstone of Fineza's operation. A total of 1.7 million flyers and 8,100 posters were distributed in 1973.[57] A series of public forums were held in various school auditoriums to address the colonos' concerns and guide them through the steps necessary to receive their land titles. Fineza's employees went door to door to secure support for the program and organized "information brigades" to promote Fineza in popular market places. Most importantly, President Echeverría visited Ciudad Neza each May 15 to mark the anniversary of Fineza and attempt to sway public opinion in its favor.

Fineza at Work

Amid all the chaos, a combination of political pressure, public will, and legal decrees gave some sense of coherence and momentum to Fineza's program. Determining the number of lots regularized by Fineza on an annual basis is a challenge for scholars. Statistics vary across different sources, along with the terms employed to categorize their respective data. After reviewing estimates more recently published, it appears as if government officials at the time reported the number of lots registered to be regularized in the future (in the process of gaining a formal land title) as actually "regularized" (a completed process). Nevertheless, roughly 1,000 lots were regularized in 1973 and 760 lots in 1974.[58] In its first year of operation (May 1973–May 1974), 39,494 people visited a Fineza office to make a payment deposit, and 15 million pesos were deposited into the land trust.[59] While 1,760 regularized lots is a minuscule number for a municipality with 150,000 lots, there were thousands of households locked into the process and making monthly payments. In 1975, the numbers rose steadily, and by the end of 1976, roughly 28,000 lots had been granted formal land titles, with an additional 20,000 in the following year (48,000 from 1973 to 1977).[60] However, numbers alone fail to paint a complete picture. The publicity achieved by tens of thousands of families who received new land titles with official stamps of approval was enough to create a sense of momentum and progress. The images of endless lines of colonos waiting to make their monthly payment in the main Fineza building reminds us of the actual people who gained formal rights for their land, even if it was founded on unjust terms.[61] The momentum generated by the land titling process was reinforced and strengthened by the numerous public works projects implemented during this period.

The physical manifestations of Fineza were also visible in the rise of public works projects. This period of urbanization in Ciudad Neza can be divided into two phases. The first half (1970–73) witnessed improvements in electrification, drainage tunnels, water piping, and road conditions for two main thoroughfares (Pantitlán and Adolfo López Mateos). These projects were carried out by the state government (Estado de México) and largely financed by loans secured by Carlos Hank from Chase Manhattan Bank.[62] In this initial phase, the piecemeal installation of water and electric services came amid the social disorder and upheaval caused by the payment strike. If they were intended to quell the unrest, the new services did little to appease Ciudad Neza's residents.

The second phase transpired after the Fineza agreements, between 1973 and 1976. Again, sizable loans were negotiated from Banobras and private banks (800–850 million pesos) to finance new infrastructure and service projects. Carlos Hank subcontracted the Associated Civil Engineers (Ingenieros Civiles Asociados, ICA), Mexico's largest private engineering firm, to begin work on water and drainage services.[63] In the first year after the Fineza agreements, seventeen primary schools were constructed, five market places were outfitted with urban services, major thoroughfares were paved, and roughly 8.5 million pesos were invested in water treatment plants.[64] Attention to human control over water increased in this period. Drainage systems linked Ciudad Neza's public utilities to surrounding canals to alleviate summer flooding and to safely expel waste from the municipality. For an area with a population of over one million people, the energy required for the electric generators to pump out the water surpassed the amount of energy consumed by the entire state of Tlaxaca.[65] In other areas, such as road work, the projects lurched forward in infrequent spurts due to financial constraints. Overall, it can be summarized that genuine advances in electrification outpaced the persistent problems of potable water; the distribution of cheap voltage was much easier than that of clean water.

The drive to urbanize Ciudad Neza was also accompanied by the launch of a new park in the eastern section of Neza. The Parque del Pueblo, a centerpiece of Fineza, was envisioned as a symbol of urban planning surrounded by the endless rows of subdivisions. Notable for its size and budget, the park featured green lawns, tree-lined walkways, an artificial lake, and its own zoo.[66] The Parque del Pueblo served several different purposes. First, it addressed a popular demand for a public park in a municipality composed of dirt roads, homes, markets, bars, bath houses, modest churches, and shoddy wrestling arenas. With the Plaza de Toros closed down, the Parque del Pueblo fulfilled a strong community demand while also helping the PRI distinguish Fineza from previous failures at reform. As a minireplica of the neighboring San Juan de Aragón, the Parque del Pueblo served a larger purpose: the projection of power through human mastery over nature. In an effort to combat social connotations associated with Ciudad Neza's flooding, dust storms, and desert plains, the image of a verdant park created through modern engineering and maintained by the parks department signaled the rationalization of space for public order.

The Mexican state's intervention in Ciudad Neza's urbanization also produced a smaller project called Acción Casa. Modest in scale, Acción Casa sold building materials (brick, cement, wood, tools) at bare-minimum costs, all subsidized by the state.[67] Acción Casa grew out of AURIS and soon established six sites in the second half of the seventies. At one of the Acción Casa sites, a new lot owner could buy all of the necessary materials to build their own home at a basic level. They also distributed manuals and literature produced by AURIS on autoconstrucción for Mexico's "popular classes."[68] The significance of Acción Casa went beyond bricks and mortar. Its launch signaled the Mexican government's open recognition and partial legitimization of autoconstrucción. With Acción Casa, Mexican leaders resigned themselves to the fact that a self-built home for a poor urban dweller was an undeniable feature of urban life in modern Mexico. Without underestimating the importance of Acción Casa, it was a minor concession to the self-help housing models promoted by the United Nations and the Organization of American States (OAS).[69] Acción Casa was a local experiment that was never elevated to a national level like CORETT or Infonavit.

Overall, the pace of Mexico's first significant drive to regularize informal settlements was gradual but steady. In Ciudad Neza, corruption, mismanagement, and dissident neighborhood associations coexisted with compliant colonos, monthly payments, land title regularization, ad campaigns, and public works projects. Momentum ebbed after 1977 yet maintained an average of 8,000 land titles regularized until the program (later renamed Plan Santugio) ended in 1991.[70] In total, Fineza granted 159,000 formal land titles over the course of eighteen years (1973–91).[71] Fineza's focused work in Ciudad Neza contributed to the overall process of land regularization in Mexico City's metropolitan area. After factoring the various agencies together (i.e., Fineza, CORETT, Fideurbe), approximately 63,255 land titles were granted to informal property lots in the Mexico City metropolitan area between 1970 and 1976. The number of land titles benefited 315,320 people.[72]

* * *

A summation of Fineza requires a multisided approach that weighs its results on various levels. This chapter has synthesized official data from government reports to serve as an empirical foundation for a social history of the events and actors surrounding Fineza's land regularization program. One of the chapter's aims was to highlight the central role of illegal land invasions and *líderes sociales* (Odón Madariaga Cruz, Rogelio Vargas Soriano, UGOCM) for future studies that take a more systematic approach to Fineza's financial consequences. At a very basic level, any summation of Fineza would have to start with the consideration that its very foundations were unjust and financially burdensome for Ciudad Neza's residents. It openly legitimated land fraud and compensated the perpetrators. The Mexican government squandered an opportunity to create humane living conditions capable of future growth and upward mobility for Ciudad Neza's residents in the 1970s. Although it was not a break from the past, Fineza did mark the beginning of a series of reforms that eventually brought about genuinely improved living conditions and reliable public services for large sections of Ciudad Neza by the 1990s. The central point here is that at the moment when these reforms began in 1973, the financial burdens placed on colonos, the toleration of Odón Madariaga's land invasions, and impunity granted to the fraccionadores were all products of policy decisions that went against legal norms and were all factors that further ensnared residents in impoverished conditions.

The 159,000 land plots regularized by Fineza / Plan Santugio did transform Ciudad Neza from an "informal city" into a proper municipality (*municipio*). Still a site of informal economies (i.e., transportation, textiles, furniture, illicit drugs, food), its land tenure and property lots had been largely incorporated into formal state agencies. At its core, the mounds of paperwork and land contracts represented the definitive insertion of public lands into the capitalist real estate market through state intervention.

For residents, their land titles prevented arbitrary evictions, afforded them legal rights in court cases, built wealth for homeowners, and provided a sense of security ("a peace of mind") for those in the most precarious sectors of the economy. The drainage systems and paved roads installed under the auspices of the Fineza Land Trust were visible and tangible reforms directly felt by residents in their everyday lives. In isolation, the introduction of new services and property titles under Fineza could be viewed as significant reforms.

When compared to families who benefited from social housing programs, the Mexican government's unjust application of the law and unequal distribution of rights becomes all the more apparent. The residents of housing complexes covered throughout this work (Unidad Santa Fe, San Juan de Aragón) were not forced to make back payments for fraudulent land titles, not required to pay for the installation of public services, and did not have to pay extortion fees to urban caciques like Odón Madariaga. Financial burdens imposed in violation of legal norms placed Ciudad Neza's residents at a disadvantage to other strata and highlight how the alleviation of poverty does not always lead to a decline in social inequality.

In the previous chapters, we have focused on how social movements commonly associated with progressive reforms—labor unions, neighborhood associations—ended up defending or perpetuating inequality. In addition, they helped reinforce the PRI's dominance and its rituals of marginality on the urban periphery. The following chapter presents an alternative to this common narrative. The arrival of a group of young Jesuits to Ciudad Neza in 1969 marks a rupture in the seemingly perpetual cycle of violence–resistance–repression that played out in Ciudad Neza for two decades. Their history demonstrates how the failure of the state to provide critical social services could create a void filled by organized sectors of civil society.

8

Serve the People
Liberation Theology in Ciudad Nezahualcóyotl

The summer of 1971 was a decisive time in the lives of Ignacio Salas Obregón and Martín de la Rosa. The two Catholic activists had recently witnessed an armed assault on student demonstrators in an incident that would become known as the Corpus Christi massacre (June 10, 1971). The massacre exacerbated the growing tensions between Martín de la Rosa and Ignacio Salas Obregón. The two activists were united in their commitment to serve the poor and had recently moved to Ciudad Nezahualcóyotl. In fact, it was a previous massacre—the October 2, 1968, Tlatelolco massacre—that brought them together and served as a catalyst for their *promoción popular* (popular promotion) project in Ciudad Neza. The project was born out of a desire to "go to the masses." Now in the summer of 1971, the question of political violence brought the young Catholics' project in Ciudad Neza to the brink of total collapse.

The young Catholics (mainly Jesuits) came of age at a time when the number of students enrolled in colleges and universities surged around the world.[1] In the mid-twentieth century, the explosion of student activism on college campuses gave rise to a smaller, yet significant, phenomenon: radicalized students abandoning their universities to organize workers in factories, mines, fields, and slums around the world. Although its history is still fragmented and anecdotal, the desire to "go to the masses" was a pervasive feature of the New Left, spanning from midwestern college towns to European cities.[2] In revolutionary Cuba and China, this phenomenon took on a more organized character. These campaigns were viewed by state officials as a means to overcome the historical divisions between the city and the countryside—for middle-class youth to shed their "petit bourgeois worldview" by living and working with the rural peasantry.[3] The young Jesuits in Ciudad Neza shared this general spirit, but their deep commitment to the church and the teachings of Christ profoundly shaped how they interpreted what it meant to "go to the masses." Nevertheless, despite all the local variants, a unifying epistemological thread emerged out of this period: in order to *know* the masses, one had to *live* among the masses.

The following chapter veers away from the previously addressed themes of land tenure and housing to highlight the rise of civil society organizations in Ciudad Neza. In the case of the young Jesuits, the origins of their work in Ciudad Neza requires a brief overview of the impact Vatican II and CELAM II had on Catholicism in Mexico. These questions must be dealt with in their own right before turning to the history of liberation theology in Ciudad Neza.

Vatican II and the Poor in Mexico

The Second Vatican Council (1962–65) was a pivotal moment in world history. In sixteen documents, Vatican II articulated and mandated a reorientation within the Catholic Church. This reorientation shifted the church's attention to the poor and vulnerable, denounced all forms of war, placed a greater emphasis on social justice, and reorganized church hierarchy to give greater responsibility to the laity. In essence, it represented "an opening up" to the world for the Catholic Church. This reorientation was most forcefully expressed in the *Pastoral Constitution on the Church in the Modern World* (1965), a pillar of Vatican II that addressed marriage, culture, war, and economic development.[4]

Vatican II magnified underlying divisions within the church while also spurring new movements, institutions, and transnational alliances. In broad strokes, the Mexican church took a cautious approach to the council's proceedings. As historian Matthew Butler observes, the Mexican church did eventually commit "to acting more upon and in the world, but was fearful of assimilating a worldly pluralism that might transform its own decidedly hierarchical religious field."[5] Mexico's "hierarchical religious field" was extraordinarily strict and structured to restrict the parishioners' role in shaping the direction of the church after the bloody Cristero uprising. This development led to an acute dilemma: the hierarchical religious field that brought Mexico's Catholic Church growth and stability was also the religious hierarchical field the Second Vatican Council sought to reform.

After two decades of relative calm (1940–60), both within the church and in broader state-church relations, Vatican II revealed the latent fissures under the church's orderly facade. These divisions persisted between individuals and across regions. Geographically, conservative opposition to reforms was strongest in Puebla, Guadalajara, León, Morelia, and locally in Texcoco. These conservative strongholds were tempered by more moderate voices in support of the Vatican's reforms in Chiapas, San Luis Potosí, and Veracruz. The country's moderate dioceses have often been overshadowed in Mexico's historiography by the more visible and controversial figures in Cuernavaca, the epicenter of progressive Catholicism in Mexico.[6] The impact of Vatican II in Mexico was most visible in three distinct spheres: education, clergy-laity relations, and foreign missionary work (specifically, foreign missionaries coming to Mexico). For the remainder of this section, I briefly highlight a key example for each sphere particularly relevant to the formation of the young Jesuits.

Universidad Iberoamericana (Ibero) was the primary meeting point for the young Jesuits. Ibero began in 1943 as a fledgling Jesuit institution under the aegis of UNAM. For much of the 1940s, it survived as a small Catholic cultural center until it gained full status as a university in 1952. Ibero's initial years were marked by financial instability and a lack of vision. In 1956, a financial board of trustees established the overall mission of the university: an academic institution designed to train Mexico's future financial leaders in a modern curriculum modeled after departments in North America and Europe.[7] The Jesuit leadership rationalized that the university could instill Mexico's next generation of businessmen and economists with social Catholic values. The church's shift and conscious realignment with the poor after Vatican II had major repercussions for the Jesuit Order's multiple educational institutions in Mexico. Vatican II ushered in an intense period of debate among Mexico's Jesuit leaders, documented most vividly in the Jesuits' publication *Pulgas*. The debates over education culminated in the summer of 1968 with the finalization of a university *ideario*, a "statement of ideals" passed by the University Council to "orient the path of the university" in a direction guided by the values of humanism and social Catholicism expressed in the documents released by the Second Vatican Council.[8] The University Council's reorientation toward the poor was most concretely manifested in two key developments between 1968 and 1970. First, the university instituted a social service program for students to make community work in Mexico City's poor neighborhoods an essential component of their educational experience. Second, the Jesuit Order ruled in favor of closing its premiere high school, Instituto Patria, after deciding its elite student body symbolized a corruption of their values and was an institution that ran counter to the reforms promulgated by Vatican II.[9]

The second sphere of change can be found in Vatican II's call for the church to engage with worldly matters, as the world is "the place and the means for the lay faithful to fulfill their Christian vocation."[10] One of the most important forces behind these efforts was the Episcopal Mutual Aid Union (Unión de Mutua Ayuda Episcopal, UMAE). Formed in 1963 and primarily based in the Gulf Coast region (Tamaulipas, Veracruz), the UMAE established training centers and published manuals to guide priests in how to apply the principles of Vatican II to Mexico's local conditions. The UMAE's mass-produced literature and training manuals accompanied several reforms implemented in the Mexican church during the period: the introduction of Spanish (instead of Latin) into church liturgy, Bible study groups among parishioners, the use of folkloric music during services, and sociological studies of local dioceses as a tool for evangelization.[11] The UMAE's literature helped facilitate this process for Mexico's clergy, even serving as a general guide for the young Jesuits during their first year of giving Mass and holding services in Ciudad Neza.

If the UMAE represented a case of local clergy attempting to assimilate Vatican II's principles into Mexico's national context, then the CIDOC was an example of foreign clergy using Mexico as a site to subvert Vatican II on a global level. The Center for Intercultural Formation (CIF, a missionary training center from 1961 to 1966) and later the Intercultural Documentation Center (Centro Intercultural de Documentatión, or CIDOC, an education center founded in 1963 as part of CIF) were part of a larger hemispheric campaign to establish several centers across Latin America to train a new generation of Catholic missionaries.[12] The Catholic centers were a product of their time—a moment when Vatican II's reorientation coincided with the U.S.-led Alliance for Progress in Latin America.[13] For Mexico, the Jesuit leadership at Fordham University in New York established a new training center for missionaries in Cuernavaca, Mexico. When Fordham University and the Pontifical Commission for Latin America invested 52,000 dollars into the Cuernavaca missionary center (CIF), they had no intention of "subverting Vatican II on a global level"—that mission resided in the mind of CIF's director, Ivan Illich.[14]

At the time of CIF's founding, Ivan Illich was a thirty-five-year-old Catholic priest rising through the ranks of the church hierarchy. When he convinced the CIF board at Fordham to relocate the center to Cuernavaca, he viewed it as a small, but significant, countermeasure to the renewed mission of cultural imperialism in Latin America.[15] The CIF was established in a former luxury hotel in 1961. Located a two-hour drive south of Mexico City, Cuernavaca was a popular destination for weekend retreats due to its charming atmosphere and close proximity to the capital. Despite the luxury hotel's ghostly traces of former decadence, the empty ballrooms, shuddered casinos, and numerous guest rooms provided an ideal setting for a long-term missionary center. Well aware of clerical oversight and convention, Illich made sure to prohibit politics from the curriculum and assembled a professional staff of Spanish-language instructors. Within these confines, however, Illich took every opportunity to counter the perceived "invasion" of missionary projects he viewed as part of an overall effort to flatten out local cultures through Western modernization. In an updated preface to his 1967 article, "The Seamy Side of Charity," he clarified his intentions for opening the center: "The first [goal] was to help diminish the damage done by the papal order. Through our education program for missionaries we intended to challenge them to face reality and themselves, and either refuse their assignments or—if they accepted—to be a little less unprepared."[16] In the later part of the 1960s, Illich's antimissionary stance found its own particular resonance with the young Jesuits as outsiders attempting to establish themselves in Ciudad Neza's unfamiliar settlements.

Illich's dissidence could only be tolerated for so long. By 1967, the publication of his controversial article, "The Seamy Side of Charity," finally placed his priesthood in question. Illich's trial and meeting in the Vatican at the beginning of 1968 would determine his future as a clergyman in the church.[17] Yet even in this moment of personal crisis, there were larger issues at stake for Illich on the horizon. After its initial conference in 1955, the main council for Latin American bishops, the Latin American Episcopal Conference (Consejo Episcopal Latinoamericano y Caribeño, CELAM), was set to meet in Bogotá, Colombia, in 1968 for the first time in thirteen years. At the time, and to this day, CELAM II was viewed as a landmark event in the history of the Catholic Church in Latin America. Illich was a key figure in a transnational group of bishops and priests who privately met in the months leading up to the conference and were largely successful in making CELAM II a definitive moment in the legitimation of liberation theology for segments of the church in Latin America. After CELAM II, Illich would return back to Cuernavaca. Due to the intervention of Sergio Méndez Arceo, the CIDOC remained open as a nonecclesiastical entity, though it was no longer permitted to engage in missionary work or training.[18] Illich renounced his priesthood, yet his faith endured. In the following year, the young Jesuits from Ciudad Neza would visit the CIDOC for the first time and find themselves among an international cohort of young activists and intellectuals. The events of 1968, both in Mexico and around the world, brought hundreds of young people to Cuernavaca in search of answers and direction in turbulent times.

Los Profetas

CELAM II convened at a time of global rebellion. In the summer of 1968, the world watched as protests overshadowed the Democratic National Convention in Chicago and tanks rolled down the streets of Prague. It was a moment when young people spoke in an "international language of dissent."[19] Yet this international language possessed regional dialects inflected by local histories, political cultures, and positions in the global economy. Mexico's language of dissent spoke less of imperialist war and more of the expansion of democratic rights under an authoritarian regime. When Mexico City's various student groups united under the banner of the National Strike Council (Consejo Nacional de Huelga, CNH) on August 2, 1968, they focused their demands on civil liberties, amnesty for political prisoners, and justice brought against repressive authorities.[20]

The Tlatelolco massacre on October 2, 1968, was the most visible and shocking act of repression by the PRI in the late 1960s. At least three hundred people were murdered and many thousands more arrested that night. Wanton violence and repression traditionally reserved for rural unrest were meted out in the center of Mexico City's largest middle-class housing complex. Far from an isolated incident, the Tlatelolco massacre was simply the most vicious and concentrated act of repression in a coordinated series of arrests, raids, and roundups in the months leading up to the 1968 Olympic Games (October 12–27).[21]

The events of '68 shook Universidad Iberoamericana to its very foundations. Students from UNAM, IPN, and Ibero made up the bulk of the roughly fifteen hundred protesters arrested in a succession of police raids throughout the summer and fall. Ibero's campus was temporarily closed in September 1968 amid the military's seizures of UNAM and IPN's campuses.[22] The student movement coincided with internal reforms within Ibero designed to cultivate a more open dialogue with secular intellectuals (including even Marxist Lombardo Toledano).[23] In this politically charged moment, Ibero's Jesuit Order was reluctant to take an official position on the student movement in the immediate aftermath of the Tlatelolco massacre. Nevertheless, individual members of Ibero signed a statement in support of the student movement along with members of the Mexican Social Secretariat (Secretariado Social Mexicano, SSM). The aforementioned grouping, along with Bishop Sergio Méndez Arceo, were among the few voices within the church to publicly condemn the October 2 Tlatelolco massacre. For Martín de la Rosa, the church's silence in the face of open bloodshed was an act of complicity.[24]

In the aftermath of the Tlatelolco massacre, a small group of Jesuits began to live in Edmundo Campion, a community created by Jesuits in a poor section of the Federal District. In 1969, the community became a meeting place for a loose collection of young Jesuits informally dubbed "Los Profetas."[25] These young Jesuits were linked together by their desire to live the teachings of Christ through their service to the poor and vulnerable. Many, such as Martín de la Rosa, Luis del Valle, and Xavier de Obeso, studied at Jesuit universities in Europe at a time of heightened political and intellectual ferment. Martín de la Rosa met Xavier de Obeso in Paris when Obeso was an organizer for the Young Catholic Workers (Juventud Obrera Católica, JOC) and a parish priest in a working-class district of Paris.[26]

At different points over the span of 1968 and 1969, "Los Profetas" returned back to Mexico after their studies concluded in Europe. Xavier de Obeso's arrival was announced in a local newspaper (*Porvenir*) and was greeted in Monterrey with crowds and a local marching band.[27] Martín de la Rosa's return was much less eventful, although just as revealing. Miguel Rico Tavera, a university student who would later move to Ciudad Neza in 1970, remembered an encounter with Martín de la Rosa in 1969: "Martín went to go study in Europe and when he came back, I saw him with all of this long hair, a long beard, sandals, jeans. I asked him, 'What happened to you? Were you so poor over there that you ran out of suits? Or what?' It was then when he [Martín] began to talk to me about the 'preferential option for the poor.'"[28]

Although exact dates do not currently exist, the group of young Jesuits who would move to Ciudad Neza in 1969 began to meet and form in the weeks following the October 1968 Tlatelolco massacre. It was a tense moment of reflection and urgency, repression, and regathering. Martín de la Rosa wrote, "Even a year after [the massacre], the student groups were confused, dispersed, and traumatized."[29] It was in this period when Martín de la Rosa met José Luis Sierra Villarreal at Universidad Iberoamericana. José Luis Sierra was a former student at the Monterrey Institute of Technology and Higher Education (Instituto Tecnológico y de Estudios Superiores de Monterrey, ITESM, more commonly known as Tec) who was active in various Catholic student groups on campus. After leaving Monterrey for Mexico City, José Luis Sierra reconnected with Ignacio Salas Obregón, also a former Tec student who was active with the Catholic group Professional Student Movement (Movimiento Estudiantil Profesional, MEP). After dropping out of Tec, Ignacio Salas Obregón traveled around Mexico as a full-time organizer for MEP and sporadically worked out of an office shared with the Catholic Association of Mexican Youth (Asociación Católica de la Juventud Mexicana, ACJM).[30] In search of direction, Ignacio Salas Obregón began to spend more time with Martín de la Rosa—mutual friends with José Luis Sierra and Xavier de Obeso.

In September 1969, Luis del Valle and De la Rosa initiated a series of meetings and discussions among a loose collection of young Catholics "in search of a more authentic Christianity."[31] The informal circle grew as they published an influential bulletin called *Liberación* (1969–72), which functioned as a collective organizer for clergy influenced by liberation theology.[32] The fall of 1969 witnessed two countervailing trends responsible for De la Rosa's move to Ciudad Neza. The first was a landmark conference organized by Sociedad Teológica Mexicana (Primer Congreso Nacional de Teología), widely considered "the birth of liberation theology in Mexico." For one week, over seven hundred people, priests, and laity worked together in small groups to discuss education, the church, politics, family life, and capitalism in Mexico through a theological worldview framed by CELAM II.[33]

The conference revitalized the young Jesuits' spirits shortly after a moment of failure and demoralization. In the fall of 1969, the grouping organized around *Liberación* planned and wrote a manifesto protesting the massacre of Tlatelolco. On October 2, 1969, one year after the massacre, not one newspaper agreed to publish the manifesto. Furthermore, Mexico City's archbishop Miguel Darío Miranda y Gómez intervened to halt the group's plans to hold commemoration events for the massacre's victims in ten churches. The group's attempt to organize church parishioners through official channels was blocked by the diocese's highest authorities.[34] In their efforts to "go to the masses," it soon became clear they would have to circumvent the bishops they once admired as seminary students. Martín de la Rosa reflected, "Unlike what happened in the 1968 movement, when students asked the masses to join their cause, at the end of 1969, the idea was the opposite: it was necessary for us to join the masses."[35] In collectively deciding to move to Ciudad Neza, the young Jesuits were replicating a phenomenon found throughout the global sixties: students and middle-class youth abandoning campus life in search of a true revolutionary agent. Unlike many of their counterparts in the New Communist Movements of Italy, France, and the United States, the young Jesuits' move to Ciudad Neza was not completely independent and of their own volition.[36] Between 1969 and 1972, they were part of the Jesuit Order's general turn toward marginalized communities and maintained some connection to the official church hierarchy. With this notable distinction, it can still be argued the young Jesuits were on their own as they ventured into Mexico's largest shantytown at the beginning of 1970.

The Young Jesuits Arrive in Ciudad Neza

The young Jesuits' project in Ciudad Neza was launched in October 1969, one year after the Tlatelolco massacre. Their arrival did not produce the kind of cinematic scene one might expect: naive youth disembarking from a bus into a strange new world. Their participation in the Sociedad Teológica Mexicana, the CIDOC, holiday services, and the need to secure a church space made their move more gradual and sporadic until January 1970.[37] By this time, the Jesuits had permanently moved to Ciudad Neza and established the Iglesia de Refugio in the Aurora section of Ciudad Neza (the same neighborhood as Odón Madariaga).[38]

The exact number of people and the chronology of when they moved to Ciudad Neza is still a matter of dispute and complicated by the fact that many individuals came and went in the first year of the project. It can be said with certainty that Martín de la Rosa, José Luis Sierra, Ignacio Salas Obregón, Carlos Garza Falla, and Miguel Rico Tavera were the first to move to Ciudad Neza in 1969–70. Two homes were secured by group members, one linked more closely to the church on Calle Cucaracha and a second rented out by Ignacio Salas Obregón and José Luis Sierra on Calle Macorina.[39] As expected, the presence of university students and young priests was quite a sight in Ciudad Neza. Martín de la Rosa remembered the group arrived in Ciudad Neza anticipating "a lot of antisocial behavior" based on the news. The community's initial suspicion of the young Jesuits was eased when Martín de la Rosa began to offer free literacy courses and after-school workshops to neighbors in Colonia Aurora.[40]

Overwhelmed and confused, the young Jesuits started to experiment with a variety of programs that were intended to cultivate a deeper relationship with the community. In their first year, they focused on three areas: pastoral work, education services, and a monthly bulletin. Of the three, their religious work formed the bedrock foundation for all other activities and projects. The young Jesuits immediately recognized the power of tradition in Ciudad Neza. For outsiders, Martín de la Rosa's status as a Jesuit priest lent them an air of legitimacy in the eyes of the residents. They carried out pastoral work in homes, community centers, and the Iglesia de Refugio. On Saturday afternoons, they held a lively Mass for youth (*misa de juventud*) where they integrated folk music into their services, developed a rapport with some local youth, and built direct links to the community in Colonia Aurora. Sermons and religious activities were centered on the social realities of Ciudad Neza and discussed from an evangelical point of view that extolled liberation for the masses.[41] In particular, the young Jesuits' sermons linked "the Christian commitment" to "the revolutionary commitment" in a spirit reminiscent of the ideas professed by Colombian priest Camilo Torres.[42]

The harsh realities of Ciudad Neza forced the young Jesuits to seek answers in new places or return to old ones with new questions. Their rooms were lined with stacks of books and littered with mimeographed pamphlets. Operating at a distance from friends, family, and clerical authorities, Ciudad Neza provided a space for rumination, study, and debate. At the same time, their isolation and autonomy were only partial, as they maintained close relations with progressive Catholics and leftist students in the Federal District. Guillermo Casas, a Jesuit who lived in Edmundo Campion in 1970, remembers, "From this period, I remember frequent visits from José Luis Sierra, Nacho [Ignacio] Salas, and Carlos Garza ... with discussions of the situation and the times, just as much about social issues as religious ones, confronting each member's own life and work. It was an intense period."[43]

Of all the members, Ignacio Salas Obregón dove the deepest into the works of Karl Marx. Mario Ramirez, an economics student at UNAM, noted that Salas Obregón "had a photographic memory for Marx's writings and a tremendous capacity for political theory. He could spend hours upon hours just sitting, typing away, and writing."[44] In 1970, Salas Obregón and De la Rosa formed the Centro Crítico Universitario (Cecrun) to act as a bridge between the young Jesuits in Ciudad Neza and universities in the Federal District. Cecrun held forums on themes surrounding liberation theology at UNAM and Ibero, primarily conceived of as the theoretical component of their project. In surveying all the forums and debates from this period, four sources stand out as the most influential: Karl Marx, Paulo Freire, Germán Zabala, and Roger Vekemans.[45]

The young Jesuit collective in Ciudad Neza engaged in a deep study of Karl Marx's work, with each individual embracing it to varying degrees. In the 1970–71 period, there was a basic consensus among members that capitalism could not exist without widespread exploitation, and it presented a fundamental barrier to achieving a society of mutual respect, dignity, and peace based on the Christian doctrine of evangelical love. The young Jesuits' openness to socialism or socialistic values, however, did not imply a wholesale adoption of Marxism, particularly its core tenets of historical materialism, atheism, and call for the abolition of the traditional family. Collectively, the group focused most of its attention on Marx's works on political economy (*Das Kapital, Grundrisse*). These foundational texts were studied concurrently with works emerging from the *dependistas* (proponents of dependency theory) such as Andre Gunder Frank, Aníbal Quijano, and Pablo González Casanova.[46] Overall, Marxism functioned more as a mode of analysis than a guide to action.

The young Jesuits' study of Marx and various dependistas manifested itself in a programmatic summation of Mexican society that was internally circulated in 1971. Enumerated in nine points, they claimed the Mexican state betrayed the revolution for a mode of capitalist development defined by external dependency, foreign capital's domination over internal markets, and the enrichment of a small number of local elites. The PRI is singled out as a repressive force and political entity responsible for a society incapable of resolving "the fundamental problems of mankind: justice, democracy, and true liberty." Their move to Ciudad Neza only reinforced their belief that "the Mexican student movement was a social explosion, a symptom of a crisis, but incapable of real social change."[47] For the young Jesuits, radical change could only be brought about by those who have "nothing to lose but their chains."[48] For Ignacio Salas in particular, it was the dispossessed campesinos and exploited workers he encountered on his trips across Mexico who would form the backbone of the revolution—a people with no stake in the current society and who would not recoil from the violence and destruction necessary to overthrow the state's repressive apparatus.

Marx's sweeping study of capitalism did not anticipate the rise of a social class represented in the colonias of Ciudad Neza. As time progressed, they were viewed by some as "the massification of the lumpenproletariat." While the notion of Neza as "lumpen" had some basis in reality, it was a misguided understanding of both lumpenproletariat as a social category and Ciudad Neza as a home to it. Marx identified the lumpenproletariat as "vagabonds, discharged, ex-convicts, runaway slaves . . . swindlers, beggars . . . pickpockets, gamblers, brothel keepers, rag-pickers, knife-grinders; in short, the entirely undefined, disintegrating mass."[49] Officials in the Soviet Union characterized the lumpen as an unorganized class composed of individuals and small groupings who tended to survive by illegal means, lacked class consciousness, and could be easily co-opted by reactionary forces.[50] For the young Jesuits, it was evident the colonos of Ciudad Neza were not proletarians in the traditional sense—factory workers, trade union members, wage laborers—yet neither did they conform to Marx's description of the lumpenproletariat. A combination of public stigma and Marxist dogma distorted the Mexican left's view of Ciudad Neza's residents and prevented them from recognizing their potential to be organized into a revolutionary movement. The Mexican Communist Party devoted little attention to mapping out the contours of the "lumpen" and failed to see large numbers of colonos did in fact labor (even if informally) in the construction, textile, furniture, and auto industries. Their exploitation was not lost on the progressive Catholics in Mexico and Latin America more broadly.

Throughout the continent, Vatican II and CELAM II reoriented the Jesuit Order toward the slums and shantytowns of major cities in larger numbers. The preferential option for the poor amplified the number of Jesuits in close contact with residents who were understudied by scholars and overlooked by political activists. Within this regional shift, there were several Catholic leaders who viewed the absence of a communist presence in poor shantytowns (Brazil being a notable exception) as a rare opportunity to organize a large base of poor shanty dwellers susceptible to communist influence and infiltration.[51] Jesuit sociologist Roger Vekemans became one of the most vocal and active proponents of this view through his work with Chile's Center of Social and Economic Development for Latin America (Centro de Desarrollo Económico y Social para América Latina, DESAL). After years of research and investigation in Santiago's "misery belt," DESAL was one of the few academic centers in Latin America to carry out systematic and comprehensive studies of the informal poor before the 1970s. DESAL's balance of sociological inquiry with Catholic morality in the pursuit of social integration (*promoción popular*) appealed to the young Jesuits in Ciudad Neza.[52] As they struggled to make sense of Ciudad Neza's inhabitants, DESAL's short-lived Marginality Project (1966–69) provoked a sharp debate among the young Jesuits and cut to the core questions of how to define the essential characteristics of this undefined social class in Latin America.

During the second half of the 1960s, the Rockefeller Foundation funded DESAL's Marginality Project. The project set out to study Chile's "marginal masses" and develop a program to address their impoverished conditions. The divisions that emerged between Roger Vekemans and Argentine José Nun were emblematic of the contending views over the nature of Latin America's hyperurbanization in the 1960s.[53] Vekemans, a Belgian Jesuit who arrived in Chile in 1956, helped establish Chile's sociology department at the Pontificia Universidad Católica de Chile in 1959. While elements of dependency theory can be found in Vekemans's analysis, he generally ascribed to a worldview closer to modernization theory. This was made evident in his belief that the marginal shanty dweller was the human face of Latin America's failure to progress to a modern level of capitalist development; marginality was the social expression of a society caught in transition between "traditional" and "modern" economies. For Vekemans, the roots of marginality could be found in the "historical continuity of economic imperialism" in which development poles concentrated in one or two urban centers produce limited growth at the expense of the hinterlands ("internal colonialism"). In a blunt description of those in the marginal class, Vekemans writes, "It can be said that they are not socially or economically integrated into society, into a class system, since they do not belong to an economic system . . . they are in neither the countryside that expels them nor the city that does not welcome them." He goes on to conclude, "They do not belong to the primary or secondary sectors, they are nobody, they do nothing more than exist, to populate a small piece of land, which is a no-man's-land."[54] In the face of this predicament, Vekemans formulated a strategy called *promoción popular* (later adopted by Christian Democrats in Chile and Venezuela) with the ultimate aim of economic and social integration of the marginal poor into Chilean society as a means to promote democracy and combat communism.

Roger Vekemans's theory of marginality addressed a major social phenomenon with a set of methodologies accepted in the social sciences and with a vision of socioeconomic integration made palpable for policy makers. His emphasis on the integration of popular sectors into the nation's development "through the organization of the marginal sectors themselves by means of the exercise of their solidarity" found an audience among Frei's administration, foreign agencies in the Alliance for Progress, and progressive Catholics around the world.[55] As a result, it also became a central target for Marxist José Nun. Nun viewed marginality as an inherent product of capitalist development in a dependent country. He postulated that the increase of foreign capital in Latin American countries produced a level of marginality that went beyond Marx's concept of an "industrial reserve army." According to Nun, the un- and underemployed in Latin America's cities constituted something else, what he called a "marginal mass." It was a term that recognized that the poor and informal urban sector in Latin America represented a more permanent, integral, and significant social class than what existed in the European societies of Marx's day.[56] The critical distinction was noted and analyzed by the young Jesuits in their study sessions but limited by the fact that Nun offered no clear solution beyond the vague mention of radical economic transformation. Ultimately, the debates over the sociological dimensions of marginality did not deter the young Jesuits' enthusiasm for taking up the mantle of promoción popular for their project in Ciudad Neza, despite the fact that they remained highly critical of Vekemans's theory of marginality. Still, the general concept of promoción popular left several unanswered questions. Promoción popular toward what end? Socialism? Social harmony? And by what means? The consensus around education as a vehicle for liberation provided some direction, but it fell short of how to conceptualize and carry out a radical education project in Ciudad Neza. Fortunately for the young Jesuits, their predicament arose at a time when Ivan Illich's CIDOC was in the process of becoming a global hub for radical pedagogy in nearby Cuernavaca.

Pedagogy of the Oppressed

The beginning of 1969 was a moment of truth for Ivan Illich. After Illich refused to comply with the secrecy oaths of his trial at the Vatican, he was subsequently cast out as a heretic. No longer funded by the CIF in New York and forbidden from training Catholic missionaries, the CIDOC's future hung in the balance. In this period, his faith in Christ never wavered.[57] For all his dissidence and subversion, Illich never went beyond the bounds of religious doctrine to justify his actions. After he renounced his public persona as a priest, he continued to carry out his priestly duties, remained celibate, and kept the Bible at the center of his life. The CIDOC, now located in a "California-style" mansion on a mountainside in Cuernavaca, was rebranded as a "humanistic institution" open to all who shared its humanist ideals and a desire to learn. With its funds cut and full-time staff to pay, student enrollment was more crucial than ever. Between the flurry of press coverage over his controversial trial at the Vatican and his soon-to-be-released manifesto *Deschooling Society* (1970), Illich's notoriety caused a stir and projected the CIDOC into the secular world of *New York Times* readers, progressive-minded educators, and radicalized students.[58] For better or worse, the notoriety also attracted a new generation of counterculture dropouts in search of "the eccentric guru of the revolution"—a title Illich thoroughly disdained.[59]

The CIDOC built upon its Spanish-language classes and expanded them for a broader audience. The staff also developed a program of courses with an overarching emphasis on Latin American studies and pedagogy. Through well-organized conferences, seminars, and workshops, the CIDOC became a beacon for individuals interested in alternative forms of education intended to foster critical thinking and erode social control. The center brought prominent education theorists such as Jonathan Kozol (*Death at an Early Age*, 1967),

Paul Goodman (*Growing Up Absurd*, 1960), John Holt (*How Children Learn*, 1967), and Paulo Freire (*Pedagogy of the Oppressed*, 1968) to Cuernavaca for intensive workshops on pedagogy.[60] At any point of the year, there could be between one hundred to five hundred students registered for classes with titles such as De-schooling the Society taught by Paul Goodman and Mary and Eve: A Political Theology for the Women's Movement by Davida Foy Crabtree (Boston Seminary Student) and lectures offered by Cuernavaca's local assortment of expats and exiles, including German psychoanalyst Erich Fromm, blacklisted communist Lini de Vries, and Brazilian Marxist Francisco Juliao.[61]

The young Jesuits were thrust into this vibrant mix in November 1969. For one week, they joined over a hundred attendees from across the Americas in a conference on alternative education. Theoretical and practical, the conference delved into questions of how to design learning spaces that did not perpetuate the same oppressive hierarchies they opposed as socially conscious educators. Teaching philosophies commonly referred to today as "student-based learning," "collaborative learning," and "problem-posing methods" were discussed, and later pioneered, by conference participants with distinctly anticapitalist aims. At the November 1969, January 1970, and March 1970 conferences, Paulo Freire demonstrated the teaching methods for adult literacy programs he cultivated in his work for the Brazilian and Chilean governments over the course of the previous decade (1961–64 and 1964–69, respectively).[62] On a practical level, the method was based on students learning a set of fifteen to twenty words that were relevant to their daily lives (e.g., *house, milk, rent, vote*). The basic mechanics of phonetic literacy were taught in connection with their social meaning and aided by visual displays (illustrations, picture slides) for deeper connections. The practical objectives served loftier ambitions: "The psycho-social method is a method of raising awareness [*conscientização*, 'critical consciousness']. It makes those who are illiterate reflect on their own reality and on the reality of humankind to bring them to a deeper understanding of these realities. Through reflection, the illiterate leaner is able to critically grasp and understand reality, form a critical conscious, act critically, and integrate themselves into that reality with the ability to consciously change it."[63] For Freire, the ends had to determine the means; the point was not to simply teach about liberation but to liberate how one taught.

Freire's seminars had a profound impact on Martín de la Rosa. The young Jesuit was not alone in this regard. Years later, Jonathan Kozol, also in attendance, told Freire of the inner turmoil Friere provoked in his life: "It has not been easy to be faced with painful choices of the kind you pose for me.... No other author, teacher, friend, ally—has left my life so different."[64] The 1969–70 CIDOC conferences represented a coming together of previously disparate individuals in the education reform movement. Inexperienced and unsure of themselves, the young Jesuits would meet two individuals at the CIDOC who would directly influence their project in Ciudad Neza. Amid the lively debates and smaller crowds of attendees scattered throughout the CIDOC's courtyards and garden terraces was Alex Morelli, a French priest of the Dominican Order. Interned in Dachau by the Nazis during the war, he later moved to Latin America (first Uruguay, then Mexico in 1967), where he published several works on violence, capitalism, and religious scripture. Their chance encounter in Cuernavaca would eventually lead to his arrival in Ciudad Neza—a development that will be detailed later in the chapter.

Secondly, the young Jesuits made a direct and ongoing connection with Colombian Germán Vladimir Zabala Archila. A close friend of Camilo Torres, Germán Zabala was a Marxist-humanist who co-founded the Golconda movement. Golconda was led by clergy in support of liberation theology who collaborated with local university students to set up several schools in Bogotá's poor neighborhoods. As a trained mathematician, Germán Zabala worked out a detailed and comprehensive program for popular education as a tool for community development. For the young Jesuits in Neza, the practical-minded Germán Zabala filled a void left by Freire's more generalized philosophical writings.[65] For the sake of brevity, I highlight a concise passage from CELAM II promoted by Germán Zabala that gets to the heart of humanism and foreshadows the future split experienced by the young Jesuits: "The uniqueness of the Christian message does not so much consist in the affirmation of the necessity for structural change, as it does in an insistence on the conversion of men and women who will bring about this change. We will not have a new continent without new and reformed structures, but above all, there will be no new continent without new people."[66] This passage inverts the traditional Marxist-Leninist dialectic of societal change—a relative minority (vanguard) leads a mass movement to overthrow the preexisting order, dismantles the power structure, and begins to transform people's consciousness on a national or regional scale through the establishment of new revolutionary structures ("The ruling ideas of each age have ever been the ideas of its ruling class").[67] The inverse of this dialectic contains a philosophical kernel with decisive implications for the kind of political work the young Jesuits were navigating in Ciudad Neza: the emphasis on people's consciousness over structures allows for a more gradual, incremental strategy as opposed to the need for radical structural change from a new revolutionary regime. This ideological difference, concomitant with the question of violence, would soon come to the fore in Ciudad Neza.

Fractures and Splits, 1971–1972

The young Jesuits began to offer an array of classes in 1970. Initially ambitious, some suffered from low attendance, while others succeeded. Night classes for workers on unionism, labor laws, and capitalism drew few attendees and failed miserably. "We clearly saw the fact that Ciudad Neza was a bedroom community, a fact that strongly conditioned the possibilities of doing work among workers," reflected Martín de la Rosa.[68] More success was found with adult literacy classes, public speaking workshops, and a theater group for neighborhood youth. A DFS report filed by a local informant notes their use of a slide projector (a direct influence of Freire's CIDOC workshop): "In the public speaking courses they motivate the participants with photographs, where one can see a poor child in the mud, a woman with an empty bucket for water, etc., with the deliberate purpose of inciting reactions against the government."[69] The young Jesuits delineated three levels of unity, starting with the broadest level of support among residents and narrowing down to a small nucleus of activists who conveyed a genuine commitment to revolutionary change.

As the project entered its second year in 1971, the slow, daily work of literacy classes and youth theater groups began to wear down the patience of the group, especially Ignacio Salas Obregón and José Luis Sierra. By this point, Salas Obregón had grown closer to Raúl Ramos Zavala, a former leader of the Communist Party's youth wing. Ramos Zavala shared a parallel history with Ignacio Salas: Ramos Zavala organized youth in Monterrey until he was reassigned to Mexico City by the Communist Party in 1969.[70] Several months later, Ramos Zavala was expelled from the party for a controversial position paper that advocated for armed self-defense. In March 1971, Salas Obregón internally circulated a scathing criticism of the promoción popular project in Ciudad Neza. In the letter, he identifies the source of their failure to mobilize the residents in Ciudad Neza: "There is no real class consciousness that questions the immediate and spontaneous interests of our class origins. . . . Our class is not only bourgeois but clerical, which assumes that the ideological indoctrination to this class is much more penetrating and has roots much deeper in us." He goes on to write, "This lack of class consciousness accounts for all of our abstract, chaotic, and idealistic ways we conceive and measure our work." Salas Obregón ends with a point that foreshadows his future direction: "The original motivation to be with the masses, motivated by bourgeois-Christian ideologies, has been modified for me in a sense that to be with the masses is not a question of being with them geographically but to be with them in their struggles . . . to engage in a struggle really capable of getting the masses out of this immense poverty."[71] It wasn't enough to live with the masses; one had to be willing to die for them as well.

The breaking point came in June 1971. On May 1, student protests boiled over and shut down the Autonomous University of Nuevo León (Universidad Autónoma de Nuevo León, UANL). Newly passed bylaws that eroded university autonomy and slashed annual budgets pitted members of the university against local politicians until President Echeverría was able to negotiate a settlement between the two sides. Despite the settlement, solidarity protests originally scheduled to be held in support of the Monterrey students proceeded as planned in Mexico City. On June 10, a crowd of ten thousand demonstrators were attacked by dozens of young men (Halcones) armed with long poles (*palos*) and high-caliber rifles. Dressed in civilian clothing, the Halcones were clandestinely trained by federal authorities to intimidate, assault, and terrorize street demonstrators. When the smoke cleared, some twenty-five students lay dead and dozens more critically wounded.[72] Salas Obregón and José Luis Sierra, who were among the protesters attacked by the Halcones, escaped relatively unscathed. Miguel Rico Tavera remembered, "José Luis and Nacho [Ignacio] went to the march where people were struck dead, and the two came back to Nezahualcóyotl later that night, furious . . . and they said, 'Real change is not possible unless it is achieved through armed struggle.' And from there, they broke with the Jesuits."[73]

Ignacio Salas Obregón and José Luis' split from the young Jesuits was not immediate. They would come and go for a few weeks, stopping by to sleep in Ciudad Neza and then leaving early the next morning. Ignacio and José Luis began to acquire guns and train with them in the mountains near Puebla (Rio Frio). Martín de la Rosa remained completely opposed to armed struggle on both practical and moral grounds. Martín commented, "Nacho and José Luis had no idea about guns, it was all really childish, they asked me to teach them how to handle weapons."[74] Father Xavier de Obeso was not as sure. In fact, Obeso played a significant role in instigating Salas Obregón to take up arms until the time came to go underground, at which point Obeso cracked under the pressure and bowed out from the struggle.

The lives of Che Guevara and Camilo Torres began to seem less abstract to Ignacio Salas Obregón. Images of revolutionaries with guns from Vietnam, Algiers, Montevideo, and Oakland circulated around the world and were reprinted in underground pamphlets distributed among Mexico's revolutionary youth. Salas Obregón looked not only abroad but also back to Mexico's own violent past. In Ignacio's case, he primarily drew inspiration not from Villa or Zapata but from the battalions of armed Catholic peasants with banners declaring their faith to the world: "¡Viva Cristo Rey!" According to Miguel Rico, Salas Obregón cited the Cristero soldiers of the 1920s as a source of inspiration and justification for taking up arms as a Catholic: "Nacho began to resort to the Cristiada, where the cristeros saw the need to take up arms to defend their religious position. . . . Ignacio said, 'We have the right to defend the dignity of the poor, our dignity as human beings.'"[75] An irrevocable division hardened between Salas Obregón and Martín de la Rosa, with contradictory influences pulling them down divergent paths. In July, Salas Obregón met with Luis del Valle, a slightly older priest in the loose collection of "Los Profetas" and a mentor figure to Ignacio. In his memoirs, del Valle recounts the last time he saw Ignacio in person: "Ignacio told me, 'From here on out, don't bother looking for me anymore,' that I wasn't going to see him anymore. He was going underground, clandestine, and that there was nothing more to say about it. He gave me a hug and left."[76] Ignacio Salas Obregón cut all ties with his former friends by not moving forward with them in the armed struggle. He was no longer Ignacio or Nacho but Vicente, a new name for a new identity.

Promoción Popular and Conservative Counterattack

The split in 1971 left the young Jesuits in shambles. Those who did not leave with Ignacio left out of frustration. Martín de la Rosa and an unnamed associate were left in the desolate plains of Ciudad Neza, their house on Calle Cucaracha, and the church across the street.[77] It could have ended then, but Martín had gone too far to turn back now. It was a period to regroup and rebuild. The anguish and turmoil provoked by Ignacio Salas Obregón's departure also clarified De la Rosa's vision and steeled his convictions. He looked outward, both in recruiting new life into the promoción popular project and in connecting that project to other segments in the progressive church.

Luis del Valle was instrumental in this transition. Initially part of the project, del Valle was assigned to a different diocese in 1970 and was not as physically present in Ciudad Neza as the other Jesuits. In the period surrounding the split, del Valle became a more permanent fixture in Ciudad Neza—holding religious services, teaching night classes, and working more closely with Martín de la Rosa to sink deeper roots into the community.[78] In the aftermath of the split, Martín de la Rosa gathered the small number of resources he could muster together and focused them entirely on popular education. Youth workshops and adult literacy courses met an expressed need of Ciudad Neza's residents and created a basis for sustained political work in the heart of Neza's fastest-growing colonia (Aurora). It was a style of political work that differed greatly from the exchanges common with the PRI's political patronage, often experienced by lining up to vote or being corralled into a rally. Instead, the young Jesuits carried out ongoing work in the realm of consciousness and focused on raising awareness of one's surroundings and the connections between one's surroundings and larger socioeconomic systems. They viewed the classroom as a space to encourage active participation (horizontal, democratic) and critical thinking among its students. This model also contrasted with the rigid and rote curriculum practiced in Ciudad Neza's public schools.

The Jesuits fared no better with the local clergy of the Catholic Church in Ciudad Neza. In 1972, there were thirty permanent priests, eight nuns, and one assistant bishop in Ciudad Neza. In reality, true power resided in the hands of three church rectors who controlled parishes of 100,000 to 150,000 members each. In Colonias Romero, Estado de México, and sections of Aurora, all fees collected from marriages, baptisms, and funerals were funneled directly to the rectors in a system where each priest was obligated to turn over the bulk of their funds to the appropriate corresponding rector. With no accountability or transparency for the collected funds, the rectors grew in wealth and power, leading to what a local priest described as "an authentic clerical caciquismo" in Ciudad Neza.[79]

The forces grouped around Martín de la Rosa represented a counterhegemonic pole to Ciudad Neza's clerical caciquismo. The arrival of Alex Morelli strengthened this counterhegemonic pole and further connected Martín de la Rosa's project to an even broader network of Dominican priests and figures in the progressive Church. Morelli's clerical position was protected by the Dominican Order and strengthened locally by his leadership role in Mexico's SSM.[80] Morelli received an invitation from "three Jesuits" in September 1971 (shortly after the split) and was given permission by his superiors to move to Ciudad Neza in March 1972.[81] Alex Morelli was a priest who grew disillusioned with developmentalism and came to view it as an impediment to individual and collective liberation. In his writings and work, he sought to dismantle the geopolitical framework of the Cold War: "The dividing line in the world today is not situated between the East and the West, between capitalist and socialist countries. . . . The separation is increasingly marked by the division between the oppressed and the oppressor: the oppressed who suffer under the yoke of imperialism, capitalism, and socialism."[82] Morelli's presence raised the profile of the promoción popular project in the eyes of progressive theologians around the world. Years later, Harvey Cox of Harvard Divinity School wrote, "Neza is the dark secret of Mexico. . . . Often its inhabitants seem to be crushed by the dust that burns the streets without shade, enveloped by the smell of rotting garbage. And Alex [Morelli], a kind and contemplative man, although an intellectual at heart, was present among them, as a sign of hope, a source of faith, recalling the promise of the Gospel of Christ."[83]

A prisoner in the Nazi concentration camps and a world traveler, Morelli was still shocked by the depths of poverty found in Ciudad Neza. In writing to a friend in France, he described Ciudad Neza as "a place without a flower, without a plant, without birds, without drinking water, without sewers, without garbage collection." He goes on to explain, "We live and bathe in dust. Right now, we live and move in mud. Imagine the infections born out of the dust, dust mixed with detritus and fecal matter, a place where pools of water are stagnant under a harsh sun; just imagine the smell."[84] Morelli viewed himself as living in a world created not by the failures of development but by the inevitable by-product of development. It only reinforced his belief in the church's preferential option for the poor: "We cannot participate in the liberation of oppressed people, confined in an intellectual office or protected by the reassuring walls of a classical convent. It appears that sharing in the problems, sufferings, and struggles of the poorest masses is an absolute condition to motivate a revolutionary praxis." He goes on to admit, "The conditions make it difficult to democratize education."[85] Morelli was clear where he stood when he arrived at Ciudad Neza in 1972: "I believe, with clear conviction, that capitalism, at its essence, is evil, while socialism is bad only in its most excessive perversions."[86] (At the time of writing, Morelli would have included the Soviet Union as an "excessive perversion" of socialism.)

The question of socialism defined the parameters of debate in 1972. Among the participants of the promoción popular project in Ciudad Neza, the question centered not on the viability of socialism but on its compatibility with the Bible. In this period, the Bible provided a possible template for a vision of an alternative society liberated from the trappings of modern capitalism. This debate was deepened with the arrival of José Porfirio Miranda in 1972.

José Porfirio Miranda moved to Ciudad Neza at a moment of existential crisis. Only a few months earlier, he gathered his family together in Torreón to announce, with deep regret, that he was leaving the priesthood to pursue his passion for philosophy. The former Jesuit was less motivated to move to Ciudad Neza as a political organizer than his colleagues: "I moved to Neza as a poor person, not to help the poor. I needed time to reflect, study, and write."[87] His work explored the notion of property in the Bible and sought to establish a direct link between Karl Marx's conception of justice and the core tenets of the Bible.

For José Porfirio Miranda, the Bible views property as not a particular good or item but the shared wealth of a community. Despite Miranda's extensive meditation on property in *Marx and the Bible* (1972), he never addresses the Bible's discussion, and approval, of slavery (a person as property).[88] Nevertheless, an extensive critique of Porfirio Miranda's work would miss its historical significance. In reading Miranda, one can see how a morality born prior to the advent of capitalism could find a degree of compatibility with a society brought about after its abolition. Surrounded by immense poverty, Porfirio Miranda sought to reconcile the precapitalist values of the Bible (communal and humanistic) with Marx's vision of postcapitalist world ("From each according to his ability to each according to his need").[89] In this period, Porfirio Miranda wrote his now classic *Marx and the Bible*—arguably the most widely read Mexican work on liberation theology and grouped among Gustavo Gutiérrez's *A Theology of Liberation* (1971) and Leonardo Boff's *Church: Charism and Power; Liberation Theology and the Institutional Church* (1981) as one of the most significant for works from Latin America on the subject.[90]

The question of socialism took on a more organizational dimension for Martín de la Rosa. In collaboration with Luis del Valle, he helped bring together an informal grouping of priests into a new organization called Sacerdotes para el Pueblo (Priests for the People). The organization was founded on April 14, 1972, and established chapters in Colima, Monterrey, Oaxaca, Mexico City, and Ciudad Neza.[91] Sacerdotes para el Pueblo was composed of priests already in conflict with their respective ecclesiastical authorities for their outspoken views on poverty, socialism, and liberation theology. The movement found counterparts in Argentina (Priests for the Third World), Colombia (Golconda), Peru (ONIS), Guatemala (Cosdegua), and Chile ("The Group of 80").[92]

These national coalitions were the driving force behind an international conference in Chile organized by the Christians for Socialism movement. One week after the founding of Sacerdotes para el Pueblo in Mexico, over four hundred clerical and lay participants packed into a textile union hall in socialist Chile to form a strategic alliance with Marxists to achieve socialism in Latin America. The *New York Times* reported, "The assembly and its final declaration were significant in the Latin American political context, wherein elements of the Catholic Church have moved beyond the Reformist and progressive position adopted in 1968 by the Latin American bishops at Medellín, Colombia [CELAM II]."[93] For Martín de la Rosa, it was "the maximum point of ideological expression of the Christian left."[94] De la Rosa was in attendance with Sergio Méndez Arceo, the only bishop present at the conference. After the conference concluded, Méndez Arceo continued his travels to Cuba for his historic meeting with Fidel Castro. Martín returned back to Ciudad Neza and prepared to face the repercussions of his daring move. In 1972, Sergio Méndez Arceo was a bishop with close connections to President Echeverría and enough authority to withstand the consequences of attending an international conference in support of socialism. Martín was not as fortunate. A bishop from Texcoco led the charge for Martín to be put on trial for excommunication. The drive to push Martín out of the priesthood was blocked by the local leadership of the Jesuit Order and parishioners in the diocese, but the damage was done.[95] Lacking in details, it appears the incident marked the beginning of Martín's disengagement with the Jesuit Order and his priestly duties. Promoción popular slowly took on a more secular character, heavily focused on popular education and democratic business cooperatives.

In the time between the Christians for Socialism conference and Martín's gradual withdrawal from the priesthood, he expanded the popular education programs and helped Luis del Valle build the Sacerdotes para el Pueblo movement. Martín had lived the solitary life of a Jesuit priest. His eventual departure was not the result of a crisis of faith. On the contrary, his faith guided him to his adoption of socialism and was fortified in his persecution. Like Ivan Illich, he abstained from the public role of a priest even as he privately maintained the beliefs of a Catholic priest. His vow to a life of poverty and commitment to the poor were unchanged. He was entering his third year in Ciudad Neza—three years of no running water, no toilet, and intermittent electricity. In Ciudad Neza, one's status as a university student or a car mechanic had no bearing on the intensity of the dust storms that whipped through its neighborhoods during the dry winter months. Nor was anyone immune to the constant swarms of mosquitoes at the height of the rainy season. Martín de la Rosa's years in the priesthood were not spent in the tranquil environs of a monastery or even the modest quarters of a church in El Centro. His faith was tested in a shack on Calle Cucaracha, only a few minutes' walk from a nearby commercial strip where pool halls, taxi stands, bathhouses, and dance halls buzzed all night with illicit activity.

Martín de la Rosa's life in Ciudad Neza nullified any accusations of youthful naivete. He was witness to both the collective solidarity between neighbors and the domestic abuse between couples. Distinct from a rural town with traditions slowly giving way to signs of modern commerce, Ciudad Neza was born from an "incomplete modernity" by residents who sought to be "modern" when they first settled its lands in the late 1940s. In this setting, Martín de la Rosa, Luis del Valle, and Alex Morelli all diverged from the Marxist or communist embrace of modern technology and mass production as mainly positive developments in humankind's struggle to move beyond material scarcity. For the progressive Catholics in Ciudad Neza, technological progress was destructive and foreign; the saturation of U.S. goods and values threatened the remnants and strains of a precapitalist culture that survived among Ciudad Neza's residents. They only looked on with dismay as their neighbors spent the little money they had on coveted Pepsi-Cola bottles and television sets.[96] The priests' outlook stemmed from a source much deeper than instinctive opposition to crass consumerism. It was an outlook rooted in the humanist tradition that strived to find a balance between individual dignity and the collective good. Modernity, in the form of Western individualism and mass-produced goods, was a source of alienation and a corrupting agent in the eyes of Martín de la Rosa.

SEPAC and Ciudad Neza's Social Movements, 1973–1976

In the spring of 1973, Ciudad Neza's MRC movement began to fray. The confusion caused by competing coalitions and bitterness over agreements to compensate the fraccionadores opened up a new opportunity for Martín de la Rosa. Initially, De la Rosa was wary of the MRC movement, as it was composed of local leaders intimately connected to the PRI and solely focused on property titles. Although supportive and sympathetic, it was a tightly controlled movement with little space to maneuver and interject the young Jesuits' brand of liberation theology. However, after the 1973 Fineza agreements, the MRC movement had split into rival factions, and several neighborhood associations held out against the Fineza agreements due to its conciliation with Ciudad Neza's fraccionadores.[97]

The most visible sign of the promoción popular project's political turn can be observed in the publication *El Despertar del Pueblo* (The awakening of the people). *El Despertar del Pueblo* was a monthly bulletin (a protozine) focused on the living conditions and local politics of Ciudad Neza.[98] It featured profiles of local residents, advertisements for their adult literacy classes, and graphic illustrations that addressed public health issues such as water contamination, diarrhea, and malnutrition. The paper dedicated several issues to the

Fineza Land Trust, primarily to expose how it perpetuated poverty in Ciudad Neza. It warned against Echeverría's "democratic opening" and closely followed the military coup as it unfolded in Chile.[99] The layout, content, and language of the bulletin were consciously designed to appeal to a broad audience; articles were short and simple, illustrations were accompanied text, and the subject matter was relevant to the day-to-day lives of residents.[100] In one example, an image utilizes a quote from Colombian priest Camilo Torres on the need for revolution, placed above an announcement for classes in music, arts, English, literacy, and sewing. In all this, Martín de la Rosa patiently worked to create and expand a space for local politics outside of the PRI's control.[101]

The beginning of 1974 witnessed Martín de la Rosa's most ambitious project to date. The sporadic education centers were solidified into several new locations under the direction of Popular Educational Services (Servicios Educativos Populares, SEPAC).[102] Two new Jesuit priests (Francisco Ornelas and Antonio Ortiz) and two local activists (Jesús Ruvalcaba and Maximiliano Iglesias) collaborated in the creation of five adult literacy centers, a community center (Casa Mater), and a cultural center in Colonia El Sol (Centro Cultural Cóyotl). The centers were pragmatic with a radical edge, designed to meet the basic needs of the community while also opening up the possibility to politically work with residents in a manner that was more participatory and democratic. The influences of Freire and Illich carried over from the classroom into community organizations and cooperatives.[103] By 1975, SEPAC continued to expand its operations with a public library in Colonia Maravillas and two more cultural centers (La Casa del Pueblo and Centro Cultural Libertad). In addition, SEPAC published a book series on education with titles that included *Popular Education and Capitalist Society* and *How a Democratic Group Works*.[104] Independent of the PRI and church authorities, SEPAC constituted a genuine expression of Mexican civil society. Its Freire-influenced schools and democratic cooperatives were limited to Ciudad Neza, but SEPAC's pioneering work formed an early outpost for the civil society organizations that would later grow into larger numbers after 1985.

The auspicious beginnings of SEPAC coincided with the tragic demise of José Luis Sierra and Ignacio Salas. Luis Sierra was hunted down by authorities and imprisoned in February 1972. He spent the remainder of the 1970s in jail until he was released by an amnesty agreement under President Lopez Portillo.[105] In February 1974, Ignacio Olivares, also a former Tec student and MEP activist, was detained and tortured to death behind closed doors.[106] Two months later, Ignacio Salas was injured in a shoot-out with two policemen. When officials realized his true identity in the hospital, Ignacio disappeared and was never seen again—*desaparecido*.[107] Martín de la Rosa learned of their fates through the news headlines. By 1974, the hundreds of students enrolled in SEPAC courses consumed his time and attention.

In retrospect, Martín and Ignacio's lives reflected a political milieu and moment much larger than their own personal trajectories. In particular, Martín's turn to popular education underscores an overlooked feature of the period: the failure to transform the urban shantytown into a staging area for the revolution did not negate its role as a progenitor to the democratic movements of the 1980s. SEPAC provided a model for how to reach Mexico's poorest communities in a manner that was practical and ideological at the same time.

The Fineza largely pacified the MRC movement, but it also spawned a smaller grassroots movement in its wake. By 1975, SEPAC was one of several independent political organizations in Ciudad Neza. Most notably, a Maoist collective formed by students at UNAM's nearby CCH-Oriente school (*prepatoria*) began to make inroads into Ciudad Neza.[108] Composed of local youth who came of age in the aftermath of '68, they eventually grew into the FPI. Initially small in numbers, working-class youth steeped in a revolutionary ideology of the times can become a powerful force when thrust into a volatile situation. The core members of FPI entered into several tenuous coalitions that split apart almost as they were formed (ULR, OIR-LM) until various social movements and organizations were finally able to unite as the Emiliano Zapata Popular Revolutionary Union (Unión Popular Revolucionaria Emiliano Zapata, UPREZ) in 1987.[109] The FPI's journey started later and moved more slowly than the young Jesuits'. Despite the irreconcilable ideological differences, both political movements were united in their use of education as a means to reach, organize, and transform Ciudad Neza's residents. In summarizing the Jesuit and Maoist groups in Ciudad Neza, scholar Andrew Selee wrote, "There were several movements in the 1970s which refused to play the rules of the game. Though they operated at a much smaller scale, their efforts also laid the groundwork for the changes that would take place in the 1980s and 1990s."[110]

In reflecting on the debates and the near implosion of the promoción popular project in 1971, Martín de la Rosa wrote, "Those who did not believe in a democratic framework were inclined to work with 'elites' [revolutionary cadre] in small circles; those who believed in working inside a legal framework placed more value on openly working with the masses on a broader level."[111] The ethical dimensions of violence and the feasibility of guerrilla warfare in a nonrevolutionary situation weighed heavily on Martín de la Rosa's thoughts in 1971.[112] However, in the end, Martín de la Rosa opposed clandestine guerrilla actions due to their isolated nature—political work limited to a small group of revolutionaries without the freedom to openly organize grassroots organizations on a democratic basis. In addition, his pastoral work and organizing experience in Ciudad Neza disabused him of the notion that Mexico's shantytown masses were eager to join a revolutionary movement led by former students.

SEPAC reached thousands of Ciudad Neza's colonos on its own terms. By 1978, SEPAC operated twenty-two adult education centers, three cultural centers, two cooperatives, a library, and several elementary schools.[113] It had evolved from a single organization into what Martín de la Rosa described as "a confederation of collectives."[114] Jesús Ruvalcaba estimated approximately two thousand adults learned to read through SEPAC's literacy classes, and three thousand children completed elementary school with SEPAC.[115] Nearly ten years earlier, Martín de la Rosa was a student himself, sitting under the shade of a tree in Cuernavaca as he listened to Paulo Freire discuss the idea of popular education as a vehicle for liberation.

In 1979, SEPAC dissolved and discontinued its operations as a result of internal disputes. Martín de la Rosa faded from view and out of the archives, only to reappear years later as a sociologist and community organizer in Tijuana. Luis del Valle continued to merge social reform with religious faith as a Jesuit priest in Mexico City's poor colonias while also campaigning for Mexico to provide refuge for Chilean activists seeking asylum during the Pinochet years. SEPAC was not only a part of Ciudad Neza's history but an interpreter of it as well. Today, SEPAC's *Netzahualcóyotl: Un fenómeno* (1974) and *Netzahualcóyotl: Testimonios históricos* (1978) offer a counternarrative to the "official" histories of Ciudad Neza's past.[116] Unlike the official histories of Ciudad Neza, mostly written by PRI functionaries who portray the residents as victims of fraccionadores, SEPAC's works interpret the misery found in Ciudad Neza as a product of the collusion between those fraccionadores and the PRI.[117]

SEPAC's own summation of their work and their analysis of Mexican society echo the voices of militant activists and scholars of the era. From this perspective, any reform short of revolution would only perpetuate the same inequality responsible for the misery and suffering of the marginal masses. The disappointment that set in after their dreams for a radical transformation dissipated partially clouded and distorted their ability to grasp the significant political developments unfolding around them. In surveying the period (1968–82), it is unquestionable that the root causes of severe poverty in Mexico's ciudades perdidas were not fundamentally, or even seriously, transformed by Echeverría or his successor, Lopez Portillo. However, with the passage of time and the power of historical analysis, it is possible to discern the stirrings of an awakened civil society under dictatorial rule in the urban social movements active throughout Mexico's urban periphery.

Conclusion

"Remember to ask about the Jesuits. . . . Don't forget to ask about the old pictures of the house." I jotted down the notes as I sat on the steps of the Palacio Municipal. Essentially Ciudad Neza's city hall, the Palacio Municipal was already buzzing with activity early in the morning. I was there to meet Rogelio Vargas at our regular spot. He lives nearby in the same house detailed in this book. Rogelio shared the home with his wife until she passed away a few years ago. Now he lives alone, though constantly surrounded by assistants, neighbors, lawyers, fellow PRI-istas, and low-level bureaucrats. At eighty-three years old, he's outlived most of his friends—and his enemies.

I greet Rogelio and we walk over to a café. He seems upbeat and buoyed by a renewed sense of vigor. Alfredo del Mazo Maza was recently declared the winner of the governor's race for the State of Mexico, following on the heels of another PRI candidate winning the governorship in Rogelio's native Oaxaca. Alejandro Murat Hinojosa's victory in Oaxaca meant more to Rogelio than a point of pride. Over the past ten years or so, Rogelio's main political work has been deeply entwined with Oaxaca. With nearly half a million Oaxacan migrants currently living in Ciudad Neza and neighboring Chalco, Rogelio plays a key role as a political organizer and deal maker for PRI candidates in Oaxaca seeking support among a massive base of Oaxacan voters now residing in the Valley of Mexico (Valle de México).[1]

It has been forty-five years since Rogelio Vargas turned against his former friends in the MRC coalition. At the time, his decision infuriated Ciudad Neza's social leaders, and two bounties were placed on his head.[2] Anytime I allude to those years, he returns to the same point: he never mobilized people to invade unsettled lands in Ciudad Neza. His commitment to abstain from land invasions ran as deep as his loyalty to the PRI. That loyalty was tested in the 1990s, when large numbers of activists and political leaders in

Ciudad Neza broke with the PRI and joined the newly formed Party of the Democratic Revolution (Partido de la Revolución Democrática, PRD). As with many former MRC leaders, Odón Madariaga Cruz drifted away from the PRI and became a governing member of the PRD. I mention to Rogelio that if Odón was still alive today, he probably would have joined MORENA by now. Rogelio lets out a chuckle. He speculates on the future of the PRI before we go over some questions that I had prepared for him. The bill is paid, and we part ways. I walk across the main plaza of the Palacio Municipal, still busy with throngs of people arriving and leaving.

Although the Palacio Municipal's architecture still resembles its original design from the 1960s, the political environment surrounding the complex has changed over the years. At the time of the Palacio Municipal's founding in 1963, the PRI dominated national politics and had consolidated its position as the only party of consequence in Mexican society. Today, there are four political parties (PRI, PAN, PRD, MORENA) vying for power. In one example, after the 2018 elections, residents of Ciudad Neza found themselves with a municipal president from the PRD, a governor from the PRI, and a president from MORENA. This transition, though considered peaceful due to the absence of military coups or conventional warfare, was still marked by assassinations, torture, kidnappings, and repression.

It is a bitter irony when the long-sought-after goal of competitive elections—the lifeblood of a healthy democracy—turns into a violent bloodletting. Ideally, competitive elections in a multiparty system are fundamental to a thriving democracy. However, the realities of political competition in Mexico cannot be disentangled from widespread violence. At this point, criminal violence cannot be viewed as some kind of political externality. It is a powerful force at the center of politics. In a recent election cycle (2018), at least 145 candidates or people related to electoral processes were murdered on the campaign trail. In Chilapa, Guerrero, both the PRI and PRD candidates were gunned down, not to mention the dozens of candidates who faced death threats and kidnappings in numerous districts across the country.[3] Though truly horrific, the spate of assassinations should come as no surprise to scholars of Mexico's recent history, given that nearly 265 PRD activists were murdered in the 1990s.[4] Ultimately, the PRI's use of lethal force in the 1980s and 1990s could not prevent the country's disillusionment with their entrenched rule.

What gave rise to a third party in Mexican politics? What factors contributed to a split in the PRI's leadership in the mid-1980s? Why was this the breaking point? These questions require a more careful analysis of the period that follows the years examined in the present study. One probable factor was a recognition, among a faction of the PRI's leadership, that a broad base of support for an alternative party existed in both organized and latent forms throughout Mexico. The urban social movements (MUP) discussed in this book represented one of the key constituencies that would rally around Cuauhtémoc Cárdenas's call for democracy and social justice.[5] By the 1980s, a national coalition of urban social movements with deep roots in Mexico's poor neighborhoods and strong opposition to the PRI provided the kind of organizational network and support necessary to launch a campaign against the ruling party's sweeping austerity measures.[6]

This book focused on the origins of one of the nation's largest mass movements for land rights and urban services in Ciudad Neza. Organized resistance in Ciudad Neza coincided with the first wave of popular urban movements in Mexico. While each city collaborated with the PRI to varying degrees, each city also established independent community organizations led by local residents.[7] In this initial stage (1968–74), we can observe some early instances of civil society groups breaking with the conventional cycle of resistance, repression, and co-option practiced in previous decades. In the present work, I have identified four factors behind this rupture. First, the inhumane conditions that gave rise to rebellion continued to exist in Mexico's major cities. Second, the PRI was unable to effectively integrate neighborhood associations (colonos) into their ruling apparatus, though they did establish ongoing ties through their CNOP federation. Third, the accumulation of historical experience exerted a strong influence on people's consciousness. In comparing Luis Echeverría to earlier leaders, it is not sufficient to simply provide the historical context for each president. Decades of betrayals, dashed hopes, violent repression, and entrenched corruption had a cumulative effect that must be factored into any analysis of the PRI's diminishing popularity in the 1970s and 1980s. And fourth, the ideological currents of the global sixties helped provide a basis for breaking from the PRI's orbit. Whether the Jesuits in Ciudad Neza or Maoist groupings in Durango, Mexico's New Left operated outside of the PRI's traditional networks and established a revolutionary pole of attraction in some of Mexico's poorest neighborhoods.[8]

Perhaps if the young Jesuits continued their pastoral work in Ciudad Neza, they would have formed an ecclesial base community (*comunidades eclesiales de base*). The emergence of ecclesial base communities in Latin America gave an organizational expression to Vatican II's general principles of engagement with lay parishioners and a commitment to social justice. These lay groups grew by the hundreds in both rural and urban areas of Mexico, contributing to the revitalization of its civil society.[9] In relation to Ciudad Neza, the dissolution of the young Jesuit grouping, along with the power of the conservative Texcoco archdiocese, proved to be effective in quelling discontent and stifling the growth of a more progressive strand of social Catholicism in the area. Like the fraccionadores in Ciudad Neza, the role of the Catholic Church in the repression, or support, of urban social movements in other locations remains largely understudied.[10]

If the late 1960s produced the first sparks of the MUP movement, 1980 represented its culmination as a major force in national politics. On May 1, 1980, thousands of activists gathered in Monterrey to form the National Coordinator of the Popular Urban Movement (Coordinadora Nacional del Movimiento Urbano Popular, CONAMUP).[11] Over sixty organizations from fifteen states established a national coalition of housing rights organizers, reaching nearly a million members in 1984.[12] Its founding document declared that the CONAMUP was "independent of the bourgeoisie, the state, the state's apparatus of control, and its political parties."[13] Ciudad Neza's Independent Popular Front (Frente Popular Independiente, FPI) played a critical role in the formation of the CONAMUP and later expanded its efforts beyond housing to create several public schools in Ciudad Neza.[14]

The founding of the CONAMUP coalition and its subsequent committees occurred on the cusp of Mexico's financial crisis. While historically high inflation rates wreaked havoc on Mexico's economy in the 1970s, the 1982 debt crisis truly marked a major turning point in Mexican history. After failing to pay its foreign debts, Mexico's economy went into a free fall and eventually enacted several structural adjustment policies demanded by creditors.[15] Budgets for food programs, medical care, and social services were slashed. State subsidies for IMSS's housing complexes were dramatically reduced, and many units were converted into privately owned condominiums. Figures charting the decline in inequality began to reverse direction and increase again after 1983.[16]

The rise of civil society amid economic turmoil provided a powerful narrative for journalists and scholars in the 1980s. The gubernatorial victories of opposition parties and the volunteer brigades who were responsible for rescuing victims from under the rubble of the 1985 earthquake represented powerful examples of democracy in action.[17] To periodize the beginning of Mexico's democratic transition in the 1980s also situates the country in a broader history of democratization around the world. Popular movements in South America, Eastern Europe, and South Africa paved the way for new democratic republics to emerge on the world scene.[18]

Informal Metropolis has argued that the roots of Mexico's democratic transition reach further back than the financial crises of the 1980s. This summation stems from a shift in methodological orientation. As opposed to viewing the past through the lens of electoral politics, it widened the scope of inquiry to include a close study of neighborhood associations and urban social movements. As a result, the archival research carried out for this book was able to detect change and nuance among certain segments of society in the 1970s that would be traditionally overshadowed by the PRI's hegemony in Mexican politics.

Beyond historical periodization, drawing attention to social movements in the 1970s has larger implications for understanding the relationship between economic conditions and political mobilization. While it is unquestionable that the economic turmoil of the 1980s spurred greater resistance, the experience of the 1970s suggests a different dynamic. Instead, it was the nation's economic growth and enlargement of its middle class that aroused a sense of frustration and anger among those excluded from the benefits of the "Mexican miracle." In urban housing, this was most evident in the government's construction of modern multifamiliares for middle-class families at the expense of the informal poor.

The divisions between the multifamiliar and the informal settlement were most clearly defined in the 1950s. In this early period, government policies toward informal settlements were at their most repressive, and criteria for acceptance into social housing programs were at their most selective.[19] Despite President Luis Echeverría's attempts to break from past practices, agencies such as Infonavit and Indeco could only push against the parameters established in the previous decades. Even when President Miguel de la Madrid created the National Fund for Popular Housing (Fideicomiso Fondo Nacional de Habitaciones Populares, FONHAPO) for unsalaried workers in 1981, underfunding limited its reach.[20] After surveying the history of urban housing in Mexico over the course of the twentieth century, the Echeverría period stands out as the most pivotal.[21] Shortly after Echeverría's presidency ended, sociologist Manuel Castells published an article on urban policy in postrevolutionary Mexico. The article identified four key features in urban policy during the Echeverría years that "represented a profound transformation in the regional and urban policies of the Mexican state." They were (1) a policy of regional decentralization and urban deconcentration, (2) legal norms for land speculation, (3) a national housing program for workers, and (4) the regularization of informal land tenure.[22] While the first two features proved to be of minor significance, the latter two did represent a "profound transformation" in urban policy.[23] Not only did Infonavit construct nearly one hundred thousand homes under Echeverría; but more importantly, it finally consolidated a mortgage lending program capable of operating on a national scale.[24] At the same time, the public fideicomisos, or land trusts, were established as a national model for land regularization in areas deemed "irregular" or "informal." Unlike Infonavit, the regularization of informal land tenure would be primarily confined to the Mexico City area during much of the 1970s, though it would later expand to other cities in future years. By 1976, roughly four hundred informal settlements had been regularized and given basic services, a feat that affected millions of residents.[25] At the time, Castells viewed this period as one of major state intervention into urban affairs. In hindsight, we can now see this as one of the last gasps of state-led development in Mexico. IMSS, Infonavit, and other public institutes continued to operate, and new ones would later appear, but the legitimacy and momentum surrounding the "revolutionary state" as a check against exploitation and foreign domination would never regain the same kind of support or stature.

While Mexico City's enormous size and complexity always allow for exceptions and counterexamples, several general conclusions can be offered about housing during the latter half of the twentieth century. First, it was in this period when the census counted more homeowners than apartment renters in Mexico City. This transition was caused mainly by a rise in self-built homes but also by a change in housing policy (FOVI, Infonavit) that encouraged home ownership after 1963. The growth of the stand-alone house (single-family detached home) was made possible by the city's rapacious sprawl. This development was reflected in the explosive population growth of the nearby State of Mexico. By 1995, the number of people in urbanized areas of the State of Mexico surpassed the Federal District, and in 2010, the Federal District's population accounted for only 45 percent of the Mexico City metropolitan area's population.[26] The pace of Mexico City's urban sprawl did eventually ease up after 1985, accompanied by an increase in population density. Finally, these decades witnessed the rise and decline of the state's role in housing matters. Although Mexico's housing institutions moved closer to a market-oriented approach in the 1980s, FOVI and Infonavit remained key actors in providing housing loans for Mexican workers. By the 1990s, Infonavit was mainly geared toward providing mortgages and aiding private-sector enterprises. Nevertheless, it was still a government agency responsible for approximately 65 percent of all housing loans in Mexico.[27]

Like the rest of Mexico City, Ciudad Neza's population density increased after the 1970s. In fact, Ciudad Neza is currently the most densely populated municipality in Mexico. As of 2020, an estimated 1.1 million people were squeezed into sixty-three square kilometers, or 18,000 inhabitants per square kilometer.[28] Images of Ciudad Neza's barren plains and muddy roads are distant memories in this highly urbanized strip of concrete on the edge of the capital.

Its high population density, combined with popular stigmatization, led Mike Davis to claim that Ciudad Neza was part of the world's largest megaslum in 2006. Grouped together with Chimalhuacán, Chalco, Iztapalapa, and fourteen other contiguous municipalities, Ciudad Neza was ranked as the most populated slum in Davis's *Planet of Slums*.[29] From a planetary perspective, this makes sense. However, if one were to zoom in to a street-level view of Ciudad Neza, the label "megaslum" is less convincing. The clusters of middle-class families in Ciudad Neza's Zona Norte and its western colonias (Porvenir, Maravillas, Las Palmas) add a layer of heterogeneity too great to be branded as such. In 1975, Ciudad Neza did constitute the world's largest shantytown. Yet the post-Fineza reforms and transformations chronicled in this work defy such labels.

Neighborhoods named after Raúl Romero or streets that bear the name Aureliano Ramos are relics of a bygone era when land developers ruled Ciudad Neza with an iron fist. The end of their rule was not a predestined outcome of modern urbanization but the result of a protracted struggle waged against difficult odds. After three years of widespread strikes supported by President Echeverría, Ciudad Neza's fraccionadores were still able to hold on to their lands. When they finally relinquished control, the land regularization produced mixed results. Inherently flawed from the beginning due to the federal government's conciliation with the fraccionadores, this book highlighted a feature of urban land regularization in both Ciudad Neza and Mexico: land titles were a central demand for millions of residents struggling to survive in the city. Though it was this demand that brought neighbors together to form associations, social movements on the urban periphery would achieve more lasting significance as precursors to the formation of a new urban citizenry in Mexico.

Table 1. Land and property in Colonias del Vaso de Texcoco / Ciudad Neza (twenty documented colonias)

Colonia name	Date authorized by local authority	Surface area (sq m)	Previous land tenure	Land developer
México	February 7, 1947	n/a	None, desiccated land from Texcoco	Raúl Romero Erazo
El Sol	October 1948	2,000,437	Federal property	César Hann Cárdenas
Estado de México	April 2, 1949	1,990,000	None, desiccated land from Texcoco	Justino Fernández Miranda
Evolución	April 18, 1949	152,321	None, desiccated land from Texcoco	Victor Manuel Villaseñor Moore
Romero	May 12, 1949	343,780	Ejido Pantitlán	Raúl Romero Erazo
Tamaulipas	November 10, 1950	400,000	None, desiccated land from Texcoco	José Lorenzo Zakany
Maravillas	July 31, 1952	248,000	Común repartimiento	Benjamín Cemaj
Porvenir	October 14, 1954	379,046	Común repartimiento	Victor Manuel Pavón Abreu
Agua Azul	October 26, 1954	210,256	Común repartimiento	Colonia Agua Azul
Las Águilas	March 17, 1955	205, 417	Común repartimiento	Compañía Fraccionadora Las Águilas
Gral. José Vicente Villada	September 12, 1955	526,660	None, desiccated land from Texcoco	Alejandro Romero Lasquetty
Los Volcanes	October 4, 1955	n/a	Común repartimiento	Fraccionadora Los Volcanes

(*continued*)

Table 1. Land and property in Colonias del Vaso de Texcoco / Ciudad Neza (twenty documented colonias) (*continued*)

Colonia name	Date authorized by local authority	Surface area (sq m)	Previous land tenure	Land developer
Loma Bonita	February 10, 1956	95,000	Común repartimiento	Ismael Valdés Salgado
Manantiales	October 6, 1956	263,340	Común repartimiento	Fraccionamientos Populares
Las Palmas	April 15, 1957	144,417	Ejido	Herald Steenbock Kock
Aurora	July 10, 1957	8,093,713 (includes all sections owned by Eckstein)	Común repartimiento	Bernardo Eckstein Salz
Aurora (sec. Romero)	1957	448,005	Común repartimiento	Raúl Romero Erazo
Pirules	August 19, 1957	293,344	Ejido	Aguas y Construcciones
Metropolitana	November 29, 1959	2,424,646	Ejido	José Lorenzo Zakany
Reforma	May 4, 1962	2,323,920	Ejido	Victor Manuel Villaseñor Moore
Modelo	November 13, 1959	175,841	Ejido	Inmobiliaria Loscar

Note: Común repartimiento is a term historically used in the State of Mexico to refer to communal lands that survived the liberal reforms of the mid-1800s and were only nominally privatized. For areas designated "desiccated land from Lake Texcoco," they were considered federal property when Fineza's land transfers began after 1973.

Sources: Figures drawn from Saucedo, "Movimientos de colonos"; and *Informe de Actividades de Fineza* (1974), held in CIDNE's library as 16-6/578-579.

NOTES

Introduction

1. The Spanish began major hydraulic projects intended to drain the lakes in 1607. See Candiani, *Dreaming of Dry Land*.
2. Rogelio Vargas Soriano, interview with author, June 12, 2018.
3. Bautista, *Camino por la Mixteca*, 34–37.
4. This work primarily draws from Székely, *Economics of Poverty*, 11–13. See also Hernández Laos, "Medición de la incidencia," 265–97; Brachet-Márquez, *Contention*; and Bértola and Williamson, "Introduction," 6.
5. Hansen, *Politics of Mexican Development*, cited in Ward, *Mexico City*, 7.
6. For a range of examples, see McCormick, *Logic of Compromise*; Padilla, *Rural Resistance*; Eckstein, *Poverty of Revolution*; and Stavenhagen, "Capitalism and the Peasantry," 27–37. For an alternative argument, see Bleyant, Challú, and Segal, "Inequality, Living Standards," 584–610. Bleyant, Challú, and Segal write, "Our finding that growth was broadly inclusive during the 'Mexican miracle' mirrors findings for Uruguay and Chile in the same period, but it is a key point of disagreement with much of the historiography for Mexico, which claims that inequality rose" (596).
7. This is similar to the process in Brazil described by sociologist Janice Perlman. See Perlman, *Myth of Marginality*, 5.
8. Anda, *Vivienda colectiva*. In addition to *multifamiliar*, *unidad habitacional* was also commonly used. By the 1960s, the term *unidad habitacional* became more common than *multifamiliar*. See Alonso and Montes, *El espacio habitacional*.
9. Bazant, *Autoconstrucción de vivienda*. Martha Schteingart has published prolifically on urban housing in Mexico. See Jaramillo and Schteingart, "Procesos Sociales," 11–28.
10. Castillo and Bassols Ricárdez, "Construcción Social," 181–212; "Cumple 20 años, todos en la miseria," *Proceso*, April 16, 1983, https://www.proceso.com.mx/135873/cumple-20-anos-todos-en-la-miseria (site no longer extant).
11. See, for example, Davis, *Planet of Slums*, 28.

12. For the most direct influence, see Wacquant, *Urban Outcasts*, 168. For a case in Mexico, see Bayón, "El 'lugar' de los pobres," 133–66.
13. Pagaza, *Anatomía de un gobierno*.
14. For more on this duality, see Sluis, *Deco Body, Deco City*.
15. This is a slight variation on Roberts, *Cities of Peasants*.
16. See Muñoz García, Oliveira, and Stern, *Migración y desigualdad social*.
17. Székely, *Economics of Poverty*, 11–13.
18. Huitron, *Netzahualcóyotl*; Schteingart, "El proceso de formación," 100–123.
19. DGIPS stands for Dirección General de Investigaciones Políticas y Sociales, or General Directorate of Political and Social Investigations. For background, see Padilla and Walker, "In the Archives," 1–10.
20. Iglesias, *Netzahualcóyotl*; Alonso, "Los movimientos sociales," 17–52.
21. The works that directly have covered Ciudad Neza are Saucedo, "Movimientos de colonos"; Castillo and Bassols Ricárdez, "Construcción Social," 181–212; Schteingart, *Los productores*; and Vélez-Ibáñez, *Rituals of Marginality*; Rosa, *Netzahualcóyotl*.
22. Two key reference points for this approach were Fischer, McCann, and Auyero, *Cities from Scratch*; and Self, *American Babylon*. Although there are many works that were published in the 1960s and 1970s that compared data on different communities, few identified connections or relations linking them together. For an exceptional work that theorized the socioeconomic relationships between the informal poor and urban middle class, see Lomnitz, *Networks and Marginality*, 23–25.
23. The use of *deprivation* and *stigmatization* draws from Wacquant, *Urban Outcasts*, 160–69.
24. Exact wording from Doreen Massey, interview with Nigel Warburton, *Social Science Bites*, podcast audio, February 1, 2013. The formulation distills Massey's work in Massey, *For Space*.
25. Derived from Tuan, *Space and Place*, 4–5; and Craib, *Cartographic Mexico*, 4.
26. See Davis, *Urban Leviathan*; Piccato, *City of Suspects*; Kuri, *La experiencia olvidada*; and Morales Martínez, *Ensayos urbanos*. See also Olsen, *Artifacts of Revolution*; Sluis, *Deco Body, Deco City*; and Tenorio-Trillo, *I Speak of the City*. A notable exception can be found in some environmental histories. See Vitz, *City on a Lake*; and the works collected in Legorreta, *La ciudad de México*.
27. Two seminal texts are Cronon, *Nature's Metropolis*; and Jackson, *Crabgrass Frontier*. See also Balakrishnan, *Shareholder Cities*; Hise, *Magnetic Los Angeles*; Murray, *Taming the Disorderly City*; and Self, *American Babylon*.
28. The direct translation would be "historical center" for *Centro Histórico* and "conurbation" for *conurbación*. For more on the lack of urban renewal in Mexico City, see Yee, "Making of Mexico."

29. Duhau and Giglia, *Las reglas del desorden*; and Vitz, *City on a Lake*. For work after the 1970s, see also Pezzoli, *Human Settlements*.
30. Caldeira, "Peripheral Urbanization," 3–4.
31. Castells and Portes, "World Underneath," 12. See also Cross, "Co-optation, Competition," 41–61; and Bleynat, *Vendors' Capitalism*.
32. Menna Agha and Léopold Lambert, "Informality Is a Fallacy," *Architectural Review*, December 16, 2022, https://www.architectural-review.com/essays/outrage/outrage-informality-is-a-fallacy?tkn=1.
33. Fraccionadores have usually been discussed in relation to a protest or social movement. For examples, see Vélez-Ibáñez, *Rituals of Marginality*; and Galván, *El Movimiento Urbano Popular*.
34. Friedrich, "Legitimacy of a Cacique," 247. This work is expanded upon in Friedrich, *Agrarian Revolt*. For an influential collection, see Brading, *Caudillo and Peasant*.
35. For different variations of urban caciquismo, see Knight and Pansters, *Caciquismo in Twentieth-Century Mexico*.
36. Pensado, *Rebel Mexico*, 38–39.
37. For the U.S., see Hirsch, *Making the Second Ghetto*; Massey and Denton, *American Apartheid*; Sugrue, *Origins of the Urban Crisis*; Rothstein, *Color of Law*; Smith, *Racial Democracy*; Menchaca, *Mexican American Experience*; and Boger, "Meaning of Neighborhood," 236–58. For South Asia, see Lewis and Harris, "Segregation and the Social," 589–607; and Rao, *House, but No Garden*. For Europe, see Arbaci, *Paradoxes of Segregation*.
38. Historian Colin Gordon utilized census data and archives with GIS mapping to detail segregation between African American and white residents in St. Louis, Missouri. Gordon, *Mapping Decline*. Another work on St. Louis using critical juncture theory and path dependence to trace racial segregation since 1865 is Benton, "'Just the Way Things Are,'" 1113–30. Lawsuits, legal petitions, and trial records are used to research racial discrimination in Walsh, *Racial Taxation*; and Taylor, *Race for Profit*. A rare case of analyzing the similarities and differences in the Americas can be found in Schteingart, "Pobreza y Políticas Sociales," 161–84.
39. Rubalcaba and Schteingart, *Ciudades Divididas*; González Liano, "Segregación social," 57–64; Sabatini, "La segregación social." Sabatini briefly compares Black ghettos in the United States to poor urban neighborhoods in Latin American cities, but only in terms of perceived social dysfunction and crime. For a study that includes more cultural dimensions of segregation, see Guillermo Aguilar and Escamilla H., *Segregación urbana*. For more recent work on spatial segregation with ethnoracial features in Baja California and Cancún, see Velasco Ortiz, "Movilidades indígenas," 32–58; and Castellanos, *Indigenous Dispossession*.

40. Murray, *Taming the Disorderly City*; Gordon, "Dividing the City"; Sugrue, *Origins of the Urban Crisis*, 41–45.
41. Data compiled in Muñoz García, Oliveira, and Stern, *Migración y desigualdad social*.
42. Yee, "Forging Mixtec Identity," 55–77. Orellana found a small community of migrants who lived around the same two-block radius but considered it too small and precarious to be an ethnic enclave or neighborhood. Orellana, "Mixtec Migrants in Mexico City," 275. On the symbolism, see Nova, "'Culture' of Exclusion," 249–68.
43. In the 1960s and 1970s, most studies focused on the continuation of village or regional social relations as a means to survive in the city. See Butterworth, "Two Small Groups," 39–41. Later, issues more directly related to racial discrimination were examined in López and Martínez, "La reproducción de la pobreza." Examples of housing material, rental applications, and social worker forms are compiled in Instituto Mexicano del Seguro Social (IMSS), *Manual de Operaciones*.
44. Eckstein, *Poverty of Revolution*, 72–73. Mexico City's history of urban housing echoes Luis Reygadas's broader argument for understanding inequality in Latin America: "Ethnic and racial markers account for a portion of inequality, but the overwhelming share is now explained by factors such as occupation, gender, place of residence, and above all, the family and individual's education. Ethno-racial determinants function not on their own but in conjunction with others." See Reygadas, "Construction of Latin American Inequality," 31–32. The classification of one's status based on multiple characteristics, including race, dress, language, occupation, income, and residency, has some parallels with the colonial period discussed in Cope, *Limits of Racial Domination*.
45. Monsiváis, *Mexican Postcards*, 97–99; Bartra, *Cage of Melancholy*, 94.
46. Lomnitz-Adler, *Modernidad Indiana*, 23.
47. Araiz, "Participación del estado," 168–73.
48. A comparative analysis of the rental fees for public housing and the monthly payments for lots in the Vaso de Texcoco reveals a great deal of overlap and similarity. Between 1957 and 1963, the average cost of a one-bedroom apartment in an IMSS housing complex was 117 pesos, plus a small monthly fee for services (15–25 pesos). Though the average monthly fees in the Vaso de Texcoco were below 100 pesos before 1950, by the early 1960s, the average payment had increased to 150 pesos per month for a plot of land, plus an average of 115 pesos was spent by each lot on water. In two specific cases, residents generally paid 225 pesos a month for a lot in Aurora and 215 a month in Agua Azul. Figures drawn from Benítez, *Viaje al centro de México*, 84–85; Secretaría General de Gobierno del Estado

de México, "Relación de Fraccionamientos de Ciudad Nezahualcóyotl," 1972, Centro de Información y Documentación de Nezahualcóyotl (CIDNE), box 16, UAE/V-15; and Palomares, *Historia de Ciudad Nezahualcóyotl*, 7. See also Ortiz Mena, "Una importante obra," 136.

49. Peña, "¿Viviendo Cada Vez Más Separados?," 57–93; Sabatini, "La segregación social." For an example that proposes a "ring" model of segregation, see Delgado, "De Los Anillos," 237–74.
50. Monsiváis, *Entrada libre*, 80. Originally cited in *Excélsior*, December 8, 1985, 4. Unless otherwise noted, all translations of Spanish-language sources are my own.
51. Monsiváis, *Entrada libre*, 80. For examples in Latin America, see Mainwaring, "Urban Popular Movements," 131–59; Oxhorn, *Organizing Civil Society*; and Irazábal, *Ordinary Places, Extraordinary Events*.
52. Huntington, *Political Order in Changing Societies*, 280–82. Janice Perlman's summation of modernization theory and the urban poor continues to be a key reference point. See Perlman, *Myth of Marginality*, 122–26. A landmark work on clientelism is Cornelius, *Politics and the Migrant Poor*.
53. Tamayo, "Del Movimiento Urbano Popular," 499–518; Tamayo, "Crítica de la ciudadanía," 113–42; Rodríguez Cortés and Ortega Breña, "Building Citizenship," 176–90.
54. The approach of moving toward a more everyday, public level of analysis is most directly influenced by Avritzer, *Democracy and the Public Space*, 4. Another important work that moves beyond a singular focus on elections is Davis and Brachet-Márquez, "Rethinking Democracy," 86–119. For work on the nineteenth century and early twentieth century, see Forment, *Democracy in Latin America*; Piccato, *Tyranny of Opinion*; and Ingwersen, "La Pata De Cabra," 1–27.
55. Smith, "Introduction," 7. See also de la Peña, "Civil Society and Popular Resistance," 304–45. For a broader view, see Arato and Cohen, *Civil Society and Political Theory*; and Edwards, *Civil Society*.
56. Shefner, *Illusion of Civil Society*; Alvarez et al., *Beyond Civil Society*. See also Holston, *Insurgent Citizenship*, 9–10.
57. Bennett, "La evolución," 89–96; Haber, *Power from Experience*. Groupings in more middle-class areas are discussed in Walker, *Waking from the Dream*, 173–200. For work on an earlier period of urban movements and neighbor associations, see Wood, *Revolution in the Street*.
58. For the case of Ciudad Neza, see Vélez-Ibáñez, *Rituals of Marginality*.
59. For an overview of the MUP, see Saiz, *El Movimiento Urbano Popular*. For more theoretical works, see Touraine, *Actores sociales*; Castells, *City and the Grassroots*.
60. For broader discussion on populism, see Kiddle and Muñoz, *Populism in Twentieth Century Mexico*.

61. Galván, "La Colonia Proletaria Rubén Jaramillo." For Monterrey, see Castells, *City and the Grassroots*, 190–99. For Durango, see Haber, *Power from Experience*.
62. Loaeza, "La Política Del Rumor," 557–86; Schmidt, *Deterioration of the Mexican Presidency*; Ovalle, *Tiempo suspendido*.
63. Pensado and Ochoa, "Introduction," 3–18.
64. Rubin, *Decentering the Regime*; Lenti, *Redeeming the Revolution*; Olcott, *International Women's Year*; Muñoz, *Stand Up and Fight*; Mendiola Garcia, *Street Democracy*.
65. Foweraker and Craig, *Popular Movements*; Escobar and Alvarez, *Making of Social Movements*.
66. See Perlman, *Myth of Marginality*; Castells, *City and the Grassroots*; Lomnitz, *Networks and Marginality*; Labbé, *Land Politics and Livelihoods*; and Fischer, McCann, and Auyero, *Cities from Scratch*.
67. Holston, "Insurgent Citizenship," 247.
68. For Brazil, see McCann, *Hard Times*; and Avritzer, *Urban Reform*. For Uruguay, see Canel, *Barrio Democracy*. For Chile, see Murphy, *For a Proper Home*; Oxhorn, *Organizing Civil Society*; and Schneider, *Shantytown Protest*. For a more contemporary work on Chile, see Pérez, *Right to Dignity*.

1. Mexico City at a Crossroads

1. Ramírez Vázquez, "Human Settlements Issues," 310.
2. Tannenbaum, "Streetwise History," 127–50.
3. Valencia, *La Merced*, 132–34.
4. Frieden, "Search for Housing Policy," 81–82.
5. Novo, *Nueva Grandeza Mexicana*, 122.
6. For different facets of public health and city planning in Mexico City, see Agostoni, *Monuments of Progress*; and Piccato, *City of Suspects*.
7. Vitz, *City on a Lake*, 23–28.
8. Agostoni, *Monuments of Progress*, 138–40. For previous attempts, see Candiani, *Dreaming of Dry Land*.
9. A. Pani, *En Camino*. For background on generational dissidence, see Matute, *El Ateneo de México*.
10. A. Pani, *Hygiene in Mexico*, 7.
11. A. Pani, *Hygiene in Mexico*, 84, 91.
12. Lear, *Workers, Neighbors*.
13. Cited in Cymet, *From Ejido to Metropolis*, 11.
14. Cymet, *From Ejido to Metropolis*, 140–41.
15. Cymet, *From Ejido to Metropolis*, 141.

16. Cymet, *From Ejido to Metropolis*, 143.
17. Haynes, "Order and Progress," 44.
18. Villarreal and Hamilton, "Residential Segregation," 74.
19. Muñoz García, Oliveira, and Stern, *Migración y desigualdad social*, 43–47.
20. Valencia, *La Merced*, 163.
21. Muñoz García, Oliveira, and Stern, *Migración y desigualdad social*, 47.
22. Davis, *Urban Leviathan*, 110.
23. Cymet, *From Ejido to Metropolis*, 22–23.
24. Frieden, "Search for Housing Policy," 93.
25. Ramírez Vázquez, "Human Settlements Issues," 310.
26. Scott, *Urban and Spatial*, 235–38. (A prior edition exists, published by the World Bank.)
27. See, for example, Aguilar, "Mexico," 175–201.
28. Scott, *Urban and Spatial*, 238.
29. Ramírez Vázquez, "Human Settlements Issues," 312.
30. For migration rates, see Butterworth, "Rural-Urban Migration," 65–67; and Muñoz García, Oliveira, and Stern, *Migración y desigualdad social*. For hometown associations, see Kemper, *Migration and Adaptation*; and Fitzgerald, "Colonies of the Little Motherland," 145–69.
31. Scott, *Urban and Spatial*, 41–42.
32. Scott, *Urban and Spatial*, 41–42.
33. Bautista, *Camino por la Mixteca*, 109.
34. Increased accessibility was documented in Orellana, "Mixtec Migrants in Mexico City," 275–76; Butterworth, "Two Small Groups," 39–41; Arizpe, *Indígenas en la ciudad*.
35. Muñoz García, Oliveira, and Stern, *Migración y desigualdad social*, 109.
36. Pilcher, *Cantinflas and the Chaos*.
37. Muñoz García, Oliveira, and Stern, *Migración y desigualdad social*, 65.
38. Arellano, *Rumores y retratos*, 28; Raul Beethoven Lomeli, "Inauguróse el Gran Edificio Multifamiliar," *Excélsior*, September 3, 1949, 1.
39. Arellano, *Rumores y retratos*, 28.
40. M. Pani, *Los multifamiliares de pensiones*, 46.
41. Nutini and Isaac, *Social Stratification in Central Mexico*, 100.
42. Nutini and Isaac, *Social Stratification in Central Mexico*, 100.
43. Nutini and Isaac, *Social Stratification in Central Mexico*, 101.
44. Nutini and Isaac, *Social Stratification in Central Mexico*, 102.
45. "La Ciudad en Peligro," *Excélsior*, March 11, 1954, 3. For earlier background on conflicts over public spaces, see Cruz, *El trabajo en las calles*. For another example of contestations in public spaces, see Jiménez, *Making an Urban Public*.

46. Frieden, "Search for Housing Policy," 81–82.
47. The compiled data can be found in Frieden, "Search for Housing Policy," 77.
48. For examples, see Carlos Vargas, "Miles de Mexicanos Viven en Espantables Viviendas," *Excélsior*, November 26, 1944, 6.
49. Victor Ceja Reyes, "De Cara al Tiempo: Refugio de Desesperados," *El Nacional*, April 6, 1955, 8.
50. Instituto Nacional de la Vivienda (INV), *Investigación nacional*, sec. 4.
51. Haynes, "Order and Progress," 207–14.
52. Banco Nacional Hipotecario Urbano y de Obras Públicas (BNHUOP), *Estudios 6*, 37–39, 256. The BNHUOP was changed to Banobras (Banco Nacional de Obras Públicas, or National Bank of Public Works) in 1966.
53. BNHUOP, *Estudios 6*, 145–46.
54. BNHUOP, *Estudios 6*, 145–46. This pattern continued into the 1960s. For later studies, see Carmona, "El Problema de la Vivienda," 79–101.
55. Carmona, "El Problema de la Vivienda," 148.
56. Carmona, "El Problema de la Vivienda," 148.
57. Carmona, "El Problema de la Vivienda," 172.
58. Adrián García Cortés, "Mas Proyectazo," *El Universal*, February 5, 1951, 5. Pulquerías are establishments in Mexico that sell the alcoholic beverage pulque.
59. Cortés, "Mas Proyectazo," 5.
60. Adrián García Cortés, "Barbarie Tecnica," *El Universal*, June 10, 1951, reprinted in Cortés, *La reforma urbana de México*, 153. Adrián García Cortés was a celebrated journalist from Sinaloa who covered urban culture and Indigenous communities for various newspapers over the course of four decades. In 1972, he published a compilation of all of the articles he wrote about Mexico City's Planning Commission meetings that took place between 1950 and 1953. Cortés's regular coverage of the Planning Commission gives a rare and valuable record of the internal meetings held among the main political body responsible for designing and implementing a new street grid for the center of Mexico City. I refer to the articles in the book compilation unless it was only published in a newspaper.
61. Cortés, "Barbarie Tecnica," 162.
62. Cortés, "Barbarie Tecnica," 162.
63. Cortés, "Barbarie Tecnica," 162.
64. Alvarez Escobar, "Violenta dimisión de la Liga de Defensa de Propietarios de Casas," *El Universal*, October 15, 1952, reprinted in Cortés, *La reforma urbana*, 365.
65. Alvarez Escobar, "Se aprueba la ampliación de las calle de Guatemala," *El Universal*, July 2, 1952, reprinted in Cortés, *La reforma urbana*, 335; and Alvarez Escobar,

"Apertura de la avenida Veinte de Noviembre, desde Catedral hasta Peralvillo," *El Universal*, July 2, 1952, reprinted in Cortés, *La reforma urbana*, 315.

66. Adrián García Cortés, "Tacuba a Salvo," *El Universal*, March 22, 1953, 3
67. Cortés, "Tacuba a Salvo," 3, includes details on the parts of Guerrero that were demolished and cleared for extension of the Paseo de la Reforma, one of the few urban renewal projects, along with Tlatelolco (1964), to be implemented under Uruchurtu.
68. For Uruchurtu's political alliances, see Davis, *Urban Leviathan*, 134–36.
69. For examples, see Zipp, *Manhattan Projects*; Smith, *Boom Cities*; Klemek, *Transatlantic Collapse*; Kwak, "Slum Clearance"; and Sivaramakrishnan, *Re-visioning Indian Cities*.
70. "Ley de Planificación del Distrito Federal," *Diario Oficial*, December 31, 1953.
71. An example can be found in the history of Colonia Militar, documented by Cornelius, *Los inmigrantes pobres*, 212–15.
72. An early example of his agenda can be observed in "Promete Uruchurtu Mejorar los Servicios Públicos y Frenar la Carestía en el D.F.," *Excélsior*, December 2, 1952, 2, 6.
73. See the special issue dedicated to UNAM's University City, *Arquitectura México*, no. 39 (September 1952).
74. Carranza and Lara, *Modern Architecture in Latin America*, 162.
75. Pani formulated an approach that called for "a city within the city," essentially urban renewal, and "a city outside the city," a planned urban community built at a distance from the city center. For more background, see Gómez Mayorga and Pani, "El problema de la habitación," 71.
76. Carranza and Lara, *Modern Architecture in Latin America*, 153.
77. Garrido, "El Destino de Ciudad Universitaria," 197–200.

2. Mass Housing in the Mexican Metropolis

1. Olsen, *Artifacts*; Leidenberger, "Los orígenes," 24–38; Fierro, "Modeling the Urban Commune," 272–99.
2. M. Pani, *Los multifamiliares de pensiones*.
3. Patron, *IMSS*, 31.
4. For background on these labor conflicts, see Dion, *Workers and Welfare*, 75–80.
5. "El Nuevo Contrato Colectivo de los Trabajadores del IMSS," *Seguro Social: Organo del Sindicato Nacional de Trabajadores del Seguro Social*, December 19, 1949, 1.

6. "Arcevo Sobre Inversiones en Colonias para Trabajadores," August 1, 1945, Archivo Histórico del Instituto Mexicano del Seguro Social (AHIMSS).
7. "Los Discursos Pronunciados en la Apertura del IMSS," *Excélsior*, July 16, 1957, 12.
8. Arellano and Pani, *Historia oral*, 75–76.
9. For broader discussion, see Latham, *Modernization as Ideology*.
10. See Escobedo, "El gran experimento humano," 42; Díaz Arias, "Santa Fe," 177–78.
11. For an example of this discourse and programming, see IMSS's Unidad Morelos complex. Instituto Mexicano del Seguro Social (IMSS), *Unidad Morelos*.
12. A sample of an application for housing through IMSS can be found in IMSS, *Manual de Operaciones*, sec. I. For figures, see "Población Amparada" in IMSS, *Mantenimiento*, 43.
13. For another example of the selection process in another IMSS housing complex, see "Inaugurará hoy el Presidente la Unidad de Servicio 'Independencia,' del IMSS," *Excélsior*, September 20, 1960, 10.
14. Díaz Arias, "Santa Fe," 177. For another example of livestock and bars being prohibited from a social housing complex in Mexico City, see Eckstein, *Poverty of Revolution*, 67. For a view that warned of the problems between health and livestock in urban settings, see Demetrio Lopez Agatangelo, "El Hombre y la Habitación, el Animal y la Salud," *El Nacional*, December 21, 1965, 7.
15. Rodríguez Rebolledo, "Trabajo social."
16. Contained in IMSS, *Manual de Operaciones*, sec. I.
17. "Inaugurará hoy," 10.
18. J. Jesus Cervantes, "Los Primeros Habitatantes: Jose Manuel Padilla, El Primero entre los Primeros," *Impacto*, August 1957, 28.
19. Cervantes, "Los Primeros Habitatantes," 29.
20. Cervantes, "Los Primeros Habitatantes," 29.
21. Cervantes, "Los Primeros Habitatantes," 29.
22. "Plano General—Unidad Santa Fe," *Arquitectura México*, no. 59 (September 1957): 138.
23. "Plano General—Unidad Santa Fe," 138.
24. Ortiz Mena, "Una importante obra," 136.
25. "Plano General—Unidad Santa Fe," 158–69.
26. Díaz Arias, "Santa Fe," 175–76.
27. Díaz Arias, "Santa Fe," 179.
28. IMSS, *Unidad Morelos*, 32–33.

29. I draw from Nathan Glazer's work on modernism for essential characteristics. Glazer, *From a Cause*.
30. "Texto de discurso de Benito Coquet," *Excélsior*, September 21, 1960, 3.
31. Glazer, *From a Cause*, 7.
32. Vaughan and Lewis, *Eagle and the Virgin*, 6. See also Pratt, *Planetary Longings*.
33. Banco Nacional de Obras y Servicios Públicos, *Conjuntos habitacionales*, 6–7.
34. See "Se Necesitan 6,000 millones al año para viviendas," *Excélsior*, August 25, 1965; and Instituto Nacional de la Vivienda (INV), *Investigación nacional*, 55–59.
35. A. Ortiz Reza, "Nace una Ciudad Para Ochenta mil Personas," *Excélsior*, November 22, 1964, 1.
36. Rabe, "Alliance for Progress."
37. This charter is known as the "The Charter of Punta Del Este: Establishing an Alliance for Progress within the Framework of Operation Pan America," established on August 17, 1961. Available from the Yale Law School's Avalon Project, http://avalon.law.yale.edu/20th_century/intam16.asp, accessed September 9, 2017.
38. "Report on Housing and Urban Development," December 31, 1962, National Archives and Records Administration (NARA), box 15, RG 207.
39. Frieden, "Search for Housing Policy," 82.
40. See INV, *Investigación nacional*; IMSS, *Manual de Operaciones*, sec. I. Frieden's study was carried out in 1963 and funded by the AID. Frieden, "Search for Housing Policy," 88–90.
41. INV, *Colonias Proletarias*; INV, *Herradura de Tugurios*; and INV, *Investigación nacional*.
42. "Authorized Public Loans to Mexico," September 3, 1964, NARA, box 1, RG 286.
43. "Fact Sheet on ALPRO Supervised Agricultural Credit Program," April 1, 1965, NARA, box 19, RG 0286.
44. "Authorized Public Loans to Mexico."
45. Regulations for FOVI can be found in "Informe de Viviendas de FOVI," July 18, 1967, Fondo de Secretaría de Hacienda y Crédito Público (SHCP), Archivo General de la Nación (AGN), box 100, exp. 101/000/1.
46. "Informe de Viviendas de FOVI."
47. Overview of the changes under FOVI outlined in David Amato, "Report on FOVI to USAID," June 12, 1964, SHCP, AGN, box 100, exp. 101/000/1.
48. Marcelo Javelly, "Informe de FOVI," July 19, 1967, SHCP, AGN, box 100, exp. 101/000/1.
49. "FOVI: Relación de Proyectos en Operación," December 1967, SHCP, AGN, box 100, exp. 101/000/1.
50. "Report on FOVI to USAID."

51. Sample application forms can be found in SHCP, AGN, box 100, exp. 101/000/1.
52. The largest natural lake was Texcoco. Current figures on San Juan de Aragón are taken from the website of the Secretaría del Medio Ambiente del Gobierno del Distrito Federal, https://www.sedema.cdmx.gob.mx/comunicacion/nota/celebra-sedema-59-aniversario-del-bosque-de-san-juan-de-aragon-con-mejoras-ambientales; and "Diseña UNAM Humedal Artificial del Lago de San Juan de Aragón," from Dirección General de Comunicación Social, http://www.dgcs.unam.mx/boletin/bdboletin/2012_768.html, both accessed June 4, 2017.
53. The early of history of San Juan de Aragón is detailed in López Sarrelangue, "Una hacienda comunal indígena."
54. "Asunto: Lago de Texcoco—Desecación," July 2, 1936, Fondo Lázaro Cárdenas del Río, AGN, box 889, exp. 545.3/48.
55. Vitz, *City on a Lake*, 306–8.
56. Figure can be found in land expropriation files. See "Ejidos D. F. San Juan de Aragón," Archivos Presidenciales, Adolfo López Mateos, AGN, box 293, exp. 404.1/1595.
57. "Expropiación de los terrenos de San Juan de Aragón," *Diario Oficial de la Federación*, March 1, 1962.
58. Cymet, *From Ejido to Metropolis*, 6–7.
59. Major investment in public works projects began to wane in the mid-1950s. See Vitz, *City on a Lake*, 306.
60. Héctor Velázquez Moreno, "Dónde vives?," *Calli*, no. 15 (February 1965), 9.
61. Noelle, "Ramón Torres Martínez," 149–52.
62. Noelle, "Ramón Torres Martínez," 124.
63. "Asuntos de San Juan de Aragón," October 1964, Archivo Histórico del Distrito Federal (AHDF), Obras Públicas (OP), box 311, exp. 2.
64. Perry, *Neighborhood and Community Planning*, 32.
65. "Costos y planes" and "Informe de Unidad Vecinal I," 1963, AHDF, OP, box 311, exp. 3.
66. "López Mateos inauguró la Primera Ciudad de Interés Social del INV," *El Día*, November 5, 1964, 9.
67. For examples, see "Nació una Nueva Ciudad en el Distrito Federal: El Conjunto San Juan de Aragón Constituye un Sistema Urbano Modelo Para Beneficio de las Clases Populares," *El Día*, November 16, 1964, 1; and "Nueva y Hermosa Ciudad Incorporada a la Capital Mexicana," *Excélsior*, November 16, 1964, 1.
68. Andrean Villalea, "Inauguró ALM la Unidad de Viviendas Presidente Kennedy," *Excélsior*, December 18, 1964, 1. The Unión de Obreros de Artes Gráficas de los

Talleres Comerciales were the Union of Graphic Arts Workers in Commercial Workshops.
69. Ortiz Reza, "Nace una Ciudad."
70. "En el Régimen de López Mateos se Edificaron 92 mil 665 Unidades de Habitación en El País," *El Día*, September 14, 1964, 7. Note the total over the course of six years was 92,665 units.
71. There are 1,010 housing contracts stored in the Federal District's archives. "Titulares," November 1965, OP, AHDF, box 96, exp. 3.
72. "Titulares."
73. "Se Convierten en Propietarios 10 mil Trabajadores," *El Día*, November 9, 1964, 9.
74. "Se Convierten en Propietarios," 9.
75. "Se Convierten en Propietarios," 15.
76. "Se Convierten en Propietarios," 9.
77. Eckstein, *Poverty of Revolution*, 67. For an example of a view that warned of the problems between health and livestock in urban settings, see Demetrio Lopez Agatangelo, "El Hombre y la Habitación," 7.
78. "Titulares."
79. "16 Familias Fueron Trasladadas de 'Los Gachupines' a San Juan de Aragón," *Excélsior*, August 10, 1965, 15.
80. "16 Familias Fueron Trasladadas," 15.
81. "40 Familias de la colonia La Cruz Sufren por las Lluvias," *El Día*, July 31, 1971, 9.
82. Sudra, "Low-Income Housing System," 132.
83. Eckstein, *Poverty of Revolution*, 65–68.
84. Eckstein, *Poverty of Revolution*, 73.
85. Eckstein, *Poverty of Revolution*, 73.
86. "Destinan 200 Lotes de la Unidad Aragón para Casas de Locutores," *El Día*, February 3, 1970, 9; and "Empleados de ASA solicitan casas en la Unidad Aragón," *El Día*, February 4, 1970, 9.
87. Luis de Cervantes, "15,000 viviendas populares se harán este año en el Distrito Federal," *Excélsior*, March 14, 1970, 6.

3. Land Politics on the Periphery

1. "Declaratoria que crea la Zona Sub-urbana del Lago de Texcoco," April 3, 1953, Centro de Información y Documentación de Nezahualcóyotl (CIDNE), box 17, exp. UAE/V-18/E-210/13.

2. Proposals for reflooding Lake Texcoco can be found in "Asunto: Lago de Texcoco y Tolvaneras," April 1953, Archivo General de la Nación (AGN), Ramas Presidenciales, Adolfo Ruiz Cortines (ARC), box 569, exp. 496/4.
3. "Transcripción de la declaración de Eduardo Chávez, secretario de Recursos Hidráulicos de 5 de diciembre de 1955," cited in Confederación Nacional Revolucionaria, August 8, 1957, AGN, ARC, box 569, exp. 496/4. See also an interview with Jorge L. Tamayo in "La Lucha Contra la Naturaleza," *El Día*, May 4, 1971, 9.
4. The 1958 Law of Sub-Divisions of Lands in the State of Mexico established the building codes and infrastructural requirements for official recognition of a new residential subdivision. Published in *Gaceta de Gobierno: Organo Oficial del Gobierno del Estado de México* (Toluca), December 20, 1958, 1–3.
5. Raúl Romero Erazo, "Problemática de la Invasión de Terrenos Colonia México," n.d., Centro de Información y Documentación de Nezahualcóyotl (CIDNE), Bibliografía no. 699/16–83, 2.
6. Montaño, *La Tierra de Ixtapalapa*, 101.
7. Romero, "Problemática de la Invasión," 4–5.
8. Romero, "Problemática de la Invasión," 8.
9. Palerm, *Obras hidráulicas prehispánicas*, 220.
10. For sources describing the area before urbanization, see Apenes, "'Tlateles' of Lake Texcoco," 29–32; Parsons, *Last Pescadores*, 129.
11. Census data list the population in 1950 at 1,287 and 1,642 for 1965. Instituto Nacional Estadística Geografía e Información (NEGI), "Cuaderno Estadístico Municipal Chimalhuacán Estado de México," 1996, CIDNE, no. 1878/50.
12. Romero, "Problemática de la Invasión," 11.
13. Romero, "Problemática de la Invasión," 12.
14. "Escritura Compra Venta de Terreno en colonia México," November 9, 1947, CIDNE, box 16, UAE/V-16/E-167.
15. "Escritura Compra."
16. "Declaratoria que crea la Zona Sub-urbana del Lago de Texcoco," *Diario Oficial de la Federación*, February 12, 1949.
17. A report featuring the history of "authorizations" for forty-seven colonias can be found in Secretaría General de Gobierno del Estado de México, "Relación de Fraccionamientos de Ciudad Nezahualcóyotl," 1972, CIDNE, box 16, UAE/V-15.
18. *Gaceta de Gobierno*, September 24, 1947, 1–2.
19. Tamayo, *Panorámica Socioeconómica 1970*, 5–6.
20. Iglesias, *Netzahualcóyotl*, 22–23; Servicios Educativos Populares (SEPAC), *El Manual del Colono*, 11.

21. "El mayor número de tolvaneras se produce en marzo en Distrito Federal," *El Día*, June 7, 1971, 9.
22. Sadot Fabila Alva, "Nezahualcóyotl: Una Ciudad que Empieza a Vivir," *El Día*, May 14, 1973, 14.
23. Pagaza, *Anatomía de un gobierno*, 158.
24. Parsons, *Last Pescadores*, 12.
25. "Oficio de la Federación de Colonos del Vaso de Texcoco, firmado por Juan Pérez M, de la colonia del Sol," September 2, 1953, AGN, Fondo de Porfirio Muñoz Ledo (PML), box 569, exp. 496/4.
26. Iglesias, *Netzahualcóyotl*, 22.
27. From an interview with Ernestina Mateos de Huerta, "Sangre, Sudor y la Vida de un Hijo," *Revista Expectativas de Actualidad*, 1994, 15. Also discussed in Ernestina Mateos de Huerta, CIDNE Oral History Collection (Audioteca), May 14, 1991.
28. The borders for the colonia are indicated on the land contracts between Justino Lopez Herrera and the party of César Hann Cárdenas and Javier Muñoz on May 24, 1949. See "Contrato de Compra Venta de Terreno en colonia El Sol," CIDNE, box 16, UAE/V-27/E-435.
29. Vitz, *City on a Lake*, 165–74.
30. Lake Texcoco and its surroundings were first deemed federal property by President Benito Juárez in 1862. After parts of the lake were drained through public works projects, Porfirio Díaz designated the lake bed as federal property. On September 9, 1912, the Secretaría de Fomento declared the land as federal property and was upheld again by President Carranza on September 17, 1917. See Luna, *Nezahualcóyotl*, 4–6.
31. I counted forty-three contracts notarized by Rafael del Paso Reinert, although that is not a complete tally. For examples relevant to Colonias El Sol and Aurora, see "Contratos de Compra Venta de un Terreno colonia El Sol," 1949, CIDNE, box 16, exp. UAE/V-16/E-168; and "Contratos de Compra Venta de Terrenos de la colonia Aurora," 1956, CIDNE, box 16, exp. UAE/V-16/E-182.
32. "Queja de colonos del Sol," December 5, 1950, Archivo de la Secretaría de Obras Públicas del Estado de México (ASOPEM), El Sol, exp. 0871208/67; and "Escrito de vecinos de la colonia del Sol," November 1950, ASOPEM, El Sol, exp. 0871208/67. Also see Iglesias, *Netzahualcóyotl*, 32.
33. Iglesias, *Netzahualcóyotl*, 31.
34. Beltran, cited in Iglesias, *Netzahualcóyotl*, 33.
35. Beltran, cited in Iglesias, *Netzahualcóyotl*, 34–35.

36. For an example of Ortega's reports, see "Informe de Rubén Ortega López, presidente del Comité de Fraccionamientos Urbanos del Distrito de Texcoco," January 1954, AGN, Fondo de Adolfo Ruiz Cortines (ARC), box 569, exp. 496/4.
37. "Escrito del Comité Pro-Mejoras de la colonia del Sol," April 6, 1953, AGN, ARC, box 569, exp. 496/4.
38. "Informe de Rubén Ortega López a Enrique Rodriguez Cano, Sec. de la Presidencia de la República," September 1953, AGN, ARC, box 569, exp. 491/4.
39. "Escrito al Presidente de la República," July 25, 1956, AGN, ARC, box 569, exp. 496/4.
40. This estimate comes from "Relacionado con 30,000 colonos que viven en las tierras resucitado al Lago de Texcoco, municipal Chimalhuacán, Estado de México," August 8, 1957, AGN, ARC, box 569, exp. 496/4.
41. Example of flyer found in "Protesta e Inconformidades en el Periodo de las Actividades Electorales," 1969, CIDNE, box 26, exp. UAE/V1/E13.
42. "Escrito de los colonos de la colonia Romero en contra del fraccionador Raúl Romero," June 30, 1953, ASOPEM, Colonia Romero, exp. 0871410/54.
43. "Queja de los colonos del Vaso de Texcoco en contra de Rubén Ortega López y de Guadalupe Ramírez Chavira," January 2, 1955, AGN, ARC, box 569, exp. 418.2/107; and "Denuncia de los Colonos de el ex-Vaso de Texcoco," *El Universal*, June 3, 1953, 9.
44. Iglesias, *Netzahualcóyotl*, 59.
45. Iglesias, *Netzahualcóyotl*, 63.
46. Taken from an interview in Alba Muñiz, "Control político," 74.
47. "Escrito de Ruben Ortega y otras organizaciones del Vaso de Texcoco," October 23, 1956, AGN, ARC, box 569, exp. 545.1/71.
48. Iglesias, *Netzahualcóyotl*, 96.
49. *Gaceta de Gobierno*, December 20, 1958.
50. "Otoragacion de Terrenos y Escrituras Constitutiva de la colonia Aurora Sur," January 1956, CIDNE, box 16, exp. UAE/V-16/E-182, 5.
51. "Relaciones Exteriores y Naturalización," *Diario Oficial de la Federación*, March 31, 1951, 2.
52. Aréchiga, *La Plaza de Toros*, 34.
53. Background to the company and its founders found in Aréchiga, *La Plaza de Toros*, 32–33.
54. Carlos Várgas, "Señalan a los judíos como instigadores de los sucesos ocurridos en Chimalhuacán," *La Extra*, May 5, 1961, 2–4.
55. Aréchiga, *La Plaza de Toros*, 35.

56. "Acuerdo del ejecutivo del Estado Relativo al Fraccionamiento Aurora Municipio de Chimalhuacán, Distrito de Texcoco," March 8, 1957, CIDNE, Secretaría de Gobierno, no. 16E-21.
57. "Informe de Víctor Manuel Pérez Mondragón al C. Procurador General de justicia del estado de México," February 1971, CIDNE, box 16, exp. UAE/V-18/E-210.
58. "Informe de Víctor Manuel Pérez Mondragón," 18.
59. Várgas, "Señalan a los judíos," 2.
60. "Oficio 201-I de la Dirección General de Gobernación," December 4, 1967, ASOPEM, Colonia Aurora, exp. 0870499/56-021008.
61. Tamayo, *Panorámica Socioeconómica 1970*, 41–49.
62. Instituto de Información e Investigación Geográfica, *Panorámica Socioeconómica*, 276.
63. Aréchiga, *La Plaza de Toros*, 27–30.
64. Aréchiga, *La Plaza de Toros*, 34–36.
65. Aréchiga, *La Plaza de Toros*, 56–57.
66. Aréchiga, interview with author, March 8, 2017.
67. "Se inaugura el cine lago," *El Gallo*, December 12, 1963, 1.
68. That rare exception was Várgas, "Señalan a los judíos," 2.
69. The source is a clipping of an article included in an untitled, self-published memoir by a resident of Colonia Maravillas found uncategorized in CIDNE's library. The clipping includes the title and article but is missing all other details. Manuel Palomares Bobadilla, "El Síndico Muñoz Protégé al Judío Cemaj," in Palomares, *Historia de Ciudad Nezahualcóyotl*, 198.
70. Bobadilla, "El Síndico Muñoz Protégé al Judío Cemaj," 198.
71. Rosa, *Promoción Popular*, 107–9.
72. An image and address for the offices in the Metropolitan Cathedral can be found in an advertisement for the Romero Brothers company in *El Gallo*, April 1963, 11.
73. Rosa, *Promoción Popular*, 107.
74. Ocotitla Saucedo, "Movimientos de colonos," 145.
75. Ocotitla Saucedo, "Movimientos de colonos," 140.
76. Comité Ejecutivo Central, Pro-Municipio Libre, "Inauguración del Municipio," *El Gallo*, April 1963, 1.
77. Comité Ejecutivo Central, "Inauguración del Municipio," 1.
78. See CIDNE, Fototeca, folder V-2/5.
79. Alan Knight identifies five levels of caciquismo: national, state, regional, municipal, and local. See Knight, "*Caciquismo* in Twentieth-Century Mexico," 20.
80. Middlebrook, "Caciquismo and Democracy," 412.

81. Along with the issue of labor unions, Salvador Maldonado Aranda also discusses the "territorial dimension that union *cacicazgos* acquire in the urban-industrial space" related to caciques or charros in organized labor. See Aranda, "Between Law and Arbitrariness," 242. Similar phenomena in urban-based universities have been examined by Pensado and Pansters, the former focusing on student organizations and *porros* in the 1950s and 1960s, the latter on institutional power of a Puebla university in the 1990s. See Pensado, *Rebel Mexico*, 5; and Pansters, "Building a Cacicazgo," 296–326.
82. Cornelius, "Contemporary Mexico," 135.
83. Cornelius, "Contemporary Mexico," 141.
84. Lewis, "Dead-End *Caudillismo*," 151–68.
85. Ocotitla Saucedo, "Movimientos de colonos," 93.

4. Autoconstrucción in Ciudad Neza

1. Boils, *Las casas campesinas*.
2. Romero, *Latinoamerica*.
3. Holston, "Autoconstruction," 450.
4. Frieden, "Search for Housing Policy," 77.
5. Harth Deneke, "Colonias Proletarias," 45.
6. Frieden, "Search for Housing Policy," 81.
7. Harth Deneke, "Colonias Proletarias," 45; Sudra, "Low-Income Housing System," 75. Matthew Vitz identifies Colonia Ex-hipódromo de Peralvillo (1923) as the first large colonia proletaria. Vitz, *City on a Lake*, 91.
8. Napier, "Core Housing," 11.
9. Raúl Torres Barrón, "La Ciudad de Cartón, a dos Cuadras del Viaducto," *Excélsior*, January 12, 1970.
10. Alí Primera, "Techos de cartón," *Alí Primera*, vol. 2 (Cigarrón: Promus, 1972), CD.
11. Gandy, "Planning, Anti-planning," 247–64; Friedmann, *China's Urban Transition*.
12. Data from the Instituto Nacional de Estadística y Geografía, Anuario estadístico (1975), reprinted in Rosa, *Promoción Popular*.
13. Alcázar, *Autoconstrucción de vivienda*; Bazant, *Autoconstrucción de vivienda*; Lomnitz, *Networks and Marginality*; Pezzoli, *Human Settlements*.
14. Ruvalcaba, *Ciudad Nezahualcóyotl*, 24.
15. Ruvalcaba, *Ciudad Nezahualcóyotl*, 24.
16. Drawn from Banco Nacional Hipotecario Urbano y de Obras Públicas, *Estudios 6*.

17. "40 mil Talleres Clandestinos de Costura Operan en el DF," *El Día*, September 7, 1972, 13.
18. "Maquiladoras Explotadas," *El Despertar del Pueblo*, August 1973, 9.
19. Instituto de Información e Investigación Geográfica, *Panorámica Socioeconómica*, 275.
20. Quote cited in Alba Muñiz, "Control político," 70.
21. Enrique Ruiz García, interview with CIDNE staff, September 3, 1990, Ciudad Nezahualcóyotl, CIDNE Oral History Collection (Audioteca).
22. Tamayo, *Panorámica Socioeconómica*, 17.
23. Tamayo, *Panorámica Socioeconómica*, 18–19.
24. Tamayo, *Panorámica Socioeconómica*, 17, 21.
25. Sudra, "Low-Income Housing System," 97; García Canclini, Castellanos, Mantecón, and López, *La ciudad de los viajeros*.
26. Iglesias, *Netzahualcóyotl*, 22.
27. Iglesias, *Netzahualcóyotl*, 20–21.
28. "Volante del Fraccionamiento Colonia Estado de México," flyer reprinted in Ocotitla Saucedo, "Movimientos de colonos," 78.
29. Interview found in Juárez y Ortega Valadéz, "El proceso de segregación," 184.
30. "Escrito de vecinos de la colonia del Sol." Copies of these reprinted letters were consulted in "Obras Públicas y Colonización," 1950–70, Archivo Histórico del Estado de México (AHEM), Fondo Fomento y Obras Públicas (OP), vol. 18, exp. 8. I cite them in the form I consulted them; however, the original letters were utilized in Ocotitla Saucedo, "Movimientos de colonos."
31. Torres, *La Plaza de Toros*, 25.
32. Torres, *La Plaza de Toros*, 31.
33. Torres, *La Plaza de Toros*, 31.
34. "La Vivienda: Los Problemas y Soluciones," *El Día*, July 8, 1972, 9.
35. Carlos Várgas, "Anuncian amplias y modernas residencias y el público hallará sólo chozas inmundas," *La Extra*, May 1961, 3.
36. "Irregularidad en Fraccionamientos del Lago de Texcoco," *El Nacional*, November 26, 1959, 4; and later, "Escrito de Abraham Zolotnik, apoderado del fraccionamiento Aurora S.A.," February 26, 1963, Colonia Aurora, ASOPEM, AHEM, vol. 18, exp. 8.
37. "Escrito de Gregorio Cervantes," December 3, 1967, Colonia Aurora, ASOPEM, AHEM, OP, vol. 18, exp. 8.
38. "Censo de la SRH de la colonia del Sol," January 21, 1959, CIDNE, box 15, UAE/V-1/E-9.
39. "Censo de la SRH."

40. Instituto Mexicano del Seguro Social (IMSS), *Investigación de vivienda*, estrato 69.
41. IMSS, *Investigación de vivienda*, estratos 48–49.
42. Lewis, "Urbanization without Breakdown," 41.
43. Bazant, *Autoconstrucción de vivienda*, 92–94.
44. Jorge Cruz Lozano, interviewed by Olga Bonilla Elizalde, October 15, 1991, Ciudad Nezahualcóyotl, CIDNE, (Audioteca). Listed as "Habitante de Cd. Nezahualcoyotl desde 1954."
45. IMSS, *Investigación de vivienda*, estrato 69.
46. Maria Martinez, interviewed with Olga Bonilla Elizalde, October 15, 1991, Audioteca, CIDNE, Ciudad Nezahualcóyotl. Listed as "Habitante de Cd. Nezahualcoyotl desde 1965." Lewis, *Five Families*, 199.
47. Bazant, *Autoconstrucción de vivienda*, 93.
48. Description based accounts from Martinez, interview; Vargas Soriano, interview; and Gustavo Alatriste, dir., *Q.R.R.: Quien resulte responsable* (Mexico City, 1971), DVD.
49. Castillo, "Produccion del Espacio Urbano," 115.
50. That work was later published in Lewis, *Five Families*.
51. Lewis, *Five Families*, 198.
52. For examples of recorded observations of livestock, see teacher-student accounts in Estrada Ayon, "Memoria," 12. CIDNE has an uncataloged collection of theses produced by students training to become teachers in Mexico.
53. Lewis, *Five Families*, 198–99.
54. Ernestina Mateos de Huerta, "Sangre, Sudor y la Vida de un Hijo," *Revista Expectativas de Actualidad*, 1994, 14–16.
55. Espinosa Castillo, "Produccion del Espacio Urbano," 121.
56. Pagaza, *Anatomía de un gobierno*, 145.
57. Pagaza, *Anatomía de un gobierno*, 145.
58. Pagaza, *Anatomía de un gobierno*, 146.
59. Auyero, "Patients of the State," 6.
60. For key works that cover these questions, see Schwartz, *Queuing and Waiting*; Levine, *Geography of Time*; Flaherty, *Watched Pot*; Clark, *Time and Power*; Munn, "Cultural Anthropology of Time," 93–123; and Thompson, "Time, Work-Discipline," 56–97.
61. Auyero, *Patients of the State*.
62. Sigal, "Marginalidad espacial," 1547–77; Sánchez-Mejorada Fernández and Torres Mora, "Cotidianidad y Modalidades," 167–200; Alonso, *Sexo, trabajo*.
63. Based on Sánchez-Mejorada Fernández and Torres Mora, "Cotidianidad y Modalidades"; Iglesias, *Netzahualcóyotl*; and Maria Martinez, interview.

64. For examples of children walking with mothers, see "Dramática Situación Provoca la Escasez de Agua Potable en Ciudad Netzahualcóyotl," *El Día*, March 6, 1969, 9; Alatriste, Q.R.R. For an extensive study of the relationship between water, gender, and class in Mexico, see the work of Bennett, "Gender, Class, and Water," 76–99.
65. In addition to the sources by Sigal, Sánchez-Mejorada Fernández and Torres Mora, Alonso, Iglesias, and Maria Martinez, see Sudra, "Low-Income Housing System," 476; Rivero Villar, "Role of Social Capital," 120–25; and Pedro Díaz G., "¿Te has preguntado cómo nació Ciudad Nezahualcóyotl?," *Excélsior*, February 13, 2017, https://www.excelsior.com.mx/comunidad/te-has-preguntado-como-nacio-ciudad-nezahualcoyotl-i/1145590.
66. "Se Agudiza la Escasez de Agua Potable en Ciudad Netzahualcóyotl," *El Día*, March 5, 1969, 9.
67. Rivero Villar, "Role of Social Capital," 121.
68. IMSS, *Mantenimiento*; "Plano General—Unidad Santa Fe," *Arquitectura México*, no. 59 (September 1957): 158–69.
69. Arellano, *Rumores y retratos*, 92.
70. Mateos de Huerta, "Sangre, Sudor," 15; Alatriste, Q.R.R.
71. Lear, *Workers, Neighbors*, 38; Piccato, *City of Suspects*, 20.
72. Departamento del Distrito Federal (DDF), *La Ciudad de México*, 34–53; Krieger, *Megalópolis*, 32–33. It should be noted that while potable water was generally distributed to middle- and upper-class areas, there were notable malfunctions and problems at times for these areas as well. See Aboites Aguilar, "Illusion of National Power," 218–44.
73. Tyler, *Stigma*; Muhammad, *Condemnation of Blackness*; Newell, *Histories of Dirt*; Freeman, *Color of Love*; Verma and Srivastana, *Routledge Handbook of Exclusion*; Wacquant, *Urban Outcasts*; Bayón, "El 'lugar' de los pobres," 133–66.
74. For two representative examples, see Clark, *Dark Ghetto*; and Glazer and Moynihan, *Beyond the Melting Pot*.
75. "Drama y Crimen en las Colonias Proletarias," *El Día*, June 19, 1969.
76. "Marginados del Progreso a un Paso de la Metrópoli," *Novedades*, August 2, 1970.
77. "Marginados del Progreso."
78. "Marginados del Progreso."
79. "Marginados del Progreso."
80. Jorge L. Tamayo, "La Lucha Contra la Naturaleza," *El Día*, May 4, 1971.
81. J. R. Gamez Teran, "Fin de una Leyenda Negra," *Novedades*, January 8, 1971.
82. "Esto es Ciudad Nezahualcóyotl," *Novedades*, September 5, 1971.
83. "Esto es Ciudad Nezahualcóyotl."

84. J. R. Gamez Teran, "Fin de una Leyenda Negra: Todo el Problema Comienza a 5 Kmts. del Zócalo; Nezahualcóyotl," *Novedades*, January 9, 1971.
85. Pagaza, *Anatomía de un gobierno*, 158.
86. Pagaza, *Anatomía de un gobierno*, 158.
87. Pagaza, *Anatomía de un gobierno*, 155.
88. Pagaza, *Anatomía de un gobierno*, 155.
89. Frieden, "Search for Housing Policy," 75–77.
90. Castells, "Apuntes," 1182.

5. Mortgaging the Revolution

1. "Llegó Allende: América Latina queremos libertad, dijo LE," *Excélsior*, 1 December 1972, 1.
2. Mancera, "Inversión en programas habitacionales," 62. Infonavit stands for Instituto del Fondo Nacional de la Vivienda para los Trabajadores / Institute of the National Housing Fund for Workers.
3. "Llegó Allende: América Latina queremos libertad, dijo LE," *Excélsior*, 1 December 1972, 1.
4. "Llegó Allende," 1.
5. Alejandro Iñigo, "'Levantar Unidades Habitacionales es Liberar' Ante Allende, Sentíes Puso en Servicio el Conjunto Vicente Guerrero," *Excélsior*, December 2, 1972, 26.
6. Garza et al., *El problema de la vivienda*.
7. Infonavit, *Primer informe*, 14.
8. Infonavit, *Primer informe*, 14.
9. "Las Ciudades Perdidas son un Reto al Infonavit," *El Universal*, August 23, 1973, 7.
10. "Ante el Problema de la Habitacion," *Excélsior*, March 22, 1972, 13. For one of the earliest articles to use the term *ciudad perdida*, see "La Llamada 'Ciudad Perdida' fue Cambiada a Ixtapalapa," *Excélsior*, December 24, 1950, 12.
11. Buelink, "Viviena para los no asalariados," 31.
12. Buelink, "Viviena para los no asalariados," 34–35.
13. For broader overview, see Walker, *Waking from the Dream*.
14. A. Ortiz Reza, "Nace una Ciudad Para Ochenta mil Personas," *Excélsior*, November 22, 1964, 1.
15. Arellano, *Modernidad habitada*.
16. Alonso and Montes, *El espacio habitacional*.
17. Héctor Velázquez Moreno, "Dónde vives?," *Calli*, no. 15 (February 1965), 9–11.
18. Prieto and Gutiérrez, "Unidad de Servicios Sociales."

19. Ramón Torres Martínez, "Una solución al problema de la vivienda," *Novedades*, December 20, 1969, 6. See also Mario Quintero Beccerra, "Urge Establecer el Plan Nacional de la Viviena," *El Universal*, June 18, 1970, 7.
20. Martínez, "Una solución," 6.
21. Martínez, "Una solución," 6.
22. "La vivienda unifamiliar, solución utiopica al problema de la vivienda," *El Día*, May 6, 1972, 9.
23. Angel Escalante Baranda, "La Vivienda," *Novedades*, February 2, 1970, 7.
24. *V Comisión de Estudio: Informe sobre la vivienda popular*, Comisión Nacional Tripartita, 1971, unpublished report, cited in Robinson, "Politics of Low-Income Housing," 36. A note of gratitude to Lisa Robinson for calling attention to the overlooked Brazilian influence on Mexico's housing policy.
25. "Discurso de Silva-Herzog," *El Universal*, May 2, 1972, 11.
26. Benmergui, "Housing Development," 218.
27. Perlman, *Myth of Marginality*, 201.
28. "Algunos comentarios sobre la vivienda popular," *Revista Mexicana de la Construcción*, no. 112 (April 1972): 37, reprinted in Buelink, "Programa de estudios," 16.
29. Pearlman, *Myth of Marginality*, 204.
30. Buelink, "Programa de estudios," 17.
31. Robinson, "Politics of Low-Income Housing," 26.
32. J. Reyes Estrada, "400,000 Puertas para Viviendas del Infonavit Serán Construidas por los Campesinos del Estado de Durango," *Excélsior*, January 24, 1973, 5.
33. Description of events can be found in Artemio Rubio y Mendizabal, "Una Indudable Habilidad Política," *El Universal*, May 2, 1972, 13.
34. "En Marcha el Plan de la Vivienda," *El Nacional*, May 3, 1972, n.p.
35. The outline for the use of these laws can be found in "Leyes, Estatutos, y Requerimientos del Infonavit," May–September 1972, AGN, Fondo de Porfirio Muñoz Ledo (PML), box G1-1, exp. 1.
36. "Oficial: Silva-Herzog Será Director del Fondo Nacional de la Viviena," *Excélsior*, April 30, 1972, 3.
37. "Discurso de Silva-Herzog," 11.
38. "Leyes, Estatutos, y Requerimientos del Infonavit," May–September 1972, AGN, PML, box G1-1, exp. 1.
39. "Cumplimos un año y . . . ," *El Día*, April 30, 1973, 11.
40. Poniatowska, *La noche de Tlatelolco*.
41. Poniatowska, *Hasta no verte*.
42. Elena Poniatowska, "El Infonavit Beneficiará a Casi Cuarto Millones de Trabajadores y sus Familias," *Novedades*, June 15, 1973, 7.

43. "Criterios para la Asignacion de los Recursos del INFONAVIT," May–September 1972, AGN, PML, box G1-1, exp. 1.
44. Poniatowska, "El Infonavit Beneficiará," 8.
45. Elena Poniatowska, "Ni Compadrazgo ni Deshonestidad para los Créditos en el Infonavit," *Novedades*, June 16, 1973, 7.
46. "Será Transformado Radicalmente el Instituto Nacional de la Vivienda," *El Universal*, December 11, 1970, 4. The INV was shut down and reopened in 1971 as INDECO, Instituto Nacional para el Desarrollo de la Comunidad Rural y la Vivienda Popular.
47. Iturriaga, "Creación y asimilación," 4–5.
48. Poniatowska, "Ni Compadrazgo," 8.
49. Poniatowska, "Ni Compadrazgo," 8.
50. Elena Poniatowska, "En Meses el Infonavit ha Hecho mas Casas que Varios Regimenes," *Novedades*, June 17, 1973, 7.
51. Poniatowska, "En Meses el Infonavit," 7.
52. Russell, *History of Mexico*, 513.
53. "Infonavit: La casa de la Discordia," *Proceso*, January 14, 1978, https://www.proceso.com.mx/122189/infonavit-la-casa-de-la-discordia (site no longer extant).
54. "Discurso de Silva-Herzog," 11.
55. Carlos A. Medina, "Pide Fidel Velázquez que Rinda Cuentas el Infonavit," *El Sol de México*, June 20, 1973, 13.
56. Medina, "Pide Fidel Velázquez," 13.
57. "El Primer Mandatario Puso en Servicio las Instalaciones del Centro de Cómputo Electrónico del Infonavit en Villa Obregón," *El Nacional*, May 2, 1973, 3.
58. "Seleccionó 23,000 Obreros para Obtener Casa, una Computadora del Infonavit," *Excélsior*, August 23, 1973, 9.
59. "V Informe Anual," Dirección Empresarial, Infonavit, 1977, 7.
60. Robinson, "Politics of Low-Income Housing," 86; "Radicalismo verbal del sindicalismo oficialista," *Proceso*, April 11, 1981, https://www.proceso.com.mx/130816/radicalismo-verbal-del-sindicalismo-oficialista (site no longer extant).
61. Felipe Vargas, "Responde Silva-Herzog con Cifras a los Ataques de la CTM al Infonavit," *Novedades*, June 28, 1973, 7.
62. "Infonavit solo ha Hecho 6 mil de las 100 mil Casas que Ofreció, dice Fidel," *Novedades*, November 16, 1973, 17.
63. "Ni el 50 percent de las Casas Prometidas ha Realizado el Infonavit: Fidel Velázquez," *Novedades*, December 22, 1975, 7.
64. "La Denuncia Contra El Infonavit," *Novedades*, June 12, 1976, 11.

65. "La Denuncia Contra El Infonavit," 11.
66. For an example, see "Unidades Habitacionales Focos de Vicio," *El Heraldo de México*, October 23, 1976, n.p.
67. "Asegura Fidel Velázquez que en el INFONAVIT no se Aplica el Tripartismo," *El Nacional*, June 4, 1976, 5.
68. "Asegura Fidel Velázquez," 5.
69. Sergio de Avila, "El Infonavit Responde a Fidel: 19 mil Millones Tiene en Lotes y Materiales," *Novedades*, December 22, 1975, 5.
70. Avila, "Responde a Fidel," 5.
71. Robinson, "Politics of Low-Income Housing," 70.
72. "Bernardo Aguirre Resuelve Problemas del Infonavit en Chihuahua," *El Universal*, September 19, 1976, 9.
73. "Al Fin del Sexenio, el INFONAVIT Habrá Entregado 120 mil Viviendas," *El Día*, May 2, 1976, 13.
74. "El INFONAVIT Trabaja en 120 Ciudades del Interior: Ha Entregado 120 Conjuntos," *El Día*, June 8, 1976, 4.
75. "Entrega el INFONAVIT las Primeras Casas de Interés Social en Juchitán, Oax.," *El Nacional*, February 28, 1974, 7; "El INFONAVIT Trabaja," 4.
76. "La Denuncia Contra El Infonavit," 13.
77. "Los sindicatos manejarán los recursos para viviendas," *Proceso*, January 19, 1980, https://www.proceso.com.mx/127785/los-sindicatos-manejaran-los-recursos-para-viviendas (site no longer extant).
78. Lenti, *Redeeming the Revolution*, 247–48.
79. "Los sindicatos manejarán."
80. Tilly, *Durable Inequality*, 10.

6. Strike

1. Rogelio Vargas Soriano, interview with author, June 13, 2018. For an account of Echeverría's visit, see "Una visita de Echeverría a Ciudad Nezahualcóyotl," *El Día*, June 20, 1970, 1.
2. "Se dará una solución rápida al problema de la tenencia de la tierra en Ciudad Nezahualcóyotl," *El Día*, August 3, 1971, 1.
3. From the *Anuario Estadistica*, 1975, tabulated in Rosa, *Promoción Popular*, 45.
4. Schmidt, *Deterioration of the Mexican Presidency*; Dillingham, *Oaxaca Resurgent*; Kiddle and Muñoz, *Populism in Twentieth Century Mexico*.
5. For an example, see Schmidt, *Deterioration of the Mexican Presidency*.
6. Camín, *Después del Milagro*, 153.

7. See Secretaría General de Gobierno del Estado de México, "Relación de Fraccionamientos de Ciudad Nezahualcóyotl," 1972, Centro de Información y Documentación de Nezahualcóyotl (CIDNE), box 16, UAE/V-15.
8. Rosa, *Promoción Popular*, 71–73.
9. Fox, "Patterns of Morbidity," 151–85.
10. The theses are uncataloged in a box in CIDNE's library under the label "Tesis de las Escuelas Normales Públicas del Estado de México."
11. Pagaza, *Anatomía de un gobierno*, 119.
12. Comité Especial de Planificación Cooperación Municipio de Nezahualcóyotl, *Informe sobre el estudio preliminar en Ciudad Nezahualcóyotl, Estado de México*, 1969, CIDNE, box 16, UAE/V-25/E382.
13. Comité Especial de Planificación, *Informe sobre el estudio preliminar*.
14. See Secretaría General de Gobierno del Estado de México, "Relación de Fraccionamientos," 83.
15. "Resumen General de Obras de Urbanización, 1971–1972," 1972, CIDNE, box 16, UAE/V-1/E-5.
16. "Resumen General."
17. "Se Agudiza la Escasez de Agua Potable en Ciudad Netzahualcóyotl," *El Día*, March 5, 1969, 9; "Dramática Situación Provoca la Escasez de Agua Potable en Ciudad Netzahualcóyotl," *El Día*, March 6, 1969, 9–12.
18. Ruvalcaba, *Ciudad Nezahualcóyotl*, 30.
19. Tabulation of deaths from the Dirección General de Epidemiología (1970), table reprinted in Rosa, *Promoción Popular*, 48.
20. "Diarrhoeal Disease," World Health Organization: Fact Sheet, accessed July 8, 2018, http://www.who.int/news-room/fact-sheets/detail/diarrhoeal-disease.
21. Rosa, *Netzahualcóyotl*, 8.
22. The origins of the MRC movement can be found in "Distrito Federal," 1970, Archivo General de la Nación (AGN), Secretaría de Gobernación, Investigación Política y Social, box 1702-B, exp. 137845/2; and "Estado de México," November 25, 1970, AGN, box 1702-B, exp. 7. For the founding date of the MRC, see "Boletín de Prensa," December 28, 1971, Personal Archive of Angel Garcia Bravo (PA/AGB).
23. "Distrito Federal," AGN, box 1702-B, exp. 137845/2.
24. Quote and description of moving to Mexico City based on Rogelio Vargas Soriano, interview with author, June 3, 2018.
25. Jong and Graf, "How a City."
26. Benítez, *Viaje al centro de México*, 84.

27. "Acuerdo del ejecutivo del Estado Relativo al Fraccionamiento Aurora Municipio de Chimalhuacán, Distrito de Texcoco," March 8, 1957, CIDNE, Secretaría de Gobierno, box 16, no. 16E-21.
28. Benítez, *Viaje al centro de México*, 85.
29. Vélez-Ibáñez, *Rituals of Marginality*, 109–10.
30. Benítez, *Viaje al centro de México*, 89.
31. Hugo Sánchez, "Proponen a Hank González un Plan de ayuda a Ciudad Netzahualcóyotl," *El Día*, February 2, 1970.
32. "Estado de México," December 27, 1970, AGN, box 1702-B, exp. 7.
33. "Folleto del Frente Zapatista de Nezahualcóyotl," October 1971, CIDNE, box 16, V-29/E-4; "Distrito Federal: Información de Netzahualcóyotl," September 15, 1970, AGN, box 1702-B, exp. 7.
34. "Justo Precio de Garantía y Regularizar el Mercado Agrícola, Ofrece Hank González," *Excélsior*, December 22, 1964, 10; Guillermo Hewett Alva, "Compra Total de Cosechas: Fueron Autorizados a la CONASUPO para ese fin dos mil Millones de Pesos," *El Universal*, October 29, 1968, 6; Guillermo Ochoa, "Las Promesas de Hank González," *Excélsior*, September 13, 1969, 7–8. For background on CONASUPO, see Ochoa, *Feeding Mexico*, 177–98. CONASUPO stands for National Company of Popular Substances/Goods, or Compañía Nacional de Subsistencias Populares. See also Villegas, *El Estilo Personal*.
35. "Letter to the Director General de Quejas de la Presidencia," October 29, 1971, PA/AGB.
36. Quote and figures cited in Gutmann, *Ser hombre de verdad*, 67. For a broader overview, see Loaeza, "Política del rumor," 575–81.
37. Saiz, *El Movimiento Urbano Popular*.
38. Odón Madariaga stated, "There was the experience of October 2 [the date of the Tlatelolco massacre], and we were not prepared to suffer a defeat." In Benítez, *Viaje al centro de México*, 92.
39. The National University (UNAM) has a collection of the periodical during the years of the strike in the Hemeroteca Nacional de México. See, for example, "Alerta contra un grupo que se hace llamar Movimiento Restaurador de Colonos, A.C.," *El Heraldo del Valle de México*, March 15, 1970, 1.
40. "Estado de México," December 27, 1970.
41. Benítez, *Viaje al centro de México*, 93.
42. "Una multitude de habitantes de Ciudad d Netzahualcóyotl se reunió," *La Prensa*, June 24, 1971, 27.
43. Arreguin, *Cuatro años de lucha*, 16. Can be found in CIDNE under the classification Bibliografía 62/B-18.

44. Hugo Sánchez, "Se Unen Comuneros y Colonos Contra los Fraccionadores," *El Día*, October 4, 1971, 9.
45. Rogelio Vargas Soriano, interview with author, June 12, 2018.
46. "Reunión de trabajo en Los Pinos para resolver el problema de la tierra en Nezahualcóyotl," 1973, CIDNE, box 16, V-21/E-264.
47. "Reunión de trabajo."
48. For estimates for the number of members before and after the split, see "Breve comentario sobre la creación del Movimiento Restaurador de Colonos de Ciudad Neza," 1974, CIDNE, box 26, V-1/E-21. A description of the events surrounding the split can be found in "Estado de México: Información de Netzahualcóyotl," July 21, 1971, AGN, box 1702-B, exp. 7. A reproduction of the flyer for the student march was printed in a local weekly, *Radar*, July 11, 1971, 4, and cited in Ocotitla Saucedo, "Movimientos de colonos," 191.
49. "Boletín de Prensa."
50. "Carta al Director de Quejas de la Presidencia de el CE-MRC," October 29, 1971, PA/AGB.
51. "Represalias por la Huegla de Pagos a Fraccionadores de Neza," *El Día*, September 24, 1971, 11.
52. Vargas Soriano, interview, June 12, 2018.
53. Hugo Sánchez, "Denuncian Atropellos de la Policía de Ciudad Nezahualcóyotl," *El Día*, August 30, 1971, 9.
54. Hugo Sánchez, "Cierran casetas de los fraccionadores en Nezahualcóyotl," *El Día*, November 10, 1971, 11.
55. "Handwritten Note by Angel Avila Jacome," August 2, 1972, PA/AGB.
56. Arreguin, *Cuatro años de lucha*, 6.
57. Amado Escalaste, "La policía de Barquín aporrea a Restauradores en la celebración de las efemérides juristas," *Radar*, April 21, 1972, 9–10.
58. "Memoria sobre la cuestión de la tierra en Ciudad Nezahualcóyotl," 1972, CIDNE, box 16, exp. V-21/E-264.
59. Parts of the meeting were publicized in Ramón Jiménez, "Quedarán regularizadas dentro de un mes las tierras de Nezahualcóyotl," *El Día*, México, July 26, 1972, 9.
60. Arreguin, *Cuatro años de lucha*, 15.
61. "El Auténtico Movimiento Restaurador de Colonos Señala de Fraude al Fideicomiso de Ciudad Nezahualcóyotl," *Mercurio*, March 25, 1974, 1. Prior to Madariaga's promotion, a small news column reported a crowd of residents were led to murder Elezar Lopez Nava, who held the position Madariaga subsequently took shortly

thereafter. "Lincharon a un Regidor en Ciudad Neza," *El Universal*, August 28, 1973, 6.
62. Ocotitla Saucedo, "Movimientos de colonos," 214.
63. "A Los Colonos de Nezahualcóyotl," March 1973, AGN, box 1702-B, exp. 8.
64. "Estado de México: Información de Ciudad Nezahualcóyotl," March 1973, AGN, box 1702-B, exp. 8.
65. "Balacera Entre Políticos en Nezahualcóyotl," *El Universal*, March 29, 1973, 19; Vargas Soriano, interview, June 3, 2018.
66. "4 Horas de Balazos en Nezahualcóyotl," *Diario de la Tarde*, March 29, 1973, 1.
67. "Distrito Federal," March 1973, AGN, box 1702-B, exp. 8.
68. Vargas Soriano, interview, June 3, 2018.
69. Jaime Reyes Estrada, "Se aceptó el Fideicomiso de Ciudad Nezahualcóyotl," *Excélsior*, April 4, 1973, 11–12; "Distrito Federal," April 1973, AGN, box 1702-B, exp. 8.
70. Estrada, "Se aceptó el Fideicomiso," 11.
71. Carlos Hank González, "Explicación del C. Gobernador Prof. Carlos Hank González respecto al Fideicomiso de Nezahualcóyotl a grupo de periodistas locales," May 5, 1973, CIDNE, Biblioteca Classification 650/16–38.
72. Sergio Calvo Navarijo, "Fiesta en Netzahualcóyotl," *La Prensa*, April 9, 1973, 2.
73. For neighborhood associations who opposed Fineza, see "En Defensa de la Justicia," *El Despertar del Pueblo*, no. 40, June 24, 1973, 6. For the events surrounding the 1953 strike over land titles and housing conditions in the Vaso de Texcoco, see Iglesias, *Netzahualcóyotl*, 40–44.
74. "Si hay una coordinación de esfuerzos, no hay problema que no podamos resolver," *El Día*, May 11, 1973, 11.
75. *Paracaidismo* is a term used in Mexico for when large groups of people illegally take over unsettled land for the purpose of establishing homes. Typically, a person is responsible for leading the land invasion and will subsequently charge a monetary fee for each plot of land. Prior to the Fineza Land Trust, most land plots were already subdivided by land developers, and very little land invasions took place during the 1950s and 1960s. "Paracaidistas Activos: Investigan 500 Denuncias Sobre Invasion de Terrenos Baldios," *Sol de Medio Día*, August 8, 1974, 6; "El Auténtico Movimiento Restaurador," 1; Hugo Sánchez, "Miles de Personas Invaden Terrenos en Ciudad Nezahualcóyotl," *El Día*, April 7, 1973, 11.

7. Fineza and Land Regularization

1. Paz Muñoz, "Confrontación de ricos y pobres en Vancouver," *El Día*, May 31, 1976, 1.

2. Echeverría, "Address by Luis Echeverría Alvarez," 114. For more background on Luis Echeverría's international ambitions, see Thornton, *Revolution in Development*, 166–188.
3. "El Auténtico Movimiento Restaurador de Colonos Señala de Fraude al Fideicomiso de Ciudad Nezahualcóyotl," *Mercurio*, March 25, 1974, 1.
4. Manuel Muñiz Moran, "Acusaron a un Diputado de Robar Lotes en Ciudad Lago," *Mercurio*, March 25, 1974, 1.
5. "Conferencia de prensa del AMRC," October 4, 1974, Centro de Información y Documentación de Nezahualcóyotl (CIDNE), box 26, UAE/V-2/E-40.
6. Rogelio Vargas Soriano, interview with author, June 12, 2018. See also "Entrevista de Rogelio Vargas Soriano," *El Despertar del Pueblo*, August 1973, 8.
7. Vargas Soriano, interview, June 12, 2018. See also "Entrevista de Rogelio Vargas Soriano," 8.
8. Description of Rogelio Vargas's house in the 1970s is based on personal photos and the oral description of the owner. Vargas Soriano, interview, June 12, 2018. See also "Entrevista de Rogelio Vargas Soriano," 8.
9. Vargas Soriano, interview, June 12, 2018. See also "Entrevista de Rogelio Vargas Soriano," 8.
10. Iglesias, *Memorias de Nezahualcóyotl*.
11. An example of this process is discussed in Vélez-Ibáñez, *Rituals of Marginality*, 170.
12. Rogelio Vargas Soriano, interview with author, June 3, 2018. For a broader context, see Villegas, *El Estilo Personal*.
13. Vargas Soriano, interview, June 3, 2018. For a broader context, see Villegas, *El Estilo Personal*.
14. Vélez-Ibáñez, *Rituals of Marginality*, 2.
15. Instituto de Acción Urbana e Integración Social (AURIS), *Auris*, 5.
16. Gyger, *Improvised Cities*, 33–40.
17. Pagaza, *Anatomía de un gobierno*, 121.
18. Description of Eibenshultz and Rotterdam-based Bouwcentrum found in Pagaza, *Anatomía de un gobierno*, 120–22.
19. Onjas, *La experiencia mexicana*.
20. Pagaza, *Anatomía de un gobierno*, 121.
21. Antochiw, *Asentamientos habitacionales planificados*. See also "Acción Casa" and "Pintura Casa," 1973, CIDNE, box 16, UAE/V-30/E-529.
22. Varley, "¿Clientelismo o tecnocracia?," 140–41.
23. Azuela, "Evolución de las políticas," 224–25.
24. "Informe de Inversion de Terrenos," 1974, CIDNE, Desarrollo Urbano y Obras Públicas, box 17, UAE/V-32/E-575.

25. "El Fideicomiso de Ciudad Nezahualcóyotl, instrumento para la regularización de la propiedad urbana," 1974, CIDNE, box 16, UAE/V-32/E-579.
26. Lauro Lopez, "Buenos Frutos del Fideicomiso de Nezahualcóyotl," *El Día*, March 3, 1974, 11.
27. "El Fideicomiso de Ciudad Nezahualcóyotl."
28. Fineza, "Informe de Actividades Desarrolladas 1974," April 1974, CIDNE, Obras Públicas, box 17, UAE/V-33/E-596.
29. Fineza, "Informe de Planeación y Actividades Desarrolladas," 1973, CIDNE, Obras Públicas, box 16, UAE/V-32/E-584.
30. Fineza, "Informe de Actividades."
31. "Actividades del Fideicomiso," June 1974, CIDNE, Obras Públicas, box 17, UAE/V-33/E-595.
32. "Actividades del Fideicomiso."
33. "Quejas de Colonos al PDTE. del COMITÉ Tecnico de Fineza," 1974, CIDNE, Obras Públicas, box 16, UAE/V-25/E379.
34. Servín, "Reclaiming Revolution," 532.
35. "Estado de México, Información de Nezahualcóyotl," October 5, 1973, Archivo General de la Nación (AGN), Dirección General de Investigaciones Políticas y Sociales (DGIPS), box 1703-B, exp. 6.
36. Nery Córdova, "Un fideicomiso oficial, legitimador de frauds," *Proceso*, April 28, 1979, https://www.proceso.com.mx/125959/un-deicomiso-o-cial-legitimador-de-fraudes (site no longer extant); "El Auténtico Movimiento Restaurador," 1.
37. "¿Qué tan legal es el fideicomiso?," *El Despertar del Pueblo*, no. 37, June 3, 1973, 1.
38. Enrique Maza, "Netzahualcóyotl: En Defensa de Justicia," *Excélsior*, June 20, 1973.
39. A published letter addressed to President Echeverría and Governor Hank González from Odón Madariaga, Rogelio Vargas Soriano, and Artermio Mora Lozada expresses their support and gratitude from Fineza. In a collection found in May 10, 1974, AGN, SG/IPS, box 1703-B, exp. 6.
40. Miguel T. Garcia, "Dirigente de Colonos Arteramente Asesinado en C. Nezahualcóyotl," *Alerta*, June 3, 1973, 3–4.
41. Enrique Maza, "¿Los Pobres, en qué términos?," *Excélsior*, October 31, 1973.
42. Fineza, "Informe de Planeación."
43. Hugo Sanchez, "Miles de Personas Invaden Terrenos en Ciudad Nezahualcóyotl," *El Día*, April 7, 1973, 13.

44. "Unos dos mil Paracaidistas Invaden Predios en Ciudad Nezahualcóyotl," *Ovaciones*, May 3, 1973, 3; "Estado de México, Información de Ciudad Neza," May 4, 1973, AGN, SG/IPS, box 1702-B, exp. 8.
45. Enrique Gonzalez, "Infame Trafico de Lotes en Ciudad Nezahualcóyotl," *Alerta*, June 30, 1973, 3–4.
46. Fineza, "Informe de Actividades."
47. "Un Fideicomiso ha Dado Tranquilidad a Habitantes de Ciudad Nezahualcóyotl," *Novedades*, March 9, 1974, 2, 5.
48. "Acusaron un Diputado de Robar Lotes en Ciudad Lago," *Mercurio*, March 25, 1974, 1.
49. Maza, "¿Los Pobres, en qué términos?"
50. Maza, "¿Los Pobres, en qué términos?"; Cuauhtémoc Melendez, "Balacera en Ciudad Nezahualcóyotl, al Ser Disuelto el Congreso de la Federación de Obreros y Campesinos," *El Día*, November 17, 1973, 9.
51. "Distrito Federal," September 25, 1973, AGN, DGIPS, box 1702-B, exp. 9.
52. "Mató a dos Hombres un Pistolero de Guerrero," *Excélsior*, September 25, 1973, 26.
53. Maza, "¿Los Pobres, en qué términos?," 7. For another example of a killing carried out over land disputes, see "Lincharon un Regidor en Ciudad Nezahualcóyotl," *El Universal*, August 28, 1973, 13.
54. "Distrito Federal."
55. Maza, "¿Los Pobres, en qué términos?," 7; "Situación que guarda el conflicto entre los colonos de Ciudad Neza, lista de detenidos," September 25, 1973, AGN, DGIPS, box 1702-B, exp. 9.
56. See flyer titled, "Agitan en Ciudad Nezahualcóyotl," September 1973, AGN, DGIPS, box 1702-B, exp. 9.
57. Fineza, "Informe de Planeación."
58. Fineza, "Informe de Actividades"; Huamán, "La regularización territorial."
59. Fineza, "Informe de Actividades."
60. Fineza, "Informe general revision efectuada al fideicomiso de Cd. Neza," 1978, CIDNE, UAE/V-29/E-503; Huamán, "La regularización territorial."
61. Huitron, *Netzahualcóyotl*, 183.
62. Huitron, *Netzahualcóyotl*, 97–100; Vélez-Ibáñez, *Rituals of Marginality*, 131.
63. Pagaza, *Anatomía de un gobierno*, 130–31.
64. Pagaza, *Anatomía de un gobierno*, 132; "Actividades del Fideicomiso."
65. Pagaza, *Anatomía de un gobierno*, 132.
66. "Mercado Adelanto en las Obras del Gran Parque Central," *Carta de Fineza*, July 1974, 1. The park still exists today relatively unaltered since the 1970s.

67. "Acción Casa," 1973, CIDNE, UAE/V-30/E-529.
68. "Acción Casa."
69. For background on these programs, see Gyger, *Improvised Cities*, 33; Abrams, *Man's Struggle for Shelter*; and Harris, "Silence of the Experts," 165–89.
70. Fineza, "Informe general"; Huamán, "La regularización territorial."
71. Huamán, "La regularización territorial."
72. "Han Sido Regularizadas un 80 por Ciento de las Colonias Proletarias del DF," *El Nacional*, September 8, 1976, 8; Huamán, "La regularización territorial"; Huitron, *Netzahualcóyotl*, 185–88.

8. Serve the People

1. Geiger, *History of American Higher Education*, 491–507; McMahon, "Higher Education," 465–68.
2. Elbaum, *Revolution in the Air*; Leonard and Gallagher, *Heavy Radicals*; Linhart, *L'etabli*.
3. Han, *Unknown Cultural Revolution*, 24–27; Cheng and Manning, "Revolution in Education," 359–91.
4. See Hughes, "Traditionalist Catholicism," 64–85; Barger, *World Come of Age*; and Terrazas, "La recepción," 57–90.
5. Butler, "Catholicism in Mexico."
6. Rosa, "La Iglesia católica," 95.
7. Espinosa, *Jesuit Student Groups*, 92–96.
8. Espinosa, *Jesuit Student Groups*, 4, 107.
9. Jean Meyer, "Disidencia jesuita," *Nexos*, December 1, 1981, https://www.nexos.com.mx/?p=3966.
10. Pope Paul VI, "Decree on the Apostolate of the Laity Apostolicam Actuositatem," November 18, 1965, Vatican.va.
11. González Gary, "Poder y presiones de la iglesia," 249–51.
12. Hartch, *Prophet of Cuernavaca*, 74.
13. Cited in Bruno-Jofré and Zaldívar, "Center for Intercultural Formation," 464.
14. "Requests for Funds: An Overview; Center for Intercultural Documentation," January 1, 1963, CIDOC Dossier, Biblioteca Daniel Cosío Villegas, El Colegio de México, CIDOC Documentos, Cuernavaca—Mexico, Centro Intercultural de Documentación, folder 370.196 C 397d.
15. Hartch, *Prophet of Cuernavaca*, 30.
16. Illich, *Celebration of Awareness*, 47–48.
17. "El juicio del padre ILLICH: Texto del interrogatorio al que fue lo sometió el Vaticano," *Excélsior*, March 3, 1969, 1, 16.

18. "El 'entredicho' del CIDOC: Índice a algunos documentos," 1969, CIDOC Dossier, Biblioteca Daniel Cosío Villegas, El Colegio de México, CIDOC Documentos, Cuernavaca—Mexico, Centro Intercultural de Documentación, folder 69/131.
19. Suri, *Power and Protest*, 3.
20. Carey, *Plaza of Sacrifices*, 60–65.
21. Carey, *Plaza of Sacrifices*, 130–33; Aguayo Quezada, *1968*.
22. Espinosa, *Jesuit Student Groups*, 120.
23. "Mensaje de episcopado al pueblo de México sobre la reforma educative," *Christus* 408 (November 1969): 1166–70.
24. Rosa, "La Iglesia católica," 99. For a statement opposed to the student protests, see Auhumada, "Mensaje pastoral."
25. Alvarez Gutiérrez, "De Católico a Guerrillero," 106–7. This work contains several important interviews with Jesuits or Catholic activists who lived in Ciudad Neza.
26. Alvarez Gutiérrez, "De Católico a Guerrillero," 71; Meyer, "Disidencia jesuita."
27. Alvarez Gutiérrez, "De Católico a Guerrillero," 71; Meyer, "Disidencia jesuita."
28. Interview with Miguel Rico Tavera reprinted in Alvarez Gutiérrez, "De Católico a Guerrillero," 107.
29. Rosa, *Promoción Popular*, 71.
30. Pensado, "El Movimiento Estudiantil," 183–85.
31. Rosa, "La Iglesia católica," 106.
32. Pensado locates Monterrey as the main base for *Liberación*. Pensado, "El Movimiento Estudiantil," 183.
33. See the special issue on the conference, "La solidaridad del Sacerdote con los pobres," *Christus*, no. 410 (January 1970).
34. Account offered in Rosa, "La Iglesia católica," 99.
35. Rosa, *Promoción Popular*, 72.
36. Elbaum, *Revolution in the Air*, 100, 112.
37. Rosa, *Promoción Popular*, 71–73.
38. Rosa, *Promoción Popular*, 73.
39. Pensado, "El Movimiento Estudiantil," 186; "El caso del fundador de la Liga 23 de Septiembre, ante la Fiscalía Especial," *Proceso*, February 21, 2002, https://www.proceso.com.mx/nacional/2002/2/21/el-caso-del-fundador-de-la-liga-23-de-septiembre-ante-la-fiscalia-especial-64616.html.
40. Rosa, *Promoción Popular*, 74.
41. A description of the group's initial activities can be found in Rosa, *Promoción Popular*, 85–87.

42. For an example of a reference to Camilo Torres, see the graphic illustration featuring Torres in SEPAC's bulletin, *El Despertar del Pueblo*, July 20, 1974, 5.
43. Gordo del Valle, *Siempre humanos*, 49.
44. "El caso del fundador."
45. Rosa, *Promoción Popular*, 78–80.
46. For Rosa's account of Marxist study circles, see Rosa, *Promoción Popular*, 77–78; and Rosa and Valle, "¿Marx y/o Jesucristo?," cited in Pensado, "El Movimiento Estudiantil," 183. For background on Salas Obregón, see "El caso del fundador." Two influential texts were González Casanova, *La democracia en México*; and Frank, *Capitalismo y subdesarrollo*.
47. The text of a nine-point statement from 1969 was reprinted under the subheading "Analysis of the Conjuncture" in Rosa, *Promoción Popular*, 81.
48. Marx and Engels, *Communist Manifesto*, 137.
49. Marx, *Eighteenth Brumaire of Louis Bonaparte*, 38.
50. *Great Soviet Encyclopedia*, 3rd ed., ed. Aleksandr Mikhaïlovich Prokhorov (New York: Macmillan, 1973), s.v. "Lumpenproletariat."
51. Brazil being an exception due the Communist Party's longer and more sustained history of organizing in several favelas. With this notable exception, informal settlements as sites for organizing political bases were largely ignored by Communist Parties in the 1950s and early 1960s. For the Brazilian exception, see Fischer, "Red Menace Reconsidered," 1–33.
52. For examples of Vekemans's work, see Vekemans and Giusti, *Tendencias ideológicas*; Vekemans and Venegas, *Seminario de promoción popular*; and Vekemans, Fuenzalida, and Giusti, *La marginalidad en América Latina*.
53. For a detailed account of the Marginality Project, see Plotkin, "US Foundations," 65–92.
54. Vekemans, Fuenzalida, and Giusti, *La marginalidad en América Latina*, 54. See also Fauré, "Entre Roger Vekemans," 56.
55. Fauré, "Entre Roger Vekemans," 57.
56. The text studied by the activists in Ciudad Neza was Nun, "Superpoblación relativa," 178–236.
57. Hartch, *Prophet of Cuernavaca*, 90.
58. Illich, "Why We Must Abolish Schooling"; Ivan Illich, "Urge una revolución cultural en las instituciones, para crear una nueva estructura de aspiraciones humanas," *Siempre*, July 8, 1970, 48–50; Edward B. Fiske, "Vatican curb aimed at reform advocate," *New York Times*, January 29, 1969, 1–2.
59. Hartch, *Prophet of Cuernavaca*, 125.

60. For different reports and speeches reprinted in the CIDOC dossier, see Cámara, "Ideología Católica contemporánea"; Reimer, "Second Annual Report"; Freire, "Real Meaning of Cultural Action"; and Holt, "Letter Advocating School Resistance."
61. Hartch, *Prophet of Cuernavaca*, 115.
62. See Paulo Freire, "Talk from Freire," CIDOC *Informa* (1970): 5–7. For a personal account of Freire's CIDOC lectures in 1970, see Spring, *Corporatism, Social Control*, 5–7; and Rosa, *Promoción Popular*, 84. For a broader background on Freire, see Kirkendall, *Paulo Freire*.
63. Fauré, "Entre Roger Vekemans," 64.
64. Cited in Kirkendall, *Paulo Freire*, 91.
65. Rosa, *Promoción Popular*, 80, 106; Alvarez Gutiérrez, "De Católico a Guerrillero," 130.
66. Consejo Episcopal Latinoamericano and Colonnese, "Church in the Present-Day Transformation," n.p., under subheading 2, "Fundamentación doctrinal."
67. Marx and Engels, *Marx and Engels Selected Works*, 123.
68. Rosa, *Promoción Popular*, 84–86.
69. "Informe," March 1970, Archivo General de la Nación (AGN), gallery 1, file 2, box 1508a, 5–6. Accessed on the website of the Ex–Comisión de la Verdad del Estado de Guerrero (COMVERDAD), https://biblioteca.archivosdelarepresion.org.
70. Pensado, "El Movimiento Estudiantil," 183–84; "El caso del fundador."
71. Reprinted in Rosa, *Promoción Popular*, 99–100.
72. Valero and Vargas, *1968*.
73. Alvarez Gutiérrez, "De Católico a Guerrillero," 148.
74. "El caso del fundador."
75. Miguel Rico Tavera interview cited in Alvarez, "De Católico a Guerrillero," 145.
76. Gordo del Valle, *Siempre humanos*, 269.
77. Rosa recounts this period in Rosa, *Promoción Popular*, 108.
78. Pensado, "El Movimiento Estudiantil," 186.
79. Alonso, Conyers, and Kerney, "Vatican Bureaucracy," 75.
80. Alonso, Conyers, and Kerney, "Vatican Bureaucracy," 77.
81. Malley and Chambon, *Le Père Morelli*, 118.
82. Morelli, *Libera a mi pueblo*, 15.
83. Malley and Chambon, *Le Père Morelli*, 132.
84. Malley and Chambon, *Le Père Morelli*, 129.
85. Malley and Chambon, *Le Père Morelli*, 128.
86. Malley and Chambon, *Le Père Morelli*, 78.
87. Oliveros de Miranda, "José Porfirio Miranda," 300.
88. Miranda, *Marx y la Biblia*.
89. Marx, "Critique of the Gotha Programme," 16.

90. Gutiérrez, *Teología de la Liberación*; Boff, *Church*.
91. Rosa, "La Iglesia católica." For more background on the Sacerdotes para el Pueblo, see Crespo, "First Latin American Encounter."
92. Dodson, "Liberation Theology," 203–22.
93. Juan de Onis, "Assembly in Chile Urges Socialism," *New York Times*, May 4, 1972, 6.
94. Rosa, "La Iglesia católica."
95. Rosa, *Promoción Popular*, 107–9.
96. Rosa, *Netzahualcóyotl*, 23–24.
97. Rosa, *Promoción Popular*, 113.
98. *El Despertar del Pueblo* was a bulletin published from August 1972 to December 1973, comprising sixty-one issues. CIDNE has fourteen issues of varying dates.
99. "Sobre el Fideicomiso," *El Despertar del Pueblo*, June 24, 1973, 1; "Que Viva Chile," *El Despertar del Pueblo*, September 15, 1974, 1.
100. *El Despertar del Pueblo*, August 31, 1974, 6.
101. *El Despertar del Pueblo*, July 20, 1974, 5.
102. Rosa, *Promoción Popular*, 128.
103. Ruvalcaba, *Ciudad Nezahualcóyotl*; Iglesias, *Memorias de Nezahualcóyotl*, classified in CIDNE as Bibliografía no. 13, A10.
104. SEPAC's activities are discussed in Rosa, *Promoción Popular*, 129–34.
105. Pensado, "El Movimiento Estudiantil," 187.
106. "El caso del fundador."
107. Robinet, "Revolutionary Group," 139–41.
108. For the evolution of the CCH Oriente student group, see Bennett and Bracho, "Orígenes del Movimiento Urbano Popular," 93–94; and Bautista González, *Movimiento Urbano Popular*, 20.
109. Robert Rico, "La Unión de Colonias Populares del Valle de México," *La Jornada*, July 19, 2013, https://www.jornada.com.mx/2013/07/19/opinion/022a1pol.
110. Selee, *Decentralization, Democratization*, 140.
111. Rosa, *Promoción Popular*, 95.
112. Rosa, *Promoción Popular*, 91–92.
113. Ruvalcaba, *Ciudad Nezahualcóyotl*, 64.
114. Rosa, *Promoción Popular*, 110.
115. Ruvalcaba, *Ciudad Nezahualcóyotl*, 65.
116. Rosa, *Netzahualcóyotl*; Iglesias, *Netzahualcóyotl*.
117. For an example of a history written in this light, see Huitron, *Netzahualcóyotl*.

Conclusion

1. Feike de Jong, "Los oaxaqueños del Valle de México pueden determinar las elecciones," *Expansión*, July 1, 2010, https://expansion.mx/nacional/2010/07/01/los-oaxaquenos-del-valle-de-mexico-pueden-determinar-las-elecciones.
2. Pagaza, *Anatomía de un gobierno*, 171.
3. For a recent statistical breakdown, see Darío Brooks, "Las decenas de políticos que han sido asesinados en México durante la campaña de la elección intermedia," BBC *News Mundo*, May 20, 2021, https://www.bbc.com/mundo/noticias-america-latina-57166582.
4. Hélène Combes, "Killing Candidates in Mexico: The PRD in the 1990s," *SciencesPo*, October 21, 2021, https://hal-sciencespo.archives-ouvertes.fr/hal-03391745.
5. Cuauhtémoc Cárdenas ran for president in 1988 in a coalition called Frente Democrático Nacional (National Democratic Front). For an important work addressing these questions, see Bruhn, *Taking on Goliath*. Also see Davis and Brachet-Márquez, "Rethinking Democracy," 101–3.
6. See Esteve, *Los Movimientos Sociales Urbanos*.
7. For an overview of the MUP, see Saiz, *El Movimiento Urbano Popular*.
8. Haber, *Power from Experience*; Crespo, "Los maoístas del norte," 200–229. See also Hernández Vélez, *El Movimiento Urbano Popular*; Hinojosa, *Participación Política*; and Meza, *Movimiento Urbano Popular*.
9. Napolitano, "Between 'Traditional' and 'New,'" 323–39; Gomez and Wright, "Bonds of Suffering," 141–57; Guzmán and Martin, "Back to Basics," 351–66.
10. Krischke, "Church Base Communities," 186–210; Adriance, "Base Communities," 163–78; Sabia, *Contradiction and Conflict*.
11. Moctezuma, "LA CONAMUP," 37.
12. Moctezuma, "Mexico's Urban Popular Movements," 38.
13. Moctezuma, "LA CONAMUP," 30.
14. Galván, *El Movimiento Urbano Popular*.
15. Walker, *Waking from the Dream*, 144.
16. Székely, *Economics of Poverty*, 11–13.
17. Specifically, this refers to the PAN's gubernatorial victory in Baja California in 1989. See also Poniatowska, *Nada, nadie*.
18. Oxhorn, *Organizing Civil Society*; Zuern, *Politics of Necessity*; Glenn, *Framing Democracy*; Huntington, *Third Wave*.
19. The repressive tactics against irregular settlements in the Federal District were legitimated through laws passed under Uruchurtu. See "Ley de Planificación del Distrito Federal," *Diario Oficial*, December 31, 1953.

20. Schteingart, "Producción habitacional," 240.
21. Although President Adolfo López Mateos's record of construction and legislation was smaller in scope, his presidency was responsible for Mexico's largest and most iconic housing projects. The Ernesto Uruchurtu period was arguably the most decisive in Mexico City's modern history, but not for the nation as a whole.
22. Castells, "Apuntes," 1179.
23. In regard to land speculation legislation, Echeverría did pass an important law (1976 Ley General de Asentamientos Humanos / 1976 Human Settlements Law), but it was mainly nominal and scrapped by José López Portillo. Mexico-Cetenal, *Información Cetenal*.
24. "El INFONAVIT Trabaja en 120 Ciudades del Interior: Ha Entregado 120 Conjuntos," *El Día*, June 8, 1976, 4.
25. Castells, "Apuntes," 1183.
26. Salazar, "Expansión y reconversión económica," 163–65. Figure drawn from Organisation for Economic Co-operation and Development (OECD), *OECD Territorial Reviews*, 16–17.
27. "INFONAVIT—Mexican State Institution for Ensuring That Families Can Exercise Their Constitutional Right to Decent Housing," federal government press release, April 26, 2016, https://www.gob.mx/epn/prensa/infonavit-is-the-main-mexican-state-institution-for-ensuring-that-families-can-exercise-their-constitutional-right-to-decent-housing-epn.
28. Instituto Nacional de Estadística y Geografía (INEGI), *Censo Nacional de Población y Vivienda 2010*, available at http://www3.inegi.org.mx/sistemas/temas/default.aspx?s=est&c=25433&t=1.
29. Davis, *Planet of Slums*, 27–28.

BIBLIOGRAPHY

Manuscripts and Archives
Archivo General de la Nación (AGN)
    Adolfo Ruiz Cortines (ARC)
    Dirección General de Investigaciones Políticas y Sociales (DGIPS)
    Fondo de Porfirio Muñoz Ledo (PML)
    Miguel Alemán Valdes (MAV)
    Secretaría de Comunicaciones y Obras Públicas (SCOP)
    Secretaría de Gobernación (SG)
    Secretaría de Hacienda y Crédito Público (SHCP)
Archivo General e Histórico Municipal de Nezahualcóyotl (AGHN)
    Fondo de Obras Públicas (OP)
Archivo Histórico del Instituto Mexicano del Seguro Social (AHIMSS)
    Vivienda
Archivo Histórico del Distrito Federal (AHDF)
    Departamento del Distrito Federal (DDF)
    Obras Públicas (OP)
Archivo Histórico del Estado de México (AHEM)
    Obras Públicas (OP)
Biblioteca Lerdo de Tejada
    Archivos Económicos
Biblioteca Nacional de México (BNM)
    Hemeroteca Nacional de México (HNM)
Centro de Información y Documentación de Nezahualcóyotl (CIDNE)
    Administración Pública
    Biblioteca
    Desarrollo Urbano y Obras Públicas
    Fototeca
    Política Interior

El Colegio de México, Biblioteca Daniel Cosío Villegas
    Centro Intercultural de Documentatión (CIDOC)
John F. Kennedy Presidential Library and Museum, Boston (NLJFK)
    Teodoro Moscoso Papers
National Archives and Records Administration (NARA)
    U.S. Agency for International Development (USAID)
Rockefeller Archive Center, Sleepy Hollow, New York (RAC)
    International Basic Economy Corporation Archives (IBEC)
United Nations Archives and Records Management Section, New York (ARMS/UN)

Published Works

Aboites Aguilar, Luis. "The Illusion of National Power: Water Infrastructure in Mexican Cities, 1930–1990." In *A Land between Waters: Environmental Histories of Modern Mexico*, edited by Christopher R. Boyer, 218–44. Tucson: University of Arizona Press, 2010.

Abrams, Charles. *Man's Struggle for Shelter in an Urbanizing World*. Cambridge: MIT Press, 1964.

Adriance, Madeleine. "Base Communities and Rural Mobilization in Northern Brazil." *Sociology of Religion* 55, no. 2 (Summer 1994): 163–78.

Agostoni, Claudia. *Monuments of Progress: Modernization and Public Health in Mexico City, 1876–1910*. Calgary: University of Calgary Press, 2003.

Aguayo Quezada, Sergio. *1968: Los archivos de la violencia*. Mexico City: Reforma, 1998.

Aguilar, Marian Angela. "Mexico." In *Social Welfare in Latin America*, edited by John Dixon and Robert P. Scheurell, 175–201. London: Routledge, 1990.

Agustín, José. *Tragicomedia mexicana 2: La vida en México de 1970 a 1988*. Mexico City: Planeta Mexicana, 1992.

Alba Muñiz, Maria Eugenia de. "Control político de los migrantes urbanos. Un caso: Los colonos de Ciudad Netzahualcóyotl, México." Master's thesis, El Colegio de México, 1976.

Alcázar, Iliana Ortega. *Autoconstrucción de vivienda, espacio y vida familiar en la Ciudad de México*. Mexico City: FLACSO México, 2016.

Almondoz, Arturo. *Planning Latin American Capital Cities, 1850–1950*. London: Routledge, 2002.

Alonso, Enrique Ayala, and Gerardo Alvarez Montes, eds. *El espacio habitacional en la arquitectura moderna*. Mexico City: UAM-Xochimilco, 2013.

Alonso, Jorge A. "Los movimientos sociales en el Valle de México. Una introducción." In *Los movimientos sociales en el Valle de México*, 17–52. Mexico City: CIESAS, 1986.

Alonso, José Antonio. *Sexo, trabajo y marginalidad urbana*. Mexico City: Editorial Edicol, 1981.

Alonso, José Antonio, Lisa Conyers, and Michael Kerney. "The Vatican Bureaucracy and Its Neo-Christian Project: Reflections from a Low-Income Parish in Mexico." *Latin American Perspectives* 13, no. 3 (Summer 1986): 75.

Alvarez, Sonia E., Jeffrey W. Rubin, Millie Thayer, Gianpaolo Baiocchi, and Agustín Laó-Montes, eds. *Beyond Civil Society: Activism, Participation, and Protest in Latin America*. Durham NC: Duke University Press, 2017.

Alvarez Gutiérrez, Ana Lucía. "De católico a guerrillero: El caso de Ignacio Salas Obregón." Bachelor's thesis, Universidad de Guanajuato, 2016.

Anda, Enrique X. de. *Vivienda colectiva de la modernidad en México: Los multifamiliares durante el periodo presidencial de Miguel Alemán (1946–1952)*. Mexico City: UNAM, Instituto de Investigaciones Estéticas, 2008.

Antochiw, Michel A. *Asentamientos habitacionales planificados y no planificados*. Naucalpan de Juárez: AURIS, 1974.

Apenes, Ola. "The 'Tlateles' of Lake Texcoco." *American Antiquity* 9, no. 1 (July 1943): 29–32.

Araiz, Héctor Nieto. "Participación del estado en el desarrollo de vivienda para no asalariados de ingresos mínimos." *Revista Vivienda* 8, no. 2 (June 1983): 168–73.

Aranda, Salvador Maldonado. "Between Law and Arbitrariness: Labour Union Caciques in Mexico." In *Caciquismo in Twentieth-Century Mexico*, edited by Alan Knight and Wil Pansters, 278–97. London: Institute for the Study of the Americas, 2005.

Arato, Andrew, and Jean L. Cohen. *Civil Society and Political Theory*. Cambridge: MIT Press, 1992.

Arbaci, Sonia. *Paradoxes of Segregation: Housing Systems, Welfare Regimes and Ethnic Residential Change in Southern European Cities*. Hoboken NJ: Wiley-Blackwell, 2019.

Arellano, Graciela de Garay, compiler. *Modernidad habitada: Multifamiliar Miguel Alemán, historia oral del Multifamiliar Miguel Alemán, 1949–1999*. México DF: Instituto Mora–UNAM, 2004.

———, compiler. *Rumores y retratos de un lugar de la modernidad: Historia oral del Multifamiliar Miguel Alemán, 1949–1999*. México DF: Instituto Mora–UNAM, 2002.

Arellano, Graciela de Garay, and Mario Pani. *Historia oral de la ciudad de México: Testimonios de sus arquitectos, 1940–1990*. México DF: Instituto Mora, 2000.

Arizpe, Lourdes. *Indigenas en la ciudad de Mexico: El caso de las "Marias."* Mexico City: Sep Diana, 1980.

Arreguin, Carlos Corona. *Cuatro años de lucha en Nezahualcóyotl*. Ciudad Nezahualcóyotl: Self-published, 1973.

Auhumada, Ernesto Corripio. "Mensaje pastoral: Sobre el movimiento estudiantil." *Christus* 398 (January 1969): 12–15.

Auyero, Javier. "Patients of the State: An Ethnographic Account of Poor People's Waiting." *Latin American Research Review* 46, no. 1 (2011): 6.

———. *Patients of the State: The Politics of Waiting in Argentina*. Durham NC: Duke University Press, 2012.

———. *Poor People's Politics: Peronist Survival Networks and the Legacy of Evita*. Durham NC: Duke University Press, 2001.

Aviña, Alexander. *Specters of Revolution: Peasant Guerrillas in the Cold War Mexican Countryside*. New York: Oxford University Press, 2014.

Avritzer, Leonardo. *Democracy and the Public Space in Latin America*. Princeton NJ: Princeton University Press, 2002.

———. *Urban Reform, Participation, and the Right to the City in Brazil*. Sussex: Institute of Development Studies, 2007.

Azuela, Antonio. "Evolución de las políticas de regularización." In *El Acceso de los Pobres al Suelo Urbano*, edited by Antonio Azuela and François Tomas, 220–32. Mexico City: Centro de Estudios Mexicanos y Centroamericanos, 2013.

Balakrishnan, Sai. *Shareholder Cities: Land Transformations along Urban Corridors in India*. Philadelphia: University of Pennsylvania Press, 2019.

Banco Nacional de Obras y Servicios Públicos. *Conjuntos habitacionales en la República Mexicana*. Mexico City: Banobras, 1970.

Banco Nacional Hipotecario Urbano y de Obras Públicas (BNHUOP). *Estudios 6: El problema de la habitación en ciudad de México*. Mexico City: BNHUOP, 1952.

Barger, Lilian Calles. *The World Come of Age: An Intellectual History of Liberation Theology*. New York: Oxford University Press, 2018.

Bartra, Roger. *The Cage of Melancholy: Identity and Metamorphosis in the Mexican Character*. New Brunswick NJ: Rutgers University Press, 1992.

Bautista, Raúl Ruiz. *Camino por la Mixteca: Un testimonio y documentos para la microhistoria de San Juan Achiutla y la Mixteca Alta en el estado de Oaxaca*. Mexico City: Self-published, 2010.

Bautista González, Raúl. *Movimiento Urbano Popular: Bitácora de Lucha*. Mexico City: Casa y Ciudad, 2015.

Bayón, María Cristina. "El 'lugar' de los pobres: Espacio, representaciones sociales y estigmas en la Ciudad de México." *Revista Mexicana de Sociología* 74, no. 1 (March 2012): 133–66.

Bazant, Jan. *Autoconstrucción de vivienda popular*. Mexico City: Trillas, 1992.

Benítez, Fernando. *Viaje al centro de México*. Mexico City: FCE, 1975.

Benmergui, Leandro. "Housing Development: Housing Policy, Slums, and Squatter Settlements in Rio de Janeiro, Brazil and Buenos Aires, Argentina, 1948–1973." PhD diss., University of Maryland, 2012.

Bennett, Vivienne. "Gender, Class, and Water: Women and the Politics of Water Service in Monterrey, Mexico." *Latin American Perspectives* 22, no. 2 (1995): 76–99.

———. "La evolución de los movimientos urbanos populares en México entre 1968 y 1988." *América Latina Hoy* 7 (January 1993): 89–96.

———. *The Politics of Water: Urban Protest Gender and Power in Monterrey, Mexico*. Pittsburgh: University of Pittsburgh Press, 1995.

Bennett, Vivienne, and Julio Bracho. "Orígenes del Movimiento Urbano Popular Mexicano: Pensamiento político y organizaciones políticas clandestinas, 1960–1980." *Revista Mexicana de Sociología* 55, no. 3 (July 1993): 93–94.

Benton, Mark. "'Just the Way Things Are around Here': Racial Segregation, Critical Junctures, and Path Dependence in Saint Louis." *Journal of Urban History* 44, no. 6 (March 2017): 1113–30.

Bértola, Luis, and Jeffrey Williamson. "Introduction." In *Has Latin American Inequality Changed Direction? Looking over the Long Run*, edited by Luis Bértola and Jeffrey Williamson, 1–16. New York: Springer, 2017.

Bleynat, Ingrid. *Vendors' Capitalism: A Political Economy of Public Markets in Mexico City*. Stanford: Stanford University Press, 2021.

Bleynat, Ingrid, Amílcar E. Challú, and Paul Segal. "Inequality, Living Standards, and Growth: Two Centuries of Economic Development in Mexico." *Economic History Review* 74, no. 3 (2021): 584–610.

Boff, Leonardo. *Church: Charism and Power; Liberation Theology and the Institutional Church*. Translated by John W. Diercksmeier. 1981. Reprint, New York: Crossroad, 1983.

Boger, Gretchen. "The Meaning of Neighborhood in the Modern City: Baltimore's Residential Segregation Ordinances, 1910–1913." *Journal of Urban History* 35, no. 2 (January 2009): 236–58.

Boils, Guillermo. *Las casas campesinas en el porfiriato*. Mexico City: M. Casillas Editores, 1982.

Bolaño, Roberto. *The Savage Detectives*. Translated by Natasha Wimmer. New York: Farrar, Straus and Giroux, 2007.

Bonilla, Frank. *Rio's Favelas: The Rural Slum within the City*. New York: American Universities Field Staff, 1961.

Boyer, Christopher. *Becoming Campesinos: Politics, Identity, and Agrarian Struggle in Postrevolutionary Michoacán, 1920–1935*. Stanford: Stanford University Press, 2000.

Brachet-Márquez, Viviane. *Contention and the Dynamics of Inequality in Mexico, 1910–2010*. Cambridge: Cambridge University Press, 2014.

Brading, David A., ed. *Caudillo and Peasant in the Mexican Revolution*. Cambridge: Cambridge University Press, 1980.

Bruhn, Kathleen. *Taking on Goliath: The Emergence of a New Left Party and the Struggle for Democracy in Mexico*. University Park: Penn State University Press, 1996.

Bruno-Jofré, Rosa, and Jon Igelmo Zaldívar. "The Center for Intercultural Formation, Cuernavaca, Mexico, Its Reports, and Illich's Critical Understanding of Mission in Latin America." *Hispania Sacra* 66, no. 2 (December 2014): 464.

Buelink, Horacio. "Programa de estudios sobre políticas nacionales de vivienda: Brasil." *Revista Vivienda Infonavit* 2, no. 11 (August 1976).

———. "Viviena para los no asalariados." *Revista Vivienda Infonavit* 1, no. 2 (February 1976).

Burian, Edward, ed. *Modernity and the Architecture of Mexico*. Austin: University of Texas Press, 1997.

Butler, Matthew. "Catholicism in Mexico, 1910 to the Present." *Oxford Research Encyclopedia of Latin American History* (November 22, 2016). https://doi.org/10.1093/acrefore/9780199366439.013.23.

Butterworth, Douglas. "Rural–Urban Migration and Microdemography: A Case Study from Mexico." *Urban Anthropology* 4, no. 3 (Fall 1975): 65–67.

———. "Two Small Groups: A Comparison of Migrants and Non-migrants in Mexico City." *Urban Anthropology* 1, no. 1 (Spring 1972): 39–41.

Caldeira, Teresa. "Peripheral Urbanization: Autoconstruction, Transversal Logics, and Politics in Cities of the Global South." *Environment and Planning D: Society and Space* 35, no. 1 (January 2017): 3–20.

Cámara, Gabriel. "Ideología Católica contemporánea respecto a la educación y Desarrollo en México." CIDOC *Informa* 8, no. 44 (July–June 1969): 1–3.

Camín, Héctor Aguilar. *Después del Milagro*. Mexico City: Cal y Arena, 1988.

Candiani, Vera. *Dreaming of Dry Land: Environmental Transformation in Colonial Mexico City*. Stanford: Stanford University Press, 2014.

Canel, Eduardo. *Barrio Democracy in Latin America: Participatory Decentralization and Community Activism in Montevideo*. University Park: Penn State University Press, 2014.

Carey, Elaine. *Plaza of Sacrifices: Gender, Power, and Terror in 1968 Mexico*. Albuquerque: University of New Mexico Press, 2005.

Carmona, Fernando. "El Problema de la Vivienda en México." *Investigación Económica* 18, no. 69 (January 1958): 79–101.

Carranza, Luis E., and Fernando Luiz Lara. *Modern Architecture in Latin America: Art, Technology, and Utopia*. Austin: University of Texas Press, 2015.

Castañeda, Luis M. *Spectacular Mexico: Design, Propaganda, and the 1968 Olympics*. Minneapolis: University of Minnesota Press, 2014.

Castellanos, María Bianet. *Indigenous Dispossession: Housing and Maya Indebtedness in Mexico*. Stanford: Stanford University Press, 2021.

Castells, Manuel. "Apuntes Para Un Análisis de Clase de La Política Urbana Del Estado Mexicano." *Revista Mexicana de Sociología* 39, no. 4 (1977): 1161–91.

———. *The City and the Grassroots: A Cross-Cultural Theory of Urban Social Movements*. Berkeley: University of California Press, 1983.

Castells, Manuel, and Alejandro Portes. "World Underneath: The Origins, Dynamics, and Effects of the Informal Economy." In *The Informal Economy: Studies in Advanced and Less Developed Countries*, edited by Manuel Castells, Alejandro Portes, and Laura Benton, 11–40. Baltimore: Johns Hopkins University Press, 1989.

Castillo, Maribel Espinosa. "Produccion del Espacio Urbano y Participacion Vecinal en el Ex-Vaso de Texcoco: Viejas y Nuevas Geografias." PhD diss., UNAM, 2004.

Castillo, Maribel Espinosa, and Mario Bassols Ricárdez. "Construcción Social Del Espacio Urbano: Ecatepec Y Nezahualcóyotl. Dos Gigantes Del Oriente." *Polis* 7, no. 2 (2011): 181–212.

Chang, Jason Oliver. *Chino: Anti-Chinese Racism in Mexico, 1880–1940*. Urbana: University of Illinois Press, 2017.

Chazkel, Amy. *Laws of Chance: Brazil's Clandestine Lottery and the Making of Urban Public Life*. Durham NC: Duke University Press, 2011.

Cheng, Yinghong, and Patrick Manning. "Revolution in Education: China and Cuba in Global Context, 1957–76." *Journal of World History* 14, no. 3 (September 2003): 359–91.

Clark, Christopher. *Time and Power: Visions of History in German Politics from the Thirty Years War to the Third Reich*. Princeton NJ: Princeton University Press, 2019.

Clark, Kenneth Bancroft. *Dark Ghetto: Dilemmas of Social Power*. New York: Harper and Row, 1965.

Consejo Episcopal Latinoamericano and Louis M. Colonnese. "The Church in the Present-Day Transformation of Latin America in the Light of the Council." Paper presented at the Second General Conference of Latin American Bishops, August 24–September 6, 1968, Bogotá, Colombia.

Contreras, Carlos Salas. *Arqueología del exconvento de la Encarnación de la ciudad de México: Edificio sede de la Secretaría de Educación Pública*. Mexico City: INAH, 2006.

Cope, Douglas R. *The Limits of Racial Domination: Plebeian Society in Colonial Mexico City, 1660–1720*. Madison: University of Wisconsin Press, 1994.

Cornelius, Wayne. "Contemporary Mexico: A Structural Analysis of Urban *Caciquismo*." In *The Caciques: Oligarchical Politics and the System of Caciquismo in the Luso-Hispanic World*, edited by Robert Kern, 135–50. Albuquerque: University of New Mexico Press, 1973.

———. *Los inmigrantes pobres en la ciudad de Mexico y la politica*. Mexico City: Fondo de Cultura Económica, 1980.

———. *Politics and the Migrant Poor in Mexico City*. Stanford: Stanford University Press, 1975.

Cortés, Adrián García. *La reforma urbana de México*. Mexico City: Bay Gráfica, 1972.

Covert, Lisa Pinley. *San Miguel de Allende: Mexicans, Foreigners, and the Making of a World Heritage Site*. Lincoln: University of Nebraska Press, 2017.

Craib, Raymond B. *Cartographic Mexico: A History of State Fixations and Fugitive Landscapes*. Durham NC: Duke University Press, 2004.

Crespo, Jorge Iván Puma. "The First Latin American Encounter of Christians for Socialism and the Rise of the Catholic Left in Mexico." Paper presented at the 68th annual conference of the Rocky Mountain Council for Latin American Studies (virtual), March 19, 2021.

———. "Los maoístas del norte de México: Breve historia de Política Popular–Línea Proletaria, 1969–1979." *Izquierdas* 27 (2016): 200–229.

Cronon, William. *Nature's Metropolis: Chicago and the Great West*. New York: W. W. Norton, 1991.

Cross, John C. "Co-optation, Competition, and Resistance: State and Street Vendors in Mexico City." *Latin American Perspectives* 25, no. 2 (1998): 41–61.

Cruz, Mario Barbosa. *El Trabajo en las Calles: Subsistencia y Negociación Política en la ciudad de México a Comienzos del Siglo XX*. Mexico City: Colegio de México–UAM Cuajimalpa, 2008.

Cymet, David. *From Ejido to Metropolis, Another Path: An Evaluation on Ejido Property Rights and Informal Land Development in Mexico City*. New York: Peter Lang, 1992.

Davis, Diane E. *Urban Leviathan: Mexico City in the Twentieth Century*. Philadelphia: Temple University Press, 1994.

Davis, Diane E., and Viviane Brachet-Márquez. "Rethinking Democracy: Mexico in Historical Perspective." *Comparative Studies in Society and History* 39, no. 1 (1997): 86–119.

Davis, Mike. *Planet of Slums*. London: Verso, 2006.

Dawson, Alexander. *Indian and Nation in Revolutionary Mexico*. Tucson: University of Arizona Press, 2004.

Degregori, Carlos Ivan. *How Difficult It Is to Be God: Shining Paths Politics of War in Peru, 1980–1999*. Translated by Steve J. Stern. Madison: University of Wisconsin Press, 2012.

de la Peña, Guillermo. "Civil Society and Popular Resistance: Mexico at the End of the Twentieth Century." In *Cycles of Conflict, Centuries of Change: Crisis, Reform, and Revolution in Mexico*, edited by Elisa Servín, Leticia Reina, and John Tutino, 304–45. Durham NC: Duke University Press, 2007.

Delgado, Javier. "De Los Anillos a La Segregación: La Ciudad de México, 1950–1987." *Estudios Demográficos y Urbanos* 5, no. 2 (1990): 237–74.

Departamento del Distrito Federal (DDF). *La Ciudad de México, 1952–1964*. Mexico City: DDF, 1964.

Díaz Arias, Julián. "Santa Fe, Una Unidad de Servicios Sociales." *Arquitectura México*, no. 59 (September 1957): 177–78.

Dillingham, Alan Shane. *Oaxaca Resurgent: Indigeneity, Development, and Inequality in Twentieth-Century Mexico*. Stanford: Stanford University Press, 2021.

Dion, Michelle L. *Workers and Welfare: Comparative Institutional Change in Twentieth-Century Mexico*. Pittsburgh: University of Pittsburgh Press, 2010.

Dodson, Michael. "Liberation Theology and Christian Radicalism in Contemporary Latin America." *Journal of Latin American Studies* 11, no. 1 (May 1979): 203–22.

Draper, Susana. *1968 Mexico: Constellations of Freedom and Democracy*. Durham NC: Duke University Press, 2018.

Duhau, Emilio, and Angela Giglia. *Las reglas del desorden: Habitar la metrópoli*. Mexico City: Siglo XXI, 2008.

Echeverría, Luis. "Address by Luis Echeverría Alvarez, President of Mexico, at the U.N. Conference on Human Settlements." *Habitat International* 1, no. 2 (1976): 114.

Eckstein, Susan. *The Poverty of Revolution: The State and the Urban Poor in Mexico*. Princeton NJ: Princeton University Press, 1977.

Edwards, Michael. *Civil Society*. Malden MA: Polity, 2004.

Elbaum, Max Elbaum. *Revolution in the Air: Sixties Radicals Turn to Lenin, Mao and Che*. London: Verso, 2002.

Escobar, Arturo. *Encountering Development: The Making and Unmaking of the Third World*. Princeton NJ: Princeton University Press, 1995.

Escobar, Arturo, and Sonia Alvarez, eds. *The Making of Social Movements in Latin America: Identity, Strategy, and Democracy*. Boulder CO: Westview Press, 1992.

Escobedo, Antonio Acevedo. "El gran experimento humano." In *Los multifamiliares de pensiones*, edited by Mario Pani. Mexico City: Editorial Arquitectura, 1952.

Espinosa, David. *Jesuit Student Groups, the Universidad Iberoamericana, and Political Resistance in Mexico, 1913–1979*. Albuquerque: University of New Mexico Press, 2014.

Esteve, Hugo. *Los Movimientos Sociales Urbanos: Un Reto Para La Modernización*. Mexico City: Instituto de Proposiciones Estratégicas, 1992.

Estrada Ayon, Maria Eloisa. "Memoria." Teacher certificate thesis, Escuela Normal para Señoritas, 1971.

Fanon, Frantz. *The Wretched of the Earth*. 1963. Reprint, New York: Grove Press, 2004.

Fauré, Daniel. "Entre Roger Vekemans y Paulo Freire: Las campañas de alfabetización de adultos en el gobierno de Eduardo Frei (Chile, 1964–1970)." *Kavilando: Revista de Ciencias Sociales* 9, no. 1 (July 2017): 56.

Fierro, Alfonso. "Modeling the Urban Commune: Collective Housing, Utopian Architecture, and Social Reproduction in the Mexican 1930s." *Mexican Studies / Estudios Mexicanos* 38, no. 2 (August 2022): 272–99.

Fischer, Brodwyn. *A Poverty of Rights: Citizenship and Inequality in Twentieth Century Rio de Janeiro*. Stanford: Stanford University Press, 2008.

———. "The Red Menace Reconsidered: A Forgotten History of Communist Mobilization in Rio's Favelas, 1946–1956." *Hispanic American Historical Review* 94, no. 1 (February 2014): 1–33.

Fischer, Brodwyn, Bryan McCann, and Javier Auyero, eds. *Cities from Scratch: Poverty and Informality in Urban Latin America*. Durham NC: Duke University Press, 2014.

Fitzgerald, David. "Colonies of the Little Motherland: Membership, Space, and Time in Mexican Migrant Hometown Associations." *Comparative Studies in Society and History* 50, no. 1 (January 2008): 145–69.

Flaherty, Michael G. *A Watched Pot: How We Experience Time*. New York: New York University Press, 1999.

Fontes, Pablo. *Migration and the Making of Industrial São Paulo*. Durham NC: Duke University Press, 2016.

Forment, Carlos A. *Democracy in Latin America, 1760–1900*. Vol. 1. Chicago: University of Chicago Press, 2013.

Foweraker, Joe, and Ann L. Craig, eds. *Popular Movements and Political Change in Mexico*. Boulder CO: L. Rienner, 1990.

Fox, David J. "Patterns of Morbidity and Mortality in Mexico City." *Geographical Review* 62, no. 2 (1972): 151–85.

Frampton, Kenneth. *Modern Architecture: A Critical History*. New York: Oxford University Press, 1980.

Franco, Jean. *The Decline and Fall of the Lettered City: Latin America in the Cold War*. Cambridge MA: Harvard University Press, 2002.

Frank, Andre Gunder. *Capitalismo y subdesarrollo en América Latina*. Buenos Aires: Siglo 21 Editores, 1970.

Freeman, Elizabeth Hordge. *The Color of Love: Racial Features, Stigma, and Socialization in Black Brazilian Families*. Austin: University of Texas Press, 2015.

Freire, Paulo. "The Real Meaning of Cultural Action: Text from Lecture Delivered at CIDOC January 1970." *CIDOC Informa* 10, no. 49 (February 1970): 1–17.

Frieden, Bernard J. "The Search for Housing Policy in Mexico City." *The Town Planning Review* 36, no. 2 (July 1965): 77–82.

Friedmann, John. *China's Urban Transition*. Minneapolis: University of Minnesota Press, 2005.

Friedrich, Paul. *Agrarian Revolt in a Mexican Village*. Englewood Cliffs NJ: Prentice-Hall, 1970.

———. "The Legitimacy of a Cacique." In *Local-Level Politics: Social and Cultural Perspectives*, edited by Marc J. Swartz, 243–69. Chicago: Aldine, 1968.

Galván, Azucena Citlalli Jaso. "La Colonia Proletaria Rubén Jaramillo: La lucha por la tenencia de la tierra y la guerra popular prolongada." Master's thesis, UNAM, 2011.

Galván, Felipe de Jesús Moreno. *El Movimiento Urbano Popular en el Valle de México*. Mexico City: Universidad Autónoma Metropolitana, 2013.

Gandy, Matthew. "Planning, Anti-planning, and the Infrastructure Crisis Facing Metropolitan Lagos." In *Cities in Contemporary Africa*, edited by Martin J. Murray and Garth Andrew Myers, 247–64. New York: Palgrave Macmillan, 2007.

García, Alfonso Sánchez. *Memorias de Nezahualcóyotl: Un pueblo, un nombre, un hombre*. Toluca: Centro de Información y documentación de Nezahualcóyotl, 1990.

García Canclini, Néstor, Alejandro Castellanos, Ana Rosas Mantecón, and Nacho López. *La ciudad de los viajeros: Travesías e imaginarios urbanos México, 1940–2000*. Mexico City: Fondo de Cultura Económica, 2013.

Garrido, Luis. "El Destino de Ciudad Universitaria." *Arquitectura México*, no. 39 (September 1952): 197–200.

Garza, Gustavo, Martha Schteingart, Jorge Legorreta, and Pedro Pírez. *El problema de la vivienda en México: La acción habitacional del Estado*. Mexico: El Colegio de Mexico, Centro de Estudios Económicos y Demográficos, Area de Estudios Urbanos, 1978.

Geiger, Roger L. *The History of American Higher Education: Learning and Culture from the Founding to World War II*. Princeton NJ: Princeton University Press, 2015.

Gilbert, Alan, and Peter Ward. *Housing, the State, and the Poor: Policy and Practice in Three Latin American Cities*. Cambridge: Cambridge University Press, 1985.

Glazer, Nathan. *From a Cause to a Style: Modernist Architecture's Encounter with the American City*. Princeton NJ: Princeton University Press, 2007.

Glazer, Nathan, and Daniel Patrick Moynihan. *Beyond the Melting Pot: The Negroes, Puerto Ricans, Jews, Italians, and Irish of New York City*. Cambridge MA: MIT Press, 1963.

Glenn, John K. *Framing Democracy: Civil Society and Civic Movements in Eastern Europe.* Stanford: Stanford University Press, 2001.

Gomez, Elba Noemi, and Bradley Wright. "Bonds of Suffering, Bonds of Hope: The Story of a Priest Committed to the Poor." *Latin Americanist* 63, no. 2 (June 2019): 141–57.

Gómez Mayorga, Mauricio, and Mario Pani. "El problema de la habitación en México: Realidad de su solución." *Arquitectura México*, no. 27 (April 1949): 71.

González Casanova, Pablo. *La democracia en México.* Mexico City: Era, 1965.

González Gary, Óscar. "Poder y presiones de la iglesia." In *México ante la crisis: El impacto social y cultural, las alternativas,* edited by Pablo González Casanova and Héctor Aguilar Camín, 249–51. Mexico City: Siglo 21 Press, 1985.

González Liano, Angel Javier. "Segregación social en la periferia urbana de la Ciudad de México: Estudio de caso de Xochimilco." *Revista Latinoamericana de Estudiantes de Geografía* 5, no. 1 (2017): 57–64.

Gootenberg, Paul, and Luis Reygadas. *Indelible Inequalities in Latin America: Insights from History, Politics, and Culture.* Durham NC: Duke University Press, 2010.

Gordo del Valle, Luis. *Siempre humanos, siempre en proceso.* Aguascalientes: Centro de Estudios Jurídicos y Sociales, 2011.

Gordon, Colin. "Dividing the City: Race-Restrictive Covenants and the Architecture of Segregation in St. Louis." *Journal of Urban History* 25, no. 2 (March 2021): 160–82.

———. *Mapping Decline: St. Louis and the Fate of the American City.* Philadelphia: University of Pennsylvania Press, 2009.

Grandin, Greg. *The Last Colonial Massacre: Latin America in the Cold War.* Chicago: University of Chicago Press, 2011.

Guillermo Aguilar, Adrián, and Irma Escamilla H., eds. *Segregación urbana y espacios de exclusion: Ejemplos de México y América Latina.* Mexico City: UNAM, 2015.

Gürel, Meltem Ö, ed. *Mid-century Modernism in Turkey: Architecture across Cultures in the 1950s and 1960s.* New York: Routledge, 2016.

Gutiérrez, Gustavo. *Teología de la Liberación: Perspectivas.* Lima: CEP, 1971.

Gutmann, Matthew C. *Ser hombre de verdad en la ciudad de México: Ni macho ni mandilón.* Mexico City: El Colegio de México, 2000.

Guzmán, Elsa, and Christopher Martin. "Back to Basics Mexican Style: Radical Catholicism and Survival on the Margins." *Bulletin of Latin American Research* 16, no. 3 (1997): 351–66.

Gyger, Helen. *Improvised Cities: Architecture, Urbanization, and Innovation in Peru.* Pittsburgh: University of Pittsburgh, 2019.

———. "The Informal as a Project: Self-Help Housing in Peru, 1954–1986." PhD diss., Columbia University, 2013.

Haber, Paul. *Power from Experience: Urban Popular Movements in Late Twentieth-Century Mexico*. University Park: Penn State University Press, 2006.

Hall, Peter. *Cities of Tomorrow: An Intellectual History of Urban Planning and Design in the Twentieth Century*. 3rd ed. Malden MA: Blackwell, 2002.

Han, Dongping. *The Unknown Cultural Revolution: Life and Change in a Chinese Village*. New York: Monthly Review, 2008.

Hansen, Roger. *The Politics of Mexican Development*. Baltimore: Johns Hopkins University Press, 1974.

Hardoy, Jorge Enrique. *Urbanization in Latin America: Approaches and Issues*. Garden City NY: Anchor Books, 1975.

Harms, Erik. *Saigon's Edge: On the Margins of Ho Chi Minh City*. Minneapolis: University of Minnesota Press, 2011.

Harris, Richard. "The Silence of the Experts: Aided Self-Help Housing, 1939–1954." *Habitat International* 22, no. 2 (June 1998): 165–89.

Hartch, Todd. *The Prophet of Cuernavaca: Ivan Illich and the Crisis of the West*. Oxford: Oxford University Press, 2015.

Harth Deneke, Jorge Alberto. "The Colonias Proletarias of Mexico City: Low Income Settlements at the Urban Fringe." PhD diss., Massachusetts Institute of Technology, 1966.

Haynes, Keith Allen. "Order and Progress: The Revolutionary Ideology of Alberto J. Pani." PhD diss., Northern Illinois University, 1981.

Hernández, Ricardo. *La Coordinadora Nacional del Movimiento Urbano Popular*. Mexico City: Praxis, Gráfica Editorial, 1987.

Hernández Laos, Enrique. "Medición de la incidencia de la pobreza y la pobreza extrema en México (1963–1988)." *Investigación Económica* 49, no. 191 (March 1990): 265–97.

Hernández Vélez, Salvador. *El Movimiento Urbano Popular En La Laguna, 1970–1980*. Torreón, Coahuila: Gobierno de Coahuila, 2013.

Hinojosa, Alejandra Rangel. *Participación Política De Las Mujeres En Un Movimiento Urbano De Nuevo León*. Mexico City: Plaza y Valdés, 2000.

Hirsch, Arnold. *Making the Second Ghetto: Race and Housing in Chicago, 1940–1960*. Cambridge: Cambridge University Press, 1983.

Hise, Greg. *Magnetic Los Angeles: Planning the Twentieth-Century Metropolis*. Baltimore: Johns Hopkins University Press, 1999.

Holston, James. "Autoconstruction in Working-Class Brazil." *Cultural Anthropology* 6, no. 4 (November 1991): 450.

———. *Insurgent Citizenship: Disjunctions of Democracy and Modernity in Brazil*. Princeton NJ: Princeton University Press, 2008.

———. "Insurgent Citizenship in an Era of Global Urban Peripheries." *City & Society* 21, no. 2 (October 2009): 247.

Holston, James, and Arjun Appuradai. "Cities and Citizenship." In *Cities and Citizenship*, edited by James Holston, 1–18. Durham NC: Duke University Press, 1999.

Holt, John. "A Letter Advocating School Resistance: Addressed to Participants in the Author's Seminar Course Held at CIDOC." *CIDOC Informa* 10, no. 49 (February 1970): 1–5.

Huamán, Elías. "La regularización territorial en la zona metropolitana de la ciudad de México (1970–2002): Un instrumento desvinculado de la política de ordenamiento territorial." *Scripta Nova: Revista Electrónica de Geografía y Ciencias Sociales* 14 (August 2010). http://www.ub.edu/geocrit/sn/sn-331/sn-331-32.htm.

Hughes, Jennifer Scheper. "Traditionalist Catholicism and Liturgical Renewal in the Diocese of Cuernavaca, Mexico." In *Catholics in the Vatican II Era: Local Histories of a Global Event*, edited by Kathleen Sprows Cummings, Timothy Matovina, and Robert A Orsi, 64–85. New York: Cambridge University Press, 2018.

Huitron, Antonio. *Netzahualcóyotl: Miseria y grandeza de una ciudad*. Toluca: Editorial Libros de México, 1975.

Huntington, Samuel P. *Political Order in Changing Societies*. New Haven CT: Yale University Press, 1968.

———. *The Third Wave: Democratization in the Late Twentieth Century*. Norman: University of Oklahoma Press, 1991.

Iglesias, Maximiliano. *Memorias de Nezahualcóyotl*. Mexico City: SEPAC, 1995.

———. *Netzahualcóyotl: Testimonios históricos, 1944–1957*. Ciudad Nezahualcóyotl: SEPAC, 1978.

Illades, Carlos. *La Inteligencia Rebelde: La izquierda en el debate público en México, 1968–1989*. Mexico City: Océano, 2012.

Illich, Ivan. *Celebration of Awareness: A Call for Institutional Revolution*. Harmondsworth: Penguin, 1973.

———. "Why We Must Abolish Schooling." *New York Review of Books* 15, no. 1 (July 2, 1970): 9–15.

Infonavit. *Primer informe anual de actividades*. Mexico City: Infonavit, 1973.

Ingwersen, Lance. "La Pata De Cabra, Satire and Free Speech in Nineteenth-Century Mexico City." *Journal of Latin American Studies* 54, no. 1 (January 2022): 1–27.

Instituto de Acción Urbana e Integración Social (AURIS). *Auris: Descripción de la organización*. Mexico City: AURIS, 1971.

Instituto de Información e Investigación Geográfica. *Panorámica Socioeconómica*. Toluca: Gobierno del Estado de México, Secretaría de Finanzas y Planeación, 1963.

Instituto Mexicano del Seguro Social (IMSS). *Investigación de vivienda en 11 ciudades del país*. Mexico City: IMSS, 1965.

———. *Mantenimiento: Unidades habitacionales, conservación-saneamiento, información*. Mexico City: IMSS, 1975.

———. *Manual de Operaciones de Unidades de Vivienda del IMSS*. Distrito Federal: IMSS, 1964.

———. *Unidad Morelos de servicios sociales: San Juan de Aragón*. Mexico City: IMSS, 1962.

Instituto Nacional de la Vivienda (INV). *Colonias Proletarias: Problemas y Soluciones*. Distrito Federal: INV, 1958.

———. *Herradura de Tugurios: Problemas y Soluciones*. Distrito Federal: INV, 1958.

———. *Investigación nacional de la vivienda mexicana, 1961-62*. Mexico City: IMSS, 1963.

Irazábal, Clara, ed. *Ordinary Places, Extraordinary Events: Citizenship, Democracy, and Public Space in Latin America*. London: Routledge, 2008.

Iturriaga, Renato. "Creación y asimilación de información tecnológica en México, un caso de estudio: Infonavit." *Revista Vivienda Infonavit* 1, no. 1 (December 1975): 2-8.

Jackson, Kenneth. *Crabgrass Frontier: The Suburbanization of America*. New York: Oxford University Press, 1985.

Jaramillo, Samuel, and Martha Schteingart. "Procesos Sociales y Producción de Vivienda en América Latina: 1960-1980 (Análisis de Casos)." *Revista Mexicana de Sociología* 45, no. 1 (1983): 11-28.

Jiménez, Christina M. *Making an Urban Public: Popular Claims to the City in Mexico, 1879-1932*. Pittsburgh: University of Pittsburgh Press, 2019.

Jong, Feike de, and Gustavo Graf. "How a City Became a Slum." CityLab, June 28, 2017. https://www.citylab.com/equity/2017/06/how-a-slum-became-a-city/529488/.

Jordan, Robert. "Flowers and Iron Fists: Ernesto P. Uruchurtu and the Contested Modernization of Mexico City, 1952-1966." PhD diss., University of Nebraska, 2013.

Joseph, Gilbert M., and Daniel Nugent, eds. *Everyday Forms of State Formation: Revolution and the Negotiation of Rule in Modern Mexico*. Durham NC: Duke University Press, 1994.

Joseph, Gilbert M., Anne Rubenstein, and Eric Zolov, eds. *Fragments of a Golden Age: The Politics of Culture in Mexico Since 1940*. Durham NC: Duke University Press, 2001.

Joseph, Gilbert M., and Mark D. Schuzman, eds. *I Saw a City Invincible: Urban Portraits of Latin America*. Wilmington DE: SR Books, 1996.

Juárez, Arturo Castro, and Ernesto Ortega Valadéz. "El proceso de segregación en el área urbana de la ciudad de México." Master's thesis, UNAM, 1983.

Kandell, Jonathan. *La Capital: The Biography of Mexico City*. New York: Random House, 1988.

Kemper, Robert V. *Migration and Adaptation: Tzintzuntzan Peasants in Mexico City*. Los Angeles: Sage, 1977.

Kiddle, Amelia, and María L. O. Muñoz, eds. *Populism in Twentieth Century Mexico: The Presidencies of Lázaro Cárdenas and Luis Echeverría*. Tucson: University of Arizona Press, 2010.

Kirkendall, Andrew J. *Paulo Freire and the Cold War Politics of Literacy*. Chapel Hill: University of North Carolina Press, 2010.

Klemek, Christopher. *The Transatlantic Collapse of Urban Renewal: Postwar Urbanism from New York to Berlin*. Chicago: University of Chicago Press, 2011.

Knight, Alan. "*Caciquismo* in Twentieth-Century Mexico." In *Caciquismo in Twentieth-Century Mexico*, edited by Alan Knight and Wil Pansters, 1–50. London: Institute for the Study of the Americas, 2005.

———. *The Mexican Revolution*. Vol. 1, *Porfirians, Liberals and Peasants*. Cambridge: Cambridge University Press, 1986.

Knight, Alan, and Wil Pansters, eds. *Caciquismo in Twentieth-Century Mexico*. London: Institute for the Study of the Americas, 2005.

Krieger, Peter. *Megalópolis: La modernización de la ciudad de México en el siglo XX*. Mexico City: UNAM, 2007.

Krischke, Paulo J. "Church Base Communities and Democratic Change in Brazilian Society." *Comparative Political Studies* 24, no. 2 (July 1991): 186–210.

Kuri, Ariel Rodríguez. *Historia Política De La Ciudad De México (Desde Su Fundación Hasta El Año 2000)*. Mexico City: El Colegio de México, 2012.

———. *La experiencia olvidada: El ayuntamiento de México; Política y gobierno, 1876–1912*. Mexico City: El Colegio de México, 1996.

Kwak, Nancy. "Slum Clearance as a Transnational Process in Globalizing Manila." In *Making Cities Global*, edited by Andrew Sandoval-Strausz and Nancy Kwak, 98–113. Philadelphia: University of Pennsylvania Press, 2018.

Kwak, Nancy, and A. K. Sandoval-Strausz, eds. *Making Cities Global: The Transnational Turn in Urban History*. Philadelphia: University of Pennsylvania Press, 2017.

Labbé, Danielle. *Land Politics and Livelihoods on the Margins of Hanoi, 1920–2010*. Vancouver: University of British Columbia, 2014.

Latham, Michael. *Modernization as Ideology: American Social Science and "Nation Building" in the Kennedy Era*. Chapel Hill: University of North Carolina Press, 2000.

Lear, John. *Workers, Neighbors, and Citizens: The Revolution in Mexico City*. Lincoln: University of Nebraska Press, 2001.

Legorreta, Jorge, ed. *Ciudad de México: Debate*. Mexico City: UNAM-Azcapotzalco, 2008.

Leidenberger, Georg. "Los orígenes de la educación urbanística en México: El Instituto de Planificación y Urbanismo dirigido por el arquitecto Hannes Meyer (1938–1941)." *Espacialidades* 8, no. 1 (May 2018): 24–38.

Lenti, Joseph U. *Redeeming the Revolution: The State and Organized Labor in Post-Tlatelolco Mexico*. Lincoln: University of Nebraska, 2017.

Leonard, Aaron, and Conor Gallagher. *Heavy Radicals: The FBI's Secret War on America's Maoists; The Revolutionary Union / Revolutionary Communist Party 1968–1980*. Winchester: Zero Books, 2015.

Levine, Robert. *A Geography of Time*. New York: Basic Books, 1997.

Lewis, Oscar. *The Children of Sanchez: Autobiography of a Mexican Family*. New York: Random House, 1961.

———. *Five Families: Mexican Case Studies in the Culture of Poverty*. New York: Basic Books, 1959.

———. "Urbanization without Breakdown: A Case Study." *Scientific Monthly* 75, no. 1 (July 1952): 41.

Lewis, Robert, and Richard Harris. "Segregation and the Social Relations of Place, Bombay, 1890–1910." *South Asia: Journal of South Asian Studies* 36, no. 4 (October 2013): 589–607.

Lewis, Stephen E. "Dead-End *Caudillismo* and Entrepreneurial *Caciquismo* in Chiapas, 1910–1955." In *Caciquismo in Twentieth-Century Mexico*, edited by Alan Knight and Wil Pansters, 151–68. London: Institute for the Study of the Americas, 2005.

———. *Rethinking Mexican Indigenismo: The INI's Coordinating Center in Highland Chiapas and the Fate of a Utopian Project*. Albuquerque: University of New Mexico Press, 2018.

Linhart, Robert. *L'etabli*. Paris: Les Editions de Minuit, 1978.

Loaeza, Soledad. "Política del rumor: México, noviembre–diciembre de 1976." *Foro Internacional* 17, no. 4 (April 1977): 575–81.

Lomnitz, Larissa Adler. *Networks and Marginality: Life in a Mexican Shantytown*. New York: Academic Press, 1977.

Lomnitz-Adler, Claudio. *Modernidad Indiana: Nueve Ensayos Sobre Nación y Mediación en México*. Mexico City: Grupo Editorial Planeta, 1999.

López, Flor M., and Patricia Martínez. "La reproducción de la pobreza de la población indígena migrante en la Ciudad de México." In *Segregación urbana y espacios de exclusion: Ejemplos de México y América Latina*, edited by Adrián Guillermo Aguilar and Irma Escamilla H., 281–97. Mexico City: UNAM, 2015.

López, Ricardo, and Barbara Weinstein, eds. *The Making of the Middle Class: Toward a Transnational History*. Durham NC: Duke University Press, 2012.

López Sarrelangue, Delfina E. "Una hacienda comunal indígena en la Nueva España: Santa Ana Aragón." *Historia Mexicana, el Colegio de México* 32, no. 11 (September 1982): 1–38.

Luna, Margarita García. *Nezahualcóyotl: Tierras que surgen de un desequilibrio ecológico*. Toluca: CIDNE, 1990.

Mainwaring, Scott. "Urban Popular Movements, Identity, and Democratization in Brazil." *Comparative Political Studies* 20, no. 2 (1987): 131–59.

Malley, François, and Albert Chambon. *Le Père Morelli, de Dachau à Net*. Paris: Éd. du Cerf, 1986.

Mancera, Ramón Plaza. "Inversión en programas habitacionales." *Revista Vivienda Infonavit* 2, no. 7 (December 1976): 60–71.

Marx, Karl. *The Eighteenth Brumaire of Louis Bonaparte*. Moscow: Progress, 1937.

Marx, Karl, and Friedrich Engels. *Marx and Engels Selected Works*. Vol. 1. Moscow: Progress, 1969.

———. *Marx and Engels Selected Works*. Vol. 3. Moscow: Progress, 1970.

Massey, Doreen. *For Space*. London: Sage, 2005.

Massey, Douglas S., and Nancy A. Denton. *American Apartheid: Segregation and the Making of the Underclass*. Cambridge MA: Harvard University Press, 2003.

Matute, Alvaro. *El Ateneo de México*. Mexico City: Fondo de Cultura Económica, 1999.

McCann, Bryan. *Hard Times in the Marvelous City: From Dictatorship to Democracy in the Favelas of Rio de Janeiro*. Durham NC: Duke University Press, 2014.

McCormick, Gladys I. *The Logic of Compromise in Mexico: How the Countryside Was Key to the Emergence of Authoritarianism*. Chapel Hill: University of North Carolina Press, 2016.

McMahon, Mary E. "Higher Education in a World Market: An Historical Look at the Global Context of International Study." *Higher Education* 24, no. 4 (December 1992): 465–68.

Menchaca, Martha. *The Mexican American Experience in Texas: Citizenship, Segregation, and the Struggle for Equality*. Austin: University of Texas Press, 2022.

Mendiola Garcia, Sandra C. *Street Democracy: Vendors Violence and Public Space in Late Twentieth-Century Mexico*. Lincoln: University of Nebraska Press, 2017.

"Mensaje de episcopado al pueblo de México sobre la reforma educative." *Christus* 408 (November 1969): 1166–77.

Mexico-Cetenal. *Información Cetenll en La Aplicación de la Ley General de Asentamientos Humanos*. Mexico City: CETENAL, 1977.

Meza, Armando. *Movimiento Urbano Popular En Durango*. Mexico City: CIESAS, 1994.

Middlebrook, Kevin J. "Caciquismo and Democracy: Mexico and Beyond." *Bulletin of Latin American Research* 28, no. 3 (July 2009): 412.
Miranda, José Porfirio. *Marx y la Biblia: Crítica a la filosofía de la opresión*. Salamanca: Sígueme, 1972.
Moctezuma, Pedro. "LA CONAMUP." *Estudios Políticos* 4-5, no. 1 (October 1985): 30-37.
———. "Mexico's Urban Popular Movements." *Environment and Urbanization* 2, no. 1 (April 1990): 35-50.
Monsiváis, Carlos. *Entrada libre: Crónicas de la sociedad que se organiza*. Mexico City: Ediciones Era, 1987.
———. *Mexican Postcards*. Translated by John Kraniauskas. London: Verso, 1997.
Montaño, Maria Cristina. *La Tierra de Ixtapalapa: Luchas Sociales*. Mexico City: UNAM-Iztapalapa, 1984.
Morales Martínez, María Dolores. *Ensayos urbanos: La Ciudad de México en el siglo XIX*. Mexico City: Universidad Autónoma Metropolitana, 2011.
Morelli, Alex. *Libera a mi pueblo*. Buenos Aires: Cuadernos Latinoamericanos, 1971.
Moreno, Héctor Velázquez. "Dónde vives?" *Calli* 15 (February 1965): 9-17.
Moya, Jose C. *Cousins and Strangers: Spanish Immigrants in Buenos Aires, 1850-1930*. Berkeley: University of California Press, 1998.
Muhammad, Khalil Gibran. *The Condemnation of Blackness: Race, Crime, and the Making of Modern Urban America*. Cambridge MA: Harvard University Press, 2011.
Mumford, Eric. *The CIAM Discourse on Urbanism, 1928-1960*. Cambridge: MIT Press, 2000.
Munn, Nancy D. "The Cultural Anthropology of Time: A Critical Essay." *Annual Review of Anthropology* 21 (1992): 93-123.
Muñoz, María L. O. *Stand Up and Fight: Participatory Indigenismo, Populism, and Mobilization in Mexico, 1970-1984*. Tucson: University of Arizona Press, 2016.
Muñoz García, Humberto, Orlandina de Oliveira, and Claudio Stern. *Migración y desigualdad social en la Ciudad de Mexico*. Mexico City: El Colegio de México, 1977.
Murphy, Edward. *For a Proper Home: Housing Rights in the Margins of Urban Chile, 1960-2010*. Pittsburgh: University of Pittsburgh Press, 2015.
Murray, Martin J. *Taming the Disorderly City: The Spatial Landscape of Johannesburg after Apartheid*. Ithaca NY: Cornell University Press, 2008.
Muzaffar, Ijlal. "The Periphery Within: Modern Architecture and the Making of the Third World." PhD diss., Massachusetts Institute of Technology, 2007.
Napier, Mark. "Core Housing, Enablement, and Urban Poverty: The Consolidation Paths of Households Living in Two South African Settlements." PhD diss., Newcastle University, 2002.

Napolitano, Valentina. "Between 'Traditional' and 'New' Catholic Church Religious Discourses in Urban, Western Mexico." *Bulletin of Latin American Research* 17, no. 3 (1998): 323–39.

———. *Migration, Mujercitas, and Medicine Men: Living in Urban Mexico*. Berkeley: University of California Press, 2002.

Newell, Stephanie. *Histories of Dirt: Media and Urban Life in Colonial and Postcolonial Lagos*. Durham NC: Duke University Press, 2020.

Niblo, Stephen. *Mexico in the 1940s: Modernity, Politics, and Corruption*. Wilmington DE: Scholarly Resources, 1999.

Noelle, Louise. *Arquitectos contemporáneos de México*. Mexico City: Trillas, 1989.

Nova, Carmen Martínez. "The 'Culture' of Exclusion: Representations of Indigenous Women Street Vendors in Tijuana, Mexico." *Bulletin of Latin American Research* 22, no. 3 (2003): 249–68.

Novo, Salvador. *Nueva Grandeza Mexicana*. Mexico City: Editorial Hermes, 1967.

Nun, José. "Superpoblación relativa, ejército industrial de reserva y masa marginal." *Revista Latinoamericana de Sociologia* 5, no. 2 (1969): 178–236.

Nutini, Hugo G., and Barry L. Isaac. *Social Stratification in Central Mexico, 1500–2000*. Austin: University of Texas Press, 2010.

Ochoa, Enrique. *Feeding Mexico: The Political Uses of Food Since 1910*. Wilmington DE: Scholarly Resources, 2000.

Olcott, Jocelyn. *International Women's Year: The Greatest Consciousness-Raising Event in History*. Oxford: Oxford University Press, 2017.

Oliveros de Miranda, María Adela. "José Porfirio Miranda de la Parra: Una vida entre Marx y la Biblia." *Signos Filosóficos*, no. 7 (June 2002): 300.

Olsen, Patrice Elizabeth. *Artifacts of Revolution: Architecture, Society, and Politics in Mexico City, 1920–1940*. Lanham MD: Rowman & Littlefield, 2008.

Onjas, Gregorio Valner. *La experiencia mexicana en materia de asentamientos humanos*. Mexico City: Secretaría de Asentamientos Humanos y Obras Públicas, 1978.

Orellana, Carlos. "Mixtec Migrants in Mexico City: A Case Study of Urbanization." *Human Organization* 3, no. 32 (Fall 1973): 273–83.

Organisation for Economic Co-operation and Development (OECD). *OECD Territorial Reviews: Valle de Mexico*. Paris: OECD Publishing, 2016.

Ortiz Mena, Antonio. "Una importante obra de habitación colectiva." *Arquitectura México*, no. 59 (September 1957): 136.

Ovalle, Camilo Vicente. *Tiempo suspendido: Una historia de la desaparición forzada en México, 1940–1980*. Mexico City: Bonilla Artigas, 2019.

Oxhorn, Philip. *Organizing Civil Society: The Popular Sectors and the Struggle for Democracy in Chile*. University Park: Penn State University Press, 1995.

Padilla, Tanalís. *Rural Resistance in the Land of Zapata: The Jaramillista Movement and the Myth of the Pax Priísta, 1940–1962*. Durham NC: Duke University Press, 2008.

Padilla, Tanalís, and Louise E. Walker. "In the Archives: History and Politics." *Journal of Iberian and Latin American Research* 19, no. 1 (2013): 1–10.

Pagaza, Ignacio Pichardo. *Anatomía de un gobierno singular: Seis años con Carlos Hank, 1969–1975*. Zinacantepec: Editorial Porrúa, 2017.

Palerm, Ángel. *Obras hidráulicas prehispánicas en el sistema lacustre del Valle de México*. Mexico City: INAH, 1973.

Palomares, Manuel. *Historia de Ciudad Nezahualcóyotl: Botín de filibusteros*. Ciudad Nezahualcóyotl: Self-published, 1985.

Pani, Alberto J. *En Camino Hacia la Democracia*. Mexico City: Direccion de talleres graficos, 1918.

———. *Hygiene in Mexico: A Study of Sanitary and Educational Problems*. New York: G. P. Putnam's Sons, 1917.

Pani, Mario, ed. *Los multifamiliares de pensiones*. Mexico City: Editorial Arquitectura, 1952.

———. "México: Un problema. Una solución." *Arquitectura México* 60 (December 1957): 198–226.

Pansters, Wil. "Building a Cacicazgo in a Neoliberal University." In *Caciquismo in Twentieth-Century Mexico*, edited by Alan Knight and Wil Pansters, 296–326. London: Institute for the Study of the Americas, 2005.

Parsons, Jeffery R. *The Last Pescadores of Chimalhuacán, Mexico: An Archaeological Ethnography*. Ann Arbor: University of Michigan Press, 2006.

Patron, Emilio Gamboa. *IMSS: Una Historia Compartida, 1943–1993*. Distrito Federal: Editorial Gustavo Casas, 1993.

Peattie, Lisa Redfield. *The View from the Barrio*. Ann Arbor: University of Michigan Press, 1968.

Peña, Landy Sánchez. "¿Viviendo Cada Vez Más Separados? Un Análisis Multigrupo de La Segregación Residencial En La Ciudad de México, 1990–2005." *Estudios Demográficos y Urbanos* 27, no. 1 (2012): 57–93.

Pensado, Jaime. "El Movimiento Estudiantil Profesional (MEP): La radicalización de la juventud católica mexicana durante la Guerra Fría." *Mexican Studies / Estudios Mexicanos* 31, no. 1 (February 2015): 183–85.

———. *Rebel Mexico: Student Unrest and Authoritarian Political Culture during the Long Sixties*. Stanford: Stanford University Press, 2013.

Pensado, Jaime, and Enrique C. Ochoa. "Introduction: Mexico beyond 1968: Revolutionaries, Radicals, and Repression." In *Mexico beyond 1968: Revolutionaries, Radicals, and Repression during the Global Sixties and Subversive Seventies*, edited by Jaime M. Pensado and Enrique C. Ochoa, 3–18. Tucson: University of Arizona Press, 2018.

———, eds. *Mexico beyond 1968: Revolutionaries, Radicals, and Repression during the Global Sixties and Subversive Seventies*. Tucson: University of Arizona, 2018.

Pérez, Miguel. *The Right to Dignity: Housing Struggles, City Making, and Citizenship in Urban Chile*. Stanford: Stanford University Press, 2022.

Perlman, Janice. *The Myth of Marginality: Urban Poverty and Politics in Rio de Janeiro*. Berkeley: University of California Press, 1976.

Perry, Clarence. *Neighborhood and Community Planning*. Vol. 7. New York: Regional Plan of New York and Its Environs, 1929.

Pezzoli, Keith. *Human Settlements and Planning for Ecological Sustainability: The Case of Mexico City*. Cambridge: MIT Press, 1998.

Piccato, Pablo. *City of Suspects: Crime in Mexico City, 1900–1931*. Durham NC: Duke University Press, 2001.

———. *A History of Infamy: Crime, Truth, and Justice in Mexico*. Oakland: University of California Press, 2017.

———. *The Tyranny of Opinion: Honor in the Construction of the Mexican Public Sphere*. Durham NC: Duke University Press, 2010.

Pilcher, Jeffrey. *Cantinflas and the Chaos of Mexican Modernity*. Wilmington DE: Scholarly Resources, 2001.

"Plano General—Unidad Santa Fe." *Arquitectura México*, no. 59 (September 1957): 138–40.

Plotkin, Mariano Ben. "US Foundations, Cultural Imperialism and Transnational Misunderstandings: The Case of the Marginality Project." *Journal of Latin American Studies* 47, no. 1 (November 2014): 65–92.

Poniatowska, Elena. *Hasta no verte Jesús mío*. Mexico City: Era, 1969.

———. *La noche de Tlatelolco: Testimonios de historia oral*. Mexico City: Era, 1971.

———. *Nada, nadie: Las voces del temblor*. Mexico City: Ediciones Era, 1988.

———. *Nothing, Nobody: The Voices of the Mexico City Earthquake*. Translated by Aurora Camacho de Schmidt and Arthur Schmidt. Philadelphia: Temple University Press, 1995.

Portes, Alejandro, Manuel Castells, and Laura A. Benton. *The Informal Economy: Studies in Advanced and Less Developed Countries*. Baltimore: Johns Hopkins University Press, 1989.

Prakash, Gyan, and Kevin M. Kruse, eds. *The Spaces of the Modern City*. Princeton NJ: Princeton University Press, 2008.

Pratt, Mary Louise. *Planetary Longings*. Durham NC: Duke University Press, 2022.

Prieto, Alejandro, and José María Gutiérrez. "Unidad de Servicios Sociales y Habitación Independencia del IMSS." *Arquitectura México*, no. 73 (March 1961): 10–13.

Ramírez Vázquez, Pedro. "Human Settlements Issues and Policies in Mexico." *Habitat International* 3, nos. 3–4 (1978): 310.

Rabe, Stephen G. "Alliance for Progress." *Oxford Research Encyclopedia of Latin American History* (March 3, 2016). https://doi.org/10.1093/acrefore/9780199366439.013.95.

Rao, Nikhil. *House, but No Garden: Apartment Living in Bombay's Suburbs, 1898–1964*. Minneapolis: University of Minnesota Press, 2012.

Redfield, Robert. *Tepoztlán, a Mexican Village: A Study of Folk Life*. Chicago: University of Chicago Press, 1930.

Reimer, Everett. "Second Annual Report of the Seminar on Alternatives in Education." *CIDOC Informa* 9, no. 45 (September 1969): 1–23.

Reygadas, Luis. "The Construction of Latin American Inequality." In *Indelible Inequalities in Latin America: Insights from History, Politics, and Culture*, edited by Luis Reygadas and Paul Gootenberg, 23–49. Durham NC: Duke University Press, 2010.

Rivero Villar, Manuel Alejandro. "The Role of Social Capital in the Resilience of Self-Help Settlements: The Case of Nezahualcóyotl in the Metropolitan Area of Mexico City." PhD diss., University College London, 2018.

Roberts, Bryan. *Cities of Peasants: The Political Economy of Urbanization in the Third World*. Beverly Hills: Sage, 1979.

Robinet, Romain. "A Revolutionary Group Fighting against a Revolutionary State: The September 23rd Communist League against the PRI-State (1973–1975)." In *Challenging Authoritarianism in Mexico: Revolutionary Struggles and the Dirty War, 1964–1982*, edited by Fernando Herrera Calderón and Adela Cedillo, 139–41. New York: Routledge, 2012.

Robinson, Lisa. "The Politics of Low-Income Housing in Mexico: A Case Study of Infonavit, the Workers' Housing Fund." PhD diss., Stanford University, 1980.

Rodríguez Cortés, Luisa F., and Mariana Ortega Breña. "Building Citizenship: The Struggle for Housing in Eastern Mexico City." *Latin American Perspectives* 44, no. 3 (May 2017): 176–90.

Rodríguez Rebolledo, María Victoria. "Trabajo social en la Unidad de Habitación Legaría del I.M.S.S." Master's thesis, UNAM, 1966.

Romero, José Luis. *Latinoamerica: Las ciudades y las ideas*. Buenos Aires: Siglo 21 Argentina Editores, 1976.

Rosa, Martín de la. "La Iglesia católica en México: Del Vaticano II a la CELAM III (1965–1979)." *Cuadernos Políticos* 19 (January 1979): 95.

———. *Netzahualcóyotl: Un fenómeno*. Mexico City: Fondo de Cultura Económica, 1974.

―――. *Promoción Popular y Lucha de Clases*. Ciudad Nezahualcóyotl: SEPAC, 1979.

Rosa, Martín de la, and Luis del Valle. "¿Marx y/o Jesucristo?" *Liberación*, no. 22 (October 1971): n.p.

Rothstein, Richard. *The Color of Law: A Forgotten History of How Our Government Segregated America*. New York: W. W. Norton, 2017.

Rubalcaba, Rosa Máría, and Martha Schteingart. *Ciudades Divididas: Desigualdad y Segregación Social en México*. Mexico City: El Colegio de México, 2014.

Rubin, Jeffrey. *Decentering the Regime: Ethnicity, Radicalism, and Democracy in Juchitán, Mexico*. Durham NC: Duke University Press, 1997.

Russell, Philip L. *The History of Mexico: From Pre-conquest to Present*. New York: Routledge, 2010.

Ruvalcaba, Jesús. *Ciudad Nezahualcóyotl: Mito y Realidad*. Mexico City: Self-published, 1990.

Sabatini, Francisco. "La segregación social del espacio en las ciudades de América Latina." Paper presented to the Inter-American Development Bank, March 2006.

Sabia, Debra. *Contradiction and Conflict: The Popular Church in Nicaragua*. Tuscaloosa: University of Alabama Press, 2014.

Saiz, Juan Ramírez. *El Movimiento Urbano Popular en México*. Mexico City: Siglo Veintiuno Editores, 1986.

Salazar, Rodolfo Montaño. "Expansión y reconversión económica de la zona metropolitana del Valle de México, una mirada de 1970 a 2000." *ACE: Architecture, City and Environment* 2 (July 2006): 163–65.

Salles, Vania, and Elsie McPhail, eds. *Textos y Pre-textos: Once estudios sobre la mujer*. Mexico City: El Colegio de México, 1991.

Sánchez-Mejorada Fernández, María Cristina, and María Teresa Torres Mora. "Cotidianidad y Modalidades de Trabajo de las Mujeres de una Colonia Popular." In *Textos y Pre-textos: Once estudios sobre la mujer*, edited by Vania Salles and Elsie McPhail, 167–200. Mexico City: El Colegio de México, 1991.

Saucedo, Pedro Ocotitla. "Movimientos de colonos en Ciudad Nezahualcóyotl: Acción colectiva y política popular 1945–1975." Master's thesis, Universidad Autónoma Metropolitana–Iztapalapa, 2000.

Schmidt, Samuel. *The Deterioration of the Mexican Presidency: The Years of Luis Echeverría*. Tucson: University of Arizona Press, 1991.

Schneider, Cathy Lisa. *Shantytown Protest in Pinochet's Chile*. Philadelphia: Temple University Press, 1995.

Schteingart, Martha. "El proceso de formación y consolidación de un asentamiento popular en México: El caso de Ciudad Nezahualcóyotl." *Revista interamericana de planificación*, no. 57 (1981): 100–123.

———, ed. *Espacio y vivienda en la ciudad de México*. Mexico City: El Colegio de México, 1991.

———. *Los productores del espacio habitable: Estado, empresa y sociedad en la ciudad de México*. Mexico City: El Colegio de México, 1989.

———. "Pobreza y Políticas Sociales en México y Estados Unidos de Norteamérica: Un Estudio Comparativo." *Revista Mexicana de Sociología* 59, no. 2 (1997): 161–84.

Schwartz, Barry. *Queuing and Waiting: Studies in the Social Organization of Access and Delay*. Chicago: University of Chicago Press, 1975.

Scott, Ian. *Urban and Spatial Development in Mexico*. Baltimore: Johns Hopkins University, 1982.

Selee, Andrew. *Decentralization, Democratization, and Informal Power in Mexico*. University Park: Penn State University Press, 2011.

Self, Robert O. *American Babylon: Race and the Struggle for Postwar Oakland*. Princeton NJ: Princeton University Press, 2003.

Servicios Educativos Populares (SEPAC). *El Manual del Colono, Ciudad Nezahualcóyotl*. Ciudad Nezahualcóyotl: SEPAC, 1978.

Servín, Elisa. "Reclaiming Revolution in Light of the 'Mexican Miracle': Celestino Gasca and the Federacionistas Leales Insurrection of 1961." *The Americas* 66, no. 4 (2010): 532.

Shefner, Jon. *The Illusion of Civil Society: Democratization and Community Mobilization in Low Income Mexico*. University Park: Penn State University Press, 2008.

Sigal, Silvia. "Marginalidad espacial, Estado, ciudadanía." *Revista Mexicana de Sociología* 43, no. 4 (1981): 1547–77.

Sivaramakrishnan, K. C. *Re-visioning Indian Cities: The urban renewal mission*. Los Angeles: Sage, 2011.

Sluis, Ageeth. *Deco Body, Deco City: Female Spectacle and Modernity in Mexico City, 1900–1939*. Lincoln: University of Nebraska Press, 2016.

Smith, Benjamin T. "Introduction." *Mexican Studies / Estudios Mexicanos* 36, nos. 1–2 (January 2020): 1–9.

Smith, Neil. *Uneven Development: Nature, Capital and the Production of Space*. New York: Blackwell, 1984.

Smith, Otto Saumarez. *Boom Cities: Architect Planners and the Politics of Radical Urban Renewal in 1960s Britain*. Oxford: Oxford University Press, 2019.

Smith, Preston H., II. *Racial Democracy and the Black Metropolis: Housing Policy in Postwar Chicago*. Minneapolis: University of Minnesota Press, 2012.

Snodgrass, Michael. *Deference and Defiance in Monterrey: Workers, Paternalism and Revolution in Mexico, 1890–1950*. Cambridge: Cambridge University Press, 2003.

Spring, Joel. *Corporatism, Social Control, and Cultural Domination in Education: From the Radical Right to Globalization.* New York: Routledge, 2013.

Stavenhagen, Rodolfo. "Capitalism and the Peasantry in Mexico." *Latin American Perspectives* 5, no. 3 (Fall 1978): 27–37.

Sudra, Tomasz Leopold. "Low-Income Housing System in Mexico City." PhD diss., Massachusetts Institute of Technology, 1976.

Sugrue, Thomas J. *The Origins of the Urban Crisis: Race and Inequality in Postwar Detroit.* Princeton NJ: Princeton University Press, 1996.

Suri, Jeremi. *Power and Protest: Global Revolution and the Rise of Détente.* Cambridge MA: Harvard University Press, 2003.

Székely, Miguel. *The Economics of Poverty, Inequality and Wealth Accumulation in Mexico.* London: Palgrave Macmillan, 1998.

Tamayo, Jorge. *Panorámica Socioeconómica 1970: Encuesta Definitiva en Nezahualcóyotl.* Toluca: Self-published, 1971.

Tamayo, Sergio. "Crítica de la ciudadanía y la democracia sin adjetivos: Ocho escenas de un conflicto ciudadano en la ciudad de México." *Secuencia*, no. 66 (December 2006): 113–42.

———. "Del Movimiento Urbano Popular al Movimiento Ciudadano." *Estudios Sociológicos* 17, no. 50 (1999): 499–518.

Tannenbaum, Barbara. "Streetwise History: The Paseo de la Reforma and the Porfirian State, 1876–1910." In *Rituals of Rule, Rituals of Resistance: Public Celebrations and Popular Culture in Mexico*, edited by William H. Beezley, Cheryl English Martin, and William E. French, 127–50. Wilmington DE: Scholarly Resource Inc., 1994.

Taylor, Keeanga-Yamahtta. *Race for Profit: How Banks and the Real Estate Industry Undermined Black Homeownership.* Chapel Hill: University of North Carolina Press, 2019.

Tenorio-Trillo, Mauricio. *I Speak of the City: Mexico City at the Turn of the Twentieth Century.* Chicago: University of Chicago Press, 2015.

Terrazas, Santiago Madrigal. "La recepción del Concilio Vaticano II." *Revista Iberoamericana de Teología* 7, no. 13 (December 2011): 57–90.

Thompson, Edward P. "Time, Work-Discipline, and Industrial Capitalism." *Past & Present* 38, no. 1 (December 1967): 56–97.

Thornton, Christy. *Revolution in Development: Mexico and the Governance of the Global Economy.* Oakland: University of California Press, 2021.

Tilly, Charles. *Durable Inequality.* Berkeley: University of California Press, 1999.

Torres, Germán Aréchiga. *La Plaza de Toros, la Aurora: Primer icono de identidad en el municipio Nezahualcóyotl.* Toluca: Fondo Editorial Estado de México, 2016.

Touraine, Alain. *Actores sociales y sistemas políticos en América Latina.* Santiago, Chile: PREALC, 1987.

Tuan, Yi-Fu. *Space and Place: The Perspective of Experience*. Minneapolis: University of Minnesota Press, 1977.
Tyler, Imogen. *Stigma: The Machinery of Inequality*. London: Zed Books, 2021.
Valencia, Enrique. *La Merced: Estudio ecológico y social de una zona de la ciudad de México*. Mexico City: Instituto Nacional de Antropología e Historia, 1965.
Valero, Ricardo, and Rafael Vargas. *1968 Aquí y Ahora: A cincuenta años del Movimiento Estudiantil, testimonios y reflexiones*. Mexico City: UNAM, 2018.
Varley, Ann. "¿Clientelismo o tecnocracia? La lógica política de la regularización de la tierra urbana, 1970–1988." *Revista Mexicana de Sociología* 56, no. 4 (December 1994): 140–41.
Vaughan, Mary K. *Cultural Politics in Revolution: Teachers, Peasants, and Schools in Mexico, 1930–1940*. Tucson: University of Arizona Press, 1997.
———. *Portrait of a Young Painter: Pepe Zúñiga and Mexico City's Rebel Generation*. Durham NC: Duke University Press, 2015.
Vaughan, Mary K., and Stephen Lewis, eds. *The Eagle and the Virgin: National and Cultural Revolution in Mexico, 1920–1940*. Durham NC: Duke University Press, 2006.
Vekemans, Roger, Ismael Silva Fuenzalida, and Jorge Giusti. *La marginalidad en América Latina: Un ensayo de conceptualización*. Santiago, Chile: CEPAL, 1970.
Vekemans, Roger, and Jorge Giusti. *Tendencias ideológicas y desarrollo latinoamericano*. Santiago, Chile: DESAL/CEPAL, 1967.
Vekemans, Roger, and Ramón Venegas. *Seminario de promoción popular*. Santiago, Chile: CEPAL, 1968.
Velasco Ortiz, Laura. "Movilidades indígenas y explotación flexible: Segregación espacial y desigualdad étnica en una región del circuito agroexportador transnacional México–Estados Unidos." *Mexican Studies / Estudios Mexicanos* 39, no. 1 (February 2023): 32–58.
Vélez-Ibáñez, Carlos. *Reflections of a Transborder Anthropologist: From Netzahualcóyotl to Aztlán*. Tucson: University of Arizona Press, 2020.
———. *Rituals of Marginality: Politics, Process, and Culture Change in Urban Central Mexico, 1969–1974*. Berkeley: University of California Press, 1983.
Verma, N. M. P., and Alpana Srivastana, eds. *The Routledge Handbook of Exclusion, Inequality and Stigma in India*. Abingdon: Routledge, 2020.
Villareal, Rachel Kram. "Gladiolas for the Children of Sanchez: Ernesto P. Uruchurtu's Mexico City, 1950–1968." PhD diss., University of Arizona, 2008.
Villarreal, Andrés, and Erin R. Hamilton. "Residential Segregation in the Mexico City Metropolitan Area, 1990–2000." In *Urban Segregation and Governance in the Americas*, edited by Bryan R. Roberts, 73–95. New York: Palgrave Macmillan, 2009.

Villegas, Daniel Cosío. *El Estilo Personal de Gobernar*. Mexico City: Editorial Joaquín Mortiz, 1974.

"V Informe Anual." Dirección Empresarial, Infonavit, 1977, 3–11.

Vitz, Matthew. *A City on a Lake: Urban Political Ecology and the Growth of Mexico City*. Durham NC: Duke University Press, 2018.

Wacquant, Loïc. *Urban Outcasts: A Comparative Sociology of Advanced Marginality*. Cambridge: Polity, 2008.

Wakild, Emily. "Resources, Communities, and Conservation: The Creation of National Parks in Revolutionary Mexico Under Lázaro Cárdenas, 1934–1940." PhD diss., University of Arizona, 2007.

Walker, Louise. *Waking from the Dream: Mexico's Middle Classes after 1968*. Stanford: Stanford University Press, 2015.

Walsh, Camille. *Racial Taxation: Schools, Segregation, and Taxpayer Citizenship, 1869–1973*. Chapel Hill: University of North Carolina Press, 2018.

Ward, Peter. *Mexico City: The Production and Reproduction of an Urban Environment*. Boston: G. K. Hall, 1990.

Wood, Andrew Grant. *Revolution in the Street: Women, Workers, and Urban Protest in Veracruz, 1870–1927*. Wilmington DE: SR Books, 2001.

Yee, David. "Forging Mixtec Identity in the Mexican Metropolis: Race, Indigenismo, and Mixtec Migrant Associations in Mexico City." *Journal of Latin American Studies* 54, no. 1 (February 2022): 55–77.

———. "The Making of Mexico City's Historic Center: National Patrimony in the Age of Urban Renewal." *Journal of Planning History* 19, no. 1 (February 2020): 90–111.

Zipp, Samuel. *Manhattan Projects: The Rise and Fall of Urban Renewal in Cold War New York*. Oxford: Oxford University Press, 2010.

Zolov, Eric. *The Last Good Neighbor: Mexico in the Global Sixties*. Durham NC: Duke University Press, 2020.

———. *Refried Elvis: The Rise of the Mexican Counterculture*. Berkeley: University of California Press, 1999.

Zuern, Elke. *The Politics of Necessity: Community Organizing and Democracy in South Africa*. Madison: University of Wisconsin Press, 2011.

INDEX

Page numbers followed by *t* refer to the table.

Abrams, Charles, 65
Acción Casa, 141
Adolfo Gurrión Street, La Merced, 16
advertising, 70–72
Aguilar, Oliverio, 138
Agustín, José, 12
Ahumada Rivera, Sergio, 99
Alberto's Hotel Reforma, 7
Alemán, Julio, 58
Alemán, Miguel, 15, 47
Aleman Garcia, Salomon, 122
Aleman Padilla, Carlota, 25–26
Allende, Salvador, 87
Alliance for Progress, 28, 29–30
Alonso, Eugenio, 51, 52
Ángeles, Luis, 17, 18
animals, in Ciudad Neza, 75
anticommunism, 24
antiurban growth platform, of Ernesto Uruchurtu, 19–21
Aréchiga Ruiz, Germán, 56, 58
Argentina, 167
Arias, Julián Díaz, 27
aristocracy, spatial distribution of, 12–13
Asociación Católica de la Juventud Mexicana (ACJM) (Catholic Association of Mexican Youth), 151

Associated Civil Engineers (Ingenieros Civiles Asociados, ICA), 140
AURIS, 108–9, 130–31
Aurora Company, 55–60, 71
Auténtico Movimiento Restaurador de Colonos (AMRC) (Authentic Restoration Movement of Settlers), 134
autoconstrucción: advertising and, 70–72; for animals and livestock, 75; architecture of necessity and, 72–76; colonia proletaria and, 65; division of labor and, 76–80; electricity in, 75–76; as family extension, 73; gender and, 76–80; materials for, 69; overview of, xv, 64–67, 83; process of, 66; roof in, 65; space and, 76–80; tabique for, 66; time constraints and, 76–80; vulgar hybridity and, 80–83. *See also* housing
Autonomous University of Nuevo León (Universidad Autónoma de Nuevo León, UANL), 162
Auyero, Javier, 76
Ávila Camacho, Manuel, 8
Ávila Jácome, Ángel, 118, 121–22, 138
Aztec Templo Mayor, 21

Banobras, 27, 82
Barquín Díaz, Gonzalo, 109
Bautista, Raúl Ruiz, xiii–xiv
Baz Prada, Gustavo, 54
Beaux-Arts mansions, 4
Beltran, Felipe Lopez, 50–55
Boff, Leonardo, 167
Bolivia, 65
Bonifaz Nuño, Rubén, 12
Bordo de Xochiaca, 47
Brazil, housing in, 91–93
Brazil's National Housing Bank (Banco Nacional da Habitação, BNH), 92
Buendía, Severiana, 117, 122
Buenos Aires, study regarding, 15
bullfighting, 58, 59
bus transportation, 67
Butler, Matthew, 145

cacique, xxi
caciquismo, xxi
Café de Tacuba, 18, 21
Calderon, Alor, 131
Calle Rosario, La Merced, 16
Campo Deportivo Francisco Zarco, San Juan de Aragón, 34
Cantiflas, 11
capitalism, 155, 167
Cárdenas, Cuauhtémoc, 177
Cárdenas, Lázaro, 7
Carmona, Jorge F., 52
Carranza, Venustiano, 6
Casa Mater, 170
Casas, Guillermo, 153–54
Casas Alemán, Fernando, 4, 17, 19
Castells, Manuel, 180
Castillo Salas, David, 80, 81
Castro, Fidel, 168

Catholic Association of Mexican Youth (Asociación Católica de la Juventud Mexicana, ACJM), 151
Catholicism, 145–49, 178
Cemaj, Benjamín, 59
Center for Intercultural Formation (CIF), 147–48
Center of Social and Economic Development for Latin America (Centro de Desarrollo Económico y Social para América Latina, DESAL), 156
Central Executive Committee for a Free Municipality in Colonias del Vaso de Texcoco, 60
centralization, 3–4, 9, 10
Centro Crítico Universitario (Cecrun), 154
Centro Cultural Cóyotl (Colonia El Sol), 47, 49, 50–55, 68, 70, 72, 170, 183*t*
Centro Cultural Libertad, 170
Centro de Cómputo Electrónico del Infonavit (Electronic Computing Center of Infonavit), 96–97, 99–100, 102
Centro de Desarrollo Económico y Social para América Latina (DESAL) (Center of Social and Economic Development for Latin America), 156
Centro Interamericano de Vivienda y Planeamiento (CINVA) (Inter-American Center for Housing and Planning), 130
Centro Intercultural de Documentatión (CIDOC) (Intercultural Documentation Center), 147–48, 149, 158–60
Cervantes, Gregorio, 72

Cervantes Sánchez, Enrique, 33, 35
charro (corrupt union boss), xxi
Chávez Ramírez, Eduardo, 43
Chavira, Guadalupe, 53
Chiapas, xxiii
Chihuahua, 103, 115
Chilapa, Guerrero, 176
Chile, 87, 156, 167
China, 66
Chinese Revolution, 135
Christians for Socialism movement, 167
Cine Aurora movie theater, 59
Cine Lago, 59
Cine Maravillas, 59
citizenry, defined, 24
Ciudad Juárez, 88
Ciudad Lago, 137
Ciudad Neza (Ciudad Nezahualcóyotl) (Colonias del Vasco de Texcoco): advertising for, 70–72; animals and livestock in, 75; architecture of necessity in, 72–76; autoconstrucción in, 64–83; as bedroom community, 161; black legend regarding, 82–83; bus transportation in, 67; as city of extremes, xv–xvi; as communal land, 120; commute times in, 69–70; criminality in, 80–81; demographics of, 61, 67; description of, 165–66; development of, 32; disadvantages of, 70; diseases and infections in, 110; division of labor and, 76–80; electricity in, 75–76; entertainment in, 58–59; evictions in, 53; expropriation of land of, 122–24; female labor in, 68, 69, 76–80; fraccionadores in, 61–62, 106, 107, 182; graffiti in, 135; growth of, xv; housing costs in, 188n48; housing survey regarding, 72–73; housing types in, 64, 109; incomplete modernity in, 169; as informal city, 132–33; infrastructure of, 107–10; inner workings of, xx–xxi; juvenile delinquents in, 80–81; labor and living in, 67–70; land and property in, 183–84t; land invasions and, 126–30, 136–37, 138; land ownership in, xiii, xvi; land regularization and, 130–32; land tenure of, 132; land titles in, 141; Ley de Fraccionamientos de Terrenos del Estado de México and, 55–60; loan failures for, 82; Luis Echeverría's visit to, 106–7, 114–15, 120; as megaslum, 181; mobilization failures in, 162; to municipality, 60–62; natural challenges of, 48; overcrowding in, 73–74; Palacio Municipal in, 175, 176; paracaidistas (parachutists) in, 80; Parque del Pueblo in, 140–41; payment strike in, 106–7, 112–13; plans regarding, 44–47; political party affiliation of, 176; population growth of, 44, 66, 107–8, 109, 181; poverty in, 165–66; private developers in, xvi; promoción popular (popular promotion) project in, 144; public health in, 107–10; ranking of, 181; reputation of, xvi; research regarding, xviii; resident abuse in, 119; resident backgrounds in, xvii; restrictions in, 37; scarcity in, 54; social class in, 155; social movements in, 169–72; space in, 76–80; statistics regarding, 109, 141; strike in, 50–55, 124; time constraints in, 76–80;

Ciudad Neza (Ciudad Nezahualcóyotl) (Colonias del Vasco de Texcoco) (*continued*)
    tradition in, 153; uncertainty in, 78; urban informality and, 130–32; urbanity lacks of, xvi–xvii; urbanization of, 139–40; violence in, 121–22, 136; vulgar hybridity of, xvii, 80–83; water distribution in, 77–80, 109; working class in, 69; Zona Norte of, 181. *See also* Fineza Land Trust; *specific locations*
ciudad perdida, 89–90
Ciudad Universitaria (University City), 20
civil society, xxiv, 179
clandestine subdivisions (*fraccionamientos clandestinos*), 20, 89–90
Coalición Depuradora de Comités del Movimiento Restaurador de Colonos (CDC-MRC), 121
Cold War, 24, 28–31
Colín, Sánchez, 52
Colombia, 167
Colonia Agrícola Oriental, 65
Colonia Agua Azul, 183*t*
Colonia Aurora, 55–60, 70–72, 112, 137, 164–65, 184*t*
Colonia El Sol (Centro Cultural Cóyotl), 47, 49, 50–55, 68, 70, 72, 170, 183*t*
Colonia Estado de México, 47, 164–65, 183*t*
Colonia Evolución, 123, 183*t*
Colonia Gral. José Vicente Villada, 183*t*
Colonia Las Águilas, 183*t*
Colonia Las Palmas, 184*t*
Colonia Loma Bonita, 184*t*
Colonia Los Volcanes, 183*t*
Colonia Manantiales, 184*t*
Colonia Maravillas, 138, 170, 183*t*
Colonia Metropolitana, 68, 184*t*
Colonia México, 46, 47, 183*t*
Colonia Modelo, 184*t*
Colonia Pirules, 184*t*
Colonia Porvenir, 183*t*
colonia proletaria, 65
Colonia Reforma, 184*t*
Colonias Romero, 164–65, 183*t*
Colonia Tamaulipas, 183*t*
colono, defined, xvii
Colono strike, 50–55
Comisión para la Regularización de la Tenencia de la Tierra (CORETT) (Commission for the Regularization of Land Tenure), 131–32
Comité de Fraccionamientos Urbanos para el Distrito de Texcoco (Committee of Urban Subdivisions for the Texcoco District), 51, 52
Comité Executivo del MRC (CE-MRC) (Executive Committee of the MRC), 118, 119–20, 121, 124, 135, 136
Comité Pro-Mejoras del la Colonia del Sol, 50
Commission for the Regularization of Land Tenure (Comisión para la Regularización de la Tenencia de la Tierra, CORETT), 131–32
Committee for the Study of the National Housing Programs Abroad, 92
Committee of Urban Subdivisions for the Texcoco District (Comité de Fraccionamientos Urbanos para el Distrito de Texcoco), 51, 52

256 Index

Compañía Nacional de Subsistencias Populares (CONASUPO) (National Company of Popular Goods), 114
comuneros, 45
Confederación Nacional Campesina (CNC) (National Peasant Confederation), 118
Confederación Nacional de Organizaciones Populares (CNOP) (National Confederation of Popular Organizations), 118
Confederation of Mexican Workers (Confederación de Trabajadores de México, CTM), xv, 11, 99, 100–101, 102–3, 104
Conjunto Urbano Presidente Alemán (multifamiliar apartment complex), 12
conscientização (critical consciousness), 159
Consejo Episcopal Latinoamericano y Caribeño (CELAM) (Latin American Episcopal Conference), 148–49, 156
Consejo Nacional de Huelga (CNH) (National Strike Council), 149
Constitution of 1917, 94
Convento de la Encarnación, 18
Coordinadora Nacional del Movimiento Urbano Popular (CONAMUP) (National Coordinator of the Popular Urban Movement), 178
COPEVI, 37
Cornelius, Wayne, 62
Corpus Christi massacre, 144
corrupt union boss (*charro*), xxi
Cortés, Hernán, 3
Cosdegua (Guatemala), 167
Cox, Harvey, 165

crime, crisis regarding, 14
critical consciousness (*conscientização*), 159
Cuautitlán Izcalli, 94
Cuban Revolution, 28, 135
Cuernavaca, 115, 147–48
Culiacán, 115

Davis, Diane, 8
Davis, Mike, 181
decentralization, 4
democracy, as on the margins, xxiii–xxvi
Democratic Tendency, 100
Departamento Agrario, 117
Departamento de Asuntos Agrarios y Colonización (DAAC) (Department of Colonization and Agrarian Affairs), 116, 118, 120, 131
Departamento del Distrito Federal (DDF), 20
Department of Colonization and Agrarian Affairs (Departamento de Asuntos Agrarios y Colonización, DAAC), 116, 120, 131
Department of Epidemiology (Dirección General de Epidemiología, DGE), 110
Department of Planning, 33
dependency theory, proponents of (*dependistas*), 154
dependistas (proponents of dependency theory), 154
developmentalism, 24
diarrhea, 110
Díaz, Porfirio, 5, 199n30
Díaz Ordaz, Gustavo, 23
Dionicio, Don, 45

Dirección General de Epidemiología (DGE) (Department of Epidemiology), 110
Dirreción de Comunicaciones y Obras Públicas, 50
disease, spread of, 14
Diversiones y Espectáculos de México (DEMSA) (Parties and Events of Mexico), 58
Duhau, Emilio, xx
Durango, 88, 115
dust storms, 32

ecclesial base communities, 178
Echeverría, Luis: ambitions of, 89; attack of, 101; in Ciudad Neza, 106–7, 114–15, 120; decentralization plan of, 93; Fineza Land Trust and, 122–24; housing reforms of, 90–91, 103; Infonavit and, 88, 93–95; land tenure problem and, 118; leadership of, 83, 179–80; middle class and, 90; Movimiento Urbano Popular and, xxv; negotiations by, 162; rally of, 123–24; reforms of, xxv; regularization reform under, xvi; support for, 113–14; travels of, 126
Echeverrismo, xxv
Eckstein, Susan, 38
Eckstein Salz, Bernardo, 55–56, 58, 59, 62, 112, 118–19
economics, 9, 179
Edmundo Campion, 150
Eibenshultz, Roberto, 130–31
ejido, 6–7, 33
El Centro, 13, 16–19
El Despertar del Pueblo (The awakening of the people) (bulletin), 169–70

El Día (periodical), 71
elections, xxiv, 176
electricity, 75–76
Electronic Computing Center of Infonavit (Centro de Cómputo Electrónico del Infonavit), 96–97, 99–100, 102
El Gallo (newspaper), 60–61
El Heraldo del Valle de México (newspaper), 62–63
El Mosquito (newspaper), 48
El Nacional (newspaper), 14
el pueblo (the people), xxiii–xxiv
El Rosario housing complex, 101–2, 103
El Universal (newspaper), 18
Emiliano Zapata Popular Revolutionary Union (Unión Popular Revolucionaria Emiliano Zapata, UPREZ), 171
employment, in Mexico City, statistics regarding, 9
entertainment industry, 10
Episcopal Mutual Aid Union (Unión de Mutua Ayuda Episcopal, UMAE), 147
Escalante Baranda, Angel, 91–92
Estudios Churubusco, 10
ethnoracial segregation, xxi

family life, strength of, 73
Federación de Colonos del Vaso de Texcoco (Federation of Colonos), 51–52, 53
Federal District. *See* Mexico City (Federal District)
Federal District Planning and Zoning Law (Ley de Plantificacíon y Zonificación del Distrito Federal), 20
Federal District Planning Commission, 17–19, 20, 192n60

Federal Labor Law of 1970, 94
Federal Law for Agrarian Reform, 7
Fernández, Freddy (El Pichi), 58
Fernández Albarrán, Juan, 113
Fideicomisco Fondo Nacional de Habitaciones Populares (FONHAPO) (National Fund for Popular Housing), 180
Fineza Land Trust: Ciudad Neza and, 132–33; conditions prior to, 213n75; disruptions to, 136; effects of, 125; in *El Despertar del Pueblo* (The awakening of the people) (bulletin), 169–70; fallout from, 126–30; *fraccionadores* and, 122–23, 132–33; movements from, 171; opposition to, 134; overview of, 142–43; payments into, 120–21; promotion of, 138–39; signing of, 122–24; work of, 139–43
flooding, 43
fogón (cooking fire pit), 74
Fondo de Operación y Financiamiento Bancario a la Vivienda (Fund for Housing Operations and Finance, FOVI), 30–31, 38
Fordham University, 147–48
Fox, David, 108
fraccionadores (land speculators): in Ciudad Neza, 61–62; Colonia Aurora and, 55–60; *doble ventas* of, 133; effects of, 182; Fineza Land Trust agreement and, 122–23, 132–33; impacts of, 62–63; land tenure systems and, 106; Law of Fraccionamientos and, 133–34; against Movimiento Restaurador de Colonos (MRC) (Settlers' Movement for Land Restoration), 115–16; overview of, xxi, 47–50; power of, 62–63, 107; strike against, 113–14
fraccionamientos clandestinos (clandestine subdivisions), 20, 89–90
France, prefabricated homes in, 91
Frank, Andre Gunder, 154
Freire, Paulo, 154, 159–60
Frente Popular Independiente (FPI) (Independent Popular Front), 134, 135, 171, 178
Fund for Housing Operations and Finance (FOVI) (Fondo de Operación y Financiamiento Bancario a la Vivienda), 30–31, 38, 181

Galván, Rafael, 100
Garcia Bravo, Angel, 111, 113, 121, 127, 135
Garcia Coll, Julio, 131
García Cortés, Adrián, 18, 192n60
Garibay, Ricardo, 12
garment industry, 68
Garza Falla, Carlos, 153, 154
General Union of Workers and Farmers of Mexico (Unión General de Obreros y Campesinos de México, UGOCM), 134–35, 137–38
Ghana, 65
Giglia, Angela, xx
Golconda (Colombia), 167
Gómez Frías, 15
Gomez Villanueva, Augusto, 122
González, Carlos Hank, 82, 114, 116, 118, 120, 123–24, 129, 130, 140
González Casanova, Pablo, 154
Goodman, Paul, 159
government assistance, supervision of, 25
Grand Canal, 5–6

Great Migration, xvii
The Group of 80 (Chile), 167
Guadalajara, 88, 146
Guadalupe Zuno, José, 117
Guaranteed Employment Fund, 92
Guatemala, 167
Guerrero Street, Mexico City, 18
Guevara, Che, 163
Gutiérrez, Gustavo, 167
Guzmán Guzmán, José, 45

Hann Cárdenas, César, 49, 70
Herrera, Nestor, 46
highway system, development of, 10–11
Holt, John, 159
hometown associations, formation of, 10
housing: at beginning of 1970s, 88–91; Brazilian connection regarding, 91–93; *colonia proletaria* as, 65; conclusions regarding, 180–81; corruption regarding, 96; costs of, 26, 188n48; failures regarding, 39; fraccionamientos clandestinos (clandestine subdivisions) as, 20, 89–90; home ownership and, 30–31; internationalization of, 28, 39; jacales (temporary structures) as, 65; labor demographics and, 89; *la crisis* of, 13–16; laws regarding, 8–9; little convents (conventillos), 5; in mid-century Mexico City, 13–16; middle-class apartments, 15; monthly fees for, xxiii; *multifamiliar*, xv, 12, 23, 91; neighborhood-unit model for, 33–34; overview of, 22; phase one of, 22; prefabricated, 91; as problem-solving tool, 94–95; reforms regarding, 20–21; rent freezes in, 8–9; roof construction in, 65; social housing programs, xxiii, 23–26, 28, 98–104; statistics regarding, 14, 26, 29, 89; stipulations in, 36–37; subdivision prohibition for, 20; tabique for, 66; tenements, 5, 14; *unidades vecinales* for, 33–34; *unidad habitacional* as, 20; as utopian, 91; *vecindad*, 5; zoning and planning for, 20–21. See also *autoconstrucción*; *specific locations*
Huasteca region, 112
hunting, 45
Hygiene in Mexico, 6

Ibargüengoitia, Jorge, 12
ideario (statement of ideals), 146
Iglesias, Maximiliano, 170
Illich, Ivan, 148–49, 158–61
income, neighborhood, study regarding, 15–16
industries, fiscal incentives to, 8
inequality, xvii, xiv, 188n44
Infonavit: accomplishments of, 103; birth of, 93–95; Brazilian connection with, 92; Centro de Cómputo Electrónico del Infonavit (Electronic Computing Center of Infonavit) of, 96–97, 99–100, 102; *ciudad perdida* challenge of, 90; dominance of, 104; failures of, 101, 103; Fidel Velázquez Sánchez and, 97–104; geographic diversity of, 95; housing production role of, 93; legal foundation of, 94; reforms of, 95–98; significance of, 88; statistics regarding, 101, 103; strategy of, 103; successes of, 180, 181
informality, xx–xxi
informal laborers, 90
infrastructure, 15–16, 107–10

Ingenieros Civiles Asociados (ICA) (Associated Civil Engineers), 140
Institute of Social Security and Services for State Workers (Instituto de Seguridad y Servicios Sociales de los Trabajadores del Estadom, ISSSTE), 89
Institutional Revolutionary Party, xvii
Instituto de Seguridad y Servicios Sociales de los Trabajadores del Estado (ISSSTE) (Institute of Social Security and Services for State Workers), 89
Instituto Mexicano del Seguro Social (IMSS) (Mexican Institute of Social Security): failures of, 39; headquarters of, 9; housing budget of, 23; housing complexes of, 20; housing survey of, 72; overview of, 22; rental costs for, xxiii; selection process of, 24–26; social housing and, 23–24; social programs of, 27; social worker program of, 25; statistics regarding, 27; Unidad Santa Fe and, 26–28; years prior to, 15
Instituto Nacional de Vivienda (INV) (National Institute of Housing), 15, 88, 96
Instituto Patria, 147
Instituto Politécnico Nacional de México (IPN) (National Polytechnic Institute of Mexico), 12, 150
Instituto Tecnológico y de Estudios Superiores de Monterrey, Tec (ITESM) (Monterrey Institute of Technology and Higher Education), 151
Inter-American Center for Housing and Planning (Centro Interamericano de Vivienda y Planeamiento, CINVA), 130
interclass relations, 38
Intercultural Documentation Center (Centro Intercultural de Documentatión, CIDOC), 147–48, 149, 158–60
International Workers' Day, 93–95
interpersonal prejudices, xxii–xxiii
Iztapalapa, 44, 87, 115

jacales (temporary structures), 65
Jalisco, 10
Jesuit Order, 108, 147, 156
Juárez, Benito, 199n30
Juchitán, 103
Junta Regional de Planificación y Zonificación (Regional Planning and Zoning Council), 47
Juventud Obrera Católica (JOC) (Young Catholic Workers), 150

Kennedy, John F., 28, 34, 87
Kennedy, Robert, 34
Kozol, Jonathan, 158, 160

labor, demographics of, 89
La Casa del Pueblo, 170
La Extra (newspaper), 71
la gente decente, 12
Lagos, Nigeria, 66
Lagunilla, 16
Lake Texcoco, xiii, 5–6, 32, 45–46, 199n30
La Merced, 8, 16
land: expropriation of, 33; fraud, 44; invasions, 126–30, 136–37, 138; regularization, 130–32; tenure system, 4–8, 118; trusts, 180

Latin American Episcopal Conference (Consejo Episcopal Latinoamericano y Caribeño, CELAM), 148–49, 156
Law of Fraccionamientos, 133–34
Law of Sub-Divisions of Lands, 198n4
León, 146
Lewis, Oscar, 73, 74, 75
Ley de Fraccionamientos de Terrenos del Estado de México, 49, 54–60
Ley de Plantificacíon y Zonificación del Distrito Federal (Federal District Planning and Zoning Law), 20
Liberación (bulletin), 151
little convents (*conventillos*), 5
livestock, in Ciudad Neza, 75
Lomas de Chapultepec, 15–16
Lopez, Margarita, 70
López Mateos, Adolfo, 23, 28, 29, 30, 34, 39, 60, 87, 89, 91, 223n21
López Moyano, Jesús, 59
Lopez Nava, Elezar, 212–13n61
Los Profetas, 149–52, 163
Loya Ramírez, Oscar, 123–24
Madariaga Cruz, Odón, 111–13, 118, 120–22, 124, 126–27, 133–39, 176
Madrid, Miguel de la, xxiii–xxiv, 180
Maldonado Aranda, Salvador, 202n81
Manza, Hugo, 131
Maravillas, 47
marginality, theory of, 157
Marginality Project, 156
marginal mass, 157
Marx, Karl, 154, 155, 166–67
Marxism, 154
May Day celebration, 93–95
Maza, Enrique, 135, 136, 138
Mazo Maza, Alfredo del, 175
Mazo Vélez, Alfredo del, 46, 50

McNamara, Robert, 82
Méndez Arceo, Sergio, 149, 150, 167–68
Mérida, 103
Mexican Communist Party, 155
Mexican Revolution, 6, 12–13
Mexican Social Secretariat (Secretariado Social Mexicano, SSM), 150
Mexico: corruption in, 46–47, 114; financial crisis in, 178–79; hierarchical religious field of, 145; inequality in, xiv; political competition in, 176; political violence in, 176; state institutions of, 130; United States assistance to, 29–30. *See also specific locations*
Mexico City (Federal District): AURIS Institute and, 130; centralization of, 3–4, 9, 10; decentralization of, 4; economic statistics regarding, 9; electricity pirating from, 75; expansion of, xv, xx, 4, 13–14; housing types in, 29, 83; master plan for, 7–8; modernization of, 5–6; as modern metropolis, 3; outward expansion of, 3; population growth of, xvii, 8; population of, 181; road development in, 10–11, 17–18; social geography of, xx, 3, 4; statistics regarding, 7, 8, 65; surveys in, 15; as unhealthy, 6; unrest in, 6; urban restoration in, 19; zoning in, 19. *See also specific locations*
middle class, 90
middle-class apartments, 15. *See also* housing
migration/migrants: arrival process of, 11; categories of, 13; causes of, 8; crosscurrent, 4; demographics of, 10, 11; diversity of, 13; impacts of, 3; as *la*

gente decente, 12; as marginal, 11; into Mexico City, 4; search for new home during, 8–13; statistics regarding, 8; of wealthy families, 4–5
Ministry of Finance and Public Credit, 9
Ministry of Hydraulic Resources (Secretaría de Recursos Hidráulicos, SRH), 47
Ministry of Public Works and Communications, 9
Miranda y Gómez, Miguel Darío, 152
modernism, 26–31
modernity, 169
Monsiváis, Carlos, xxiii
Monterrey, 88, 115
Monterrey Institute of Technology and Higher Education (Instituto Tecnológico y de Estudios Superiores de Monterrey, Tec, ITESM), 151
Morales Rodriguez, Abel, 23
Mora Lozada, Artemio, 110, 114, 118, 122
Morelia, 146
Morelli, Alex, 160, 165–66, 169
mortgage loans, xxiii, 30, 92, 180
mosquitoes, 48
movie industry, 59
Movimiento Estudiantil Profesional (MEP) (Professional Student Movement), 151
Movimiento Restaurador de Colonos (MRC) (Settlers' Movement for Land Restoration): attacks against, 118–19; decline of, 169; demands of, 108–9; division of, 118; effectiveness of, 124; *fraccionadores* against, 115–16; growth of, 113; impacts of, 114; land trust agreement and, 121; meeting regarding, 106–7; movement of waves and, 116; origins of, 110–12; rally of, 113–14, 116–17
Movimiento Urbano Popular (MUP) (Popular Urban Movement), xxv, 115
Multifamiliar Alemán, 23, 91
multifamiliar (multifamily) housing, xv, 12, 23, 91. *See also* housing
Multifamiliar Juárez, 23
Murat Hinojosa, Alejandro, 175

naco, xxii
Nafinsa, 114
Narvarte, 14
National Autonomous University of Mexico (Universidad Nacional Autónoma de México, UNAM), 12
National Company of Popular Goods (Compañía Nacional de Subsistencias Populares, CONASUPO), 114
National Confederation of Popular Organizations (Confederación Nacional de Organizaciones Populares, CNOP), 118
National Coordinator of the Popular Urban Movement (Coordinadora Nacional del Movimiento Urbano Popular, CONAMUP), 178
National Fund for Housing, 93
National Fund for Popular Housing (Fideicomiso Fondo Nacional de Habitaciones Populares, FONHAPO), 180
National Hydrocarbons Commission, 9
National Indigenous Institute, xiv, 9
National Institute of Anthropology and History (Instituto Nacional de Antropología e Historia, INAH), 18

National Institute of Housing (Instituto Nacional de Vivienda, INV), 15, 88, 96
National Museum of Anthropology, 10
National Peasant Confederation (Confederación Nacional Campesina, CNC), 118
National Polytechnic Institute of Mexico (Instituto Politécnico Nacional de México, IPN), 12
National Strike Council (Consejo Nacional de Huelga, CNH), 149
National Tripartite Commission, 98
National Urban Mortgage and Public Works Bank (Banco Nacional Hipotecario Urbano y de Obras Públicas, BNHUOP), 15
Nava Méndez, Salvador, 82
neighborhood associations, xvii, xxiv–xxv, 47–50
neighborhood-unit model, 33–34
New York Times (newspaper), 167
Novedades (newspaper), 18, 80, 81–82
Novo, Salvador, 5
Novoa, Carlos, 17
Nun, José, 156, 157
Nutini, Hugo, 12–13

Oaxaca, xxiii, 10, 103, 175
Obeso, Xavier de, 150, 163
Ocotitla Saucedo, Pedro, 60
Oficina de Colonias, 49
Oficina de Habitación Popular (Office of Popular Housing), 33
Olivares, Ignacio, 171
ONIS (Peru), 167
oppressed, pedagogy of, 158–61
Ordoñez, José Luis, 102

organized labor, social housing and, 98–104
Ornelas, Francisco, 170
Ortega, Castro, 70
Ortega Lopez, Ruben, 51, 52, 53–54, 56
Ortiz, Antonio, 170

Padilla González, José Manuel, 25–26
Palacio Municipal, 175, 176
Palma Street, Mexico City, 18
Pani, Alberto J., 6, 7, 15
Pani, Mario, 7, 12, 17, 20, 22, 23, 33, 120, 193n75
paracaidismo, 213n75
paracaidistas (parachutists), 80, 136–37
Parque del Pueblo, Ciudad Neza, 140–41
Partido de la Revolución Democrática (PRD) (Party of the Democratic Revolution), 176
Partido Revolucionario Institucional (PRI) (Institutional Revolutionary Party): collaborations with, 177; dominance of, xxiv–xxv, 176; Fineza Land Trust and, 138–39; leadership split of, 177; lethal force of, 176; Odón Madariaga and, 134; patronage system of, xxv; reforms of, 113; as responsive force, 155; rupture factors regarding, 177; threats to, 29
Parties and Events of Mexico (Diversiones y Espectáculos de México, DEMSA), 58
Party of the Democratic Revolution (Partido de la Revolución Democrática, PRD), 176
Paseo de la Reforma boulevard, Mexico City, 4, 18

Paso Reinert, Rafael del, 50, 57
Pastoral Constitution on the Church in the Modern World (Vatican II), 145
payment strike, Ciudad Neza, 106–7, 110–22, 124
payroll tax, 93, 95, 110–11
Pearl River Delta, China, 66
Pemex, 9
Pensado, Jaime, xxi
Pérez López, Aristeo, 122, 127, 136, 138
peripheral urbanization, xx
Perla, 123
Perry, Clarence, 33
Peru, 167
petate (bedroll), 74
Pichardo Pagaza, Ignacio, 75–76, 82
pistoleros (hired gunman), xxi
Pitol, Sergio, 12
place, in Mexican history, xix–xxiii
Planning Commission. *See* Federal District Planning Commission
Plaza de la Candelaria, La Merced, 16
Plaza de Toros, Colonia Aurora, 58
Polanco, 15
political mobilization, economic conditions and, 179
political violence, 176
politics, of urban poor, xxvi
Poniatowska, Elena, 95–98
Pontifical Commission for Latin America, 147–48
poor/poverty, in Mexico, 145–49, 158–61
poor settlements, influence of, xxv
Popular Educational Services (Servicios Educativos Populares, SEPAC), 170–73
popular promotion (promoción popular) project, 144, 156–58, 164–69

Popular Urban Movement (Movimiento Urbano Popular, MUP), xxv, 115
Porfiriato, 5–6
Porfirio Miranda, José, 166–67
Portales, 14
Portillo, López, 104, 171, 173
presidencialismo, power of, xxiv
Priests for the Third World (Argentina), 167
Primera, Alí, 65
Primer Congreso Nacional de Teología (Sociedad Teológica Mexicana), 151
private developers, impunity to, xvi
Professional Student Movement (Movimiento Estudiantil Profesional, MEP), 151
promoción popular (popular promotion) project, 144, 156–58, 164–69
protesting, 162
public behavior, unsanitary conditions and, 5
public health, 5, 14, 107–10
public transportation, 11
public works, 5–6
Puebla, 146
Pulgas (Jesuit publication), 146

Querétaro, 88, 103
Quijano, Aníbal, 154

race, in Mexican history, xix–xxiii
Radiant City housing complex, 22, 23
railroad, 10–11
Ramirez, Angel, 75
Ramirez, Mario, 154
Ramírez Vázquez, Pedro, 17, 120
Ramos, Aureliano, 53
Ramos Zavala, Raúl, 161–62

Raúl Romero, Erazo, 44–47, 61, 62
Real Seminario de Minería, 18
Reforma, 137
Regional Planning and Zoning Council (Junta Regional de Planificación y Zonificación), 47
Reglamento de Colonias en el Distrito Federal, 49
religious field, hierarchical, 145
rent freezes, 8–9
residential segregation, xxi–xxii
Rico Tavera, Miguel, 153, 163
Rincón Gallardo, Eduardo, 131
Rivera, Diego, 7
roadway system, 17–18
Robinson, Lisa, 100
Rockefeller Foundation, 156
Romero, Raúl, 52, 112–13, 118–19
roofs, cardboard, 65
Rosa, Martín de la, 110, 144, 150–54, 160–61, 163–64, 165, 167–69, 170–72
Ruiz Cortines, Adolfo, 43, 52
Ruvalcaba, Jesús, 170, 172

Sabines, Jaime, 12
Sacerdotes para el Pueblo (Priests for the People), 167, 168
Sáenz Knoth, Jorge, 61
Salas Obregón, Ignacio, 144, 151, 153, 154, 155, 161–63, 170–71
Sánchez, Hugo, 117
Sánchez Colín, Salvador, 50–51, 54, 56
San Juan de Aragón, xv, 31–39
San Juan de Aragón Lake, 31
Santa María la Ribera, 15–16, 72–73
"The Seamy Side of Charity" (Illich), 148–49

Secretaría de Hacienda y Crédito Pública, 71
Secretariado Social Mexicano (SSM) (Mexican Social Secretariat), 150
segregation, residential, xxi–xxii
Selee, Andrew, 171–72
Semo, Ilán, xxi
Servicios Educativos Populares (SEPAC) (Popular Educational Services), 170–73
Settlers' Movement for Land Restoration (Movimiento Restaurador de Colonos, MRC). See Movimiento Restaurador de Colonos (MRC) (Settlers' Movement for Land Restoration)
shantytowns, survey of, 15
Shilinsky, 59
Sierra Villarreal, José Luis, 151, 153, 154, 161, 162–63, 170–71
Silva-Herzog, Jesús, 94, 95–104
Slotnik, Abraham, 55–56, 58, 59, 112
social class, in Ciudad Neza, 155
social geography, of Mexico City, xx
social housing programs, xxiii, 23–26, 28, 98–104. See also housing; specific locations
social housing project (*unidad habitacional*), 20
social inequality, rise and decline of, xvii
social integration (*promoción popular*), 156–58
socialism, 166, 167
social movements, in Ciudad Neza, 169–72
social security system, 23
social stigmas, xvi
social worker program, 25

Solís, Javier, 58
Soto la Marina, Armando (El Chicote), 59
space, in Mexican history, xix–xxiii
squatter, defined, xvi
Stein, Clarence, 33
strikes, 106–7, 110–22, 124
student movement, 115, 144–45, 149

tabique, 66
Tacuba Street, Mexico City, 18, 19, 21
Tamaulipas, 47
Tamayo, Jorge, 69
Tavera, MiguelRico, 162
telarañas, 75–76
Telesistma Mexico, 10
Televisa, 10
temporary structures (*jacales*), 65
tenements, 5, 14, 15
Tepito, 15, 16
Texcoco, 146
theory of marginality, 157
Tlatelolco, San Juan de Aragón, 35
Tlatelolco massacre, 144, 149, 152
Toledano, Lombardo, 150
Toluca, Mexico, 66, 88, 104
Torres, Camilo, 163
Torres Martínez, Ramón, 91
trabajadores no asalariados (TNA) (unsalaried workers), 90
Tuan, Yi-Fu, xix

Ugarte, Juan, 116
unidades vecinales, 33–34
unidad habitacional (social housing project), 20
Unidad Habitacional Vicente Guerrero, 87, 88, 94
Unidad Independencia, 87, 91

Unidad Kennedy, San Juan de Aragón, 30, 34–35
Unidad Modelo, 23
Unidad Morelos, San Juan de Aragón, 34
Unidad Nonoalco-Tlatelolco, San Juan de Aragón, 35
Unidad Santa Fe, 24–28
Unidad Vecinal I, San Juan de Aragón, 34
unifamiliar housing, 91
Unión de Mutua Ayuda Episcopal (UMAE) (Episcopal Mutual Aid Union), 147
Unión de Obreros de Artes Gráficas de los Talleres Comerciales, San Juan de Aragón, 34
Unión General de Obreros y Campesinos de México (UGOCM) (General Union of Workers and Farmers of Mexico), 134–35, 137–38
Unión Popular Revolucionaria Emiliano Zapata (UPREZ) (Emiliano Zapata Popular Revolutionary Union), 171
United Nations Charter of Economic Rights and Duties of States, 87
United States Agency for International Development (USAID), 29
Universidad Autónoma de Nuevo León (UANL) (Autonomous University of Nuevo León), 162
Universidad Iberoamericana (Ibero), 146–47, 150
Universidad Nacional Autónoma de México (UNAM) (National Autonomous University of Mexico), 12, 20, 150
University City (Ciudad Universitaria), 20

University Council (Universidad Iberoamericana, Ibero), 146–47
unsalaried workers (*trabajadores no asalariados*, TNA), 90
urban colonization, 54
urban informality, 130–32
urbanismo, 33
urbanization, 7
urban renewal project, 4
urban social movements, xvii, xxv, 177
Uruchurtu, Ernesto, 18–21, 223n21
utopianism, 91

Valdés, Fernando, 17
Valle, Luis del, 150, 164, 167, 168, 169, 172
Valner, Gregorio, 108, 130–31
Vargas, Carlos, 14
Vargas, Soledad, 128, 129
Vargas Soriano, Rogelio, xiii, 106–7, 111–12, 117–19, 121–22, 124, 127–29, 138, 175–76
Vaso de Texcoco, 28–31, 32, 43, 47, 188n48. *See also* Ciudad Neza (Ciudad Nezahualcóyotl) (Colonias del Vasco de Texcoco)
Vatican II, 145–49, 156
Vazquez, Angel, 58
vecindad, 5
Veinte de Noviembre Avenue, Mexico City, 18

Vekemans, Roger, 154, 156–57
Velázquez Moreno, Héctor, 33, 35
Velázquez Sánchez, Fidel, 97–104
Vélez-Ibáñez, Carlos, 129
Veracruz, 104
Villada, 123, 137
Vitz, Matthew, xx, 32
Viveros de la Loma, San Juan de Aragón, 34
vulgar hybridity, xvii, 80–83

water supply, 77–80, 109, 110
wealthy condominiums, survey of, 15
women, 68, 69, 76–80
workers' movement, 6
working-class settlements, 15

Young Catholic Workers (Juventud Obrera Católica, JOC), 150
young Jesuits: in Ciudad Neza, 152–58; commitment of, 144–45; conference of, 151–52, 158–59; conservative comeback and, 164–69; in Edmundo Campion, 150; fractures and splits of, 161–63; impact of, 135; programs of, 153; *promoción popular* (popular promotion) and, 164–69

Zabala, Germán, 154, 160
Zócalo Square, 3, 110
Zona Norte, Ciudad Neza, 181
Zuno, María Esther, 117

In the Confluencias series:

The Sonoran Dynasty in Mexico: Revolution, Reform, and Repression
By Jürgen Buchenau

The Enlightened Patrolman: Early Law Enforcement in Mexico City
By Nicole von Germeten

Men of God: Mendicant Orders in Colonial Mexico
Asunción Lavrin

Strength from the Waters: A History of Indigenous Mobilization in Northwest Mexico
By James V. Mestaz

Informal Metropolis: Life on the Edge of Mexico City, 1940–1976
By David Yee

To order or obtain more information on these or other University of Nebraska Press titles, visit nebraskapress.unl.edu.

www.ingramcontent.com/pod-product-compliance
Lightning Source LLC
Chambersburg PA
CBHW021958220426
43663CB00007B/860